A Nude Singularity
Lily Peter of Arkansas

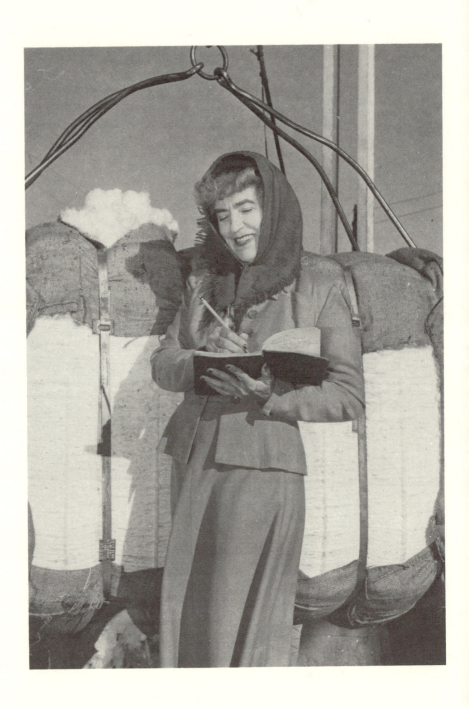

A Nude Singularity

Lily Peter of Arkansas

A Biography

by

AnnieLaura M. Jaggers

UCA Press
Conway, AR
1993

Library of Congress Cataloging-in-Publication Data

Jaggers, AnnieLaura M.
    A nude singularity : Lily Peter of Arkansas : a biography / by AnnieLaura
M. Jaggers.
          416p. 23.5cm.
    Includes bibliographical references and index.
    ISBN 0-944436-13-7 : $35.95
    1. Peter, Lily-Biography. 2. Poets, American-20th century—Biography.
3. Women plantation owners-Arkansas—Biography.
I. Title.
PS3566.E75Z74 1992
811'.54-dc20
[B]   92-24449
                                                              CIP

© 1993 by UCA Press
Manufactured in the United States of America

ISBN 0-944436-13-7

Printed on acid-free paper

To Carl

Contents

Acknowledgements

This project, the writing of a biography of Lily Peter, was financed in part by a grant from the Arkansas Endowment for the Humanities, made possible by a sabbatical leave from Arkansas Tech University, whose administration and Board of Trustees also made available office space, supplies, and services for the duration of the sabbatical year. For this support, my gratitude is immeasurable.

I acknowledge the unremitting cooperation and encouragement of Lily Peter, without which the project would have been impossible.

My project made extra work for these members of the Arkansas Tech staff, but they helped enthusiastically: Daisey Briscoe, Mittie Small, Joyce Newsom, Sue Pitts, Billie Loveless, Beth Foster, Ann Woody, Marge Coffey, and Lawrence Carter.

My writing office was housed in the library of Arkansas Tech University, and Head Librarian, Bill Vaughn, and his assistant, Shannon Henderson, and the entire staff were totally cooperative. Troy Anderson saved me many a minute and step in checking a quick reference, and Mary L. Hudson, the mailing room director, also saved me steps.

My department head, Dr. Kenneth Walker, and Dean of the School of Liberal and Fine Arts, Dr. William Seidensticker, never withheld encouragement and cooperation.

I am grateful for the patience and painstaking help of my editing consultants, Dr. Earl F. Schrock, Jr., Clarence Hall, and

Anne Courtemanche-Ellis. I acknowledge the valuable skills of Ann Smith, tape transcriber, and Ginnie Tyson, manuscript typist. The latter possesses a master's degree in English, no small measure of what she was able to give over and beyond typing skills. I thank my proof-reader, Beckie Tyson Riley, and acknowledge the photographic skills of Andy Anders and Charles Ellis.

To the members of my household, my husband, Carl Jaggers, and my sister, Verrell Shell, I am forever obliged for tons of small tasks done and ounces of crucially needed revitalization. Another indispensable ingredient to this work was the fact that my sister, Margaret, and her late husband, Garland Triplett, gave me a key to their home in Marvell, Arkansas, allowing me easy access to Lily Peter's home only ten miles away.

And this is stopping short of naming hosts of other relatives and friends who have given much in listening and well-wishing. I am truly grateful for all that has gone toward making this a fascinating project.

Foreword

When astronomers and physicists study the photographic records of their huge telescopes which sweep the heavens, they occasionally discover a phenomenon which is without visible causality and which fits no extant theory. Such a phenomenon is labeled a nude or a naked singularity.

The life of Lily Peter was such a phenomenon. The extraordinary fact of her life is not that she was a self-made millionaire, not that she was a gifted poet, photographer, and musician, not that she was a precedent-setting conservationist and environmentalist, nor that she was an indefatigable patron of the arts, nor is it that she was a childless mother to untold causes, nor that she was a spinster who never forgot she had been loved. What is extraordinary about Lily is that she became all these things when all odds were against her becoming any one of them.

This millionaire was raised on a poverty-stricken farm where she was taught at home until she was eleven by her mother, who bore eight more children. This conservationist learned at an early age how whimsical nature could be when her family survived the annual flooding of the Mississippi River during the 1890s. This rhapsodic patron of the arts received her first violin lessons through the mail. Of all the brave battles Lily fought, none could have been more frightening than those she observed her father wage when his innovative farming experiments rewarded him with disaster after disaster; yet Lily managed a four-thousand acre plantation and successfully experimented without using pesticides on her crops (on a small acreage), an alarming practice to her agri-business peers. This spinster has inspired more love than most of us in a lifetime, while her own love remained sometimes unrequited, always unfulfilled, yet vital, nurturing and sustaining others throughout her long life.

Lily Peter was a much-sought-after speaker, teacher, entertainer, hostess, guest, and consultant well into her nineties, and in all these capacities her expertise ranged among subjects as diverse as poetry and cotton farming. It's no wonder her carefully guarded age was surprising to many, because her appearance, most often viewed from the distance of an audience, looked the same for years. Face to face with Lily, her light complexion was so dramatic a contrast to the darkness of her eyes, her thick lashes and full sweeping brows that one felt she had encountered a ballet dancer whose makeup was designed for viewing from a distance. However, Lily's dramatic visage was natural (except for the cosmetic brown and curl of her hair), and, as if in keeping with her capacity to project herself, one did naturally keep at a distance from her, even though one felt important because of her ability to give her undivided attention.

Her day-to-day mode of living was as much a study of contrasts as was her profile. A Chanel suit was as unlikely a costume for the counter of cotton bales on a gin yard as is a 1963 pick-up truck an unlikely vehicle for a lady who would bring the Philadelphia Orchestra to the Arkansas hinterland at her own expense.

Since she was born only a few miles down Big Cypress Bayou, Lily's home on its banks was as permanent as her youth, as disarming as her lifestyle. The simple frame structure covered with asbestos siding was hidden among a tangle of native trees, nineteenth-century flowering shrubs, and an array of day lilies so totally immodest as to make nameplates laughable. It was so modest with its added-on rooms, its screened porch askew, its make-shift steps, and such that it suggested poverty and was indistinguishable from most tenant farmers' homes. Its interior was utterly haphazard: some sheer shabbiness and some pearls of quality and good taste. One could describe every room as a cluttered desk top reflecting a busy schedule and an owner who possessed a photographic memory which wants no "tidying up" until "gotten around to." Lily said, "If my friends choose to criticize my housekeeping, I have the blessed consolation of knowing they cannot possibly describe it as bad as it actually is." The eclectic variety of furnishings reflected the accumulation of years, from a homemade bookcase to the natural mahogany Baldwin grand piano. The walls were lined with paintings and her own color photographs, interspersed with plaques, awards, citations, and proclamations; some are elaborate, some crude and modest; but all were displayed without discrimination. Lily once said she loved owls; owls of pewter, jade, alabaster, crystal, and cedar were in every room in the house, along with owls of tapestry, collage, macrame, and straw—all of them gifts.

This unprepossessing home (still a part of her estate) lies in the heart of the Arkansas Delta, about a hundred miles south of Memphis and about twenty miles west of the Mississippi River, which is typical of one of the three types of terrain included in Arkansas. Thus a traveler from Memphis, Tennessee, to Fort Smith, Arkansas (on the Oklahoma border of the state), sees vast fields of cotton and soybeans, then acres of rice on the Grand Prairie, then finally orchards of peaches, apples, and pears which break the Ozark Mountain skyline of scrub oaks and cedars.

Lily was an anachronistic symbol of the pioneering spirit of all Americans and particularly of Arkansas, a state that is a haven for contrasts and extremes. Her life reflected the state's dichotomy of being neither South nor West. She was reared by a Yankee father and a Rebel mother; yet, she always felt at home with her relatives in Ohio, nonetheless identifying with the southern spirit to survive and prevail.

It never occurred to Lily that she was not fully responsible for herself and her actions. She was a decision maker. Perceiving her imminent death from a rare anemia, she cured herself by going to Webster's Second International Dictionary and finding that she needed peanut butter in her diet. One saw not a shred of longing for "peace and rest," until the very last days of her life. She possessed a perfervid enthusiasm for creative work, considering that pride in creativity is humankind's only compensation for mortality. She thought nothing of challenging the U. S. Corps of Engineers which, along with a local drainage district, proposed channelization of Big Creek, which connects with Big Cypress Bayou. She was the epitome of the independent woman, yet totally atypical in the graceful way she invaded the most conservative of worlds, that of rural plantation farmers, cotton ginners, and dealers in farm equipment.

Yet it is no single factor of appearance, lifestyle, environment, or accomplishment which accounts for the power of Lily's personality. She held the crowded audiences of small amphitheatres enrapt as she read her poetry. She stood like a miniature southern belle, about to be swallowed up by the huge stage that held the Philadelphia Orchestra, thanking Eugene Ormandy for accepting her invitation to play in the Arkansas wilderness. And she stood barely five feet tall in a heated courtroom of Corps of Engineer advocates, describing the ecology of a stream and its death from channelization as convincingly as she should, had she been bringing the news and describing the death of the judge's dearest relative. The size or status of Lily's audience didn't diminish her passion for her topic. The biographer once witnessed her in her den telling two little girls about another little girl who grew up in Arkansas swamps and went on to marry a member of the British peerage, expanding forever the horizons of those two little girls.

"Her words flow forth like the waters of the streams she's

saved. They move, now gently, then turbulently, according to the levels of circumstance. They reflect all the nuance, light, and shade of the anachronistic cypress woods, the futuristic Delta sky. Listeners are confident the source-spring is omnifluent and stable, like the Mississippi itself. When the flow of her words encounters the rocks of opposition, the gleam of glancing spray bursts forth in rainbow color, like the cotton gin she designed and built, looking like a Calder mobile of blazing turquoise against the Delta sky. And the droplets return to the stream as if they know they are going to the ocean and the future, which paradoxically might lie here in Lily Peter's hinterland." These words were written and spoken by the biographer prior to Lily's death.

When is a tiny metaphor drawn from the ocean of words equal to its task? When is a personality drawn from the ocean of human personality worthy of isolation for a reader's world?

The following chronicle not only lays the ground for judgment, but speaks to the limitless possibilities of human endeavor.

Chapter I

ANCESTRY, 16TH CENTURY-1891

How and when did I begin to become what I am?
Whence, indeed, came this dull Jackdaw,
Identity,
That has built its nest under my small breastbone?
> Lily Peter
> from "The Jackdaw"
> *News from Camelot*, unpublished

The contrast between Lily's mother's family and her father's family is striking. Her father's family arrived in the new world well over a hundred years before her mother's, in the 1740s, and within that first generation established themselves as local leaders in touch with national figures. The Peters lived long lives for their times, had many progeny, and within the family's second generation of Americans is a nationally recognized composer, John Frederick Peter, who is credited with composing a minuet before Mozart and a polonaise before Chopin. Most of Lily's mother's family, on the other hand, arrived in New Orleans only three generations ago, and, according to Lily, both sets of her maternal great-grandparents died young during one of the many yellow-fever flare-ups so indigenous to the malaria-ridden South of those years, each leaving only one child. The orphan, John Glensbeckle (or Mowbray), married the orphan, Pauline Hardy, and gave birth to Lily's mother, Florence. John eventually died penniless on skid row.

Lily's father journeyed across the American continent, and one can almost trace his travels in loops, from Ohio to California and back again to Ohio; from eastern Ohio to Arkansas and finally to settle in the seemingly unlikely floodlands of the western banks of the Mississippi at Indian Bay, Arkansas. Lily's mother's forebears, on the other hand, did not wander from New Orleans until their second generation, and then only a comparitively short distance away to Greenville, Mississippi — still near the banks of the great river.

Lily's father had a good education for his time and seems to have retained his forebears' genius for experimentation as he applied it to his land-clearing and farming, but it was almost as if he pushed that strain of genius too deep into the frontier and in the end died on those western banks of the Mississippi, leaving his family in dire poverty. His father was a renegade in his family, having stood up for women's rights in his church at a time when they were not considered to have any. As a result he ostracized himself from their church and home town.

Lily's mother was poorly schooled, yet despite poverty, illness, and difficulty in childbearing, lived to see five of her children educated and established in professional or productive activities. On center stage of a very desperate family, with disparate heritages, appeared Lily Peter, balancing the music of the spheres of her forebears — upholding the talent the Peters spawned in Pennsylvania over two hundred years before, overcoming misfortunes of the Mowbrays whom fate hardly gave a chance just a generation ago. Ironically, Lily was closer to her mother, felt a greater responsibility to her than to her first and probably only love, yet she identified with her father's role, which was fearless. How is a millionaire cotton grower who makes poems, music, and photographs made?

Lily's paternal ancestors were German from Austria and

were some of the earliest members of the Moravian Church. Her great-great-grandfather, John Frederick Peter, was trained in a Moravian Seminary in Germany and was chosen to go to Holland, where he was the leader of one of the country's largest missions at Herrndyjk. When he was called to the Central Moravian Church in Bethlehem, Pennsylvania, in 1760, he was fifty-four years old, a widower with three grown children whom he left in Europe. In 1761, he married a young widow, Anna Marie Engel, who bore him a daughter and a son, and he served as the senior pastor at Bethlehem until a few years before his death in 1791. His responsibilities included the administration of the Moravian boarding school for girls, the first such school anywhere in North America. He wrote a congratulatory letter from the Moravian Church to George Washington when he became president in 1789, a letter which is filed in the National Archives and signed by John Frederick Peter. [1]

Two of John Frederick's sons were composers in addition to being Moravian missionaries. Simon is listed as one of the ten American composers of the era, but it is his brother, John Frederick, the younger, who attained the greatest musical acclaim for the Peter family. John Frederick was sent to the Salem Mission in Carolina in 1780, and his first duty was as minister of music.[2] He composed many anthems for the church, all of them including small orchestral accompaniments for organ, strings, and wind instruments. He and his wife were reputed to have an exceptionally happy marriage, and Lily considered his six quintets a celebration of the marital bliss of that union, a kind of epithalamion.

Some time between 1786 and 1789, he completed the scores of these secular quintets for two violins, two violas, and a cello, actually his first essay into composing chamber music. Ranked high by musicologists, these works have been compared favorably with the first works of Beethoven and other composers of similar ability. The music is filled with joy and sunshine, like the works of Haydn;

yet the quintets are clearly original.

The completion and performance of these compositions led to a very important episode in his life, both fulfilling and disheartening. A beautiful minuet is part of one quintet, having been written long before Mozart included the minuet in his music, and a polonaise is included in another quintet, long before Chopin composed works based on that dance form.

The Moravian Church leaders frowned upon dancing in any form; therefore, when this music came to the attention of the bishop, he disapproved of it thoroughly. He was offended that an ordained minister of the church would write secular music of any kind. He summoned the young composer and threatened him with excommunication. John Frederick obediently refrained from ever writing any more music which was not for the church services, composing only hymns and anthems. Lily's favorite was "It Is a Precious Thing," a celebration of the love of God.

Lily and others considered the church's penalty to have been cruel to John Frederick and a loss to the library of early American music. He wrote in his autobiography late in life that he had tried to serve the Lord as best he could but felt that perhaps the ill health which he suffered in his later years was a punishment for his too-great love of music. [3]

Fortunately, this strict attitude of the church leaders was local and confined to that time. Today Moravians play the chamber music of Peter, Haydn, and like composers with impunity.

Lily, with the Moravian Music Foundation, subsidized the recording of the Peter quintets in 1951 and their publication by the New York Public Library in 1952. She often said that the experience of someone's finding these quintets among the music of the church of that era must have been like suddenly coming upon April blossoms on a February bough.

John Frederick's life had a poignant ending in 1813. While he was playing the organ in church for the pleasure of a small group, he suffered a fatal heart attack.

Baker's *Biographical Dictionary of Musicians* includes the following about Peter: "All told, Peter wrote some 105 sacred anthems and arias of various sizes and styles, and they are, in all probability, some of the finest and most elaborate concerted sacred works written in contemporary America. Of particular significance are Peter's copies of over two hundred chamber and symphonic works by about fifty relatively obscure European composers of the period (c. 1764-69). Included also is the earliest known (1766) copy of Haydn's Symphony No. 17."

In spite of the rigors of the period, the Moravian missionary efforts were effective and their church grew. In the 1760s a mission was begun farther west of Pennsylvania on the Tuscarawas River (also known by another Indian name, Muskingum), on land which would eventually be part of Ohio. The mission, which was named Schoenbrun, did not survive the border fighting which occurred during the American Revolution. Some of the British soldiers were under the impression that the Christian Indians were acting as spies for the patriots, and despite the fact that the Indians were completely innocent, the British totally destroyed the mission. A small remnant of the faithful survived, so in 1798 the Moravians re-established the mission on a site a little farther down the river. They called it Gnadenhutten — Tents of Grace. Longfellow refers to the mission in his poem of exodus, "Evangeline."[4]

The restoration of this mission in the 1790s called for a business manager for the trading station. Such a store provided the necessities from the outside world as well as a means of disposition of what was produced there. It provided a valuable contact for establishing a relationship of confidence and friendship which would make the Indians lend willing ears to the evangelical message of the Moravians. The church leaders regarded this function as such an integral part of the mission that they were quite demanding about the qualifications of the manager, and it is a point of pride to Lily that her great-grandfather, David Peter, half-brother to John Frederick, the younger, was chosen.

At first David refused the position. He was teaching Greek and Latin in the school for boys at Nazareth near Bethlehem and enjoying it. He and his young wife, Dorcas Chitty from Carolina, were happily married. He would not have accepted the post had it not for his best friend, John Heckewelder, whom the elders had persuaded to intervene on their behalf. Heckewelder spent one entire night plying David with persuasive arguments and praying with him. When the dawn came, David acceded to Heckewelder's wishes.

David and his wife moved to Gnadenhutten, remaining there as business manager until the position was discontinued many years later. He kept a very detailed record of every transaction at the post. Lily was able to look at this log and appreciate his refined penmanship. She noted the emergence of the term *dollar* from the German *thaler*, interrupted by a period of the use of the English system of pounds, shillings, and pence. She noted how many items changed hands and how many were new to the wilderness, including cashmere wool. The records show that one Indian whose name was Ka bought yards and yards of red cashmere material, scarlet ribbons, buttons, and other trinkets "to make himself look grand," said Lily. A common commodity at the post was bear grease, sold or bartered in large quantities along with fine furs offered for sale by the Indians. Gnadenhutten was a busy, thriving community. Ohio had not yet become a state, and the only other settlement in it was Marietta, founded on the Ohio River in 1791.

The first piano in Ohio was bought by cousins of Lily's great-grandmother, the Ruyseckers. David Peter had brought from Nazareth a harpsichord which he played well. In order to make his instrument portable for the trip west, he sawed off the legs and hinged them back. He left it portable so that he could take it to the church when services were held. David Peter also brought with him and continued to accumulate an extensive library of scholarly books.

David's young wife died not long after they had settled in Gnadenhutten, and he then married into the Leinbach family as his older brother, John Frederick, had done. The Leinbachs were craftsmen and organ builders in Germany, and in the new world had become proprietors of landed estates. [5]

David and his second wife, Susanna, had a large family which included a son, Lewis, who was Lily's grandfather. Lewis married Sarah Louisa Blickensderfer in 1830. [6] Sarah's father owned a 1,500-acre estate near Gnadenhutten, and for a wedding present he gave Sarah and Lewis a town residence built in the New England salt-box style. The same year, Lewis's father, David, built the first brick house in Gnadenhutten, a handsome three-story residence. Both of these ancestral homes were still standing and were both occupied until recent years.

Of the ten children of Lewis and Sarah Louisa Peter, Mary, who married Joseph Allen Hamilton, was the only one to remain in Gnadenhutten. Lily lived at her home while she finished high school. Her daughter, Laura, was not only a cousin to Lily, but a life-long friend.

Another of Lewis's children, Lily's Aunt Adelaide, married the only son of a wealthy German industrialist, Augustus Schultze. Fluent in eight languages, including Eskimo, he served in the Moravian mission in Alaska and wrote in the 1870s the first grammar of the Eskimo language ever published. Aunt Adelaide was much loved by Lily because her letters and gifts to her Brother Will's family in the Arkansas wilderness were always a source of happiness. The children could expect to receive a big box every Christmas from this aunt way off in Pennsylvania, filled with gifts for every member of the family. It was through

Aunt Adelaide's family that Lily developed her close ties with Bethlehem and the Moravian College there. Adelaide was educated at the Moravian seminary for girls, and her husband, Augustus Schultze, became president of Moravian College. [7]

Lewis Peter's son, William Oliver Peter, was Lily's father. He grew up in Gnadenhutten and received his education there. He earned his living as a draftsman and was good with engines. Will was profoundly affected by a controversy which involved his father and the bishop of the Moravian church. Though not a minister, Lewis Peter held a number of responsible lay positions in the church and publicly supported the proposition that it was not only godly for a woman to pray publicly in church, but also that it was highly commendable. The church elders disagreed, and Lewis lost in the fight. He was so piqued that he took his entire family and moved to the Methodist Church.

This move from one church to another placed Lily's grandfather's entire family in an atmosphere of defense. None of Lewis's brothers, sisters, or cousins sided with him; they remained faithful to the *Unitas Fratrum* (the original name of the Moravian Church). His wife, Sarah Louisa, whose cousin was the dissenting bishop of the church, was sympathetic to her husband, but efforts to dissuade him from drastic action or to convert opponents to his view were fruitless.

Because Lewis's quarrel with the church was so bitter and deep, resulting in total alienation from family and friends, all his children except Mary eventually moved away from Gnadenhutten, unusual at the time because from the beginning theirs was a "first family" whose members benefited from the stability of such status. Lily's father, Will Peter, like the rest of Lewis's children, did not adjust well to their new church, and although he was a deeply religious and moral man, Will was never active in church affairs again in his life.

The break with the Moravian church seemed to have affected Will Peter more than the other members of his family. It so happened later that he fell in love with a young girl in the Methodist Church named Ella Hamilton. When he asked her to marry him, she rejected his proposal, not because she did not love him, but because she did not wish to act over-eager. Will Peter was so sensitive to the family position that he mistook her behavior to be an indication that she didn't approve of his father's stand; therefore, he did not pursue her as Ella hoped he would and soon afterward left the town. [8]

He and his cousin, James, had built a small steam-powered boat for travelling down the Ohio and Mississippi waterways to Memphis. They were going to seek work and their fortune. Will kept a log of this journey; some excerpts of it follow:

> The Boat Tuscarawas left Gnadenhutten on Tuesday afternoon about half past three o'clock, Oct. 17th, 1876. Dimentions [sic] of the steamer are nineteen feet long by five ft. beam. Size of engine 2-3/4 bore by 4-1/2 in. stroke, geared with a bolt to the paddle shaft proportion one to five. Paddle wheels four feet diameter, paddles seven inches wide & sixteen inches long. Speed six to eight miles per hour. Having started, we ran down the Tuscarawas river a few miles and camped on the Honey Comb bottom, sleeping on the bank in the open air under a large tree. When getting our blankets ready, some coon hunters came along; had a little chat with them.

Will gave an interesting and detailed account of their trip. It included their searches for food, their "swampings" by larger vessels, their "hitch-hikers" (there were several), and their eventual landing at Memphis on December 3 of the same year. He told something of his stay in Memphis and of his eventually selling the boat for $100, $50 of which he sent home to his brother, Jesse. On Sunday, December 10, he told of going to church, his first time since leaving Gnadenhutten. He said, "It truly did me good. It seemed more civilized, and more like living right. Was in the Central M. E. Church. "

The two cousins were unsuccessful in finding jobs in Memphis, so they separated. Will went east up the Tennessee River, and James went south down the Mississippi, each promising to notify the other if good work was found. Will had not heard from James by May, 1877, so he decided to go and look for him. He traveled south as far as Helena, Arkansas, where he learned that James was rafting on the St. Francis River nearby. Will made a skiff with a friend and went to Indian Bay (up the White River), arriving on May 24. He wrote in his log:

> . . . Got employment [in Indian Bay] as engineer. Will go to work in the morning. . . .
> . . . I and Willie Spencer went out and got a fill of mulberries, also some dew berries. This is an incorporated town. There is no Church here. When anybody comes along that will preach, they have a meeting in the school house.
> July 3. Tuesday. Am to give Louis Silverman lessons to the amount of 20 hours for six dollars. Gave him first lesson today from one till two.

These were the final entries in the log. What kind of lessons was Will giving? It could have been literacy, or arithmetic, or engine building and maintenance, or violin because he was capable in all these areas. [9]

Will Peter and his cousin, James, did not stay long in Arkansas. Being idealistic and adventuresome, they continued their travels and settlings going as far west as California. Will returned to Arkansas in 1883 and settled near Indian Bay on the White River about twenty-five miles from the Mississippi.

At that time Indian Bay boasted a hotel, several boarding houses, and twenty-nine stores, most of which doubled as saloons. It was a center for timber cutting, logging, trapping, and farming on the land when cleared. At the peak of its liveliness, in the 1880s, as many as 15,000 bales of cotton a year were shipped out by steamboat. Will Peter had set up a lumber business because many families were eager to improve upon building log houses. He was able to buy a large acreage of land, both for farming and timber, and he had the first custom steam-engine-operated gin in the area. Robert Smalley had a gin before Will Peter had one, but its energy was provided by a mule-drawn wheel, much like the old-fashioned sorghum molasses presses. Will Peter had a prosperous beginning until a series of floods spelled disaster for the life of Indian Bay and many of its inhabitants in the surrounding area.

The first flood in the series occurred in 1883, the one which spurred the folks in Mississippi to begin building levees on their side of the river. Another one came in 1888, worse for Arkansas because the levees were pushing the water to the Arkansas side. Indian Bay felt the effects of the levees with backwater from the White River. An even higher flood came in 1890.

But this did not deter Will Peter from taking for his bride Florence Mowbray from Greenville, Mississippi. Dorothy Crisp writes in her book, *Neighbors of Crisp's Crossing, Creigh and Connell's Point, Arkansas*, that besides timber and farm land, Will Peter bought a spacious old log house from the heirs of Robert Connell. Robert had built it some sixty years earlier near the junction of Big Cypress Bayou and Big Creek. [10] This was the first home of Will and Florence Peter, who married on March 3, 1890.

During the decade of the 1890s, the floods came annually. The citizens of Arkansas finally started building levees, but it was too late for Indian Bay and many other people of the area. They began leaving at a rapid rate, so the lumber business declined drastically. The flood waters remained so high so long that it was impossible to plant crops. The river traffic slowed down. Land on higher ground was so cheap that people could buy it and move for less money than it would take to stay with the land in those river bottoms and sustain crop losses year after year. If they had bought by mortgage, it was particularly prudent to abandon the land and let it return to the mortgage holder. By 1900, except for a store or two, Indian Bay had become a ghost town.

But Lily's father thought that the area had a future, that prosperity would return, so he borrowed money year after year to bolster up his financial condition, accumulating such a great indebtedness that he was never able to fully recover from it. He had extended credit to many customers who never were able to pay him. He suffered another reverse when the boiler of the steam engine of his lumber mill blew up, damaging his building and equipment and, more seriously, injuring him. It took him a long time to recover, but he kept working hard and long.

Lily considered that her father had a marvelous physique and that he was extremely good looking. He was about 5'11", slender, quite strong, never taking on excess weight. Lily was told by his contemporaries that Will Peter could stand in a dug-out boat, hold up his rifle, and hit a bird or animal a good hundred yards ashore or in the air. She often wished she had inherited his sense of balance. She said that her father's rifle was made in the early years of the eighteenth century, was hand crafted, muzzle loading, and very heavy. It had been given to Will by his father, Lewis. It had a terrific kick, and Lily marveled at the feat of shooting it while standing in a dug-out boat.

What of Lily's mother's ancestors? There is a dearth of records, quite opposite to the situation in her father's family. Lily told the following.

Florence Mowbray Peter's paternal grandparents were a young couple, John and Maria Glensbeckle, who came to the United States from Germany, landing at the port of New Orleans in 1844. A few days after the birth of their first child, John, Maria died, possibly from child-bed fever. It was not long until the young widower married a woman who was apparently a loving step-mother, but when his son was only four years old, the father died of yellow fever. So young John was orphaned of both natural parents. His step-mother remarried soon to another John — John Mowbray.

Lily speculated that young John must have been a winsome child because of his step-mother's devotion to him and the fact that his step-father declared his intentions to adopt him. The step-father died, however, before this was accomplished, but the child was known by the name John Mowbray anyway. He was educated in the Catholic schools in New Orleans.

Tradition in the family has it that John Mowbray was intending to enter the priesthood until he met Pauline Hardy and changed his mind. They were married in 1868 when he was twenty-four and she was eighteen. Lily's mother was their first child, born in 1869. The couple lived in New Orleans several years, later moving to Greenville, Mississippi, where John bought a plantation. Unfortunately, in one of the great floods, it was entirely sanded, making it unproductive and a total loss to them.

There were six children born to John and Pauline Mowbray: three sons and three daughters. Two young boys, John and William, died in early childhood. Lily's Aunt Nellie (Eleanor) was the first person to die of yellow fever in the great epidemic of '77-'78, which swept the town of Greenville. Lily's mother, Florence, about nine years old, caught the disease, and the doctor had given her up to die, but she managed to survive.

Lily's grandfather, John Mowbray, died penniless, actually on skid row, having given over completely to alcohol following the loss of his plantation which held the promise of what he wished to do for his family. Lily surmised that he must have been keenly intelligent and sensitive, obviously loving the classics, borne out by the fact that he named Florence for the Italian city, Eleanor (Nellie) for Eleanor of Acquitaine, Brutus for the Roman senator, and Lorenza for the great di Medici. Lily never saw her grandfather, John Mowbray, and she saw only one picture of him which, she said, showed him to be handsome with a long, stern, arrogant-looking face reflecting a strong will. She said she knew of no other case of alcoholism in her family on either side. She thought that Edwin Arlington Robinson's poem, "Miniver Cheevy," described very well her grandfather as is illustrated by the following verses:

> Miniver loved the days of old
> When swords were bright and steeds were
>   prancing;
> The vision of a warrior bold
> Would set him dancing.
>
> . . .
>
> Miniver loved the Medici,
> Albeit he had never seen one;
> He would have sinned incessantly
> Could he have been one.
>
> . . .
>
> Miniver Cheevy, born too late,
> Scratched his head and kept on thinking;
> Miniver coughed, and cursed his fate,
> And kept on drinking.

Pauline Hardy Mowbray's mother (Lily's great-grandmother) was Sara Soniac, the only daughter of a wealthy French family living in East Feliciana Parish across the river from New Orleans. This was the one branch of Lily's mother's family that came early to the new country. The *-iac* ending is an indication that the family probably came from Djonne Province in the extreme southern part of France. Among the patrician French families of that day, marriages were arranged by the parents. Sara's parents had actually chosen for her the son of a rich planter; however, Sara met a young artist, Clements Hardy, and fell in love with him. Lily knew nothing of Hardy's parents or where in England

Father, Will Peter

Mother, Florence Peter

Will Peter bought a spacious log house from the heirs of Robert Connell

he came from; she knew only that Sara rejected her parents' choice of a husband and eloped with Hardy. Her parents were so furious that they disinherited her and never forgave her, so that they were never reconciled. The young couple went to New Orleans to live, but within two years, both they and Sara's parents were dead from yellow fever, leaving the baby girl, Pauline, who was reared by some friends of her parents in New Orleans. Lily admitted, "The end of this story sounds like a folk tale with the Soniac estate taken over by some wicked uncles as indeed happened in this case."

Pauline, Lily's maternal grandmother, unquestionably had a very unhappy life until her later years. Shortly after Florence married Will Peter, Pauline moved to the Connell's Point-Creigh neighborhood bringing her daughter, Lorenza, with her. Her only other child at home, Brutus, had gone to work on river boats.[11]

Lily's forebears on each side were representatives of all of the European social classes, the aristocracy, middle class, and peasantry, coming from Germany, Holland, England, Scotland, Ireland, France, Belgium, Norway, Hungary, and possibly Spain through the Soniacs from southern France.

The only support for Lily's confidence of her Celtic heritage was her poetic imagination and inclination toward all things Gaelic. She did not mind being alone and claimed she could conduct inner dialogues rather pleasurably. As one who chose to remain single and one who was practically isolated in childhood, she considered that her inner resources stood her in good stead, yet she never recommended singularity or an isolated childhood and believed that most people need peers and life companions. She regarded her lack of each as "a thorn in the flesh," but she took consolation from the old Chinese proverb which says, "Wherever a man dwells, he will find a thornbush growing by his door."[12]

NOTES

[1]John Frederick Peter, the younger, half-brother to David (Lily's great-grandfather), and his brother, Simon, joined the Pennsylvania group of missions in 1770, ten years after their father had joined the group. They were ordained ministers and worked in various capacities in Bethlehem, Nazareth, Litiz, each furnishing leadership in music. Donald M. McCorkle lists the places and positions of John Frederick's service which include teacher, youth worker, accountant, protocollist (secretary) of the boards and clerk of the congregation, principal of the boy's school, chaplain, diarist (Donald M. McCorkle. *Moravian Music in Salem: A German-American Heritage* [Ann Arbor: Univ. Microfilms, 1958] p. 117). Simon surely held similar positions. Lily saw many of these original documents, and they helped her to know and value her paternal ancestry.

[2]In 1790 John Frederick was called from Salem to be minister of music in Bethlehem. The call was a promotion, and he spent the remainder of his life there. In his *lebenslauf*, John Frederick recorded that he left Salem with sorrow at his separation from the brethren and, after a sojourn in New Jersey at the mission, Hope, he arrived at Bethlehem. "I had the joy of meeting again my dear father and mother [step-mother] and finding them well. But four days later my father was taken down with a burning chest fever and on April 28 he went gently and blissfully to the Savior to my deep grief. Yet I was glad that I had been able to see and speak with him once again" (McCorkle. op. cit., p. 300). He does not mention seeing his half-brother, David, Lily's great grandfather, but it is reasonable to assume that this was also a happy reunion. He would never see his brother Simon again, having left him in Salem. David would soon be going to Ohio.

[3]McCorkle's quotation and summation of information from Baker's dictionary (op. cit., p. 109). The entry in the dictionary lists Peter with the original German spelling of his given names, Johann Friedrich (*Baker's Biographical Dictionary of Music* [New York: G. Shirmer, 1940] p. 1232).

[4]*The Complete Works of Longfellow*. Medallion Edition. (Cambridge: Houghton-Mifflin, 1922) p. 95.

[5]Among the genealogical lines in the Peter family not bearing the Peter name is the Levering line from Leverington, England. John Wygard Levering, a paternal grandparent to Lily's father, was the first of her ancestors in that line to come to this country. He came by way of Holland and settled in Philadelphia and are known to be among the first citizens of Roxborough Township, the seat of Philadelphia. A brother of his, Gerhardt,

came across the Atlantic also and settled in Virginia.

The John Leverings' oldest daughter, Anna Katherine, married Heinrich Frey, a German, who had immigrated to Pennsylvania before Penn received it. The first Hungarian to come to America, according to tradition in Lily's family, was Kristoff Paus. His daughter married a cousin to Lily's great-grandmother. Although this connection is distant, Lily regards it as a part of her heritage and did not hesitate to tell Eugene Ormandy that she had an ancestor from Hungary. His reply was, "Then we're kin!"

[6]Sarah Louisa Blickensderfer, Lily's paternal grandmother, was a daughter of the third generation of men with given name, Christian. They were all devout members of the United Brethren, but were not ministers; they turned their attention to the land.

[7]Lewis and Sarah Louisa Peter had nine children besides Lily's father who lived to adulthood, and Lily had some relationship with all of them. There were four sons: Simon, William Oliver, Jesse, and Joseph Lewis; six daughters: Emily, Sarah, Clara, Naomi, Mary, and Adelaide.

[8]Ella Hamilton waited for several years before she married someone else, hoping Will would return and propose again. He never did and did not marry until seventeen years later when he was forty-three. Years later when Lily was living with her Aunt Mary (who married Ella's brother, Joseph Hamilton), Ella came to visit on the occasion of a Hamilton family reunion. When she found out that Lily was Will Peter's daughter, she talked with her at length, looking at Lily ever so intensely and asking endless questions about her father. To Lily, this is further indication that she really did care for him. Lily could not understand Ella's behavior until she returned home the next year when her mother told her about the love affair which was never consummated.

[9]The original copy of the "Memoranda" from which these selections were taken was passed, at Will Peter's death, to his elder son, Jesse, at whose death it was bequeathed to the younger brother, Theodore Edward. It is now in the possession of his son, Theodore Charles. One year as a Christmas present, the brother, Ted, had copies made for each of his sisters, Lily, Oma, and Ethel. It is in Lily's archives.

[10]Dorothy Crisp, *Neighbors of Crisp's Crossing, Creigh, and Connell's Point* (Little Rock, Arkansas: Pioneer Printing Company, 1976) p. 47.

[11]While interviewing in the neighborhood in the summer and fall of 1980, several persons, none of whom were willing to be quoted, told the biographer that Florence Peter had been married to a Crisp before she mar-

ried Will Peter and told of several deprecatory rumors about her background which were circulated, never proven nor laid to rest. These facts called for some research and yielded the following:

W. O. Peter, 43, married Mrs. Florence Crisp, 21, March 3, 1890, at the Turner Methodist Church by Thomas Whitaker (Monroe Co., AR Marriage Book E, p. 602).

W. R. Crisp married Florence Gleansbeckle [sic], July 25, 1887. Stevenson Archer, Preacher, officiating (Marriage Book 9, p. 220, Washington Co., Miss.).

Bob (W. R.) Crisp was a widower who died shortly before Florence married Will Peter.

Louisiana census records were examined. The name *Soniac* was not found. The 1860 census revealed:

> Clements Hardy, 80, artist, living alone,
> born So.Car. (LA, W. Feliciana Parish)

If this is the Clements Hardy who married Sara Soniac, he would have to have been seventy years old when Pauline was born.

The 1870 census showed this entry:

> John C. Moberry, 29, boarding house-saloon,
> b. Denmark. A wife Mary, 28, born Ireland,
> a bookkeeper, and a servant were listed
> (Ward 7, New Orleans Parish, p. 556).

This could hardly be the John Glensbeckle-Mowbray who married Pauline Hardy in 1868. No Gleansbeckle entries were found.

The 1880 Census-Index, Vol. 22, E.D. 91, Sheet 7, Line 46, Washington Co., MI, tells this:

> Pauline Mowbray, w, 30. Trout St., Greenville,
> Other members: Florence,dau.,11,born.LA.
> Brutus,son,4,born MI
> Willie,son,8\12, born MI.

Found on the 1900 AR Census, Monroe Co., Montgomery Township, HH179, was the listings for Wm. O., Florence, Lillie, Naomia, Joseph, Ethel, and Pauline Moberry (M-in-law) Sept 1850, LA.

On the 1900 AR Census, Phillips Co., Cleveland Twp, HH 201-207, there appears in the household of Annie Lightfoot, a sister, Betty Wellborn, and three boarders, one of whom was Glennbeckle [sic}, Lorenza, Dec 1882 17 single, born MI, and three laborers.

There is no accounting for the fact that Pauline Hardy who married John Glensbeckle (his legally correct name, but who went by Mowbray) did name her older children Mowbray but named her last one Glensbeckle, as Lorenza was known, or the reason why Florence used the name Gleansbeckle on the record of her marriage to Crisp. There is no accounting for the many different spellings other than that people themselves often changed spellings and that many census-takers could not spell. Also, many people slipped through the net of census workers.

A hundred years ago . . .*came from a fine old family* and . . . *shows good breeding* were everyday descriptive terms, and the definitive distinction between *lady* and *woman* was finely honed. It is a fact that, in the tradition of those who regarded themselves as aristocracy in the deep South, Lily set a great store on family heritage. She took great pride in her father's ancestors and far more shame than was called for in her mother's, despite having a deep, seemingly compensatory love for Florence, Uncle Brutus, and Aunt Rene. She could hardly bear to discuss them at all, and then she romanticized facts.

Neither Lily nor her sisters ever mentioned their grandmother, Pauline, in their letters, even though she was in and out of the home. Pauline was reputedly good at assisting mothers when babies were born and would stay in the mothers' homes weeks at a time. It takes little imagination to understand the cruelty to a sensitive child which snobbery and gossip could engender, and her suffering from it accounts in part for Lily's determination to "do something and be somebody." Could she have seen with a modern eye, she could have well characterized her grandmother and mother as courageous, resourceful women, true "survivors" in an age in which no welfare programs existed and in which charity was whimsical at best.

[12]Personal interviews with Lily Peter. Tapes 1, 2, 3, 4, 7, 8, 10. Torreyson Library Archives, University of Central Arkansas.

Chapter II

CHILDHOOD, 1891-1908

Blackberry Picking
Comes a memory of blackberry picking, like a caress,
out of my childhood, in the June sun and shade
of a brambled pasture, where a rainy spring
had made rich grass, the berries dewy sweet.
There was much to see in such a pasture as this,
and much to make one happy: puddles to wade —
rain pools under the trees where mosses cling,
cool, grass-grown pools delicious to bare young feet!
. . .
A morning of joy to remember: and with a tiny pail
of berries to surprise my mother, for her to praise —
"Where did you find such big ones, Lily? How fine!"
"In the pasture, Mother, down near the old rail fence."
All this comes back to me now, like a fairy tale,
or the songs my mother sang in my childhood days.
What has blown away all of this beauty, ashine?
What but the winds of Time, that blow hither and
hence!

> Lily Peter
> *Delta Country*, unpublished

    The dirt road to Lily's birthplace is rarely used, and it is not
red like the clay further south, nor black like the plowed fields
stretching endlessly beyond the hedgerows that line the road. The

two-rutted road is pale yellow, yellow as a dusty day lily. To negotiate this road, one needs to pick a dry summer day and a high-frame vehicle, for the only travelling companion is Big Cypress Bayou that snakes along the level of the road until you reach the swamp. There the road tops an ancient levee and make-shift bridges and finally comes to stop at Big Creek, into which Big Cypress flows.

A rise in the land at the edge of the swamp is the place where a large hand-hewn log house was built in the early 1800s by Robert S. Connell, and although it has since been destroyed by fire, the branches of the oaks and elms along the bayou still pass on those singular Delta breezes. The fringed green limbs of the cypresses towering above the swamp hint at the abundant wildlife that had been here: deer, bear, squirrel, raccoon, opossum, owl, hawk, quail, dove, rookeries of crane, songbird. Lily has heard the panther scream.[1]

By the time Lily's father bought the log cabin in the late 1880s, the trees Connell had left were large and handsome. The house faced Big Cypress Bayou, toward the south and west, its hand-laid foundation high upon a gentle slope of land, making it easy to imagine the reason for the choice of this spot for a home. Above the spring rise of water, the log house was near enough to the creek for easy access to the boat transportation available on the creek in the 1830s.[2]

It was in this house that Lily was born on June 2, 1891, and she claimed memories of the house, even of being in her cradle. This cradle was made of hand-carved and finished walnut wood. A frame about a foot off the floor provided tracks for the rockers. Its rails and posts were decorated with turnings and carvings. Lily slept in it until she was three years old. She recalled wanting her mother to put the cradle nearer the window so she could look out at the world bathed in moonlight. When the moon was right, its light would shine into Lily's cradle, and she could make finger shadows on the wall or on the sheets.[3]

Lily also remembered a red high chair with a picture of a lady painted on its seat. She would never sit all the way back in the seat for fear of hurting the lady's face.

The only time her father ever took for relaxation during the day was on Sundays. He would sit on the gallery (the roofed passageway between the two large rooms of the log house) in his rocking chair, holding Lily on his lap. Often the weather would be perfect, the vista down to the bayou would be lovely, and the murmur of conversation would be pleasant as her father talked to her and her mother, who would be working in one of the adjoining rooms. She remembered wearing a little sleeveless white dress edged with lace at the neck.

. . . Born to W. O. and Florence M. Peter, an infant, November 2, 1892. Died shortly after birth. Buried Turner.

When Lily was two years old, her father had some business at Indian Bay and allowed her to ride over with him in the buggy. It was in the fall of the year. One of the several wagons at the edge of town held a load of watermelons. It belonged to a very old colored man who had gone into one of the stores. Another Negro came along and decided to tease the old man by calling, "Somebody is stealin' yo' watermelons, fella." He repeated it several times. The tone of his voice had such a rare, plangent quality that Lily never forgot it.

During the winter of 1893, Will Peter ordered some thoroughbred Poland-China hogs from Ohio, where this breed was raised extensively with good results. Having come from Ohio, he knew that the hogs grew immensely fat, a condition any farmer wanted since lard was useful not only in cooking but in soap making as well. To Lily, those hogs were monstrous. Early in the spring when the woods were showing only the faintest green, Lily followed her mother out into the barn lot. Florence Peter had gone to the corn crib for a pan of corn for the chickens and was returning when Tom Whitfield and another neighbor rode up to the gate. They asked to see Will Peter, and Florence explained that he was away. Lily was playing at a little distance along the fence row aware of the hogs across the lot. Attracted by the corn, suddenly several of the pigs started toward Lily and her mother. Lily ran to her mother and caught hold of her apron. Mr. Whitfield laughed and said, "You're afraid of the big pig, are you, child?" Lily was quite embarrassed by her fear so clung to her mother's skirt and said nothing.

The fine hogs had a sad fate other than the one they were destined for. That summer they took cholera, and every one of them died. What Will Peter had not realized was that, because of their immense size and crossbreeding, they were more subject to maladies and much more suited to the cold winters and mild summers in Ohio than the climate of Arkansas. It was an expensive venture for him and a disappointing one, as were several of his efforts to have the best. Lily says that her father farmed more like a creative, experimental scientist than like the practical-minded business person one must be to succeed in an occupation so subject to the whims of nature. If he had had unlimited resources, this trait might well have led to some valuable agricultural innovations. As it was, his ambitions only led to the slow deterioration of his profit and savings.

. . . Born to William Oliver Peter and Florence Mobrey Peter, Naomi Cecilia Peter, October 3, 1893.

On account of the floods which were coming each year, Will Peter, as a lumberman, selected the best logs and sawed out lumber for another home for his family. He acquired the most elevated piece of land in the area for its site, and on it, he built a lumber shed for drying and seasoning the planks. The site was four miles north of the log home but was still in sight of Big Cypress Bayou.

In March of 1894, Lily's father saw that a severe flood was advancing rapidly. He took what workmen he had and set about making the lumber shed habitable. In one day, they put in floors and made steps of split logs, but they had no time for windows. Room dividers were made by throwing blankets over the rafters left exposed for the purpose. The family moved that very day because the water was rising so rapidly. One of the workmen who helped move was Ben Catlett, a friendly man who loved to tease children. When Catlett told Lily that they were going to put her into a piece of stove pipe to move her to the new house, she made it a point to stay as far away from him as she could. She was quite relieved when she found that there was a chair for her in the wagon beside Aunt Rene (Lorenza) behind her father and mother, who sat on the spring seat. Her mother held the baby, Oma, and Aunt Rene held their large Ansonia mantel clock.

When Lily was four years old, her father wanted to have a herd of Jersey cows, reputed to be the best breed for producing adequate milk with a high butterfat content. He acquired some cows and a high priced bull. All Jersey bulls are considered mean-tempered, but this one was particularly irascible and had not been dehorned. Will Peter decided that the best way to control him would be to put a ring in his nose. He ordered one, and it arrived on a day when a much needed rain had come. He had it in his pocket and was walking around the farm looking at the crops. He found the young bull down in the corner of the pasture and thought it would be a good time to catch him and put the ring in his nose. Will Peter was courageous enough to be foolhardy. As he was holding the bull around the neck trying to insert the ring, of course he met with resistance from the bull. The grass was still slippery from the rain, and Will lost his footing. One of the bull's horns caught his right arm and ripped the flesh from the wrist to the elbow. The main artery was severed. He could have bled to death had he not grasped the artery and pinched it together as he walked the mile back to the house. No one was around to come to his aid, since a rainy day meant that the hands went to town or the local country store.

When Will Peter arrived home in that condition, Lily was sitting on the front porch step playing with her china doll. The sight of her ghastly white, bloody father whose face reflected the abnormal look of fear and pain frightened her speechless. He told her to go into the house and bring her mother's scissors. When she returned with them, he instructed her to cut off a piece of flesh which was hanging from his arm at the wrist. She obeyed her father, but the sight of blood for the rest of her life demanded the pain of reliving that episode.

Her father then instructed her to find and bring her mother. Florence Peter, of course, was quite upset and immediately sent for the nearest doctor, but the doctor's ministrations did not prevent blood-poisoning from developing. Will Peter ran a high temperature for two weeks, and everyone thought he would die. He survived but was never as healthy again.

. . . Born to William Oliver Peter and Florence Mobrey Peter, a little girl, named Nellie, October 1, 1895. Died, December 18, 1895. Buried Turner.

Lily remembers a time when Tom Hamilton came for his annual visit with Will Peter. They gathered in the living room after supper, and "Mr. Tom" turned to his favorite topic, religious doctrine. In any group, he would bring up religion no matter what subject anyone else tried to introduce. He loved to argue points of doctrine, convinced that by so doing he was promoting the Lord's work. This time he chose the theme of the millennium from the Book of Revelation, as if anybody ever knew for sure what that metaphor was all about. Will and Florence Peter attempted to keep the conversation on a level of rational discussion, but with poor success; Hamilton continued to argue regardless of his hosts' disinclination.

Lily's Aunt Lorenza attempted to cool Hamilton's warmth to his subject. She said, "Last week someone sent Brother Will a book on the millennium. Let's see what the writer of the book has to say." She went over to the bookcase and took out the book, which had a cover of a rare shade of blue.

All this time, Lily was hidden under a library table covered with a Victorian table cloth which reached to the floor on all sides. Her dolls were with her, and she was pretending that they were all in a tent. But she heard her aunt read the title, *The Millennial Dawn*, and she thought that the words *millennium* and *millennial* were the most beautiful words she had ever heard, and she said them over and over to herself in a whisper for fear of forgetting them. The next day she went to the bookcase and took down the book just to look at the words. Lily, who was only five years old, had been taught to read by her mother, and she could read many words phonetically without knowing their meanings.

She loved the sounds of words. She would identify wild flowers with fanciful names she made up for them. In the fall, she discovered a beautiful wild flower growing in the fence corners near her house; because it was the same appealing shade of blue as the cover of the book, *The Millennial Dawn*, she named it that. Later she learned that her "Millennial Dawn" was the wild ageratum.

The Peters were able to have only one photograph made of Lily as a child. Her mother told her that they planned many trips to Clarendon, the location of the nearest photographer, but something always prevented them from going. The floods not only curtailed travel; they drained the family pocketbook to the point

Lily, age 4, standing next to her sister Oma

that little was left for anything beyond the bare necessities. However, David Womack, a Cypert neighbor who had a camera, came to the Peter home and made a photograph of Lily and her little sister, Naomi, whose name had been shortened to Oma. Mrs. Peter had cleaned up her little girls, who were grimy from play, put a fresh dress on each of them, and tied ribbons in their hair. She brought the red high chair out into the yard, threw an afghan over it, set the toddler, Oma, in it, and placed Lily beside the chair. Lily asked if she might hold her fan, a treasured gift from Aunt Emily, showing at an early age her sense of coquetry. All Lily's life she liked a blossom or a silk scarf or a fan in her hand when the occasion called for her to be the center of attention.

Lily's fifth birthday happened to coincide with the visit of one of her father's best friends, John Black, from Clarendon. For some unknown reason, a turkey gobbler, which was intended for Christmas, hadn't been eaten, so Florence Peter decided to save him for Lily's birthday on June 2. They had a special dinner, and much ado was made over the celebration.

But Lily was not happy. She had a preconceived notion about her fifth birthday that came from her reading of *Alice in Wonderland.* She thought that on the day she became five years old she would be as tall as her mother, that she would have grown up over the previous night. She had pictured herself going around the house doing the work that her mother did, identifying with her strength, grace, and beauty. Lily had a special task she wanted to perform on her birthday — not a feminine one nor one she had ever seen her mother do. She wanted to clean the barn. It was made of rough cypress and oak, and wisps of hay and shucks and cobwebs clung to the walls, especially in the corners. She had promised herself that, when she was five, she would sweep down all that trash. When she awoke on her birthday morning and was no bigger, she was so disappointed that she wept. The mood hung over her all day.

. . . Born to William Oliver Peter and Florence Mobrey Peter on October 26, 1896, a boy, named Joseph Lewis. Died August 26, 1905.

Florence Peter was a diplomat in dealing with her growing family. Once Lily and Oma decided they could choose other names for themselves. Florence said, "My dears, you can change your names. Just select ones you like and get every other member of the family to call you by the new name for a week, and we will change them officially." Oma chose to be named Mary for Aunt Mary who wrote often to the family. Lily went to the dictionary her mother had used in school because it contained a list of names and their meanings. Her first choice was Triphena or Tryphosa because both of these names meant the dawn of day; however, they were so odd she didn't dare tell anyone for fear of ridicule. Instead, she announced that she would like to be called Evangeline Victoria. No one managed to stick with the new names a day, let alone a week, so the girls learned the difficulty of changing habits and decided to accept the names they had.[4]

During Lily's sixth year another buggy ride with her father filled her with both pleasure and spine-chilling fright. Florence had told Will that she had time to make muscadine jelly and preserves if he could take time to go to the woods and pick some. He asked Lily to go with him. Prior to this, Lily had been asking many questions about the shape of the world. She was told that it was round, and she conceived of it as a round disk, not very thick, because she also had been told that if one dug a hole deep enough in the ground, one would come out in China. This was confusing since Florence referred to their best dishes as "china." Lily was thinking these things as her father drove farther and farther into the woods. She was so afraid that they would drive to the edge of the world and fall off that she sat rigid with her toes curled up tight in her shoes. Her fear was somewhat alleviated when her father explained that the world was round like an orange and that people and things were held in their places by the law of gravity. All of her understanding of the law came from phrases she had heard such as outlaws, in-laws, and law-breakers, and then this new law, the law of gravitation. Then her anxiety transferred to what would happen if someone broke the law of gravity. Would people and things fall off the world?

Florence Peter was ambitious for her children and fervently believed that the best means of improvement of self and circumstance lay in self-control and education. Louise Mixon Griffin, who lived in the neighborhood and knew the family well, referred to Florence as "a Spartan mother." She scolded her children for giving in to their feelings, even when hurt or ill, and praised them for any evidence of self-control under stress.[5] She started teaching them from the books which she and Will Peter had used when they were children with no inhibitions about "a right age to begin" other than whether or not they were able to recite from what they had studied.

Their home education was necessary, if the children were to have any education at all, because the public schools in Monroe County were available for only two months in the summer, and at a walking distance of three and a half miles, quite far for small children. Florence had some help teaching from her husband and her sister, Lorenza.

Lily's first readers were by Barnes; then came McGuffey's Third, Fourth, and Fifth. There were Long's language books, then Reed and Kellogg's Grammar. Just about nine years old, Lily loved Kellogg's book, especially the very first lesson, "A word is a sign of an idea." From it she learned to diagram the following sentence which she liked because it had an unusual inversion at the end: *The fly sat on the axle of the chariot wheel and said, "What a dust do I raise."* This sentence gave her an excellent opportunity to show that she knew the subject and predicate. *Morn purples the East,* a sentence showing the objective complement, was another she would diagram over and over to herself. She loved the dawn, loved the use of the adjective as a verb, and she loved the sound of the sentence. She did not know until years later that the sentence came from Milton's *Paradise Lost.*

Following Reed and Kellogg's, she was taught Harvey's

Grammar and then Meiklejohn's Grammar by her first full-year teacher, William Arthur Owens. When she finally went to Ohio at age fifteen, she was ready for Halleck's Rhetoric.

Arithmetic lessons came with the Ray series while Lily was studying at home. There were Ray's New Primary, Ray's New Intellectual, Ray's New Elementary, Ray's New Practical, and finally Ray's New Higher Arithmetic. This last one was a big book containing problems of calculus. Lily was ready for it by the time she was eleven. She had found only one difficulty. Then Florence said to her husband, "Will, you will just have to take over Lily's education in mathematics. I have been trying in vain to teach her about the greatest common divisor and the least common multiple for days, and I am making no headway at all." Lily did not know why her father was able to make it clearer to her than her mother, just that she finally learned it.

Rounding out Lily's home studies were the books, Quackenbos' *History of the United States* and Maury's *Eclectic Geography*. The latter was a big book which belonged to Aunt Rene. Lily studied the many maps and made many mispronunciations. For example, she called Chesapeake Bay "Sheepstake Bay." She read and reread all these books, because her family could afford few additions to their library. Reading was one of Lily's greatest childhood pleasures, not only in winter, when she could not be outdoors, but also during the summers when it was nothing unusual for her to take a book to some cool spot by the bayou, on the meadow, in or under a tree.

The only children to play with outside of the family were the three little Kornegay boys who lived near. They were about the same age as the Peter children, and they were allowed to exchange visits occasionally, but not often. Except at lesson time, the Peter children had to entertain themselves. Lily made up some imaginary playmates who were quite real to her. Their names were Sarah, Rose, Beau, Flower, Apple, and Popla. It never occurred to her that they did not exist. She even wrote letters to them, just as she wrote her aunts and her grandma.

One winter her Uncle Brutus had come to visit. There came a storm, and he and Will Peter went out through the pasture to see about the livestock. When they returned, Uncle Brutus, who loved to tease, said to Lily, "You know, Lily, down the road a piece on Vinegar Hill I saw Popla sitting under a red haw tree. He was barefoot and so cold he was about to freeze to death." Lily cried so hard and long with sorrow at this news that Uncle Brutus regretted his words.

Lily wrote her first poem when she was six. Silent letters of the alphabet inspired it. In McGuffey's Spelling Book, every vowel had a diacritical mark over it just as in Webster's Dictionary. From the time she began spelling the words of one syllable, such as *am, as, at, in, it, if, of, but,* her mother would require her to call the name of every diacritical mark. She also had Lily divide the words into syllables and tell which syllable was accented. In this way, Lily learned to spell with considerable accuracy. One of the most fascinating things to her was the use of silent letters. In the McGuffey speller, every silent letter was marked through with a diagonal line which Lily thought made them look especially impressive. Her first poem follows:

> Spring has come, oh, spring
> has come
> With birds that sing and bees
> that hum
> And the earth with flowers
> seems to be numb

Lily knew that the word *numb* made no sense there, but she thought she just had to use it because of that beautiful silent *b* at the end of the line.

The family post office was at Turner four miles away. In

those days there was no mail delivery to their home. If Lily's parents were able to save any extra money at all, they would subscribe to a magazine or two. At a time when they were receiving only one, *The Orange Judd Farmer*, Lily experienced her first literary disappointment, one almost strong enough to end her literary career at age eight.

This magazine included a column for children, publishing their letters and verses. Lily read that column eagerly. She noted a verse written by a boy who wrote about a squirrel which, according to him, had been out courting the night before and left some tracks in the snow. Lily considered his account a mistake. Her father had experienced a devastating loss that winter. Another of Will Peter's efforts to produce the abundant life in the Arkansas wilderness had failed. He had put every penny he could spare into fruit trees for an orchard, but the winter was so bitter that the rabbits came and stripped all the bark off the trees, killing most of them. Lily had seen the rabbit tracks in the snow, so she composed a verse to refute the claims of the young man. With no instruction, just her ear to guide her, she came up with this poem:

> 'Twas not the squirrel who
> went calling
> on his neighbor through the
> night.
> For the squirrel was a-sleeping
> His winter home within.
>
> And the rabbit was not calling
> On his own true love bedight
> But to the farmer's fruit trees
> He had been.

She knew to put the hyphen in *a-sleeping* and was proud of the big word *bedight*. But she was naive about addressing letters. She wrote to her kinfolk, for example, addressing her letter,

"Dear Grandma, Greenville, Miss." She must have addressed her letter to *The Orange Judd Farmer* the same way, because she was heartbroken that her letter was never acknowledged, that her poem was never printed, and that the little boy was not properly corrected. The letter may never have left the house, having been tossed aside as "some more of Lily's foolishness."

One of Lily's fondest memories was of her parents sitting on the porch on pleasant evenings making music, her father playing the violin and her mother singing. After his accident with the bull, he seldom played the violin because of the pain of lifting his arm, yet he did occasionally. Lily loved to hear her father tune the *g* string. It sent shivers all over her body. Wishing to emulate her father, she begged for a violin of her own.

Finally, before the Christmas when she was seven, her mother told her that Santa Claus would bring her a violin. When a big package came by express the day before Christmas, it was opened at once. Lily was sure that, if she ever got to heaven, she could be no happier than she was on that evening. Exceptions to the eight o'clock bedtime rule were made on holidays, so Lily sat up until 11:00 p.m. just holding her little violin on her lap, looking at it and loving it. Within a week she was playing simple tunes on it. She longed for a teacher. Her father taught her as much as he could verbally, but could not demonstrate for any length of time because of the pain in his injured arm. But Lily persisted, and when she finally went to school at age twelve, her teacher asked her to prepare something for the Thanksgiving program. She rehearsed an old-fashioned tune she had heard her father play, "Red Bud." At one point, her father overheard her playing a *c* instead of a *c#* and gave her a lesson on the half-step that stayed with her the rest of her life. The response of her first audience at the Thanksgiving program was quite satisfying. She played the violin all of her life until the final decade, studying, practicing, and fantasizing that she might one day perform a concerto with a great orchestra to a distinguished audience.

. . . Born to William Oliver Peter and Florence Mobrey Peter, a daughter, Ethel Louise, on October 17, 1898.

Early in the year, 1898, the community experienced an epidemic of typhoid fever caused by the devastating flood of 1897. Aunt Lorenza had it first. Next Lily's father had it, and he nearly died. The little sister, Oma, had it next, lying unconscious for two months. There was no medicine for it; she was cared for with patience and concern and perseverance. Oma must have had a strong constitution, because she recovered, having to learn to walk all over again and being nothing but skin and bones. It was amazing that she had no brain damage. When she graduated from the University of Arkansas in 1934, she ranked second in her class of more than two hundred.

The summer was hot and miserable. Lily was ill for two weeks with either a light case of typhoid or malaria. Mrs. Peter managed to hold up either because of or in spite of the fact that she was pregnant with Ethel. Will Peter never fully recovered from the effects of his bout with typhoid fever. He became an overly serious, dour person, seemingly quite distant. He was suffering also from terrible financial reverses. In 1896, cotton had gone down to five cents a pound and was several years recovering in price. The lumber business had lost customers, many of whom left owing Will Peter money. Lily thinks that it was her mother's resourcefulness and optimism in the face of seeming hopelessness that made them survive during those years.

Lily published her first book, an edition of one copy, when she was nine years old. It was her enterprise entirely. Its title was *Poems, Essays, and Stories*. She wrote its contents out in longhand as neatly as possible. For the cover, she used a sample of wallpaper left over from papering one of the bedrooms. The pattern was of pastel pink and blue flowers on a pale pink background. She cut out the letters for the title and her name from tinfoil and painstakingly pasted them on the floral cover. Lily at the tine thought the little book quite elegant and often wished she had kept it.

. . . Born to William Oliver Peter and Florence Mobrey Peter, a son, August 26, 1900, named Jesse Charles Peter.

Creativity was necessary for Lily's survival during her childhood. As the oldest child, she was usually the inspiration for most of the fun in the family. One problem she was determined to solve was the destruction of precious dolls that were left out in the yard when it rained on their home-made doll houses. She conceived of a stick doll that could live outdoors, rain or shine. Her little four-year-old brother Joe helped her to bring the stick doll into being. They chose a board about eighteen inches long for the body which would fit the clothes of Ethel's large doll, Polly Pine. They found a small piece of shingle to nail crossways for the doll's face. Joe nailed, and Lily painted the face. With a paring knife, Lily dug out holes for the eyes, which she wanted to be blue. The liquid from her mother's bluing bottle did not accomplish a nice shade of blue, so she got an entire stick of bluing and plugged the holes full of it. Lily mashed poke berries and with their deep red juice painted on an indelible nose and mouth. Even though armless, when dressed, Suzy Lucy Bunch of Roses looked like a doll. She was weather-proof too.

Lily remembered these lines from a poem she composed about her:

> Her monstrous round eyes are colored with dyes
> Made with bluing and water we got from the sluice,
> And her lips are made rosy with poke-berry juice.

The verse required a bit of poetic license. The family had no sluice (What else would rhyme with juice?) but carried their water in buckets from the pump.[6]

One of Lily's reading adventures caused some consternation. She read one of her father's books by some famous eighteenth century natural philosopher who was an agnostic, causing her to become an atheist at age nine. She dared not express this new attitude because she knew her parents would be shocked. She finally found out that what that writer did not believe in was the idea of God which was prevalent at the time. Lily was relieved and said the experience taught her that it is usually fruitless to question anyone's idea of God since most people's concept of God will usually change a number of times during their lives.

In the summer of 1901 when Lily was ten years old, she went to school for the first time on Connell's Point, about three miles and a half from the Peter home. It was a one-room school taught by Erastus Smalley, a nineteen-year-old neighbor. His father, Tom, having grown up after the Civil War when there were no schools at all in the area, was determined that his son would have an education. He had helped with the building of the first school on the point. It was called the Grider School after the donor of the land. Will Peter donated the lumber and supervised the construction by volunteer community labor.

Lily's first schooling and Erastus' first teaching job coincided. The year before, his father had sent him up to Trenton (about fourteen miles north) to a private academy established there by Professor Lee Price Anderson, who had come from Virginia. Anderson was a well qualified teacher and was determined to educate his pupils in the classical tradition. All the students had to take Latin, but Erastus did not do well at all in that subject. He had no grammar; he did not understand declensions or conjugations. When Professor Anderson found out Erastus had been given the summer teaching job at Grider School, he said, "Erastus, the thing for you to do to learn Latin is to teach it. When I come to visit your school, I will expect to observe your Latin class and see how

The first school built at Connell's Point, about 1880,
named the Grider school served as both the school house
and the meeting hall for the Sanctified Church

you and your students are getting along. If you do not have a Latin
class, I will be very disappointed."

Poor Erastus dreaded the notion of teaching Latin, but he
dreaded Professor Anderson's disapproval more. He formed a
Latin class of the only child interested, Lily. He ordered for her
a Collier and Daniels First Latin Book just like his and gave her
an assignment every day. She memorized the vocabulary and re-
cited the words and meanings to him in the few minutes he had
for her. She conjugated verbs and declined nouns as written as-
signments and handed the papers to him each day. He accepted
them gravely, but he never did return any of them.

In that short term, Lily memorized all the regular conjuga-
tions and declensions, as well as some of the more difficult ones.
She was so excited about her new knowledge that she wrote "A
Latin Love Story," illustrating the old proverb that true love never
does run smoothly. She printed the story on a scroll, tied a red
ribbon around it, and put it in her trunk, the depository of all her
treasures.

... Born to William Oliver Peter and Florence Mobrey Peter on November 6, 1901, a son, named William Harold. Died November 1, 1904. Buried Turner.

The next summer when Lily was eleven, she went to school again at the Point, but the teacher, George Porter, made no attempt to teach Latin. Lily only began to understand Latin when she started to school the next spring at Turner, a four mile walk from her home, where she had a capable teacher, William Arthur Owens. He took much interest in the progress of all his students and did everything he could to help them. He had just graduated from Hendrix College, Conway, Arkansas. He explained Latin as he taught it, and Lily learned what those declensions and conjugations were all about. Later she was to teach Latin for many years in the Marvell High School.

The first day of school at Turner was memorable for Lily. It was a bright April morning. She had walked to school with Jesse and Willie Kornegay and their stepbrother, Joel Crisp, who had stopped at her house for her. Birds were singing, and the redbud and dogwood trees were in bloom. She was excited at the prospect of meeting children she had never seen before.

As she and the boys approached the school house, she could see Mr. Owens standing on the steps. A little girl, younger than Lily, handed him a bunch of flowers, and he said, "How pretty! Pretty flowers and a pretty girl." Lily was impressed with his charming manner. The little girl was pretty, and Lily thought it was nice of Mr. Owens to tell her so.

The bell rang soon, and the children gathered inside the one-room school. Mr. Owens examined Lily's books and assigned her to the advanced class. She felt ill-equipped to adjust the other members because the one nearest her age was a fifteen-year-old, four years older than she. The ages of the others ranged from sixteen to nineteen, and all of them were dating and considering marriage.

There were only about twenty-five students in the school that day, but it wasn't long before Mr. Owens' fame as a kind and capable teacher began to spread, and the numbers increased. Eventually there were so many that he asked the school board to let his sister, Artie Mae, be his assistant. The board members agreed to do so for the summer, but not for the fall, since many children would drop out to pick cotton.

Miss Owens taught the lower grades, and Mr. Owens taught the higher ones. Toward the end of the summer, he took a little vacation for a week, moving Miss Artie Mae to the higher classes and asking Lily to take the lower ones. One of her projects for the week was to teach the first graders to count to one hundred. One of them was Jack Wells, a boy about as old as Lily, who had never been to school before.

Twelve-year-old Lily tried to behave in a very grown-up manner. She told each of them that, when they learned to count to one hundred, she would bring them, as a prize, an apple from her father's orchard. On Wednesday, Lily and the neighborhood children were walking to school when along came a man in a wagon and offered them a ride. There were about eight of them, so they had to stand up in the wagon. Jack Wells was in the group. In spite of the fact that he towered over her, she asked her pupil if he could count to one hundred. With a scowl on his face, he replied, "Naw, kin you?" That look made her feel the small seventy-two pounds that she was. Someone at school teased her and told her that she wasn't any bigger than a bar of soap after a hard day's washing, giving Lily her first knowledge of that cliche.

The children from Connell's Point found lots of entertainment walking the four-mile distance to the Turner School. There was a cabin lying at the edge of the woods by the Little Cypress Bayou that was called the Dookey Place. It was owned by the Mayo family, but an old black man named Dewey Dookey lived there. He was a friendly old man who played the fiddle for dances. A common expression was, "Let's go over to Dookey's and get him to play for us." He died in the early years of the century, but the phrase, "Dookey's place" lived on.[7]

One day the children were going by the Dookey place, then inhabited by a man named Taff Hawkins, who had a big yearling calf tied with a heavy log chain to a little calf just weaned. The big calf had jerked the little calf around until its neck was rubbed raw, and it fretted and bawled miserably. That was just Hawkins' way of keeping up with his little calf, but the children thought it was cruel. They decided to mend matters by taking off the log chain. It did not occur to them they were doing anything wrong. After quite a chase, Lily and the three Kornegay boys caught the big calf and worked the chain off his head. Then it was easy to release the younger calf.

They all felt virtuous for having done such a good deed; however, they realized that their intentions might be suspect, so they decided to get rid of the chain in order to cover up their noble deed. Lily thought of a hollow beech tree that had a hole in it they could reach. They pushed the chain into the hole, link by link, and hid it completely. They never told a soul.

Several years afterward the land was sold, and the buyer cut all the timber. The sawing crew came forward with a weird tale. They cut into a hollow beech tree which contained a heavy, rusty chain with blood on it. They surmised that it was one the Yankees used during the Civil War to torture Southern captives. (The Yankee army had marched through Eastern Arkansas and crossed the Mississippi below Vicksburg in order to surprise the garrison in Vicksburg by coming up from the south.)[8]

When the Turner School began in September of 1905, Mr. Owens decided that his one advanced class (the one Lily was in) needed to go through their books again. Lily was sure that she knew the books thoroughly; and because her mother was ill most of the time (a situation that concerned Lily greatly), she begged to be allowed to stay at home. Her parents consented. She helped in every way she could at the household and farm tasks, but she read everything she could lay her hands on.[9]

Even though she had never studied music herself, Florence Peter loved it and encouraged all the Peter children to learn and appreciate it. In spite of the floods and poverty, in 1905, she persuaded Will to buy an old-fashioned cottage pump-organ which had to be pedaled. Lily, Oma, and Ethel learned to play it.

... Born to William Oliver Peter and Florence Mobrey Peter, a son, named Theodore Edward, October 10, 1904.

When Lily was about thirteen, she read in a magazine an advertisement that said that the U. S. School of Music would give instruction by mail in violin, piano, organ — even voice. She asked her mother if she might send for the violin instruction. Mrs. Peter said she could but warned her that the lessons might not be satisfactory because the violin was such a difficult instrument. Nevertheless, Lily picked blackberries from the fence-rows, sold them, and made enough money to pay for the lessons. She misunderstood most of the instructions and formed more bad habits to go along with the ones she already had, habits which plagued her all her life because the violin teachers she had later did not bother to correct them until she went to Juilliard and studied with Louis Bostelman.

From the time Lily had been given her violin, unless it was bitter cold, she had gone to the barn to practice on it. She went of her own accord. For one thing, she wanted her pieces to be heard only after she had perfected them to the best of her ability; another reason was that the open passage-way was the coolest place she could find in the summer heat. The hay loft provided excellent insulation in summers and winters. But the story went around the neighborhood that her parents made her go to the barn to practice to relieve themselves of the noise. This offended Lily who considered her parents to be extremely patient.[10]

Lily's parents were gravely concerned about her not being in school and discussed it often. They considered Galloway, a boarding school at Searcy, Arkansas, about one hundred twenty-five miles away from their home, but felt she was too young to be away from family and that they really couldn't afford it. The next year, however, they decided they must do something.

It was in August of 1906 that Will Peter and Lily got on the train at Helena and made the long trip to Gnadenhutten, Ohio, where Lily was to live with her Aunt Mary and Uncle Joe Hamilton as family and complete her high school education.[11] She enjoyed the undivided attention of her father, and she sensed his eagerness to visit his home, which he hadn't seen since 1883. Lily felt that she was in the midst of an unending dream as she watched the new vistas from the train windows. She loved school so much that the prospect of completing high school was one of sheer delight.

Will's sister, Clara, and her husband, Miniver Belt, lived at Newark, Ohio, so they stopped there for a short visit. Lily was pleased to meet this family of relatives and thought their house the handsomest she had ever seen. Aunt Clara was a tiny woman, but quite strong and she and Uncle Miniver were most gracious. When she arrived at the Hamiltons, she found them equally gracious. The whole family welcomed her and her father and made her feel genuinely comfortable, a reception she appreciated because she had become self-conscious about her changing body and worried because she had too few clothes and too little spending money.

When she entered the high school in Gnadenhutten, she felt as if every eye was on her all the time. Although she had always liked attention, this was more than she wanted. She was the first person from the South that many of the students had ever heard speak. They would get her to talk just to listen to her accent.

Lily as a high school student

Nonetheless, she did outstanding school work. Confident of her accomplishments in Latin with Mr. Owens, she had enrolled in the advanced Latin class. When it came to the thirteenth chapter of Caesar's *Gallic Wars*, Lily was the only class member who could read those subjunctives as if they were English. When she did so, all the other students turned around and stared at her as if she were a freak.

Not long after she arrived, one of the girls asked her where she lived. Lily told her that she was from Arkansas, that she had come by train, but that she had stopped off at Newark for a little while. Her pronunciation did not coincide with the local one in Ohio. The natives said, "Noork," and Lily said, "New-ark." The girl thought Lily had said, "Europe," and "New York" and she passed the word around that Lily had recently come from abroad.

Had Aunt Mary's family not been sweet and kind to her, Lily could not have borne the grief of February 1907. She received a letter from her mother telling her of her father's death by accident. Her father had bought a new team of mules for the farm. They were not well broken, and the hands were afraid of them. Typically unafraid, Will Peter directed the men to help him harness the team to a wagon for the first time. The mules were scared and very skittish. They started out fairly well with Will at the reins, but something made the mules bolt, one in one direction, one in another. The stress broke the traces of one mule, and the imbalance caused the wagon to turn over. Two men in the wagon with Will Peter were thrown clear, but he was pinned under it and crushed. In two days he took pneumonia and died at age fifty-seven.[12]

Florence Peter wrote Lily that she must stay in Ohio and finish school because there was no way she could come home in time for the funeral; besides, she would be much more help to her mother if she came home qualified to teach school. A diploma from a good high school was considered excellent qualification for teaching a country school, unless one failed miserably the examina-

46

tion given by the County School Superintendent.

Lily graduated from Gnadenhutten High School as valedictorian of the class in May of 1908. That Sunday after her graduation, in spite of the good years of study there and the honors, she felt as if she had sunk into a horrible pit of blackness. She thought, "Here I have finished high school and now have to go out into a world I know nearly nothing about and have had little contact with. I am returning to a home that cannot possibly be the same as it was when I left it two years ago. I am going to be teaching school, and I have no idea how to begin." She felt as if she were at the bottom of the universe, even though it was lovely weather and the atmosphere was perfect on the lawn of her aunt's home, a pretty place about a mile out in the country. Lily felt like crying, but she couldn't. She had never cried as much as other children, because when she did, it was traumatic.

Lily was sad to be leaving Gnadenhutten and her friends and relatives there. She had not been allowed to date but had a "boy friend" relationship with Foster Lickey, cousin to the Hamilton children, but not to her. They had promised to write each other. All who came to the station to see her off on the train wept. (Partings in those days were often for the last time.) Cousin Laura and her cousin, Jessie Hamilton, rode with Lily about twenty miles of the journey to the little town of New Philadelphia. When they left the train, Lily felt desolate.

As she and her father had done before, she stopped and visited with her Aunt Clara and family at Newark. When she left there, she felt even more desolate because she feared she might not make train connections at St. Louis, but a friendly lady helped her do this, and as she came nearer home she began to feel better.[13]

On the train between Wynne and Helena, Arkansas, a distance of about sixty miles, a young man came to her rescue in putting down a window which was stuck. She had noticed with

47

a sweep of her eyes that he was watching her, and when he asked if he could sit down by her, she assented. He complimented her by telling her that she did not look like a native or act like one. He also said that she looked very nice and had a sweet name. He promised her that he would vote for Taft. Lily recorded in her diary:

> It all happened as such things do in story books, such as "Ramona" and "Traumerei," and we said story-book things. But I wouldn't tell him my address.

(Ironically, Lily saw the young man again on her next train ride. She boarded the train at Postelle to go to Holly Grove for the purpose of taking her qualifying teacher's examination. She wrote:

> I knew someone behind was looking at me, . . . but I did not "rubber" any to see who it was. By and by someone came up the aisle and leaned over my seat and asked me if I was the young lady he had seen on the train to Helena. He had a kind of perfume on him that I dislike, and I pretended at first that I did not recognize him. He talked a little bit and hinted that he wanted to sit by me. I didn't move though and he took the seat right behind me. Then we got to talking and talked and talked. He finally came and sat with me so we could talk better. The train went so slow I could count the fence posts so we had almost an hour, I guess. He said his name was T. L. Cooper. He is an agent for some kind of pictures. He has travelled around a good bit and been electrician and manager for several telephone companies. He asked me twice to come to a big barbecue in Clarendon the 29th. They are going to have a league ballgame. I said I couldn't because I'd be teaching school. . . . He offered to see about getting a school in Clarendon for me so I guess I will hear from him as he said he would write. He said he liked black hair and black eyes.)

48

Lily's was apprehensive as she rode on the train from Helena to Marvell on the last leg of her journey. She had just turned seventeen on June 2. She prepared herself to act very grown up and be, at all times, a comfort to her mother, whose health had become frail, and a model for two young brothers and two young sisters. It was as if, in the two years she was away, the roles of her and her mother had reversed: she would become the caretaker; her mother would become the dependent. But there is no evidence that either mother or daughter was aware of their changed roles. Perhaps Lily was motivated by a strong, subconscious desire to emulate her father, or maybe she was following her impulses as a nurturing female.

Mr. Lee Kornegay, an old friend of the family, was on the train to Marvell, and he drove Lily to Turner where Aunt Lorenza and Uncle Harve (Harvey Whitfield) lived. Grandma Glennsbeckle also lived there. Lily wrote in her diary, "Every one seems glad to see me sweet, pure, and nice." When Uncle Harve drove her home the next day, she was flooded with emotion at seeing her family. Oma had developed a lovely voice and had learned to play the organ. Lily talked until she wondered what would become of her tongue. Some neighbors stopped by to see her, and she found out for sure that the school district on the Point wanted her to teach if she passed the examination, and everyone was confident that she would.

There was a protracted meeting going on at the Sanctified Church in the Connell's Point School House. One of her school mates, Clint Hartsfield, had "gotten religion" and talked it all the time. She would have liked to discuss it with him, but because everyone used to say he was "sweet on her," she decided against it. The Sanctified Church was new in the community. Mr. Boone Crisp, father of twelve children, was concerned about not having a church in the community. He talked to a drummer and found out that an evangelical group from the Sanctified Church of Christ from Georgia was in Helena and would come out and hold services in any community, provided folks would house and feed them and provide transportation to the nearest train station. Crisp sent word by the drummer for them to come to his home. The congregation which the group established is still in existence today, and it is the only one of its kind in Arkansas. Lily wrote in her diary about her first night attending the Sanctified preaching services, "I kissed about seven hundred people." Lily attended several of the services that summer and concluded that the church's doctrinal appeal was too emotional for her.

Lily was experiencing a range of emotions: she was happy to be home, lonesome for her friends in Gnadenhutten, and apprehensive about teaching for the first time. A school board member told her not to try to please everybody and not to have any pets. She wrote many letters that summer.

Her diary for that summer includes tales of the farm animals. It was a habit of the Peter family to name all of them. That summer they included a duck named Sir Thomas and calves named Daisy, Janus, Dilly, and Amelia Bedelia, and Opechancanough, the name of an Indian chief. Lily would entertain people throughout her life with tales of personified domestic animals.

Lily attended the Turner Methodist Church, where her Uncle Harve and Aunt Lorenza worshipped. (She had become a member when she was fourteen.) Uncle Harve gave her a Sunday School class. He brought her a pony to ride. The beauty of the countryside struck her poignantly. She woke up to "birds nearly bursting their throats with song." She wrote this couplet in her diary:

> Didst ever wake at dawn in Southern woods
> When all things yet lay wrapped in cool gray dusk?

Another entry read, "It is a beautiful moonlight night, a lovely twilight, followed by a full moon. The mosquitos are awful." She described her grandmother, Pauline Glennsbeckle (Mobray):

> Grandma came. She certainly makes a slave of herself. She is an old woman, rather stout, nearing 60 with heavy iron gray hair twisted around loosely on the crown of her head. She usually keeps her head bent slightly. Her face is long and rather large and she has a very dark complexion and large piercing black eyes. She is easily offended, has a Jew accent and a fretful, yet resigned, way of speaking. She is always complaining, but still she says it is God's will. . . .

Lily and her mother walked to and from the Sanctified meeting one night and had a long conversation about their affairs. Lily reported:

> It seems to me that I am in the position girls in storybooks are placed. I hope I can work my problems out so they will end in a storybook manner. I have been out and seen some of the world, have come home to the backwoods. We are poor and there are four besides me to educate.

The church revival meeting was taking place in the school house in which Lily would start teaching in just eight days. She described the interior:

> There weren't very many at the schoolhouse when we got there. The school house is a small poorly built frame building with 3 windows in each side, a door at each end and over the pulpit at the back end which was elevated about a foot and had 3 rude pillars at the outer edge. . . . 2 sections of homemade wooden benches were ranged on either side of an aisle which was the only one up to within 10 or 12 feet of the pulpit, and on either side a single bench stood with its back against the

wall. There were a few old fashioned school desks in front of
the benches. In one corner of the room was a bucket of water.
2 or 3 lamps were fastened to the wall on each side and a lamp
stood on top of the rude square pulpit columns. People were
standing talking in little knots. We went around and spoke to
most of the people. Mr. Caviness told me again he wanted me
to get sanctified. . . . A number of the little girls crowded around
me, and I talked to them until the service opened. All of the
sanctified people bunched up in front and commenced to sing.
As they sang, they slapped their hands to beat time and brought
their heels down. Then they prayed, sang again, prayed and
sang. Mr. Brown then got up and made a talk. It was good.
After that, they had more singing and praying and talking and
by and by an experience meeting. As the evening progressed,
some of the mothers who had brought their children with them
spread quilts down on the floor between and in front of the seats
and spread the children on top of them. One woman who had
two very small children had brought a small wooden bed to the
school house and placed her two babies in it under the friendly
shelter of a mosquito bar. The spirit of God was certainly there.
One fellow who used to be one of the awfullest toughs around
was "seeking." He said, "Friends I want to tell you that I've
found the right way and I want to keep it. The devil had me
going his way for a good many years an' he's tryin' his best to
keep a hold on me yet. He's tryin' to keep me from talkin' now
but I'm going to talk if [it] takes the head off my shoulders. I
want you all to pray for me." He was a handsome young man
of a dark type, a little above medium height, well built with a
reckless dare-devil air about him and a careless graceful car-
riage. He was very poorly educated. . . . Clint brought us home
and I was dying to argue with him but didn't dare to.

It was the next day that Lily went to Holly Grove to take
her teacher's examination. She and her mother had to get up at
four o'clock in the morning to make the horse-and-buggy drive
to the train at Postelle, the last stop on the line. The train was two

hours late departing. It was a freight train with a two-compartment coach for the last car. The dirty, tedious ride was alleviated somewhat by her visit with Cooper, the young man she had encountered the second time aboard a train.[14]

About taking her examination on eleven subjects at Holly Grove she said:

> I wrote up about 30 sheets of foolscap, completing them in about 8 1/2 hours. The thermometer was 98° in the shade on the North porch where the sun never touched it and I was sick besides.

The trip home had hardly gotten under way when the train stopped and backed up about a half a mile. Someone had dropped his gold watch out the window and had actually been able to find it. Lily got to Postelle, and Mr. Sanders, the station master, told her she would have a good long wait for her mother to pick her up. She wrote in her diary:

> He offered to get a rig for me but I thought it cost too much. He took a couple of magazines from the mail for me to read, talked some and got a couple of drinks for me. It was rather romantic, sitting there in the depot. The little yellow depot was deserted & quiet save for an occasional Negro who came in to ask for "potati's" or "Liz Broewstah's" mail. About 8 or 10 low whitewashed houses and a couple of dingy little stores with Negroes loafing around on the rickety steps comprised the town. I sat facing the door with my back to the window and read. Thru the door I could catch a glimpse of a wooded lot in which a scarce-looking mule grazed aimlessly around, but the greater part of the scenery which I could see thru the door consisted of a yellow building situated opposite the depot on the other side of the track . . . which building was decorated with advertisements of "Star Tobacco" and a certain "liver regulator" which was fully guaranteed. Back of the de-

pot ran the dusty road, with one of the hereinbefore mentioned department stores situated on the other side. In front of the store was a large white oak tree which had several rude benches around it. On one of these a Negro girl in a pink dress was picking a guitar. A few Negro kids were playing ball in the road and now and then a fitful gust of talk and laughter from the Negroes on the store porch behind was borne to my ears. Otherwise, save for the buzz of the flies the place was very quiet and the warm morning sun shone down very much as it shone at the same moment on Wall St. Of course, Postelle was a somewhat noisier place than Wall St.

The depot man invited Lily to go home with him for dinner. She did, and, of course, she describes the people she met and the conversation. Her mother was at the station when they got back. Lily told that she was "as gray as a bat," undoubtedly frightened as to Lily's whereabouts. Lily continues:

A crowd of Negroes collected in front and one was playing the guitar. Presently one Negro boy stepped out from the crowd and began to dance. He said he would give us "the buck and some of the dough." It certainly was great. Once he showed how he walked up to the preacher when he went to church on Sun. morning. It amused Rev. Blevin so he gave the Negro a dime. He threw it and the Negro couldn't catch it so he picked it up off the ground without stopping and did a handspring in perfect time and showed how the young fellows and the girls showed off when they went to church. When he got thru he passed around his hat. Said he was out of "bacca." He cracked jokes a good part of the time. One of the Negros sang a song that went something like this:

> "Git yo' laigs in tune
> " " " " "
> " ready to run
> An' we'll have some fun."

It drizzled a little bit and looked like rain so Mom and I waited awhile and then started. Mom was afraid we were going to get caught in a hard rain but we weren't on the way to Turner . . . Auntie lent us some wraps. Just as we got down to Mayo's it commenced to pour and we stopped there. Mr. Mayo is such a nice old Southern gentleman. He "proposed" to me and I accepted. Mama says she thinks I made a pretty good impression. Mr. Mayo bows nicely. . . . After the rain was over we left. I read my letter on the way home and Mom and I had a delightful conversation. I have 6 letters to read.

Lily started teaching July 20 (her certificate arrived on July 23), and she described her first days of school:

Today was my first day as a school teacher. It poured rain this a.m. I dressed up in the family rain wardrobe, and split the mud for school. Mr. B. was the only one there. By & by Clem came and we signed the contract. The kids straggled in one by one & by & by I took up school. Clem made a valedictory address and I shook hands with him. . . . I was pretty shaky but I managed to get their names written down. I had 26 today. Calvin said he liked me fine. A lot of the kids asked me to go home with them.

July 21st. Asked Vinda Hill today if their dog was a hound dog and she said he was a he-dog. Wore my pink hat and waist today. Got awfully sleepy. I am hot and tired. . . . The sanctified girls won't play. Cecil Catlett gave me a tomato. . . . The kids bring me all kinds of leaves and stuff. July 23rd. Got a "love letter" today from one of the kids. Willie and Sing came this evening to invite Omie & me to an ice cream supper at Stewart's. They stayed about an hour & we ate figs & grapes & picked zinnias. July 24th. Had to settle a scrap this evening between Charlie Grider and Calvin Goins. Got some dust in my eye and couldn't cry it out. I'm tired . . . July 26th. Went to church this A.M. We got there a little bit late. . . . Willie asked me to go to church tonight. Louis F. went down to the buggy with us and talked a good while. We saw 20 black birds on a telephone wire this A.M. holding S. S. W. & Sing were called down for talking in church and I was so furious I almost died. . . . He [Willie] was surprised when I said I had never fallen in love. Asked me if I could learn to love. I was sleepy. July 27th. Had 44 pupils today. They are a pretty good bunch for a kid of 17 to manage. . . . Frankie Catlett wrote a note to Myrtle today telling her she was the prettiest girl that went to school here but not to let anyone see it. This evening the boys killed a little garter snake 1 foot long that was trying to swallow a pretty good-sized toad . . . July 28th. Today Myrtle & Lucy wrote on the board "I love my teacher better than any. She hears my lessons, she is good to me. She is pretty. She is good to let me write.". . . Have 47 pupils now. Got my table today. . . July 29th. Learned some classical poetry today.

> "Roses are red
>   "   " yellow
> I'm going to ship you
> And get another fellow."

> "I love you better than a pig likes slop."

> "While you are courting
> It's honey and pie
> When you get married
> It's root, hog, or die."

. . . Why wasn't I made a boy so I could go to West Point? And not have to say nice things to people I don't like? . . . July 30th. The kids brought me a Jack-in-the-pulpit, a silk worm and offered me apples and peaches. Henry & Frankie wrote on the board, "I love my teacher.". . . July 31st. Went to the party at Hall's tonight. . . . Wore my white dress. . . Willie took me. I like him a little better but not much. Had a pretty good time. Met a number of people. Fell down the steps and got my commencement dress dirty.

That was the last sentence of Lily's diary that summer of 1908. A phase of her life was over, and she had started on another, that of teacher-scholar. But she never turned away from the land and farming.[15]

Notes

[1]Dorothy Crisp. *Neighbors*, op. cit., p. 3.

[2]Telephone interview with Louise Mixon Griffin, 5 July 1981.

[3]Jesse Peter later bought this place from the Mayos, Lily inherited it, and her great-great-nephew by marriage (to Sherry Crisp), Mike Wooten, farms it and has re-named it "The Cypress Lily Farm."

[4]There follows a letter from Naomi Bishop (Will Peter's sister and widow of Rufus Bishop, Moravian missionary to Jamaica) to Florence Peter, dated and postmarked March 3, 1907, Bethlehem, Pennsylvania:

> My Dear Florence, A letter from Mary yesterday brought the sad news of your bereavement. O Dear Florence I only hope that brother Will died trusting in the Lord, then he is far better off than we who remain. Crippled in his arm & with poor health and the ill fortune that so often overtook him, life was a hard struggle at best. And perhaps he would never have gotten over the effects of that fall, so the Lord only spared him more misery and suffering.
>
> But I know how hard it must have been for him to think he was leaving his dear ones unprovided for. I know from experience what it means for the mother to rear a family alone, and I had only two while you have four. I do not count your brave little girlie in Ohio for she will soon be able to care for herself, but it will be some time till the others do not need you.
>
> ... With ever so much love and the prayer that our loving Father will help and comfort and guide you, I must close. Affectionately, Omie

Will Peter had had to borrow money from his sister, Adelaide

Schultze, whose husband was president of Moravian College, Bethlehem, Pennsylvania. Florence Peter received this letter from her May 22, 1907:

> Dear Sister Florence: . . . We will <u>gladly wait</u> for a year & a half in order to give you more time to make a good sale of the timber in order to pay the debt.
>
> We are anxious to hear whether anyone rented a part or all of the <u>farm</u> so that you will have something to live on during this fall & winter. — Have you a good garden with plenty of potatoes & sweetcorn for the summer? What church did you & Will belong to? And are the members willing to give a "helping hand" now in finding some one to rent the place? — for if the church members & your brothers & sisters will all take an interest in finding the right person or persons to rent the farm, there is more hope than if you must do it yourself. . . .
>
> With love & good wishes to you all, your aff. sister,
>
> Addie
>
> I forgot to say that we fully intended to throw off all the interest that has been accumulating for a number of years.

[5]Lily kept a diary of June, July, and August during that year, 1908, in which she records her last days at Gnadenhutten and her journey home. It records her leaving there on Jun 29 and arriving in Helena on June 30.

[6]Personal interviews with Lily Peter. Tapes 7, 8, 12, 14, 17, 11, 13, 17, 19, 21, 33, 40, 44, 48, 62, 63, 64. Torreyson Library Archives, University of Central Arkansas.

Chapter III

ON HER OWN:
ONE-ROOM SCHOOLS, FIRST LOVE,
AND BOLL WEEVIL SHOOTOUTS, 1908-1935

. . .

Utterly invisible, itself its own alembic,
the Psyche dwelling in its lonely cavern
within the skull works an incessant alchemy,
striving to identify its insecure existence
with vestiges from the panoply of Matter,
wrapped in the subtle envelope of Form.

In this isolate, mysterious cloud-chamber,
where alchemy and alchemist are one,
fueled by the burning idants of the spirit,
sometimes a shining miracle is wrought:
the Number comes to its quintessential form in music:
the Word is transmuted to its ultimate in Song.
Love in this narrow space finds his domain,
title and timber for the building of his mansion,
the rich stuffs for the pitching of his pavilion,
and in Love's quicksilver shadow is our only wholeness.

Lily Peter
from "Rootless Among Molecules"
The Mad Queen, unpublished

The first salary Lily earned in her long teaching career of
forty years was forty-five dollars a month, and Lily budgeted that

sum like the provider of a poverty-stricken family (which she was). When she accepted the one-room school at Good Luck in the fall, she paid one of the neighbors of her landlady fifteen dollars a month for her sister Oma's board so that Oma could live nearby while Lily tutored her for high school. Lily helped with the housework of the family she lived with so that she could pay her own board, and she gave her mother most of the remaining thirty dollars. Her two new dresses that year, which she made herself, were cotton gingham and cost less than a dollar each.[1]

The next year, 1909-10, Lily taught in La Grange, a small town surrounded by plantations and just north of her home county. For the first time in her life, she felt completely on her own. Her salary was raised to fifty dollars a month, and she was hired by the La Grange School District because the school couldn't find a male or a married female teacher. Lily was the best candidate available.

Her family and reputation were unknown in Lee County, and Lily felt compelled to avoid any conduct or companionship in La Grange which would raise the slightest question of her propriety. She dated some, but mostly with Harry Wilkins, whom she knew to be in love with someone else. However, her friendship with him developed, and he would often "walk her home" from school to the front gate of her boarding house about a mile out of town. Harry was employed in a store there, and his sister was one of Lily's pupils.

Harry's family had a retainer, an ancient black man called Uncle Isom, who was born before the Civil War. He was friendly and witty, and everyone in town liked him. One day Harry had sent Lily a note telling her that he would like to walk home with her that afternoon, and she had replied that she would meet him at the post office where she usually checked her mail box every afternoon. On that day she greeted Uncle Isom and asked about his health. Harry said the next day Uncle Isom asked, "Mr. Harry, who is dat young lady you was walkin' wid yesty eenin'?" Harry replied that it was Miss Lily Peter, the new school teacher and asked why he was inquiring. Old Uncle Isom commented, "Well Suh, Mr. Harry, dat young lady, she walked like she owned St. Louis and was jist a-fixin' to buy New York."

While Lily lived in La Grange in the home of the Wimberley family, she learned about the adaptability of the human body and never forgot the following story when she wanted to make that point. All of the drinking, cooking, and washing water came from an old-fashioned stone cistern, the reservoir for the rain water that ran off the roof of the house. One day Collins Jones (a nephew who lived in the home) was bringing up a bucket of water, and in it was the remains of "old mother black cat." Two weeks earlier everyone had discussed her disappearance and decided that the dogs had killed her. The whole family had used that water which contained the decaying remains of the black cat all that time, but no one suffered any ill effects.

It was a bleak year teaching at La Grange. Not only did Lily fail to feel at home there, but also her mother was sick, and Lily felt guilty being away from her. To add to her frustration, she had been offered a job at Marvell closer to home which she could not accept because of her contract in La Grange. Before the school year ended, she applied for a job at the Good Luck School, since it was closer to home. Instead of boarding with a family near the school, as she had done during her first year of teaching there, she lived at home and drove the distance to school in a light-weight, open buggy twice daily. The dirt road was deep mud in wet weather. On many of the short days of winter, she would leave home before dawn and arrive home after dark.

Lily's typical day that year began at 4:30 or 5:00 a.m. She would prepare breakfast for herself and the children at home: Jesse, Ethel, and Ted. Oma was still in the demonstration high school at the University of Arkansas at Fayetteville. Then she would prepare lunches for everyone going to school. Ted stayed at home where his mother taught him. An unavoidable duty for Lily was combing and brushing Ethel's hair, which was so long and thick the child could not do it herself. Just before leaving, Lily served her mother a hot breakfast. Then she and Jesse would hitch up the pony to the buggy and take off. After a mile or two, Ethel and Jesse would leave Lily (where the road turned north) and walk on to their school at Turner.

Lily was nearly always at the school by 7:30 a.m. The first chore was to build a fire, and the next to sweep and dust. She began teaching at 8:00 a.m. and dismissed the pupils at 4:00 p.m. Two fifteen-minute recesses and an hour for lunch gave her some diversion, but no relief from the supervision and responsibility for the children. There were forty-eight children enrolled that year, but the attendance would vary drastically and would average around thirty-eight. There were no uniform book requirements. Children would bring what books they had at home, usually "hand-me-downs" from other schools, and the teacher had to utilize them. In one of her reading classes, three different reading texts were being used. Lily said that there has been no job in the history of humanity requiring more adaptation and creative resources than the handling of a one-room school.

As soon after 4:00 p.m. as possible, she hitched up the pony for the return trip home. (One winter she counted thirty-nine mudholes and three sloughs which could have tipped over the buggy.)

If Lily's mother had had a good day, she would have started the evening meal; if not, Lily would have to cook it. After supper Lily would grade papers until she finished them, at times quite late. They had the simplest and best of country food, all of which was produced at home: poultry, home-cured pork, and "put-up" sausage, canned garden vegetables and fruits, milk, butter, and eggs. The preparation of so much food called for a great deal of cooperation which wasn't always easy to muster. But Florence Peter was a conciliator and a capable household executive.

Beyond the family needs for food, very little was being produced on the farm of four hundred eighty acres, the amount left by Will Peter. There were some tenants on the cleared land. Most of them took advantage of Mrs. Peter because she knew so little about farming. She was at the mercy of the tenants' knowledge of amounts of seed needed per acre and number of days required for land preparation and cultivation, and she did not know what to expect in the way of yield. It was Lily's teaching money which paid small amounts on the principal and interest on the mortgages against their land. Another potential source of income was the sale of timber, yet this never worked out for Florence Peter, because she had neither time nor the stamina to supervise the cutting and assure herself that she was getting paid for the footage removed. Further, in that time in a thinly-populated area, out-and-out timber thievery was notoriously common — the practice of some loggers of just going in and cutting timber and removing it without any report to the owner whatsoever. Most farming operations in the area had more manpower with more knowledge, experience, and time than did either Florence or Lily. It was unquestionably a difficult time. It was a strain to keep Oma at the university model high school. Lily also taught in the summers of 1910 and 1912, in addition to the regular nine-months term. Every cent of cash counted.

A small source of interest, but not income, was a project Lily took on voluntarily for the *Brinkley Argus*, a weekly newspaper. For it, she wrote poetry and essays about the countryside and interesting people in the neighborhood, not local news. Most of the poetry was light verse, for example, "The Soliloquy of the Thanksgiving Turkey." In it, Lily had an educated turkey meditating on his impending demise. But another more serious poem which she wrote for the newspaper, "December Sunset," foreshadowed her intense relationship with nature. The heated competition among newspapers which had been a feature of the late nineteenth century had diminished, but every town which was a county seat had at least one weekly. Only the heavily populated areas had daily papers.[2]

Lily wrote a diary from January to November of 1911. Despite hard work, she told of many happy times, including how she relished the beauties of spring on her drive to school. She recorded untiringly the illnesses, births and deaths in the neighborhood and embellished her diary with an occasional couplet or quatrain. She wrote about the two weeks when her school was closed because of measles. It was no vacation for Lily, even though she'd had the measles in Ohio and had become immune to it, because she had to take care of her mother, her siblings, and a neighbor family, all of whom had been infected by the measles. No private sentiment or behavior is expressed in the diary because Lily was not disposed to write anything which could not be read by others. Typical notations in this diary follow:

> April 7th. Mother was sick in bed all day today. Myrtle, May, and Nannie [Ethel's playmates] came down this evening.
> April 9th. Nancy has a little calf and I had to milk her this morning. Such kicking you never saw. I didn't get the house cleaned until way after twelve. The girls went home from Sunday School. We had a lunch dinner. Mother is feeling somewhat better. It is a lovely day, but cool. I'm having lots to do this spring, but I shall always look back on it as one of the pleasantest ones in my life. My home is delightful and I have one of the best mothers in the world.

Lily recorded in her diary that she was receiving attention from several young men. She dated Jimmie Jackson, from across Cypress Bayou toward Indian Bay, when he was home from Henderson College at Arkadelphia, Arkansas. They corresponded.

He sent many picture post cards. When he came home on holidays, one dating activity was looking at the post cards. She received many letters from Foster Lickey (her Gnadenhutten high school sweetheart). She went to church, to parties, and on buggy rides with Fred Brown.

She had many girl friends and described in her diary the wedding of one, noting that the "bride's hat is white trimmed with a willow plume and her dress is white mull — long white kid gloves and suede slippers to match. . . . I played Brahms' *Melting Tones. . .*" [at the wedding].

Lily attended a normal school for teachers at Conway, Arkansas, during the summer of 1911.[3] After she returned, she and her sisters persuaded their mother to buy a piano on the installment plan. That is the one and only time Florence Peter ever allowed anyone in the family to make purchases in that way. The piano was delivered on July 31. It rained all day, making the dirt roads nearly impassable, but neighbor Alf Kornegay went for the piano anyway. Lily wrote in her diary, "We were all worried about it, but nobody let on to anybody else. It was funny. We all looked like we had swallowed a sledge hammer apiece, but everybody tried to keep busy and crack jokes. The piano was a beauty. We sat up until late playing."

Lily also wrote in her diary about neighbors bringing in portable instruments. Lily began to skip days, noting that she was tired of writing the same old things. When she did write, she filled in with some details of the days skipped, for example:

> August 26th. . . I cleaned out my trunk Wednesday afternoon. It was a job. Looked over some old letters and burned a lot. Such a silly mess some of them were. Foster's are all fine. I saved them and re-read them all. My, I wish I could see him. [Foster Lickey, Gnadenhutten]

65

A blot on the summer happiness was her mother's persistent illness. Lily wrote:

> Sept. 4th. Mother was better that evening and I was glad. One night she was so sick she couldn't sleep, so I sat up and read and read and read until my throat ached. She was real sick that night and a screech owl kept squealing by the window. I shivered and prayed at the same time.

For the 1911-12 school year, Lily accepted the job of teaching the first three grades at Trenton (about thirteen miles north of home). She boarded at the McClure's home, and among several callers were Will Bishop and Jimmie Jackson. One time Jimmie brought her a box of candy, and Lily wrote in her diary, "Gladys McClure ate nearly half of it." This was on Tuesday. Friday morning, Lily and Mayme, her roommate and colleague, were wakened by Mrs. McClure. Gladys, a ten-year-old, had been taken quite ill. The girls and the mother attended her from 3:00 a.m. Friday morning until her death at 1:00 p.m. Saturday afternoon. It was an experience they would never forget. No one knew the cause of her death or whether the candy had anything to do with it.

That Christmas, Jimmie's sisters, Sophie and Mattie, invited Lily and Oma to come and have dinner with them. They accepted in spite of warnings that they would never make it over Big Cypress because of the condition of the road on the levee. When Lily was told she could not make the trip, it only served to spur her on. She hitched up the horse and buggy, and she and Oma took off. There were three bridges over the bayou with levees in between them. With difficulty, they made it over the first bridge and through the mudholes atop the levee and over the second bridge. But between the second and third bridge, they came upon such a deep mudhole that Lily told Oma they'd never get through it with both of them in the buggy, that one must walk the tiny ridge on the edge of the levee, and that the other must drive. Oma chose to drive and made it through onto the bridge by sitting on the high side of the tilted buggy. Lily found the mud so deep and sticky that she could not wade through it. Oma couldn't turn the buggy around to get back to Lily because she didn't know how to un-hitch a horse. So they were stranded, Oma on the third bridge, Lily in the mud on the levee, until a young Negro whom they knew came along. He was able to unhitch the horse and turn the buggy so that Oma could drive back through the mudhole, but the ordeal had taken so much time that they decided it was un-wise to continue to the Jacksons. Lily found a piece of wrapping paper in the buggy, wrote a note on it, and gave the boy a piece of money for his promise to deliver it. The note had to be thrown across the mudhole.

When the roads cleared and they saw the Jacksons again, Lily found that the note had not been delivered until late in the afternoon.

That next teaching year at Trenton Lily dated a young man, John Bishop (Will Bishop's younger brother), who asked her to marry him. She liked his good mind and sense of humor, but she didn't take his proposal seriously because he was several years younger than she. This was a more difficult year for Lily because the teaching staff at Trenton was reduced to two teachers for the entire school — herself and Mr. McCarty, a quiet, shy young man who didn't waste words on anyone and who gave no one the opportunity to waste words on him.

A few days before April 1, 1912, some of the older students at Trenton told Lily that they had decided to play truants on April Fools' Day and asked her to bring her students and come along. She flatly refused unless they obtained permission from McCarty. Fearing his refusal, the students went on anyway when the bell rang. At the bridge at the edge of the school ground they met the school board president's daughter. They invited her to come along, but because she had not been included in the planning, she refused, threatening to tell on them. Seeing the situation, McCarty came for Lily and her pupils, and they all went walking. Those who brought their lunches declared their willingness to share with those who had no lunch. It was a warm spring day, and it wasn't long until the older children and the younger ones were separated, the former wanting to go to the woods, the latter wanting to go to Big Creek, hoping to find a boat to ride. This called for cutting across the fields and through the woods, and since some of them had come barefoot, Lily pulled out many a cocklebur. She had to carry one child awhile. Lily prayed that no farmer who liked to fish had left a boat on the creek bank because spring waters were up, and her prayer was answered. No boats were found. An early eating of lunches and some games consoled them. They made their way back to the road through the sweet gum balls, stickers, and thorns. Lily could hardly restrain her sympathy for the somber McCarty, who walked with her behind the children hardly speaking a word. She knew he was concerned about the possible repercussions of neglecting his school duties that day. He might be severely reprimanded or even fired. He made no attempt to conduct classes that day.

Lily was pleased at this April Fools' afternoon break because it gave her time to make a new dress. She cut it out and started sewing on the "middie" blouse (white with a sailor collar trimmed with blue braid) for a pleated skirt. Her landlady, Mrs. Kirkland, came to the door and said, "Lily, you are going to marry a lazy man sure as you live because you are so industrious."

Lily was so tired after supper that she undressed to go to bed early, but she had barely done so when there was a knock on her door. All the high schoolers had come to continue their holiday by partying with her. She redressed, and they played games until late that April Fools' Day.

May of 1913 marked the end of Lily's two-year stint of teaching at Trenton, and during those two years she gained a new perspective on society in Helena, the hub for social life in the area. In Trenton, about twenty-five miles out in the county, Lily observed that the doings of Helena's "first families" were the main topic of conversation at the homes of her friends. Helena had been a thriving river town for nearly a hundred years, and during "The Gilded Age," approximately 1880 to 1910, wealthy families had built beautiful homes, kept them landscaped with readily available cheap labor, upheld high ideals of classical education, and displayed excellent taste in clothing and other accoutrements, so that Helena's elite presented an attractive facade to rural towns like Trenton, as evidenced by the social reportage in the *Helena World* at that time, one of the oldest papers in the state. Lily says some of the best-known families were the Hornors, the Pillows, the Tappans, the Solomons, the Keesees, the Coolidges, the Bruces, the Lockwoods, the Cloptons, and the Stephenses. Lily would never own that she herself was impressed by Helena society or cared what they thought.

The accidental burning of the Mount Vernon Academy in Trenton had driven its director, Professor Lee Price Anderson, into public school administration at Brinkley, Arkansas. It was not long until Marvell, also a growing community, called him to be the head of its school system, and he accepted because he was also offered the position of Phillips County Supervisor of Schools. In the latter capacity, Anderson became aware of Lily's ability and offered her the position of teacher of the first four grades in Marvell, and Lily gladly accepted. Marvell was to become Lily's official post office for the rest of her life.

Anderson was concerned that Lily become educated to her full capacity, and because of his encouragement, and despite the worst financial straits her family had yet endured, she went to the

University of Tennessee at Knoxville for a six-week summer course.[4] By the time she arrived there, paid for her tuition, books, and board, she realized that she didn't have the money to stay in Knoxville more than one month. It would be impossible for her to get her college credit hours. Nonetheless, she decided to stay the month and has never regretted it. She said, "I got the knowledge which is more important than the credit."

She also said that it could be considered the most important summer in her life because she heard a series of lectures by a young man, a visiting lecturer, provocative both in his personal projection and his subject matter. He introduced her to Greek philosophy, poetry, and drama in such a charming manner that she had never lost interest in it. She said, "He was handsome and eloquent and well informed and loved his topic so much himself that his enthusiasm was contagious. I came home loving it. My mind was just glowing with the brilliance of Greek civilization and what it meant to the world with its magnificence of thought and approach to life. This knowledge made a tremendous impact on my thinking." Lily soon acquired and read the works of Homer and studied the life and poetry of Sappho. She was convinced that Sappho's alleged homosexuality was a scandal perpetrated by the Hellenistic Age. She presented a long lecture to the Tennessee Poetry Society on the topic.[5] The young lecturer also inspired a study of Greek mythology, which led to the study of other mythologies, and Lily's eventual completion of a book of poetry based on nine mythologies. The work, *In The Beginning*, was published by the University of Arkansas Press in 1983. The first sentence of Lily's prologue to the book says, "Myth is the antiphon of poet and seer, orchestrated by Everyman in the culture and age of its origin: an achievement more worthy of study than many a muddled page in his history."

The summer in Knoxville was valuable to Lily also because she studied speech from a Mrs. Emerson, one of the founders of the Emerson School of Oratory in Boston. She was a meticulous teacher who demanded correct articulation and who knew how to elicit it from her students. This was a life-long boon to Lily, who spoke very rapidly, always racing to keep up with her thought. She took two helpful courses in primary teaching methods, but she found Mrs. Emerson's instruction in phonetics equally valuable.

Knoxville also gave Lily her first opportunity to encounter attitudes not commonly shared in Arkansas, especially not in rural places like her home. Her dormitory included women from all over the United States and from some foreign countries. Their vision of the world was often inspiring to her, but it also made her aware that people besides Arkansans could arrive at preconceived notions about distant people and places. Once a young woman who had found out Lily was from Arkansas asked her, "Why aren't you yellow?" Appalled, Lily countered, "Do you think all Arkansans are yellow?" The girl said, "Yes. I always heard that everyone in Arkansas had malaria which made them jaundiced." The numerous concerts Lily attended in Knoxville reinforced her determination to become more proficient on the violin.

On her twenty-second birthday, June 2, 1913, she received a gift from Foster Lickey. It was a Kodak camera, just a simple one with a box made of leather-like material which was collapsible so that it could be pulled out when in use and folded back into its flat case when not in use. Lily and Foster had corresponded during the five years since she left Gnadenhatten. He had gone to Purdue University and graduated in engineering and worked long enough to be able to ask Lily to marry him. Lily felt that she was not in love with him and rejected his proposal. She offered to return the camera to him, but he insisted that she keep it. Lily expected her true love to be overwhelming, an expectation that revealed her innate romantic temperament.

Florence Peter's health began to worsen in 1914. Lily made

no attempt to go to school that summer, nor during any subsequent summer until 1928. Lily's sister, Oma, found work in a country school near home for the year 1914-1915 and began dating Lewis Thompson. They were married at the Salem Baptist Church at Cypert in the summer of 1915. An eventual life-long friend of Lily's, Margaret Van Meter Triplett, remembers Oma's wedding. It was held after Sunday School, and the entire one-room building was decorated with field and garden flowers. Lily played the violin for the service, accompanied by her sister, Ethel, on the pump-organ. The little church and everyone in it looked beautiful to five-year-old Margaret, and the wedding is one of her most vivid memories.

In 1915, Lily lent her brother Jesse (age fifteen) money for seed to make his first crop, and he was successful enough to pay her back. The amount was forty dollars. It was an eight- or ten-acre corn crop which he planted and cultivated after school hours and during the summer. As it turned out, Lily's loan to her brother may have been one of the wisest investments in her life, since he eventually become a successful farmer. In 1918, he made enough money to attend Hendrix one year with a supplement from Lily. He loved college, particularly history, and would have loved to go on and become a teacher of that subject, but his mother's need of his assistance at farming caused him to decide to go to Monticello A and M in 1919-20 and study agriculture. The next year, he become a full-time farmer.

During the summer of 1916, Florence Peter's health failed so drastically that she was confined to her bed. Lily stayed with her and rarely left the house until she had to return to teaching. The summer of '17 was the same. Lily's teaching and life at Marvell had become fairly routine except for the excitement of watching the events of World War I. Her main indulgence was a trip on the train to Helena on occasional Saturdays to take violin lessons from Leonard G. Fristrom, a native of Australia, who had

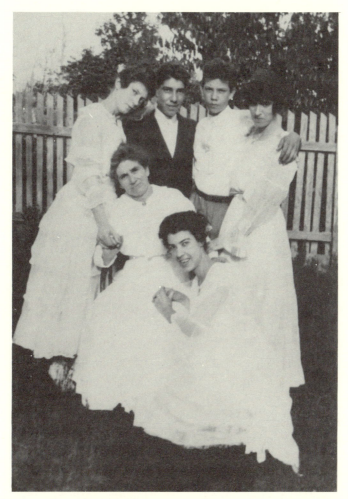

Florence Peter and her children, around the time of Oma's wedding,
(clockwise) Oma, Jesse, Ted, Lily, and Ethel

come there to teach music.

In 1918, a physician who came to Marvell told Florence
Peter that she must have surgery. It was arranged for in the fall,
and Lily took leave from teaching to go with her to St. Vincent's
hospital in Little Rock. Oma's time was taken with her infant

daughter, Marjorie, who had been born in March. Ethel was teaching in the community, but it is doubtful that Lily would have allowed anyone else to attend her mother.

Florence Peter, who was forty-nine years old, had a complete hysterectomy, quite serious considering her weakened condition. To make the event an even more strenuous ordeal, an epidemic of influenza, which took thousands of lives and is still talked about, was raging all over the South. Nurses were at a high premium, if available at all, and Lily stayed at her mother's side constantly with the exception of going to her room at the Marion Hotel for two or three hours' sleep around 3:00 a.m. An entire ward on the hospital floor above Florence's room was given over to men whose illnesses had moved from flu to pneumonia and who were dying. Their moans and screams were constant. All the corridors were jammed with frightened and grieving people. Florence's life hung in the balance many days. Lily was never more scared or miserable. Lily's relief was unimaginable when she was able to take her mother home after a stay of three weeks. The operation was successful; her recovery was rapid.

Lily's involvement in World War I was fairly inconsequential, comparatively speaking. No beau went to the service; what little of making of Red Cross boxes, wrapping bandages, and the like, that was done in Marvell, was done while she was teaching. On the day of the news of the outbreak of the war, Lily and her mother were having a picnic in the yard. Mr. John Palmer, owner of one of the two cars in Marvell, an Overland Whippet, brought the Goodwin family to spend the day.[6] On Armistice Day, school was dismissed, and Alice Ward invited Lily and several other teachers to her home to play cards, a game called Five Hundred.

During the fall of 1918 the Peter family was saddened by their awareness that Oma's marriage was failing. The next year Oma and Marjorie came home where Mrs. Peter could help with the child and Oma could teach locally. Lily was able to think about more education for herself for the first time in seven years. These family concerns caused Lily to hardly notice the women's suffrage movement, let alone participate. The famous Elaine riots of 1919, resulting from efforts of Negro tenants to unionize, escaped her attention because they affected none of the blacks she knew in Marvell or her neighborhood. None of the Peter tenants were involved.

The summer and fall of 1920 were, for Lily, the source of some of her most precious memories, yet they were laced with pain and poignancy. The time gave Lily two sources of self-confidence: one, that she possessed genuine musical talent; the other, that she had the capacity to attract, receive, and return the love of an admirable and handsome man.

Rebecca Owens, the daughter of her childhood teacher, had attended the Peabody School of Music in Baltimore, Maryland, and in correspondence with Lily, Rebecca had praised the school highly. With considerable trepidation, Lily made arrangements and enrolled. She borrowed five hundred dollars to put with her savings, intending to go just for the summer. She made over her wardrobe, packed, and traveled up East by train. She took only violin at Peabody and went to Johns-Hopkins University for two courses in journalism to further her writing ability. The university assisted her with housing, finding a room for her in a dignified neighborhood nearby. She took her meals at an excellent boarding house run by the Misses Shuttleworth. They served such delicious food that often faculty members came to eat, making Lily's company at meals often stimulating.

Lily's violin teacher was a Mr. VanHulsteyn from Holland. At her first lesson, he asked her several questions, out of courtesy, including where she was from. When she told him Arkansas, he said he had never heard of it; when she told him that it was just west of the Mississippi River, he admitted he had never heard of the river either. He spoke with a foreign accent which called for careful listening, but Lily thought he was by far the best violin teacher she had ever had.

Many social occasions were provided by both Peabody and Johns-Hopkins. One of these was a recreational tour on the Potomac River to Mt. Vernon. It was on this tour that she met Porter Gale Perrin. She and he happened to be sitting near enough to exchange glances. They realized that they were fellow students in Dr. French's journalism class. They introduced themselves and began an enthusiastic conversation that lasted the entire tour.

Just as they landed at Mt. Vernon, a violent thunderstorm occurred so they had to run the long, up-hill distance to the estate, slipping and sliding as they went. Laughing and breathless, they took refuge in the first open door, the kitchen, which was in a separate building from the big house. They stayed there for the duration of the storm, leaving them time for only a quick walk-through look at the mansion and no time for the gardens; however, the storm lent a sort of intimacy to their time together. The atmosphere of a kitchen is somewhat less than romantic, yet Lily remembers vividly how pretty were the strings of dried red peppers, onions, and other vegetables hanging in neat rows, the glass jars of herbs, and the variety of stone crocks, the gleaming copper and black iron cookware. They quickly moved into a first-name relationship (he was called by his second name), and Gale and Lily stayed together all the way back to Baltimore.

Sharing the journalism class made daily contact and conversation come easy and naturally for them. They began taking all their recreation together. Both of them lacked money, so they took advantage of all inexpensive pursuits. They attended concerts (mainly the free offerings of Peabody and Johns-Hopkins), but their favorite activity was sight-seeing. They viewed every historic site in the area. One day Gale wanted to visit Edgar Allan Poe's grave located in the cemetery next to the Presbyterian Church. They arrived to find the gate locked. Disappointed, Gale scouted around and found a hole where the fence joined a corner of the church. They scrambled through and enjoyed the solitude of the grave yard while reading the tombstones. Because the fence did not "give" in the same way, their exit proved much more difficult than their entry, and they thought for a while that they were stranded. Nevertheless, strenuous effort proved effective, and it was a laughing matter afterward.

Lily learned that Gale was the son of a Congregational minister in Vermont and that he had a bachelor's degree with an English major from Middlebury College in Connecticut. He was around five feet, eleven inches tall, of slender build so that his movements were exceedingly graceful. Lily thought his facial features were beautifully delineated and distinguished-looking. His wearing of glasses didn't distract from his expressive, blue-gray eyes. He had brown hair with a bronze tone and a light-olive complexion. The timbre of his voice and his manner of speaking were so winsome, touched by a light sense of humor, that Lily never noticed that he had a Yankee accent. She found Gale to be open-minded, harboring no preconceptions about people from Arkansas or the South.

They discussed literature endlessly, their favorite topic. Their first gifts to one another were books. Lily does not remember what books she gave Gale, but she recalls that the first one he gave her was the collected works of Edward J. N. D. Plunkett, Lord Dunsany, the English poet.[7] Another he gave her which they read and discussed together was a book of literary criticism, *New Voices*, by Marguerite Wilkinson. Gale was vitally interested in all the new movements in literature, actually more than she, but she loved discussing them with him. Although they became engaged, poverty kept them from exchanging any jewelry. Once Lily gave him a nice fountain pen.

In September, Gale had to return to his teaching position at the University of Maine, where he was a graduate assistant. Was it then, because of her love of Gale, or was it because Mr. VanHulsteyn praised her violin playing and assured her of a fall scholarship, that Lily decided to stay on in Baltimore for the fall? Certainly both situations contributed. She began to scrimp and save as soon as VanHulsteyn offered her the scholarship.

Gale came to see her in Baltimore once in the fall and at Christmas time. They wrote often. This is a letter Gale wrote on October 7, 1920:

> Hello, Lily-girl! This is to be just a *note* for the week-end. I don't know how long it takes to get a letter to Balto, but this is aimed for sometime Saturday.
>
> Busy is the word in these parts. Conferences — these glorious afternoons when everyone ought to be out making the most of our fast-disappearing foliage.
>
> I met the expected fifth class today. Had to jump into the middle of A Midsummer Night's Dream — which I hadn't thought of for over five years until the 50-minute period just before class. By telling stories of Queen Bess & other Elizabethans, & by talking very loud, we got through the period. Talked mostly about *love* and *fairies*. I'm not any more of an authority on those subjects than on Shakespeare! — Wonder what I'd do if I ever had to face a little person like you in a class.
>
> Tomorrow it's Sir Gawain & the Green Knight, among other things.
>
> A meeting of the Contributors' club tonight. We elected ten new members, eight students & two faculty. That makes 24 members. Looks like a prosperous year.
>
> How have you found "Our Baltimore"? I've often thought of your getting settled & finding where you are *at*. What courses are you taking at both places? But you know I want to know all about things, & I'm not going to ask questions. Wonder how many times you have heard of Dr. Bethesda, the house across the street, and divers nice young men. The world needs all of us.

The last set of themes was really rather interesting. One girl wrote about her gladiolus bed — 500 bulbs. This is my first experience with girls' themes. All my folks were boys last year.

But this was to be just a note — I must get to work on those blamed romances. Don't worry about my letters. When you have the time, drop us some lines.

It is 11:30 already — time for us to say Good Night

On Gale's Christmas visit, he proposed to Lily. She readily accepted, and they became engaged. It was painful for Lily to talk to the biographer about Gale, and no more letters have been found (Lily kept the others for years and doesn't remember throwing them away, but thought she might have, accidentally), but one can be sure that Lily was extremely happy that fall. Her love poems are rhapsodic; her romantic bent is evident. One can consider Lily's despair all the more wretched when by Christmas the bottom had dropped out of the cotton market, sister Oma, at home, was in the process of divorce, and her mother's health was taking a turn for the worse despite the successful surgery of 1918. Lily came home after Gale's Christmas visit in Baltimore, knowing she could not return. She had studied only at Peabody in the fall, so that academic credits were not at stake, but the disappointment of not being able to continue with violin was a pain that never left her. It did not occur to her then that the engagement would not survive the distance from Arkansas to Maine.

Hurt, disappointed, and frustrated, Lily arrived home without a job. The Connell's Point School District near her country home had progressed from offering two months' school in the summer to offering a four-month winter term, and the district needed a teacher. The directors offered Lily the position, and she gladly accepted it. She lived at home and continued to job hunt.

While she was teaching school in Marvell, Lily had learned

from friends that there were many openings for teachers in Zachary, Louisiana, because the town was only eighteen miles from Baton Rouge, and it was growing rapidly. On the chance that the situation might be the same, Lily wrote to them; they were happy to recommend her, and she secured a position in Louisiana for 1921-22.

Every Saturday Lily took the train from Zachary to Baton Rouge. She enjoyed going out to Louisiana State University. At that time it was housed in old buildings reminiscent of Spanish cloisters. The lawns were abundantly full of bay trees and magnolias draped with long sweeps of Spanish moss. Lily took violin lessons from Professor E. H. Charlton. She was discouraged at his manner, his lack of interest, and because he never once demonstrated with the instrument. On top of all that, he put her through the torture of learning a purely virtuoso piece, Schubert's *The Bee*, to perform on the year's end program. She knew that she couldn't really play it well and that it was purely for show anyway. Her only consolation was that the others were as poorly instructed as she.

Because of her association with the violin teacher, Lily was invited to play with the LSU orchestra, which included three or four good players, except for a cellist from Belgium who "inspired" the rest of the players. Beginning in the second violin section, after three weeks Lily was promoted to the first. The orchestra rehearsed regularly and gave free concerts on Sunday afternoons. It gave three formal concerts a season. This made a heavy schedule for Lily, but it was her most involved musical experience to date, and she loved it. She had a contract to be paid fifty dollars, but was required to buy a season ticket for $2.50 and was fined if she missed any rehearsals or concerts. She missed two, costing her two dollars. Since she was engaged, she had no interest in the local young men or the male musicians.

Gale Perrin came to Zachary to visit Lily during his Easter break in the spring of 1922. Lily showed him the points of interest around Baton Rouge. He agreed with her that the old Louisiana State University campus was charming because of its Spanish flavor. A picnicking day was spent with two other couples in a natural park by the Mississippi River. (One couple was Lily's roommate, Mary Lou, and her date.) Gale praised the lush balminess of the Louisiana spring. On Sunday afternoon he went with Lily to hear her perform in the orchestra. His return to Maine was a poignant parting even though neither of them realized that

Gale Perrin on the porch of Lily's boarding house, Zachary, Louisiana, 1922

it would be their last time to see one another.

They corresponded for a few more years. Lily finally broke the engagement. We can only speculate on the several factors which might have been present in the decision, but Lily said that she could not bring herself to go so far away from her mother. Although Florence Peter never demanded or even suggested that her children sacrifice for her, Lily felt strongly that her mother needed her. Lily's emotional ties to her mother were abnormally strong for several reasons, the main one being, in her opinion, the isolation of the family during her early childhood years. After all, the support and nurture, received by all loved children, was not divided in her case, especially since she was Florence's first child. It was from her mother that Lily received the tenderness and affectionate gestures needed by a sensitive child. Will Peter, although caring, was distant and undemonstrative of affection. Florence was

Lily's provider, teacher, doctor, nurse, dentist, and playmate. She gave to Lily a genuine feeling of worth by giving her the main role of being "mother's helper," expressed in many words of compliment and endearment.

The year in Louisiana seemed long, and Lily was homesick. As much as she loved to travel, she was never able to rid herself completely of some deep-seated anxiety when far from home because she felt so strongly that her mother needed her. Then, too, her father died when she was far from home, and she was unable to be at his funeral, a ritual which helps many to accept the finality of death. It seemed that Lily had gradually assumed the role of "mother's keeper." And there were some compensating factors to rejecting marriage; certainly, she was enjoying near-autonomy, and she had a strong hunger for further schooling.

Through the years Lily would speculate, or perhaps rationalize, that she had been more in love with love than with Gale; however, she took pride in the knowledge that he had an impressive career potential; she knew that he married a few years after she broke their engagement and eventually had a family. She knew that he completed his master's degree in English at the University of Maine, taught a few years at Northwestern in Chicago, and then moved to Colgate University. This was her last knowledge of him when she was interviewed in 1981.

Returning from Zachary to a summer of household and farm work, Lily began teaching at Turner, only four miles from home, in the fall of 1922. She earned $100 a month, a good salary for the times. The one-room school had a sign in front of it which read *Cypress Academy,* lettered in old English style. Lily rode to and from school, as well as all over the community, on horseback. She visited the homes of her pupils, determined to do everything possible to know the needs and families of each child. She kept a record of her riding mileage and found that, at the end of that school year, she had ridden a distance equivalent to the width of the United States. Dorothy Crisp (Mrs. Chesterfield Crisp), a neighbor, remembers this period when Lily rode so much and says that she envied Lily's horsemanship, as well as her talent and intelligence. Lily had a good pony and rode astride rather than side-saddle, but always wore over her regular clothing a great voluminous wool overskirt, full enough to drape down to her feet. Dorothy envied not only her horsemanship, but her courage to take the freedom to ride over the countryside alone in order to enjoy a gentle rain, a sunset, or the moonlight. Lily was not afraid of anything or anybody.[8]

Again Lily had eight grades to teach singlehandedly. Before consolidation, the school was the very heart of the community. Few, if any, musicians, preachers, or money-raisers were denied use of the building outside school hours. Lily provided lots of programs of music and recitation in the school house, especially on holiday occasions.

She tried to bring to her students more subject matter than ordinarily taught and experimented with short classes of fifteen or twenty minutes, relying heavily on written assignments. It was that year that she had the idea for a question box. She took a cigar box, cut a slot in the top, placed it in an accessible place, and told the students that she world attempt to answer any question that they thought of. They must write it on a slip of paper and sign their names, because she wanted no questions they might be ashamed of. One question was, "What makes a person sneeze when he looks at the sun?" Lily recalls having taken it seriously, out of her lifelong respect for a child's ruthless curiosity about things adults hardly notice, let alone question.

The Connell's Point School District had an opening for a teacher the next year, and Lily took it because it was nearer home. She still rode horseback, even though the school was only a mile away, giving her more free time. The year before she had persuaded the Turner directors to buy a piano, but this year her persuasive powers failed because the money was lacking at Connell's Point. She had to buy a piano for the school herself if she was to have one in the eighth-grade schoolroom. She found a used one for around forty dollars, and it was not "greatshakes" (actually a wretched instrument), but Lily was determined to give the students all the exposure to music she could. She played every morning for their singing hymns, patriotic songs, and a variety of others from *The Golden Song Book*. Every child who would respond to her encouragement to play simple pieces on the piano gave up his recess so Lily could teach them the notation. Parents of these children, who didn't have pianos in their homes, had a wonderful surprise when they came to a program and heard their children play.

Lily taught the summer terms as well. Her mother's health was improved, but she was not completely well, and Lily helped with the household work. She was never without some duties about the farm management. Florence Peter was always the titular head of the family, but Jesse had most of the responsibility of the farming, which wasn't too profitable in those years. Lily would often let him have the cash for the "furnish." She gave her mother twenty dollars a month to use as she wished, but it mainly went toward her brother Ted's education. He started at Monticello A and M that fall of 1923. Oma was divorced that year, was at home, and contributed what she could.

Lily and Ethel helped Jesse with the farming in the summer of 1923. Cotton had come to be the one crop which farmers depended upon for their cash income. It was planted throughout the South down through Texas into the Rio Grande Valley. It is no wonder that the Mexican boll weevil migrated right up into Arkansas. There was an ominous invasion that year. All the farmers were panicky and were willing to try anything to rid themselves of this infestation.

The Agriculture Department of the University of Arkansas

had extension agents in every county. They advised a solution which now sounds ridiculous, but it worked if one could manage it. They advised mixing a solution of calcium arsenate and water in a barrel and adding some black strap molasses to make the poison stick on the cotton when sprayed on the plants. What they couldn't advise was how to keep the molasses from "gumming up" any spraying mechanism one might invent.

Jesse had bought as much seed of the finest quality registered cotton as he could afford and had enough to plant a little four-acre field near the house, hoping to yield enough to expand his quantity of seed each year. All were concerned with helping him save that field from the boll weevils, so Lily and Ethel attacked the problem. They made up the solution in an old wash tub, found some big bottles with cork stoppers and punched holes through the stoppers. By giving the bottle a jerk, they could make a small amount come through. Cotton produces a white bloom, which turns pink the second day and red the third. The girls went to the field and, row by row, "shot" each white bloom. They went up and down those rows all during the months of June and July and made fun out of the task. They made up jingles about what they were doing, for example:

> The boll weevil is a lively beast
> On cotton he does love to feast
> He came to us from Mexico,
> And back to that land we wish he'd go.
>
> And since we don't like what he's doing
> We're giving him some of our own homebrewing.
> It's made of calcium arsenate
> With H_2O at a proper rate
> And black strap molasses to make it sweet.
> We hope Mr. Weevil will eat and eat

And eat until he has his fill
And go on to boll weevil heaven
Before any one can say nine times seven.

By means of that slow, crude, and tedious method, they were able to save that patch of cotton so their brother could have some good seed for the next year. That was the beginning of the use of chemicals in fighting pests which has become such a highly developed and expensive process prevalent today, and which Lily regarded as deplorable.

The spring of 1924 is remembered as "the spring of the buffalo gnat plague." It was nothing unusual, just more severe. When one occurred, everybody made smudgepots for protection. An old ten-pound lard bucket with tar in the bottom for burning would suffice and provided the most effective defense. Farmers kept them burning day and night in the fields around the livestock. The mules and horses had buckets rigged around their necks. The buffalo gnats went for the eyes of any animal or human being, and enough stings could blind or even kill. Many mornings Lily found herself and her pony, even with his bucket, in thick swarms of gnats, and she always found the experience frightening. She rarely could give the pupils their much-desired recess. The extensive clearing of swamp lands brought an end to the plagues of buffalo gnats.

In a letter that Lily wrote to her brother Ted that spring, she describes an unusual school project:

> March 26, 1924. . . . We have been planting flowers at school this week—jonquils, bridal wreath, burning bush, chrysanthemums, roses, and beds of zinnias and touch-me-nots. We have a lot more to plant, and we'll have the whole school ground looking lovely by and by, if they grow. . . .

The children brought so many plants and seeds that the planting flowed from the school yard to nearly a mile down the road. Everyone in the neighborhood enjoyed the effort. An occasional tangle of climbing roses can be seen along the fence rows even today.

Another letter to Ted indicates that Gale was on her mind, in spite of the broken engagement:

> May 29. . . . By the way, did you ever ask your English instructor about Gale — P. G. Perrin? If you did, you forgot to tell me what he said. And if you haven't, don't forget to mention this to him sometime. I'd like to know how well he likes Gale. . . .

Lily was still corresponding with Gale as is indicated by the letter she received from his father in August, 1923, headed "The Mountain Parsonage," West Newbury, Vermont:

> Dear Miss Peter: — As a second letter from you has come to this address for our son, Porter — and this second one is registered — I will send you a word of explanation. Porter left home July 16th on one of his lone hiking tours. He passed through northern N. H., and then spent quite a little time in Maine, making his headquarters for some days at his old stamping ground of Maine Univ. He is now somewhere in Nova Scotia. The last we heard from him he was in historic old "Acadie." When he reaches Halifax he returns as far as he can by St. Lawrence boat, as we understand it. As mail for him has been collecting in his absence, we conclude that he slipped away without giving his friends other places of address, and, indeed, we at his home have known of no certain one. He was due to have been back here the 15th; is now expected any day, and will find his mail awaiting him. Very sincerely yours, J. Newton Perrin

It was the fall of 1924 that Lily packed her trunk and took

a train to Memphis to begin a college program at West Tennessee State Normal College. She planned to stay at least a school year. She had wanted to go to the University of Texas because of its reputation for becoming a research center, but the need to conserve every penny made her choose the school nearest home.

Parts of letters from her mother and sisters that first year in college illustrate the closeness of her home ties. Florence wrote on September 29:

> Dear Daughter We received your long letter. My but you must of burnt [sic] some midnight oil writing it. I certainly wish I could of been with you at the Fair. . . . Jesse is working in hay and trying to have his peas picked. He has six bales ginned and he thinks he will get two more. He will sell four more tomorrow if it don't frost tonight. . . .
>
> Your gray dress came today. I will send it to you right away. It certainly is a beauty. . . .
>
> Timbo has howled for you and comes to me so much more to be petted. The other day he wanted to get in the lot where Jesse was. He came to me and all but asked me to open the gate for him.

Ethel wrote on November 13 one of her light-hearted, witty letters:

> Dear Girl, — Your last letter was very much appreciated, especially as I know how limited is your time for writing. Mother is getting the coat. I'm glad. I'm anxious to see Mother in a coat really bought for her.
>
> I am surely glad you are doing so well with your work, but then I always knew you had twice as much brains as you need. I don't see why I didn't inherit a little of it. I'm terribly afraid I'll disgrace you when I come to Memphis either by thinking Muscle [sic] Shoals is some kind of salad or by wondering whether Davis or Coolidge was elected president.

> I'm learning the newspapers, almost by heart, and sit up nights with the dictionary (on my table) so you see if worst comes to worst it won't be my fault. . . . Much love always, . . .

Florence Peter visited Lily at her dormitory, Mynders Hall, on the first of December. On December 7, she wrote:

> Dear Lily Girl, Well tonight a week ago I was in your dear room. What a good time I had while I was with you. . . .

In February, Florence wrote that someone had tried to poison Timbo (they thought), an offense to all of them. She said:

> Dear Lily, Timbo seems to be much better. For some days he could not eat or drink, just stand over a pan of water. He now can eat boild [sic] meat mashed up fine with some bread in it. They killed the dog that bit him, but he was not mad, only had the black tongue. To keep up Timbo's strength we drenched him with olive oil and washed out his mouth. Dr. Wilkerson had no hopes for him at first. You see, he has always been well fed and cared for— is what helped to save him. Twice I thought Jesse would have to shoot him. In fact one time I told him to. . . .

Timbo was sick for five weeks. Florence wrote on March 3 that Timbo was as frisky as ever and that they found that someone had tried to poison him with calomel. She was glad after all that he had not had the disease, black tongue.

Lily's outstanding scholastic ability at West Tennessee State Normal soon became so obvious that the head of the English department, Mr. C. C. McClure, offered her a scholarship to grade freshman English compositions, even while taking the course herself. Lily's themes are all marked A or A+. The scholarship was extended for two years, enabling her to complete her bachelor's degree there.

For her research paper in the spring of '25, she had the idea of writing a composition to be named, "The Trousseau of a Girl of Memphis" (Memphis, Egypt, Twentieth Century B. C.). She had always been fascinated by the history of ancient Egypt and had read much on her own. But she combed the libraries of both the Normal and the Goodwin Institute and could not find enough material on that topic "to grease a child's skillet." Disappointed, she chose to write an essay, "The Evolution of the Violin." She explained how the violin developed from the use of the bow and arrow. She completed her paper of approximately thirty pages in her small, delicate handwriting and submitted it. The teacher inscribed on the back of it: "A+ A real contribution. Your form is almost flawless." Lily was overjoyed.

She made arrangements to take violin lessons from an Italian, Joseph Cortese. He was considered to be the best violinist in Memphis, but he was not a teacher. Lily practiced three hours a day, giving up many pleasant times with her fellow students, because she was so starved for good instruction and wanted to master the violin so badly. Cortese used the Ovid Music School of violin playing, which published four books of instruction. He thought Lily could omit the first and started her assignments in the second one. All he did was listen to her play the exercises with little comment and no correction or praise. The series contained every kind of difficult technique a violinist should have: scales, arpeggios, double-stops, and all kinds of bowing. It even contained a caprice by Paganini. But it was one thing to read and practice on one's own and another to hear works and have them demonstrated, yet Cortese never demonstrated. Lily wanted to progress and to please him. She continued her practice and at her final lesson asked him to give her extra time, for which she paid, because she had a surprise for him. She played through the entire fourth book from memory without missing a note. He was impressed enough to write a note of praise on the back of the book. A friend of Lily's told her that later Cortese remarked,

"Those little girls from Arkansas come here and take music, but they go back home in a couple of years and get married and forget all about it. I really don't know why I take my time with them." This cut Lily to the quick because she was the only girl-pupil he had from Arkansas.

Cortese taught her so poorly that she never would have continued lessons with him had she had any basis for comparison. Her study with Van Hulsteyn at Peabody was far too short a time and had to be on too elemental a level. Although Lily was never satisfied with the sound she was getting, she was invited often to perform at various civic and social functions in Memphis and got some pleasure from it. Once she played a short program on a local radio station. Letters reflect the pride of her family and her home neighborhood and Marvell friends. The Peter family had no radio then, and Mrs. Watt McKinney invited Florence Peter to spend the day with her so they could listen to Lily's program together.

Lily enjoyed all of her liberal arts courses but found the teaching methods courses tedious and of little value. Because of her interest in farming, she went into the Agriculture Department and took a course in soils which proved to be priceless.

Lack of money compelled her to teach summer sessions at home at Connell's Point and Good Luck. In the summer of 1926, she had an unusual accident. While riding her pony to school one day, she was bitten on the ankle by a horsefly. It was extremely painful, but in her usual way she did not stop for treatment. A short time later she was bitten on the exact spot by a mosquito, and a sore developed which refused to heal. She continued her work in an attempt to "wear it out." She went back to Memphis in the fall, but it was not long until her ankle was so inflamed from infection that she was hospitalized. Before healing took place, she had surgery and skin grafts three times. This nonattendance to classes, even though friends brought her assignments, caused her to make the only two grades below *A* which she made at the Normal.

She took one of her favorite courses in the summer of 1927. To teach a drama course, the college had invited a guest lecturer who had been a broadway producer. He directed the Shakespeare play, *Much Ado About Nothing*, with a student cast. Lily had a bit part, one of Dogberry's henchmen, and by practicing the proper English accent, blacking out a front tooth, and inventing some stage effects, she said she "stole the show" in that scene. She also helped with the sets, costumes, and properties and spent enough time with the director for him to find out about her proficiency in Spanish, developed in courses at the Normal. He asked her to translate the *El Cid las Niños*, a famous seventeenth century play, because he wanted to present it in New York.

Lily never fulfilled his request, although she was flattered to have it. She started the translation and took the work with her when she began teaching in Helena the next fall, but soon found that there was no more connection between teaching English in school and making a translation of a Spanish play than there was in "working in a boiler factory all day and playing a concert every evening."

The flood of 1927 arrived that spring, the like of which had never occurred before. It lasted six weeks. It took many attempts by phone for Lily to contact her mother. The news media were full of accounts of it. Lily finally found Florence Peter at the home of Abe and Sarah Davidson, who had invited Florence, Oma, and Marjorie to stay with them for the duration. Lily was so concerned that she wanted to come home, but her mother told her not to, that Lily would only be another refugee to be housed. The three stayed at the Davidsons' in Marvell for nearly a month. It was during the Passover season. Often the Davidsons, who were Jews, would notice Florence Peter weeping silently as they performed their ritual Seders. Abe Davidson told the biographer that he firmly believed that Florence was Jewish, but when he asked her, she said she was not and explained that she had close Jewish connections in New Orleans and Greenville and that the rituals brought back tender memories from her childhood. This stay strengthened their friendship. Florence often consulted Abe on various matters of farming and finance.[9]

Lily as Verges in
Much Ado About Nothing

During the flood Jesse and a friend, Elisha Whitfield, stayed in the Peter home, where the water got eight inches deep. They literally slept with their boots on, managed to prepare their food, and guarded the house against looting. They carried feed to the livestock in boats.

All involved in that flood witnessed that such disasters bring out the best and worst in people. There was robbery and pillaging and violence, but people also showed courage, endurance and generosity. The Red Cross came and issued grocery orders to stranded families. The levees were lined with Red Cross tents for men who worked day and night sandbagging the levees to make them hold. Everyone who had room at all took families in. Frank and Louise Griffin lived on one of the highest ridges in that part of the county and wanted to house "Miss Florence" but just didn't have room. They had two small boys, Frank, Jr., and Brooks, and were expecting another. Louise was relieved when she found that the Davidsons had invited Florence and her daughter and grand-daughter to stay with them. Louise said that the wagons rolled by their house just south of Cypert, one after another, filled with distraught people and all their goods, creating such an atmosphere of distress that she could hardly do her work. One day Frank, Jr. called to her to come out at once to see a pony colt thrashing around in the household equipment atop one wagon. This was just one pitiful scene among many during the flood. Many a farmer longed for enough money to buy land elsewhere.[10]

Florence Peter told the following story about the flood to her daughter-in-law, Mary Lu. When two boats doing rescue work came to Florence's house, the rescuers told her she was in-vited to the Davidsons, and she decided quickly to accept. The water was rising, the people in the boats were waiting, and there was no time to pack clothes. She put all her important papers, some trinkets with sentimental value, "all her worldly posses-sions," in one sack; she put a large ham bone for Timbo in an-other. In the scurrying of boarding the boats, she and the girls got in one boat, and Timbo got into the other. Not being sure whether they would ever get back together, she tossed what she thought was the sack with the bone in it into the boat with Timbo. When she got to dry land, she looked into her sack for something and discovered that she had the bone and that she had thrown "all her worldly possessions" after Timbo. One can imagine her relief when the other boat arrived and she found Timbo and sack in-tact.[11]

Lily was able to receive her diploma from college at the end of the summer of 1927. John Crowe Ransom was invited from

Vanderbilt that summer to teach a composition course, and Lily planned to take it because of his prestige. The course was so popular that there was an overflow of students, and Lily was invited to teach them. She missed studying with Ransom, but was pleased to be paid the salary of a beginning teacher and complete her course work at the same time.

While at the Normal, now Memphis State University, Lily was administered an IQ test. The person administering it told her that she was a genius. She wasn't particularly impressed by it. She thought that many people could have answered those questions, had they tried. She considered that the making of wise decisions, rather than academic achievement, was the mark of genius, and that she had already made a number of poor choices in her life.

With diploma in hand, August 1927, Lily had a choice of vacancies at White Haven, Tennessee, and Helena, Arkansas. White Haven was a suburb of Memphis, and its proximity to city life made Lily seriously consider it, but, as usual, the sensed need to be near home prevailed, and she chose Helena. Ethel had enough college work from State Teachers College, Conway, Arkansas, to qualify as an elementary teacher in Helena and had procured a position there.

Lily taught in Helena from 1927 to 1935, and on the whole, the experience was satisfying. During that time she taught an assortment of junior high school subjects, next the fifth and sixth grades, followed by teaching junior high English students the last three years she was there.

By her late thirties or early forties, Lily had given up dating and was finding that her greatest personal pleasure came from artistic creativity. The first year she was in Helena she decided to see whether her English research paper was publishable. She sent "The Evolution of the Violin" to *Etude*, the music magazine published by the Theodore Presser Company in Philadelphia. She sent the usual self-addressed, stamped envelope, so she was surprised that she heard nothing after a few months' time. She wrote a follow-up letter to the editor and received a reply immediately. The editor apologized, said that the article had been lost in some drawer, that it had not been read, but that she could expect a response soon. About three weeks later, Lily received a letter of acceptance and a check for thirty dollars. With a salary at less than a hundred per month, Lily thought it was a handsome sum. The article was published in 1930.[13]

The stock market crash of 1929 had little effect on the most of the people in Arkansas. The economy of Southern agriculture had gradually worsened throughout the twenties so that the farmers were already having a difficult time. This is reflected in Lily's salary which was less in 1929 than in 1922. It was the closing of banks that truly brought the situation home to the Peters. Florence Peter wrote her daughters in Helena the following letter on January 5, 1931:

> Dear Girls, I have missed you both so much today. It took Jesse till nearly noon to settel [sic] with Louis Snyder. Then he went to Creigh. Anyway he got three hogs and beef dressed.
>
> The Red Cross is going to bring some clothes down to the school tomorrow.
>
> As soon as Mr. Watkins heard that the Bank in Helena had closed its doors he went over to the school house and told Mrs. Myrtal Miles that she cold teach on and she would get her salary next fall when this years taxes came in or she could close the school. She will continue to teach and wait till fall.
>
> I wonder if it will be the same in Helena. If it is you girls stay with your job.
>
> I heard something else that may interest you both. Boon Crisp gave Ira Krow a check on the Marvell bank for $100.00 Saturday and Mr. Krow cashed it, so maby [sic] you can manage to get enough by close economy to pay your

room rent and get you something to eat. Some is putting there [sic] money in the post office. You both do the best you can. Don't buy anything but something to eat and pay your room rent.

Different men were here talking [that] things are in a critical condition. I heard too from Mr. Blyth that Mr. Howe said the Interstate Bank would open if he lost all Wabash, so Ethel you may not lose all your money.

A Negro came here today and asked for some cracklings as he had nothing to eat but corn bread. I gave another one some pig feet and ears and another one some eggs. All the off-fall of the hogs and beef were carried off. Mr. Hopper is going to cut me some wood for a dollar a rank. I thought I would have six ranks cut. That will help them some and I will have enough cut to last me the winter.

May Our Heavenly Father bless and care and keep you both. Mother

The Helena School District managed to pay its teachers, but in many parts of the state, teachers had to accept warrants which few banks or businesses would accept, and if they did so, the warrants would often be discounted up to twenty-five percent. It was a time when post office workers (who received checks from the federal government) were considered the richest folks in town. And to teach for a school district which could pay its salaries was considered lucky, as were Lily and Ethel.

To continually improve her performance on her violin was just as important to Lily as academic achievement, once she had obtained her bachelor's degree. Since her brother Ted had finished the university in '29, she thought she might study that summer and sent for a catalog from the Chicago Music College, which she had heard of through one of her colleagues in Helena who had studied there in 1928. When the time came for Lily to go, however, Florence Peter was so ill that all in the family felt something should be done. It was decided that she might benefit from spending the summer in Hot Springs, the Arkansas spa, and that Ethel should go with her while Lily stayed at home and ran the household.

Toward the end of the summer, Lily came across the little catalog and thought how the school had wasted its postage on her request. She wrote a courteous letter, thanking the school for the catalog and explaining her failure to attend. To her utter surprise, she immediately received a reply from the president, Dr. Carl Kinsey, telling her that she might have a position on the clerical staff to help pay her expenses while there the next summer. The job paid only ten dollars a week, but she was pleased enough to accept without hesitation.

Much of her spare time during the next teaching year was spent making over old clothes for that summer of 1930. She made one new school dress from a remnant of cotton dimity costing ninety-eight cents. A five-cent spool of thread, a package of blue bias tape at ten cents, and a pattern for fifteen cents ran the cost to $1.28. Her colleague had told her that there would be a concert at the end of the term in Chicago in which all enrolled would have to perform and that formal dress was mandatory. Lily went down to Ware and Solomon, one of the best stores in Helena, and bought a yellow net formal embroidered with daisies. It cost thirty dollars, which she considered a gross extravagance. One can imagine how disappointed she was that the school's remodeling job on the recital hall precluded having the concert that summer.

In addition to studying at the musical college, Lily went to the University of Chicago and took American literature from Dr. Percy Holmes Boynton. He possessed such contagious enthusiasm for his subject that Lily determined to make it her major when she continued work on her master's degree.

Lily's first clerical assignment at the college was helping prepare fifty thousand packets for mailing to potential students. When this task was finished, each of the staff was assigned to one of several visiting artists who had been recruited for the summer staff. They were conducting auditions for students applying to the school for scholarships. Lily was assigned to staff member Percy Grainger, whose composition "Country Gardens" had been played and loved by nearly every piano student in the United States and Australia, Grainger's home. He had a thick shock of bright red hair topping a short and stocky build. He was a health enthusiast long before it was fashionable. He would run along Michigan Avenue every morning in his shorts, a sight that came as near to stopping traffic as a "streaker" would now. He was a vegetarian and took all his meals in a vegetarian restaurant near the school. A large picture of him was kept on display in the window of the restaurant.

Lily, too, had heard "Country Gardens" and liked being assigned to Grainger. She sat outside the door of his studio in the hallway and ushered students in and out. She could complete her assignments in American literature and do that job too. She was awed by Grainger's testy disposition. One day when a student had failed to come and he was angry about it, he appeared at the door with a huge bunch of snapdragons which he had taken from a large container in his studio, a dripping wet mass, and practically threw them into Lily's arms. The composer of "Country Gardens" exclaimed, "I don't like flowers," and popped back into his studio like a jack-in-the-box. Despite the wetness of her dress, Lily distributed the flowers around the school using every container she could find.

Her next assignment was to a Mr. Demarest, a famous organ teacher, but she had only helped him a few days when she was summoned by the president, Dr. Kinsey. She reported to his office, fearful she had done something offensive, only to find out from his secretary that he wanted her to take the position of assistant librarian. She was relieved and pleased because she loved books, and the library was the prettiest room in the college. It was Dr. Kinsey's pride and joy because he had furnished it himself with his own collection of antique furniture. She explained that she had no library experience, but the secretary said that it did not matter because the library had low usage during the summer on account of the heat.

Lily later found out why she was offered the job. One day Dr. Kinsey's secretary asked her if she would like to know why she was chosen to assist the librarian. Lily, of course, was glad to be told because she liked the job so well. The secretary said, "Dr. Kinsey told me to look over the clerical force and pick out the one that was the best dressed, provided she looked as if she had sense enough to sit in the library." Lily enjoyed telling the story that she had been chosen as the best dressed girl in the clerical staff with a ten-year-old wardrobe of made-over clothes excepting a new homemade dress that cost $1.28. Lily made friends with most of the students in the work group, all of whom were trying to live on their ten dollars a week. They often compared notes on their food expenses (the school did not have a dining room, but there were plenty of restaurants nearby, and they often went together to inexpensive cafes.) They got their weekly checks on Thursday. One Tuesday Lily found that she had only thirty-three cents to last until Thursday. That evening Lily was going with some student friends to a program of Russian music for which they already had tickets. She left off supper because she knew she would be absorbed in the music. The next morning she spent ten cents for a roll and a cup of coffee; at noon, she thought she might get more for her money if she tried the Vegetaria, where Grainger ate. Her twenty-three cents bought her a bowl of soup, quite watery, colored with a bit of caramel and containing a few tomatoes and carrots. She wondered where Grainger got his energy.

That evening she had a date which her brother Ted had arranged for her. Ted was working in Pine Bluff, Arkansas, for the Arkansas Power and Light Company and was staying with a family whose son, Stanley, was going to Chicago on business for the bank where he worked. Ted insisted that Stanley visit Lily. When he appeared at the school, famished as she was, she went to a picture show with him even though her hunger distracted her from enjoying the movie. Afterward, he very formally asked her if she would like some "ice refreshments." They found an ice cream parlor, and Lily ordered the most extravagant concoction on the list. She got her check the next morning, and she made sure she was never penniless again.

The year 1935 saw the end of Lily's eight-year teaching stint at Helena, where she "worked like a galley-slave." The country was still in the depths of economic depression, but all of Lily's siblings were now fairly well established. Oma had graduated from the University of Arkansas in home economics, had done a residency in institutional nutrition at Barnes Hospital in St. Louis, and had a good job. Her daughter, Marjorie, married her first sweetheart, Daniel Crisp, in 1932. Ted, while in Pine Bluff, had met and married Mary Lu DeFord, and they had moved to Vicksburg, Mississippi, where he worked for the Mississippi River Commission. That Lily's mother was still in ill health was her primary concern; however, because of her voracious appetite for learning, Lily made plans to go to graduate school at Columbia University in New York City in the fall. She was confident that, with the master's degree, she could get a job teaching in a college. She planned that when she did receive her degree, her mother would live with her in some nice college town where she could receive better and more convenient medical care.

With excitement and high hopes, in June Lily boarded the train in Helena bound for New York. Even though she could have finished her degree in nine months, she wanted to start her graduate program in the summer so that she would have more time to absorb everything in New York that she could not find at home. These experiences proved to be many.

NOTES

[1]The summer of 1908, the Connell's Point school board offered Lily a position at forty dollars a month with the promise that, if they were pleased with her work, she would receive a five-dollar raise for the second month. Teaching was the only occupation offered to young women in the area, and it did not occur to Lily to leave home with that summer job available. Lily received the five-dollar raise the second month and has never been more proud of any accomplishment. In a personal interview 11 August 1980, Pearl Crisp Lane, Marvell, Arkansas, said, "I was eight years old when Lily came back from Ohio and began teaching. She was my first teacher. She was very pretty, sweet and good. All of us children loved her."

[2]Fred W. Allsopp, *History of the Arkansas Press for a Hundred Years and More* (Little Rock, Ark. Parke-Harper, 1922) p. 14.

[3]During the spring of 1911, Lily made arrangements to go to Arkansas State Teachers' College at Conway, a town in the central part of the state (thirty miles northwest of Little Rock) about one hundred forty miles from her home. She enrolled for one of the college's summer Normal (a term no longer in use which indicated teacher training) courses. In preparation she began sewing clothes every minute of her spare time. Lily arrived in Conway on June 10. She took art and reading and observed in the Model School. She formed a lively circle of girl friends right away. She and several of them joined the Story Tellers' Club at Hendrix College, also in Conway. Lily was frightened when her turn came to tell a story. She also went to every public forum or entertainment that either of the two colleges offered. A lot of her social activities centered on the Epworth League, an organization for youth in the Methodist Church.

At Hendrix, Lily met Will Bishop, a student who was to teach the next school year at Cypert, a small community just five miles north of Lily's home in Eastern Arkansas. While in Conway, Lily signed a contract to teach the next fall at Trenton, a town just eight or ten miles east of Cypert. Lily and Will made plans to spend some time together.

[4]Personal interview with Maude Anderson Orme, (daughter of Lee Price Anderson), 9 Aug. 1980. Maude Orme was born March 3, 1990, the day Florence and Will Peter married. She died July 20, 1986.

[5]In a letter to the biographer (20 Jan. 1981) Kenneth Beaudoin said, ". . . Miss Lily came over to Southwestern in Memphis to hold forth on Sappho at one of our workshops. Miss Lily went to great lengths to de-

fend the morality of Sappho and her girls on Lesbos and tried to persuade us her relations with those young ladies was very like that of a teacher in any American girl's school. Needless to say, we were not completely convinced. . . ." Lily's account of the occasion was that she sensed that some members had a personal stake in a discussion of Sappho and that she purposely "held forth" over two hours until after eleven in the evening. By that time most chairs were empty, and those present were too tired for challenges. (Beaudoin's statement came as a reply to the biographer's question as to what amusing incidents he had shared with Lily.)

[6]Whitelaw Burton owned the other car, an Oldsmobile Phaeton, a two-seat touring car. Margaret Hawks, Burton's daughter, remembered riding all over the country tied in the back seat, but couldn't remember the make of the car. However, Ben Davison, a Marvell car dealer and amateur historian, knew because he had learned about those early cars from Charlie Hendrix, a Negro, who worked for the Burtons. (Telephone interview with Ben Davidson, 2 Jan. 1982.)

[7]According to Martin S. Day, author of *History of English Literature, 1829 to the Present*, Edward John Noreton Drax Plunkett, 18th Baron Dunsany, 1878-1957, was a poet and playwright. Day said, "The English speaking world was overwhelmed by Dunsany during the first quarter of the century. It reacted from this position and came to look on Dunsany as a sort of museum piece." (Garden City, N. Y.: Doubleday, 1964) p. 254.

[8]Personal interview with Dorothy Crisp, 18 July 1980.

[9]Personal interview with Abe and Sarah Davidson, 26 Sept. 1980. A. Davidson died January 10, 1984. S. Davidson died January 20, 1985.

[10]Telephone interview with Louise Mixon Griffin, 16 Oct. 1981.

[11]Personal interview with Mary Lu DeFord Peter, 22 May 1981. Mary Lu died December 27, 1990.

[12]The sisters took room and board in the Wilford White home the first year. However, Lily, who was saving money for graduate school, persuaded Ethel to move to a place where they could do some light housekeeping and save money. They found such an arrangement in the Crabtree home, where they lived for two years. Then a larger, more commodious place became available with Judge and Mrs. E. D. Robertson. Boarders were treated like members of the family in many places and this was one of them. Edgar Robertson, Marianna, Arkansas, has vivid memories of Lily's outgoing personality and her many entertaining stories. His wife, an English teacher at Moro, Arkansas, came to be a friend of Lily through

Poetry Roundtable during the forties and sixties. Marnell Robertson, as editor of a poetry column in the *Courier-Index* at Marianna, published many of Lily's poems and treasured her friendship. (Personal interview with Marnell and Ed Robertson, 5 Aug. 1980)

Ivey Gladin, local Helena photographer, is one of the students who was Lily's pupil for five years. He was studying violin at the time and was the instigator of one of the many ruses the students would concoct to get Lily off the subject or delay a test. If her violin was in the classroom for her playing in assembly, a common occurrence, he would think up some problem he was having with his technique and ask her to help him with it. Other students would do similar things. They really thought they were putting something over on her, but they later realized that they were not, that they were merely giving themselves longer outside assignments. Lily thought she could accomplish more by responding to their various initiations which she could often capitalize upon. She was fully aware of their spurious motives. Ivey Gladin said that he had never had a teacher who wanted more to teach them the finer things of life. Sometimes they would ask her to sing for them. She did, particularly if she knew a poem set to music. Gladin has enjoyed his association with her all through the years since he was her student, having done a lot of photography and developing for her. (Personal interview with Ivey Gladin, 17 Sept. 1980)

Charles Conditt, an insurance man in Helena and representative to the state legislature, was another of her pupils. He remembers that he and other boys loved to tantalize her. One favorite trick was to toss a black board eraser up into the pan of the lighting fixture where it would heat up and, although not flammable, create an awful stink. This would put her into an entertaining dither. She despised disciplinary confrontations with the students and would strenuously avoid them; however, she occasionally resorted to applying a one-foot ruler to an open hand. He praised her ability and told with pride that he was the one who introduced a bill into the state legislature in 1970 to make her the poet laureate of the state. (Personal interview with Charles Conditt, 17 Sept. 1980)

Fern Williams Lyford, a Latin teacher, taught in the room next door to Lily during a number of those Helena years. She and Julia Camp, the French and social studies teacher, and Bobbsey Ferguson, the history teacher, and Lily spent a lot of time together and had many good times. They enjoyed going to LIly's home in the country where Mrs. Peter would always entertain them with a delicious dinner. All of them, including Mr. Wall, knew of Lily's "digressions," but felt the students were getting instruction they would get nowhere else. Wall praised her enthusiastically and often. Ethel also came in for much respect and praise. She and Lily were considered an unusual pair of sisters. (Telephone interview with Fern Lyford, 12, Jan. 1981)

Betty Woods, a reporter for the *Arkansas Democrat*, a native of Helena, told the writer that Lily considered her a star pupil in English because she (Betty) was an avid reader. One afternoon she was walking home with Lily who said, "Betty, Dear, what good literature are you reading right now?" Betty replied, "Faith Baldwin." Betty said that Lily's face fell momentarily, but that she recovered her pleasantness and said, "Oh, my dear, I'm a bit disappointed in your choice of authors, but it is good that you read a lot." (Personal interview with Betty Woods, 1 Jan. 1982)

[13]*Etude* divided Lily's writing into two parts, each to fill one of its fairly large pages (the size of the old *Saturday Evening Post*), and published one part in February, 1930, and the other in March, 1930. The layout planners added three small illustrative etchings and off-set the section headings of each part, making the articles neat and attractive. Lily's byline is prominent.

[14]Personal interviews with Lily Peter, tapes 7, 14, 23, 24, 27, 28, 29, 31, 35, 40, 42, 43, 44, 46, 49, 50, 51, 53, 54, 58, 59, 64, 66. Torreyson Library Archives, University of Central Arkansas.

Chapter IV

COLUMBIA, VANDERBILT
AND FOUR THOUSAND ACRES, 1935-1948

Let us honor the mystery of the written word,
That holds what man has thought or felt or heard!

Here are lost shrines, where, on ancient altars
Upcurl the flames of the fine word of scorn
For the ignoble: the spirit's Epiphany,
That, defying life's most dire assaulters,
Provides the courage for the ashen morn
That waits for each man in his destiny.

Sordidness shows. The dross in human nature
May make the word filthy, foolish, sick, insane.
But the high wind of Time, that winnows all,
Drives out the debris. Man, the only creature
That notes its history for its good and gain,
Distinguishes birdsong from caterwaul.

All honor to the written word, that keeps unbroken
The best that man has thought or heard or spoken!
        Lily Peter
        from "Colophon for a Bookplate"
        unpublished

Before Lily left for New York City, she arranged to live at
King's College Club across the street from Columbia University

on Amsterdam Avenue. She did not begin classes at Columbia until fall, but she settled herself quickly and registered at the Juilliard Institute of Musical Art. Lily took voice from Bernard Taylor and piano from Guy Maier, a young man who was already making his mark as a capable teacher when he died in his early thirties.

Columbia required its candidates for the master's degree in English to take thirty hours of course work plus a short thesis. This disappointed Lily because she was interested in doing in-depth research, and she did not give up the idea.

Influenced by the course in American literature taught by Dr. Boynton taken at the University of Chicago, Lily decided to concentrate on the same subject at Columbia. She was assigned Lawrence Roger Thompson as her faculty advisor. He was a graduate assistant working on his Ph.D. in English. He made a reputation later as a philologist and became the definitive biographer of Robert Frost, chosen by Frost. She called on Thompson early in the fall to seek his advice in choosing a topic for the thesis. By this time she had heard through the grapevine that a thesis for a master's degree at Columbia should be a minor affair that wouldn't compete with research being done by candidates for doctorates, for whom all the major writers were reserved. This left candidates for a master's degree like Lily with the more obscure authors and their works. She was forewarned that the main purpose of her thesis should be to gather large amounts of data and that very little literary criticism would be allowed.

Thompson's first suggestion was that she write about the unpublished poetry of Edwin Arlington Robinson. Lily asked how she could get access to it, and he responded that the answer to her question would constitute her research. She half-heartedly accepted the topic. Further discussions with him made her realize that she was not happy with the assignment, and she told him so. He questioned her further about her interests, and when he found that she wrote poetry, he asked to see some of it. She brought him some, including one poem she had written after she had arrived, "New York Skyline."[1] He was sufficiently impressed to tell her that anyone who was writing poetry of that caliber should be allowed to present a book of her own poetry to fulfill the thesis requirement. He asked if she were willing to have him present the idea to those making such decisions, and she was so pleased that she told him to go ahead and release the E. A. Robinson topic to someone else.

This request, however, caused a tempest in a teapot, or at least a great deal of arguing behind closed doors, for Columbia was not ready for such a radical idea. After several weeks of conflict, the idea was rejected, and Thompson was so offended that he transferred to Princeton the next semester.[2]

Lily was not far into the fall semester until she was having second thoughts about majoring in American Literature. She had enrolled in the required course on the subject taught by Dr. Ralph Rusk. He was both literally and figuratively a monumental man: six feet, four inches tall, possessing broad shoulders with a frame to go with them. He was monumental in his mental powers with a memory for a myriad of details. Yet Lily found that he did not relate any of this body of knowledge to life, had no more compassion for humanity "than an old shingle," and, despite a compelling, stentorian voice, was utterly dull. At first she attributed the dullness to his repetition of subject matter she already knew, but when he entered into the analysis of minor figures she had never heard of, she realized that it was just his approach to literature.

At the same time, with research in mind, Lily studied the course offerings and found that Dr. Rusk was also offering a seminar on Emerson. She feared his displeasure for having dropped his other course, yet she went ahead and asked for admittance. Much to her surprise, he greeted her like a long-lost daughter and told her he would be only too glad to have her. Because she loved

Emerson, and because she thought the seminar would enhance her research course, Lily was delighted.

An acquaintance studying for his doctorate, Paul O'Halloran, was a native New Yorker from the Bronx and was intrigued with Lily because she was from Arkansas. Lily found him to be exceptionally open-minded and non-prejudiced about people from outside New York City.

It was to Paul that Lily expressed her elation at being admitted to Dr. Rusk's seminar on Emerson. He replied, "I do hate to discourage you, but if you plan to continue your music and take in all the museums and concerts and side trips around New York, you had better not enter that seminar. Dr. Rusk is planning to write the definitive work on Emerson, and he gives his students such huge research assignments that they have little time for anything else. I've had several friends who have taken it, and they tell of harrowing experiences completing their work."

Lily was grateful for this advice and hurriedly went back to Dr. Rusk once again and withdrew as gracefully as she could, escaping his tedious lectures.

Many years later Lily read with a great deal of interest a lengthy review of Dr. Rusk's *Life of Ralph Waldo Emerson*, realizing how near she had come to being an active contributor to the research. It was amusing to her that the reviewer commented that Dr. Rusk had done a thorough job of ferreting out the details of Emerson's life, but that he (the reviewer) was surprised to find that poor Mr. Emerson had lived such a dull life.

Lily was still faced with deciding upon an area of concentration. She was thoroughly enjoying a Victorian literature course under Dr. Emory Edward Neff, despite her thinking the first time she saw him that he had to be the most unprepossessing personality she had ever seen at a college lectern. He was a tiny, skinny man, stoop-shouldered "under the burden of knowledge he carried around in his head," near-sighted, with his head thrust forward so that he always seemed to be scurrying down the corridors on important business with both arms laden with books and papers. Lily assumed that she was doomed to boredom, particularly the first day when he started reading from lecture material. She soon found, however, that those lectures were so filled with humanity, wit, imagination, compassion, and charm that they were among the most satisfying lectures she heard the whole year at Columbia. A short time before, he had spent a sabbatical year in England, where he came heavily under the influence of the Bloomsbury group of writers, and he loved to talk about them.

For a major, Lily finally settled on Modern English literature, which was lectured by Dr. William York Tindall, whom she asked to be her faculty advisor. He had completed his Ph.D. just the year before in 1934 and would eventually be considered a prominent authority on James Joyce. His book, *A Reader's Guide to James Joyce*, is a major contribution to Joyce scholarship. He had a deadpan, subtle sense of humor. One day he abruptly interrupted his lecture with this *bon mot*: "One of the traditions of Columbia University is that Dr. Neff once saw Virginia Woolf mail a letter." He then resumed his lecture.

Lily's request that Tindall advise her was granted, and together they chose a British writer who would pass as a nonentity, Alfred Austin, poet laureate of England following the death of Lord Tennyson. He had been a war correspondent during the Boer War and had done some creditable reporting and written reams of verse, but, thought Lily, not one line of sheer beauty. Prime Minister Lord Salisbury nominated him, and Queen Victoria ratified his appointment, but Lily's research revealed that neither the prime minister nor the queen gave serious thought to it. Lily found an interesting, although apocryphal, story which revealed that when Lord Salisbury was asked why he had nominated Austin, he replied that it was because the *d-a-m-n* fool wanted it so badly. Lily worked on this thesis steadily, but she didn't give it top priority.

As an elective, Lily had chosen to take Creative Writing of Poetry from Dr. Joseph Auslander. A graduate of Harvard University, he had published several books of poetry by this time and was gaining prominence as a translator from both French and Italian. He praised Lily's poetry and even encouraged her to push for publication, but she consistently refused because she felt she was not ready. Of one poem which she submitted, "Requiem for an Age of Disillusion," he said, "I wish to heaven I had written that." Lily has included this poem in one of her unpublished books, *News from Camelot.*[3]

Dr. Auslander persuaded Lily to enter the annual poetry competition at Columbia for the Mariana Griswold Van Rensselaer Prize. Those were the days when professors were not reprimanded for fraternizing with students. Many of them entertained students in their homes and became acquainted on a personal level. Such was the case with Lily and the Auslanders. She came to know Audrey, the wife, also a poet who used her maiden name, Wurdemann. Audrey won the Pulitzer Prize in 1934 for a book entitled *Seven Sins.* For fun Lily emulated her format in miniature and wrote a septet, "Seven Tortures." The poem Lily submitted for the competition was "Memory." She was told that it was runner-up to the winner.

Lily would have taken poetry from Auslander again in the spring had he not had an accident which immobilized him. It happened on January 16, 1936, when New York City was struggling with a deep snow followed by a glazing freeze. Street equipment had dug to the street bed, piling huge chunks of ice along the curbs. That day, Dr. and Mrs. Auslander were standing in a pedestrian area waiting to hail a cab. One came by at such a rate of speed that when its bumper grazed one of the heavy chunks of ice, it was thrown against Dr. Auslander's legs so hard that one of them sustained a compound fracture. The setting of the bones was so difficult that the leg had to be rebroken twice before

Auslander could use his leg properly. He was in traction until May, the last time Lily saw him. She had gone to visit the Auslanders often that spring.

Lily enjoyed many experiences during her stay at Columbia and Juilliard. During her month break between the summer and fall sessions, she took a weekend steamship tour to Boston. She wrote her mother:

> Boston. Monday evening. August 19.
> Dearest Mother:
> You ought to get a real thrill over receiving this letter. My first ever written from a ship at sea — and from a real ship — an ocean liner! I sent you a card Saturday morning telling you I was going up to Boston for a week-end. There was a special excursion rate of $7.50 for the week-end trip to Boston so I thought that would be a good time to go, since Boston is a city I've always wanted to see.
>
> The trip has been altogether delightful. I left New York Saturday afternoon at 5:30 on the steamship *New York* of the Eastern Steamship Lines, which, I am told, is the best line out of New York for cities along the coast, and we reached Boston Sunday morning about nine o'clock. I had never been on the ocean before, and I'm sure that no one on this boat could have had a greater thrill out of it than I had.
>
> The weather was ideal, the sea smooth as glass, a gorgeous moon Saturday night, and the whole trip has been all I could have wished for. The moonlight on the ocean is indescribably lovely. I sat up on deck until after midnight looking at the stars and the moon laying down a track of fire across the black, opaque water.
>
> Sunday I took a bus sight seeing tour over Boston, Cambridge, Lexington, and Concord that took more than half the day. This trip was most delightful, and on it we saw dozens of famous historical places. The rest of the afternoon I did some sight-seeing on foot, which was interesting, but took a lot of

walking. The streets of Boston are the narrowest, crookedest streets I ever saw, and it's very hard, for that reason, to find one's way around, but I managed to see a number of interesting places without a guide. The Boston Common, the Public Gardens, the Esplanade along the Charles River, the old State House, Kings' Chapel, the old Granary Burying Ground, where are buried many of the people famous in the early history of Boston -- Benjamin Franklin's parents, Mother Goose, Samuel Adams, John Hancock, many of the early governors, and so on — and I saw a number of other interesting places.

This morning I took a sightseeing bus trip over North Boston, to Bunker Hill, out to the Navy Yard, and to other interesting places. Then I went out to the Boston Public Library, which is a really magnificent place, and spent more time there than at any other single place, looking at the beautiful mural paintings, those by Sargent "Judaism and Christianity," and the ones in the Holy Grail sequence. I wish you could have seen them with me.

The boat left this afternoon at 5:30 from India Wharf — doesn't that sound romantic? — and will reach New York tomorrow morning about 8:30.

This has been a delightful trip, and I'm so glad I took it. Boston, you remember, was founded about 1630, so with three hundred years of history back of it naturally it has no end of interesting historical places, and the ocean is too beautiful for words.

I've been up on deck looking at the ocean all evening, and now it's rather late, so I must tell you good night, dear Mother. ... A world of love for you all. Devotedly, Lily.

When Lily felt the swell of the ocean as the ship moved out of New York harbor, she remembered her Viking ancestors and felt a kinship with them. She loved the sight of Cape Cod as the ship moved through the locks of Cape Cod Canal. She thought the lawn of Lexington the neatest and most well-kept she had ever seen. It was this trip that inspired "August: New England Hillside" in *The Green Linen of Summer,* Lily's first published book of poetry.

Lily's Christmas in New York City was filled with family love even though she was so far from home. She received a Christmas letter from her mother, together with a package of pecans. She was invited to Bethlehem for the holidays by her Cousin Clara, and four days before Christmas she wrote her mother a very long letter, aware that only her brother, Jesse, was home with her. Trying to comfort her, Lily recommended reading the Psalms and *Imitation of Christ* by Thomas Á Kempis, saying, ". . . that will be a fine enriching tonic for your spirit." She closed her letter with the following:

> I wish you'd give Reuben [Wilson, a loyal colored hand] a few eggs or some sugar or a little something like that for me and tell him I wish him a Merry Christmas. . . .
> A good night kiss and the happiest of Christmases — happy in the thought of our love for each other and the happy memories of the past, — and how I wish I could be with you, dear Mother, Devotedly,

Lily's Christmas in Bethlehem that year and a later visit are described by her cousin, Lee Butterfield:

> Mother told us her Arkansas cousin was coming, We pretended consternation: she was coming to see the ancestral home and we lived in a rented half-a-double. How disillusioning! However the visit did not get arranged until summer and she came to see us at our summer cabin on the Delaware at the remote area called by the unlikely name of Foul Rift (which is old English for bad rapids). We hoped she would be comfortable in our very rustic cabin and tents. We love this place but we have camped there every summer since my father decided it was good for his growing family. Newcomers at first sight

of the primitive conditions sometimes found sudden excuses to go home.

It turned out that Mother's cousin was an excellent sport, and that despite a week of discouraging rain. My mental picture of her is of a very thin woman, black hair done in a bun at the back of the head, a very thin face with great dark eyes. As the rain continued she told us about life in Arkansas, about the path of DeSoto across her father's land, about the thesis she was working on . . . marvelous stories and descriptions. And we marveled at the way she could interject related details but always pick up the main thread. We also were in awe of her delightful ability to transform hard work into an interesting adventure.

I don't think I saw her again until the first Moravian Music Festival, which was held in Bethlehem. By now I was a young married woman with assorted small children. Mother had an apartment on the second floor of our house. Miss Lily stayed with us—a transformed Lily Peter, her gray hair nicely curled, her clothes very stylish, and generally she looked ten years younger than when we had last seen her. She entranced our children and us with many more stories.

I think it was on this visit that she proved what a great person she is. We were serving dessert and wanted to top it off with the new marvelous contrivance of RediWhip. We were somewhat in a hurry because we were bound for a concert that evening and Lily was dressed most beautifully for it. My husband showed her the cream canister and pressed the nozzle as directed but instead of a puff of cream decorating her strawberries the entire canful shot out, bounced from the dessert dish to completely plaster Lily, dress, face, hair, and the wall behind her up to the ceiling. There followed a shocked silence while all of us were frozen with consternation. And then—and then, SHE LAUGHED! The little notes of laughter released us and we got napkins and towels to mop up the foam from her hair, face, bodice. And she retired to dress again for the concert. . . .[4]

Unquestionably, Lily had a variety of new experiences the year she spent at Columbia. That her association with the august school hadn't turned her into an effete intellectual can be seen by her enrollment in the Arthur Murray School of Dance. She loved to dance, although there were few opportunities in eastern Arkansas, and she wanted to dance well enough that any partner would enjoy dancing with her. One of her teachers was reputed to be an exiled Russian Prince, a rumor, Lily believed, based solely on his aloofness. Lily remembered him as being tall, handsome, saturnine, seeming to display the reputed Russian melancholy, and that he danced extremely well. After only three months of lessons, Lily was asked to take the teaching course which would qualify her to become a member of the Arthur Murray staff, and, although she was flattered, she had to decline because of her full schedule.

When Lily was in New York in 1935-36, she met Donald Hotchkiss Brooks at Juilliard, a young pianist from Hapsburg, New York. Many thought him talented enough to have a concert career, but he wanted to be a banker and became one. His engineer father died and left an inheritance not only to his mother, who was Canadian and very English, but also to his brother and himself, making him wealthy enough to have many options in his life. Don opted to study music solely for his own pleasure. He and Lily dated frequently, and their friendship existed until his death. In addition to piano, Don studied composition, and through him, Lily renewed and strengthened her life-long interest in composition. In later years, they composed songs in collaboration with each other.[5]

Lily resolved that she was not going to indulge in going home for a visit, because of the expense, until she finished her degree. However, things were not going well at home. Her mother's health was failing rapidly. Jesse had experienced a whirlwind romance with a beautiful young girl which ended in marriage, but a short-lived, unhappy one. They were divorced. Ethel and Oma both had jobs outside of Arkansas. At the end of the summer of 1936, Lily only lacked six hours of residency and the thesis on Austin for her degree. But in her homesickness and concern for her mother and Jesse, she went home in August.

It was a comforting reunion. Lily's brother Ted and wife, Mary Lu, came up from Vicksburg and invited Florence Peter to go back with them. This arrangement made Lily feel better about returning to Columbia to finish her work. Actually Mrs. Peter seemed fairly well and in good spirits, not seeming as ill as events would prove her to be.

In October, she became quite ill, and a Vicksburg doctor diagnosed her condition as a malignancy and said she must have surgery. She went to Memphis for this operation. Lily dropped her studies and rushed home only to find that her mother was at death's door from kidney failure that occurred during the surgery. Lily got to spend an hour with her before her death, and Florence recognized Lily. She died on October 16, 1936, at age sixty-seven.[6]

Lily was traumatized. Her dream of giving her mother a kind of renaissance in life, living in some pleasant college town, was obliterated. She also suffered from a horrible guilt complex about having been away from her mother the last year of her life. Later Lily realized, in retrospect, that the death was merciful because of the inadequacies of cancer treatment in that day. At that time, death from cancer meant a long, drawn-out illness that was excruciatingly painful. And she finally realized that she should not have felt so guilty. Mrs. Peter was a resourceful woman who enjoyed her social relationships outside her family, who was creative, making item after item of exquisite needlework and crochet, who wanted her children to develop their potential to the highest levels. She was, perhaps, too emotionally dependent on her children because of having widowhood thrust upon her so early in life.

Bob Smalley and his ox team, used into the 1940's.
Behind him stands Alvin King and seated on the wagon
is Ethel Peter

After ginning, the bales of cotton were stored in the street
at the railroad station at Marvell, Arkansas

But no amount of rationalizing soothed Lily for a long time.

Florence Peter left no will, and the estate was not divided among her children, except that in a few years Oma was given her portion of the land so she could deed eighty acres to her daughter Marjorie and son-in-law, Daniel Crisp, for a home place.

When Lily left Columbia, it was with a promise to return in the spring. But by mid-January it was obvious that a flood was coming. It began raining in November; it rained all of December, did not stop in January, and the waters kept rising. With her home in danger, Lily could not imagine herself studying, so she canceled her commitment to Columbia. She and Jesse fought together the devastating flood of 1937, near-equal in violence to the one in 1927.

Distress was widespread. The Red Cross came again and this time, besides issuing grocery orders, set up a tent city in Barton, a small town with the highest elevation in the county. The Griffin boys, Frank, Jr., Brooks, and Buron, helped Jesse with getting his livestock to high ground and removing all the grain and hay from the barns. On the sixteenth of February, the flood waters finally crested, but it was days before they began to fall. On February 14, Lily and Jesse were having dinner with neighbors across the field, the Bill Browns, who were celebrating the birthday of their one daughter, Elizabeth Ann. Lily received a phone call from the superintendent of the Marvell High School, asking her if she would finish out the term for the Spanish teacher who had asked for a leave of absence because of illness. Lily discussed it with Jesse. She told him that she certainly did not want to go off and leave him when he obviously needed all the help he could get in the midst of the flood. He responded, "Yes, I need you. But those students need you, too. If you don't go, they will lose their language credit and the work they've already done." He even offered to take her to Marvell, but she wouldn't let him. She called the administrator and told him that she would accept the position if he would arrange for weekly transportation since the journey called for both boat and car.

Such arrangements were made, but Lily had many difficult times going to and from school. She had to walk some distance to a place where she met Ben Davison, the driver and a friend she had taught the fourth grade. It was bitter cold, and there were six or seven long stretches she had to wade through. She could not get on enough woolen socks to keep her feet warm in her rubber boots. There were two sloughs off Big Cypress Bayou which could only be crossed in boats. Jesse kept one at each place. Anyone who came along used them. Often Lily would find one of them on the opposite side and would have to wait for someone to come along and paddle it across to her. One morning she stood there and screamed until someone heard her and came from a house across the field. An extra burden was that families remaining on the bayou would ask her to shop for them. On weekends she would try to cook adequate food to last Jesse the five days.

When the flood waters subsided, Jesse decided that they should move up to the Creigh farm and live in a farm house next door to the store (on higher ground). He had bought the place in 1928. By degrees they moved from the home place where Lily had lived since she was two years old. The farm house was less than two miles north and in sight of Big Cypress Bayou. Lily lived there until 1990.

Because she had never given up wanting further education, Lily made arrangements to finish her master's degree. She had wanted to attend Vanderbilt University ever since she had been associated with John Crowe Ransom at the Memphis Normal. Also, enthusiastic praise for Vanderbilt came from Denver Baughn, one of Lily's English teachers at the Normal. With those incentives, Lily entered the fall of 1937. Lily came to love Vanderbilt more than Columbia, but she was never sorry she went to Columbia first because of the cosmopolitan experiences it gave her.

Dr. Edwin Mims, head of the graduate school at Vanderbilt, was impressed enough with Lily's transcript from Columbia that he and Mrs. Mims arranged for her to stay in their home, an old Victorian house, formerly that of the chancellor. They installed her in a large bedroom upstairs.

Sarah Hamilton arrived at Vanderbilt, having graduated from Berea College in Kentucky, and having worked three years in Birmingham. She was entering into a graduate program in biology, and she had been told that she would have a large room for herself in Dr. Mims' home. When she found Lily ensconced in the room, she was annoyed enough to go to her advising professor and tell him that she just did not wish to spend the year with that elderly lady from Arkansas (Lily was forty-six, Sarah, twenty-two), even though Lily seemed more than courteous and affable. Her advisor said he had complained already, but that Dr. Mims had adamantly responded that the room was plenty large for two ladies, both of whom were so promising that he wanted to keep his eye on them. Miss Hamilton, not wishing to antagonize either her advisor or the dean, accepted her situation. Lily did not learn of this until years later. She and Sally (as Sarah was called by her friends) often laughed about the matter.

Mildred Stoeves lived alone in the other smaller, yet large, upstairs bedroom. She had graduated from Vanderbilt in sociology and had a job doing social service work in Nashville. She was a good friend of Katherine Mims, the professor's daughter. The three "roomers" spent a good deal of time together because they took most of their meals in the cafeteria in the basement of Kissam Hall, a dormitory nearby. Mildred and Sally both went through the autumn months thinking that Lily was quite poor. She would eat a large breakfast: two bowls of oatmeal with two pitchers of cream, a glass of prune juice, a glass of orange juice, four pieces of toast and two cups of coffee. All of this could be purchased for twenty-five cents. The rest of the day she would eat soup and salad, if she took time for that. She tried to get by on a dollar a day. She saved string and paper. Mildred and Sally, both of whom also needed to watch their pennies, would pool their resources and take Lily out to dinner. Sally said she wanted to see that Lily got some meat to eat. They also observed how studious she was, that she would often work until after midnight; and thinking that Lily needed a break, they would send Puryear (Dr. Mims' son and now a recognized sculptor) after tickets for some kind of entertainment and tell Lily that they had been given to them. That was the only way they could get her to go out.

Her grief over her mother's death, her concern for her brother, Jesse, and her study of the poet, John Donne, were the main topics of her contributions to their mealtime conversations. Both of them told how surprised they were when she announced that she would be late coming back from the Christmas holiday because she would have to settle the accounts for fifty-two families of tenant farmers and wrap Christmas packages for all of them. They vowed they would not worry about her finances anymore, but they did sympathize with the great deal of stress that she was so obviously suffering.[7]

Lily thought of her year at Vanderbilt as possibly the most important year of her life. It gave her containment at a time when she felt she might well have come apart at the seams because of the heavy cloud of guilt which hung over her. She could not drive out the thought that she should not have gone to New York, that she should have perceived the condition of her mother's health, that she had let her mother down the last year of her life. She had terrible oppressive dreams at night, and they interrupted her sleep to the extent that she was fatigued most of the time. Nevertheless, her commitment to study kept her going and got her through this strenuous period. Actually it was the thesis that imposed the limitations on Lily and kept her driving ahead.

During her first week at Vanderbilt, she went to her faculty advisor, Dr. Claude Finney, and told him of her experience at Columbia and that she had no intentions of working another hour on researching Alfred Austin and would like to start all over. Dr. Finney was professor of romantic literature, and she had enrolled in one of his classes. He had just finished a work on Keats, having spent a year in England doing research for it. He offered the material he did not use in his work to Lily, saying that she could build a thesis on any part of the unused material. She promised to examine the data.

She enrolled in two more classes, one in the literature of the seventeenth century with Dr. Finney, and one in the medieval miracle plays with Dr. Walter Clyde Curry. She had been in Dr. Finney's literature class only two weeks when he brought to class a list of term paper topics and asked for volunteers for them. When he read, "The Medieval Physick in the Poetry of John Donne," she raised her hand for the topic.

She later apologized to Dr. Finney for not accepting his offer of the Keats material, but he was not at all offended. In fact, he was delighted that she chose the topic on Donne because no one had ever attempted it, and he had had it on the list for some time. She immediately added Dr. Curry's course in Anglo-Saxon. It met every Wednesday afternoon from four to six. Every Wednesday for the entire nine months at Vanderbilt was devoted to Anglo-Saxon. She would go to her room after breakfast and study until class time without stopping for lunch. The course helped her research tremendously. For her term paper in that class, she traced the background for the measurement of an acre and found that it was based on the number symbolism of the Druid priests.[8]

Lily entered into her research on medieval medicine with the enthusiasm of a love affair and spent hours in the library. She went to the medical school and studied many of its historical works. On her first reading of Donne's lyric poetry, she found seventeen or eighteen references to medicine and began to search them out. By the time she had done this and re-read the poetry, she found she recognized about fifty more references. This took her deeper into her research. She was the first student to avail herself of the microfilm service which had just come into use. The librarians procured the equipment for her; in fact, all of them, as well as Dr. Curry and Dr. Finney, were involved in helping Lily in every way they could. Toward the end of the semester, she realized that there was so much more to be done that she asked that this topic become her thesis, rather than a term paper. This met the approval of both professors.

She extended her readings of Donne's works to the prose meditations. Upon her fourth reading, she found more than two hundred references to medicine which she verified. It took her until the deadline, two weeks before graduation, to polish and finish her thesis manuscript, *Mediaeval Physick in the Poetry of John Donne*. Dr. Curry declared it to be the finest ever produced by a student at Vanderbilt or anywhere else he knew of and the only one that he ever received that he would recommend for publication without altering a letter. It contains one hundred seventy-five pages of manuscript, nine pages of bibliography, six pages listing primary sources, and three pages of secondary sources. It includes three basic divisions: the conditions of disease prevalent, the conditions of the medical practice prevalent, and the orthodox treatments prevalent. Lily came away from the study in a state of wonder that the human species survived the era.

Lily left Vanderbilt in the spring of 1938 thinking that she would return. Dr. Curry assured her that an addition of two chapters to her thesis would make it an acceptable dissertation. She agreed, thinking it needed one chapter on astrological medicine, in high favor during the Elizabethan period in England, and another on chemical medicine, just in its beginnings under Paracelsus (sixteenth-century alchemist and physician). But she chose not to return to Vanderbilt, and that choice would always make her wonder what her life might have been like had she made a different decision.[9]

Why did Lily not return and finish her doctor's degree? Her summer at home in 1938 convinced her that her loyalty lay with helping Jesse farm. The government's efforts to subsidize farmers were helpful, but they also complicated the process considerably. Any time a piece of good land had come up for sale, Jesse had bought it. Even Lily had bought some. Both of them were struggling to pay for land. Lily thought that Jesse was a genius at farming: always buying the best of seed and stock and feed, always experimenting with the best methods of utilizing the soil or capitalizing on phenomenal weather; however, he had two traits which made her feel obligated to say close by and help him. One was that he refused to keep accurate records, considering it a waste of time, literally farming out of his hip pocket or the glove compartment of his truck. Had he not achieved superior production and been relatively frugal in his personal expenses, he probably would have failed. The other trait was his generosity, which caused him to help anyone who came along who was in need or had a hard luck story, regardless of how lazy or inefficient the person was. Further, he had an unreasonable trust in his peers and business associates, many of whom did not hesitate to take advantage of his trust and good nature.[10]

Lily accepted again the position of teaching school at Connell's Point, and this time she was made principal. She, Elizabeth Kinkle, and Daisey Richardson handled all the teaching. She lived at home with Jesse, relieving him of a number of duties and enabling him to have more social life. Lily would not admit it, but she delicately assumed a supervisory as well as a nurturing role. Further, Lily knew and appreciated the potential for their making money in a farming partnership. Lily respected money. Although frugal in many areas, Lily was lavish in support of the things she valued and would grow more so in years to come. Jesse was a congenial companion who loved history and literature and music and never tired of listening to her poetry or violin playing. He encouraged her at all times. Their relationship survived their occasional heated spats.

She taught at Connell's Point four years, engaging in various projects as in the past. The children brought plants and seed, and flowers again bloomed around the school yard and down the road. Daisy Richardson (now Middleton) pointed out that Lily, too, was generous and trusting of her students and that they often took advantage of her in harmless fun. One time the boys asked permission to play baseball in the adjoining pasture, which belonged to Jesse. She obtained Jesse's permission, and the playing proved to be good recreation until one day the boys accidentally caught the pasture on fire. Lily "had a fit" with much hurrying, scurrying, and excitement until the blaze was extinguished. The boys so loved that uproar that it wasn't long until they repeated the "accident." Their third production got out of hand, and Lily was so distraught that the students were thoroughly frightened, and a couple of them ran for Jesse as fast as they could, telling, "Miss Lily's gone plumb mad. She's out in the pasture in the midst of the fire, holding up the limbs of a big tree, praying aloud to God to save the wonderful tree and others nearby." Jesse and a number of hands came and put out the fire and told the boys they could not play ball in the pasture anymore until enough time elapsed to prove that they could play ball without starting a fire. Such a time did come.

Lily had little spare time during those years, but she took time for music practice and performance, and she took time for her personal correspondence which had grown considerably because of the friends she had made at Columbia and Vanderbilt. One of her most satisfying collections of letters is from Donald H. Brooks, a fellow student at Juilliard. During the summer of

1942, Ethel was working on her master's degree at Peabody College in Nashville. More to give herself a bit of a holiday than anything else, Lily joined Ethel and enrolled in a summer term. She took general biology and advanced swimming. She spent much time with her friends at Vanderbilt, and through them she met O. B. Emerson, a doctoral student doing his dissertation on William Faulkner. They dated often, and Lily helped him with his research for a term paper on another topic in order to give him time to work with his Faulkner research. Emerson finished his doctorate and joined the staff of the University of Alabama. He and Lily corresponded until their late years.[12]

By this time Lily was teaching again at Marvell. She seriously considered an offer made to her by William and Mary College at Williamsburg to teach at its Richmond Professional Institute. The administration paid her expenses to come for a personal interview. They received her cordially and explained her duties: she would have a freshman and two sophomore sections of English and an advanced course of journalism; she would have to handle the press relations of the school; she would supervise the print shop and sponsor the school paper. She said to herself, "That would kill anybody, and I'm not prepared to die." The final straw was that the salary would be less than she was making at Marvell High School. So she declined the position.

Lily accepted the position at Marvell because consolidation was taking place, a gravel road had been built, and she could stay at home and commute, either by driving herself or going on the school bus. Besides teaching Spanish, she was to fill in any vacancy that occurred on the teaching staff. By the time she resigned from the Marvell school in 1948, she had taught English, Spanish, Latin, world history, and American history, general science, biology, and algebra. And often geometry. The principal taught geometry at the same time Lily kept study hall and would often send her a note, telling her to take over the class because he had to leave the school, an interruption which annoyed her considerably because she had to improvise as best she could.[13]

Still, these were not easy years for Lily. She was in her fifties, a transitional time for several reasons. Could she continue to give as much time and energy as she had been giving to teaching? She always did more then was required. One of her projects was the starting of a high school newspaper. It included the news of the community to the extent that when she gave up teaching, the town started its own newspaper with the same name, *The Marvell Messenger*. She was also active in community organizations.

Lily and Jesse had a faithful cook who took care of this aspect of homemaking for more than twenty years. But Lily was responsible for the management of the household. Gracie Wilson, one of the maids, said that she could tell that "Miss Lily" was often upset. She would say nothing for hours and would often go walking in the rain without an umbrella. Gracie figured it was "because then folks couldn't tell the tears from the rain." Lily prided herself in keeping herself composed in the presence of others.

Gracie told the story about the time she went to the chicken coop to catch a fryer and dress it for Mr. Jesse's dinner. He loved fried chicken, and they always kept a few in a coop to "weaken them down and fatten them up." She discovered a large chicken snake in the coop and ran back for Miss Lily. Lily told her not to be afraid, that the old snake was too full to hurt anybody. It had crawled into the coop, eaten a fryer, and was so enlarged that it couldn't get out. Lily opened the little door, reached right in and grasped "Mr. Chicken Snake" back of the head and carried it over to the store to show "the boys" and weigh it. It weighed sixteen pounds. Lily wanted it taken down to the back lot and turned loose, but the "killers" prevailed.[14]

Lily continued to teach at Marvell High School until 1948. She took more responsibility with the farming, the store keeping and bookkeeping. During the war years labor for farming was difficult to come by. For a brief period Jesse used prisoners of war. The family letters contain one to Jesse from Stafan Taremczak, written on June 10, 1948, from P.O.W. Camp 30, Carpenters Road, Stratford, London. He told of the several camps in the United States he had been in and of having been in England thirteen months. He said:

> ... I would prefer to live 2 years in America to be only one year here. We have been divided into groups according to the length of our P.O.W. time. I belong to group 25 and my turn will be August 1948, I suppose. I often think of this day we were talking that if we were repatriated you would take some prisoners as your labourers. If you still have the same plan I am willing to work with you if I am able to reach America. ...

Taremczak's penmanship exhibited the discipline and precision of a well-educated person.

Of course, the financial advantages for farming during the war accrued to both Lily and Jesse; however, the time of Lily's big decision came in 1948. Jordan "Jurdy" Lambert, a Helena real estate man, had approached Jesse about buying Ratio Plantation. This four-thousand-acre tract of land lay some five miles southwest of Elaine. It was bordered on the east by the Mississippi River. It was approximately twenty miles as the crow flies from the Peter home, but via the roads, which then were few, the land was forty-five miles from the Peters.

In the first decade of this century, a German family named Fathauer, who operated a furniture manufacturing company in Illinois, heard of the huge tracts of virgin hardwood timber that grew in the bottom land between the White River in Arkansas and the Mississippi River. They sent a timber cruiser down to inspect the forests, and his report was so favorable that they bought fourteen thousand acres of it. This inspector was a Spaniard who generated many adventure stories, some of which are no doubt apocryphal, but he was certainly capable. It was he who named the area *Ratio*, the Spanish word for reason, a misnomer if there ever was one, in that after the timber was gone, development of it as a farm land was so extremely difficult that the attempt could have been regarded as irrational. Yellow Bank Bayou, a stream which cut through the land, ran in two different directions because of its relationship to a ridge of land heaved up by the New Madrid earthquakes; its soil types included a kind of mud called gumbo that required years to be rendered productive; the whole place grew the finest Johnson grass in Arkansas, which took years to control.

But Señor Pedro effectively handled the timber cutting, thousands of feet of virgin cypress, oak, hickory, ash — the finest of hardwoods. The Fathauers engaged hordes of cutters, mule drivers, mules, sleds, wagons, and even some oxen for working in spots where the mud was too deep for mules. Oxen can bog down to their fetlocks and still extricate their feet because of their cloven hooves. The Fathauers managed to have a spur railroad track built down to Ratio, and a post office was designated.

After they cleared about six thousand acres, they decided to farm it and hired a local man, Harlan Rawlings, to manage the operation. He was a tall, powerful man who always carried a gun and managed to put some order into a lawless area, supervising the building of at least one hundred tenant houses; however, he never achieved a profit for the landowners. The Fathauers decided to sell, and a prominent Helena businessman bought it for a million dollars. He retained Rawlings and proceeded to farm "from Cherry Street" (Cherry Street is the name of Helena's main street, and the expression is locally common to indicate absentee management). After a few years, the place bankrupted the owner, so that he had to let it revert to the Fathauers.

This time they sold it to a rich Illinois family named Swift.

They sent one of their young heirs down to run the plantation. He had an expensive roadster which he drove at such speeds on the existing dirt roads that he soon became known as "Speedy" Swift. This was during the early thirties when Lily was teaching in Helena, and she remembers that he "cut an impressive swath" in Elaine and Helena society. He had wealthy kinfolk up north, and he lived high in the Arkansas lowlands. He was kin to one or more of the executives of International Harvester Company. When the company sought to develop a cotton-picking machine, it sent one to be tested at Ratio. It was a crude affair with vacuum suction devices affixed to cotton sacks draped around and attached to a small tractor. It is unbelievable that the huge mechanism of today which sells for nearly one hundred thousand dollars could have evolved from the contraption, but it was a start, and a picture of it hung in the office of the Elaine Implement Company, a dealer for International Harvester. Lily was a director, stockholder, and vice-president of the board of the implement company until it was sold.

The Swifts did not make any money either. "Speedy" lacked the skills to deal with the many problems of the place, including his relationship with many sharecroppers. The land, again, reverted to the Fathauers, heirs who wished nothing this time but to dispose of it. They first tried to sell it to J. P. Countiss, the largest land holder around Elaine; he rejected, but pointed to a brother in Texas. This Countiss said he would buy only four thousand of the best acres. This was surveyed out, but during the negotiations of the deal, he had a severe heart attack. After a long delay, he finally gave up his earnest money because his doctor advised against such a project.

By this time the Fathauer heirs were desperate enough to allow Lambert (a real estate man) to offer the four thousand acres to Jesse for $348,000, about one-third their previous price. They had, after all, collected many a mortgage payment.

Lily and Jesse discussed this purchase often and at length.

Jesse said that, if he bought it, he would have to be down there most of the time and suggested that they sell the land around home and move to Ratio. Lily responded, "Jesse, let's not do that. All this land we have here is paid for. We don't owe a dime on it. And we don't know how Ratio is going to turn out. I think you are getting a great bargain in the land at that price. But on the other hand, we don't know what kind of conditions we may have to face down there. There may be more floods and no telling what. So let's do it this way: You go down to Ratio and do what has to be done down there, and I will stay up here and look after this the best I can."

"Well," he said, "You will have to stop teaching, because you can't look after this and teach too."

Lily said, "Well, I know that, but I won't mind stopping teaching. I would rather do it that way than for us to sell this land."

They proceeded with that plan. Jesse bought the land. Using caution, Lily asked the Marvell School District for a semester's leave. Obviously angry with her for resigning, the superintendant granted the semester's leave provided she paid for a substitute. She agreed, but shortly afterward he changed his mind and said she must take a year's leave or no time at all. She agreed to all his stipulations, but never returned to the Marvell school as a teacher. With no fanfare, farewell dinners, or such, Lily closed out a long career of forty years of teaching.[15]

[1]Lily's poem, "New York Skyline," unpublished:

> Here on the blackstone tableland
> Cast up by Chaos in the beginning,
> Hemmed in by sullen waters,
> Stand the great towers,
> But no wild swans rise,
> Wheeling from these moted waters,
> And there are no doves circling about their windows.

[2]Thompson was curator of rare books at Princeton University from 1937 to 1942. He completed his Ph.D. at Columbia in 1939. (*Directory of American Scholars*, Vol. II, 4th Ed. [New York: R. R. Bowker, 1964])

[3]Lily's poem, "Requiem for and Age of Disillusion," from *News from Camelot*, unpublished:

> When all the brittle talk is done,
> And all the candles guttered,
> And all our ribald jibes are spun,
> And all our oaths are uttered,
> Will some brave soul in the silence then
> That comes when talking's over
> Propose a test for the bitterest jest
> The sky may be said to cover?
>
> Tongues will be loosed as tongues will be,
> When someone speaks of the matter
> That's back of all the repartee
> And all of the silly chatter.
> And if they're a set of honest men
> And made on the modern pattern,
> The things you'd hear would singe your ear
> And curl up the rings of Saturn!
>
> One will speak of Love and Faith,
> And another of Hope and Duty —

Funerals, all, to the recent death
And martyrdom of Beauty.
Someone will speak of the grave of God,
And some hard-spoken sinner
Will save his curse for the universe
That disagrees with his dinner.

[4]Letter to biographer, March 1981. Lee Shields Butterfield was the granddaughter of Lily's Aunt Adelaide Peter Schultze, whose daughter, Emilie, married a Shields, cousin to Thomas Edgar Shields, who was head of the music department of Lehigh University, Bethlehem, Pennsylvania, and organist for both the Bethlehem Bach Choir and the Episcopal Church of the Nativity. Lily said that her first cousin, Emilie, was more like an aunt to her (Will Peter married so much later than most of his siblings) and Lee more like a cousin. Lee had two sisters: Gertrude (Trudy) married to Colin Ward, an Englishman, a petroleum chemist with Standard Oil; and Margaret (Peggy) married to Boyd King, an executive in radio communications and later television at Prince Frederick, Maryland. Lee was married to Thomas E. Butterfield, a lawyer in Bethlehem. Lily spent her time at Bethlehem, Christmas, 1935, with the Clara Schultze Rights family, who was a sister to Emilie Schultze Shields, Lee Butterfield's mother.

[5]Another of Lily's friendships, besides that of D. H. Brooks, which developed during her association with Juilliard, was one with John Carter. They also became life-long friends, corresponding enough through the years to keep in touch. He became head of the music department at Rollins College, Winter Park, Florida, where he remained until retirement. He died a few years ago.

[6]D. H. Brooks wrote to this biographer that he and two or three others who lived at the Kings College Club accompanied Lily to Pennsylvania Station to board a train for Arkansas when she received word that her mother was dying. Although she was composed, he said it was the saddest, most poignant experience he shared with her (Letter, 9 June 1981). D. H. Brooks wrote Lily several times a year until illness prevailed. The letters may be found in her archives and make fascinating reading for anyone interested in the fine arts.

[7]Personal interviews with Dr Sarah Sell and Mildred Stoeves, 28 Aug. 1980. On September 25, 1959, Mrs. Mims wrote a letter to Lily referring to Lily's visits to them and of Dr. Mims' death.

[8]Dr. Curry, whose Ph.D. was from University of California, Berkley, was a medievalist and author of several books. He was a consultant on Anglo-Saxon words in Webster's 2nd Edition of its *International Dictionary*.

[9]Dr. Rob Roy Purdy, current Vice-Chancellor Emeritus of Vanderbilt (also Professor Emeritus of English Literature) and Lily's classmate, told this biographer of Dr. Curry's opinion of Lily's thesis (*Mediaeval Physick in the Poetry of John Donne*) which came to him first hand. He also corroborated Lily's account of her long, hard work on the thesis. He said there were only twelve or fifteen master's-degree candidates and about four doctoral candidates during the 1937-38 school year and that many of them came to know one another quite well. It was, however, the small group in Dr. Curry's medieval drama class that became Lily's life-long friends, among whom were Purdy; Frances Edwards, who eventually became Purdy's wife; Ivar Lou Myhr, who would later marry Edgar Hill Duncan, another member of the medieval drama class. Purdy said that Lily set the pace for all of them, that she was nearly through with her thesis before he had even started his (Personal interview with Rob Roy Purdy, 27 Aug. 1980).

Dr. Edgar Hill Duncan, former Head of the Department of English and Professor Emeritus of English Literature, Vanderbilt, Nashville, Tennessee, told this writer that one day after he had given a paper in class, all the students went into the lounge. Lily greeted him with the exclamation, "Oh, Mr. Duncan, you give the very best papers," continuing with varied effusions. He responded by mimicking her exact words, "Oh, Miss Peter, you give the very best papers, etc." There was something about their expressions which brought the whole group to that sort of unstoppable laughter that lasted so long the evocation was forgotten. The incident became the subject of many remember-the-time-that reminiscences. Duncan was impressed with Lily's drive to achieve the highest standards in scholarship. He said that none of Lily's fellow students knew that she owned land. They just thought she was a bright school teacher who wished to advance her career by having an advanced degree (Personal interview with Edgar Hill Duncan, 27 Aug. 1980).

Lily enjoyed a number of nice social occasions at Vanderbilt. Dr. Finney and his wife had parties for the students each semester and would present their children "all decked out," an amenity Lily thought winsome. Ivar Lou Myhr entertained her fellow students on Thanksgiving in the country home of her family at Bellevue, a small town near Nashville (now included in it). Her father, Dr. A. T. Myhr, a native Norwegian, was pastor at the Christian Church at Bellevue for many years. Lily dated Dr. Bowles (on the staff of the English department) who lived next door to the Mimses. He would invite her over to play the violin to his accompaniments, but it was not long until she became too involved in her thesis to accept any more invitations from Dr. Bowles.

At Vanderbilt Lily felt that she had experienced the best atmosphere for graduate work that was available anywhere. She thought Dr. Curry and Dr. Finney to be unquestionably the kindest and most helpful teachers imaginable, yet demanding in a way that brought out the best scholarship. They strove to clarify the distinction between the genuine and the spurious. Dr. Mims, though head of the graduate school, taught only undergraduate classes, but he knew every student, and all students knew he cared what they accomplished.

[10]Frank Griffin, Jr., told that he could name over a dozen young men to whom Jesse Peter had loaned money with no collateral whatsoever which enabled them to buy their first tracts of land, a number which included himself and his brother Brooks. He knew of several who never repaid Jesse. He once asked Jesse why had continued to do that and Jesse replied, "Well, they deserve a chance, and everybody knows that everybody won't make good with their chances or their promises" (Personal interview with Griffin, 23 May 1981).

Daisey Middleton told this story corroborating Jesse's carelessness with money. One afternoon when she was boarding with the Peters, she walked out to the plantation store and found Jesse stretched out on a counter asleep. (He had taken a group of students to a distant ball game the night before.) A roll of bills "large enough to choke a horse" was lying on the floor in plain sight between the counter and the wood stove. She woke him up immediately and chided him, reminded him that anyone so of mind could have walked in the store and out with that money and that he never would have known what happened (Personal interview with Middleton, cited).

[11]Lily never kept copies of the letters she wrote, which occasioned much effort by this biographer to obtain copies of her correspondence. O. B. Emerson was the one person contacted who had kept a "Lily Peter" file. He graciously forwarded it for use and to be placed in her archives.

[12]Several of Lily's former students contributed to the general image of her during those last years of teaching. Louise (Totsie) Scaife Smith took ninth grade science from her and said that, although she loved "Miss

Lily," she didn't learn a thing because she was not interested. In later years she regaled Lily, saying, "Miss Lily, why didn't you just shake me and make me pay attention?" Lily answered, "Darling, that's not the way learning takes place. And besides, my dear, you have a lovely home and a fine husband, and you're undoubtedly doing just what it was intended that you do. . ." (Personal interview, 1 Aug. 1980).

Elton Batchelor, who also took science from Lily for two years, said that he learned things that weren't being taught anywhere else, that Lily could talk on any subject whatsoever. One time, one of his classmates asked her what she knew about splitting an atom, thinking it would result in one of Lily's "digressions." He was correct, because she stopped right where they were in the text and spent a week on the atom, giving them information she had gleaned from scientific journals. He said that later, when many were shocked by the development and use of the atomic bomb, he was able to say, "Miss Lily prepared her students for that several years ago." He remembers from the time he spent in her home room that she never simply chose random Bible readings, but rather chose topics lasting for days, such as the patriarchs, etc. Among other topics she presented was one on the kings of England (Personal interview with Elton Batchelor, 27 Sept. 1980).

Patsy Weeks Plumley was chosen to portray "Miss Lily" in a school entertainment. She was scared to death that she would make Lily angry or hurt her feelings, but she went ahead and mimicked her speech, tone, gestures as best she could, only to be sought out by Lily and congratulated for doing such a "splendid replica" of a personality (Personal interview with Plumley, 6 Aug. 1980).

Essie May Paschal Lumpkin wrote Lily a letter on March 25, 1980, that was so essentially student devotion to Lily that it was included in the tributes to Lily, a part of the program on Lily Peter Day, January, 1981. There are others similar in her files.

[13]Personal interviews with Grace Brown Wilson and Reuben Wilson, 16 August 1980.

[14]Personal interviews with Lily Peter, Tapes 6, 10, 16, 18, 19, 24, 30, 31, 33, 36, 41, 46, 54, 55, 60, 67, 68. Torreyson Library Archives, University of Central Arkansas.

Chapter V

WATCHING JESSE DIE AND
RUNNING A COTTON PLANTATION, 1948-1962

I went out into the wood to consult an oracle
old as the dew, old as the summer rain,
to inquire if it might be possible for a miracle
to be wrought upon a heart that was heavy with bane,
and bring it into a flowering April canticle.

The oracle I went to see was the green and intricate,
proud honeysuckle growing against a wall,
its nectar-filled corollas sculptured and delicate,
holding more honey after the dark rain fall
than ever they did when they were fresh and inviolate.

And the oracle murmured: The miracle and the canticle
are not impossible to the bane-bound spirit,
if it can bear the dark rain,
if it will yield to the spring the frozen pain,
and bring to the wood and the wall
such fragrance as it can let fall.

> Lily Peter
> "Song for a Mood"
> *Earth's Shadow*, unpublished

There is no evidence that in 1948 Lily consulted the oracle
to see what miracle could be wrought during the remaining years

of her life or that her spirit was, as she writes in the above poem, "bane-bound." Yet the mood, however fleeting, was appropriate to her realization that her child-bearing years were over and that she had no progeny. The fact was a sorrow she would always acknowledge. She believed she could only alleviate the pain caused by her childlessness through creative activity. She was extremely busy filling every moment with activity which would yield gratifying results. At age fifty-seven she did not feel old or less capable; so she looked forward to the future with excitement.

Lily plunged into helping Jesse farm the autumn of 1948. At Ratio Jesse found room and board in the plantation store manager's household, but he came home on weekends. One advantage to Lily was that James King, who had been a faithful and efficient farm employee for Jesse since 1930, remained with her and was made manager of the farming operations. Managing the gin was a new and strenuous task for Lily. She was determined to learn every phase of the operation without revealing that she knew absolutely nothing at all about it at the onset. This took years of observation and questioning. One way she accomplished this was to do the weighing that often went on until after midnight, at times all night long. Lily weighed incoming cotton during many subsequent harvest seasons. Her largest annual ginning output was 4,000 bales. Her most apprehensive experience occurred when a railway strike embargo caused two hundred bales of cotton to be tied up on the gin yard, necessitating the purchase of fire insurance at high rates. Luckily, no fire occurred.

She mastered the ginning and eventually came to know every nut, bolt, wheel, and "cyclone" essential to the operation and to know that dust and lint were enemies to be fought in the summertime. Thoroughly clean machinery was indispensable to avoidance of waste. Many times she thought that it was no job for a woman. When she took over, the head ginner was prejudiced against working for a woman. She could detect purposive, though very subtle, harassment. He would curse the men under his supervision at the least provocation, never in her presence, but in her hearing. One time he put in a whole set of equipment backward to see if she knew the difference, nearly causing thousands of dollars worth of damage. She determined that this man was going to fire himself, for she had a deliberate, well-thought-out policy of never giving anyone a "dressing down." It took several years. He had a way of beginning each season by asking for a raise, claiming that he had been offered a good job somewhere else. Lily chose for his replacement two young, reliable men, a white, J. R. Smith, and a Negro, Loydell Wilson, and posted them where they could watch the man and learn all about his job. She endured him the rest of the season, gave the observers more training in the summer, and when the ginner came with his tale of a good offer, she congratulated him, telling him that she didn't feel right about keeping him away from a better job any longer and that she had arranged for other labor. It was too late for him to retract his statement, so he departed and the young men took over his job.

Lily's full-time farm supervision came during the last years of hand picking cotton. Getting the cotton out in marketable condition was a difficult aspect of raising it. The picking usually began in August and often lasted until February, even March. Lily saw on April 13, 1946, both picking and planting occur at the same time in the same field. The cotton could not be picked wet or it would rot. She saw one season when twenty-three days of rain in September caused the cotton seeds to sprout in the bolls. So she learned to expect the many interruptions that the weather would impose every season.

Another problem for Lily was the scarcity of labor in those post-war years. The cotton crop of 1948 was the largest ever grown in Phillips County. The farmers formed an association to provide additional labor for harvesting, even engaging the help of Washington. Observing the legalities, which involved all sorts of commitments for the care and treatment of the hands, they managed to import labor from Mexico. In the following excerpts from a letter Lily wrote to O. B. Emerson on November 11, 1948, we see her description of her farm work, as well as the pleasure she took in discussing literature with him:

Dear Mr. Emerson, . . . [She thanks him for a book he has sent] I must be telling you two thank yous in one, for I enjoyed very much your letter giving the outcome of the term paper, with Dr. Purdy's gracious comment. My good friend and classmate Bob Purdy will never know the good trick we played on him! . . .

For years I had been helping Jesse some with the plantation business, but never until this fall have I had practically the full responsibility of taking charge of it during the rush season, and it is the most exciting adventure I have ever had. . . . I am here by myself most of the time, and there is so much to do I never stop working from early till late. We have in Phillips and Monroe Counties the finest crop ever made in this part of the country, which is very wonderful and a great blessing, but to tell the truth, there is so much cotton this fall it is about to kill us all off trying to handle it. We have about seventy-odd families on our plantation here, and there are more than that number down at Ratio. We have a hundred Mexicans picking cotton, in addition to all these families. We have 25 Mexicans and an interpreter here — I look after these — and 75 at Ratio. . . . I keep up with all the cotton picking here, and the Mexicans, and do the pay roll, and look after the store business here, and help some in looking after the gin, and sell cotton, and settle the accounts at the store with the tenants on our place, and do just anything and everything that comes up to be done when there is no one else to do it, even to driving one of the plantation trucks. . . .

The way Faulkner handles the stream-of-consciousness technique is amazing. But you have to go quite a piece with

141

him before you can give all the willing suspension of disbelief that he demands. Poor Benjy is supposed to be an idiot, but for a five-year-old child the perceptiveness recorded in the chapter, "April 7, 1928," and mirrored in the twenty-eight-year-old consciousness, is astonishing to say the least. The children's talk is so real you can hear it, and the plantation negroes are so real they are there before you to see and to hear — Dilsey, Roskus, Luster (We have a colored boy on our place named Luster.), T. P., Versh. Faulkner dips his pen mostly in brimstone and wormwood, but when he writes of these it is wild honey he uses, for their gentleness and the ancient wisdom and patience that are theirs. It is interesting to compare Faulkner's treatment of the stream-of-consciousness with that of Virginia Woolf. But, after all, there can be no comparison, for Faulkner is dredging in far different waters, in waters more turbid, in minds more inchoate.

Another letter to O. B. written January 29, 1949, was four-page, single-spaced. She told him more details of her farm operation, including the item of news that she nearly had an axe murder among the Mexicans and that she was regent of the James Bate Chapter of the Daughters of the American Revolution at Helena, but most of the letter was devoted to the discussion of poetry and her response to his criticism of one of her poems. She said:

> You don't realize, I'm sure, that you are doing the nicest thing in the world for me in giving me the most penetrating criticism you can think of. I hope you will let me send you a few more poems some time for your reaction to them — will you let me do this?
>
> . . . If ever I can write better poetry, and this I desire most deeply, it will be the result of this inspiration you have given me and your guidance in showing me how to avoid certain pitfalls. And do write to me again soon!

Literary subjects would continue to be the main topic of their correspondence, and Lily relied on O. B. Emerson throughout her life as a peer she could depend upon for honest, caring criticism of her writing.

During the four years Lily had the Mexican laborers on her place, she found all but a few of them energetic, law-abiding, agreeable people who did good work. She was required to provide minimal, but adequate, housing for them rent free. One tool essential to their "furnish" was an axe for chopping their stove wood, and it was this article which caused Lily considerable anxiety on one occasion. One middle-aged man was a natural trouble maker, indulging in rough, menacing horse play. On one cold October morning, he went over to the bunk of a young man and jerked all the covers off his bed and threw a bucket of cold water on him to make him get up. This resulted in a row with axes in the hands of each of them. Observers ran for her and James King, and they, with the help of the other frightened Mexicans, managed to quell the riot and extricate the weapons. She told the offender that, since this wasn't the first instance of incensing other workers, he could just prepare his belongings for deportation. Lily called the appropriate officers and they sent for him. There are many versions of Lily's dealing with fractious Mexicans, some even going so far as to say that Lily drove one to Forrest City holding a gun on another one of them in the middle of the night, but she said such tales were highly exaggerated.

Her dealing with them was considered the most successful in the county. She could converse with them fluently in their native tongue. After their first year working for Lily and Jesse, many begged to be assigned each year to "la Senorita Lili." And each year, many of the crew would beg her to figure out a way for them to stay with her permanently. She enjoyed them — their good manners, their singing, their general bent toward making hard work as pleasant as possible.

Even while the Mexicans were imported, some attention was given to machine picking. In 1949 Jesse hired such a machine. In 1952 they bought a cotton picker, but that model was not perfected, so they sold it. In 1954 they bought a large, two-row John Deere machine, and that was the last of depending on hand picking. But it never ceased to bother Lily to leave those little spots of cotton that were inaccessible to the picking machine. If she could, she would hire someone to pick it, but many times she would do it herself. She sometimes got as much as five hundred pounds that way. She despised even minute waste. Partly for that reason, partly for exercise, and partly because she liked to be outdoors, she picked cotton for six days in October, 1980, not giving in to her age (eighty-nine years), nor forgetting the dramatic effect.

In 1950 Lily responded to the summons to all interested in performing Moravian music to come to a festival in Bethlehem, Pennsylvania, led by Thor Johnson, the son of a Moravian minister from Winston-Salem, North Carolina, at that time director of the Cincinnati Symphony. Lily enjoyed her identity in Bethlehem as a collateral descendant of her great uncle, John Frederick Peter. Everyone there knew of his ability and accomplishments. Lily suggested to Thor that a recording of the Peter Quintets be made, that she would gladly commit her support of the project if he would help. He agreed, and for a minimal fee of $3,000 arranged for the musicians, two violins, two violas, and a cello. The recording was made in May of 1951. Lily went up to New York City for the event. The first violinist, Isador Cohen, who was later the leading violinist for the Juilliard Quartet and the Beaux Arts Trio, talked with Lily about her uncle's quintets. He told her that they had "sweated blood" during the rehearsals because the quintets were so subtly complex, full of Baroque trills and embellishments. They laughed over the inconsistency that the second part for viola was simple enough for a beginner; J. F. Peter mostly had good musicians, but had only one advanced viola player. The other viola player could barely play, so Peter wrote that part so that it was easy for him. Lily engaged the New York Public Library to publish the score of the quintet for a fee of $2,250. She also spent some time in New York with her friend, Don Brooks.[1]

Lily accepted more and more speaking engagements as she gained a reputation for being a good entertainer. She became famous for her many stories about black people, although none were ever risque or intentionally derogatory. She shared the same attitude as that of William Alexander Percy, expressed in his book, *Lanterns on the Levee*; he said that most Negroes were graced with wit, charm, and good manners, their natural means of coping in a land where they were stripped of their history and had little hope of a future.[2] Lily's mother knew Percy's father, Leroy, and remembered W. A. as a lad in school in Greenville, Mississippi. He was eight years younger than she. Lily was familiar with his poetry and prose works.

A typical day for Lily in the early fifties was recorded in her letter to Mrs. Mills, a writer for the *Progressive Farmer*:

> You ask what my day on the plantation is like? It varies, of course, with the seasons, the periods of most complicated activity being the spring planting, the cotton chopping in early summer, and cotton picking through the fall.
>
> On our plantation are about eighty families, most of whom have been with us for many years. Among these families, a number of the third generation are now farming upon our farms, and in one family the fourth generation is still with us. This stability makes for pleasant and understanding relationships and a general good neighborliness.
>
> In operating the plantation, I keep the books, look after the payroll, pay all bills for the plantation and plantation store, including doctor bills, hospital bills, drugstore bills, supply and

145

repair bills of every kind. I look after the gin, seeing that the cotton goes to the compress, the seed to the oil mills, with a day crew and a night crew during the busy season in the fall, and I have to take care of the gin pay roll and the gin bills and repairs. I have to see that the plantation houses and other buildings are repaired and the new ones built when necessary. Fences must be fixed, ditching done, commercial fertilizer hauled in by car load, and tractors and other heavy equipment, from combines to cotton pickers, must be kept in repair.

But all of this sounds very general, and you don't get from it a picture of what each day is like. This is difficult to convey, for one of the joys of farming is that no two days are alike. There are a few fixed points, like the payroll on Saturday, and Sunday morning, when I gather up the neighborhood children in a pick-up truck from three or four to a dozen or more, and take them to Sunday School; but for the most part my day is made up of an endless succession of small and constantly varying duties. Here are some of the items that have come before me today, which might be considered a typical day in late winter or early spring.

I am up early and at the plantation store to see that everyone has what is needed to begin the day's work and to talk over with our farm manager, James King, whatever plans may be necessary. The trucks go to haul fertilizer or freight or lumber and other building supplies for some houses that are being repaired. The carpenters are off to the houses. Mr. Brown, who has charge of the commissary, comes in time to help with the morning rush, and when this is over I go to eat breakfast which Carrie, the cook, has ready.

Most of our tenants are colored. They are willing, kindly, and industrious, but all of their problems come to me. By the time breakfast is over, someone will be waiting to see me. This time it is Isaac, who wants to borrow $10.35 to get a C.O.D. package of shoes from the post office. Plato came to tell me that he has a sick mule and needs an order to the veterinary in Marvell.

Ernest has come to do some yard work for me, and I set him

146

to work, keeping a vigilant eye on him no matter what else I may be doing, for although Ernest's intentions are of the best, he does not know a flower from a weed, and his ministrations at any moment may turn out to be disastrous.

William comes with a long face. One of his tractor tires has gone to pieces and another is about to follow suit. Tractor tires put a crimp in anyone's budget, but one can't do tractor farming without them. So I write an order for William to take to the dealer in Helena for the two tires.

In comes one of the hands from the field with the melancholy news that the pump on the liquid fertilizer distributor is not working, in spite of the combined efforts of the farm crew to persuade it to do its duty. A liquid fertilizer pump is a remarkable invention, only slightly sub-human. It is set by means of algebraic equations, and is as temperamental as a prima donna, the slightest deviation in the arrangement of its complexes being sufficient to induce a moody perverseness that only a psychiatrist can fathom. The neurosis of the liquid fertilizer pump now holding all the local psychiatrists at bay, it is necessary to call a specialist from Helena, who sells these machines. The girl in the office tells me that he is out in the country and will be home in a little while. I leave word for him to call me collect, but nothing happens. I call again, and still the pump expert is not in. The girl in the office tells me that they have a boy working for them who knows all about liquid fertilizer pumps and can doubtless fix it, but he is out in the country, too, and as soon as she can find him, she will send him out here.

Since we are three weeks behind schedule in putting out liquid fertilizer, on account of the torrential rains, and the fertilizer pump drearily refuses to cooperate, the situation has a frantic look. I go to and fro on other errands, turning to the telephone every half hour or so, but the pump expert is still in the country and the boy with the headfull of knowledge never materializes. However, after several hours of psychoanalysis by our farm mechanics, someone finally gets the right spring in the right place, and the liquid fertilizer pump forgets its secret sorrow and goes merrily to work, to the relief of everyone concerned.

One of our gin customers comes to tell me he has some cotton he has not sold and he has lost his class cards—would I please get some duplicate class cards for him? I take down the gin numbers and write the Production and Marketing Administration in Little Rock for the duplicate cards.

A telephone call from our plantation at Ratio, and I am told that a colored boy down there has gone crazy and what do they do with him? His name is Willie B., and he is subject to these spells of moon madness. They tell me all he wants to do is to plow around and around in a circle in the same part of the field, under the hallucination that he is making a garden. He has been doing this all morning and all of yesterday, which was Sunday. My brother, who looks after Ratio plantation, is in Helena on business, and they can't locate him, so what do they do with Willie B. I tell them that as long as Willie is not hurting the mule or bothering anybody, just to leave him alone until my brother comes.

One of the tenants from the Pillow farm asks to have his month's account figured. He also needs some money for farm supplies and to have the account of his share-cropper figured. I go over to the store and spend about half an hour doing this. A woman on the place who has been with us for more than twenty years sends a note by her boy to ask me would I please let her have $23.85 to get her a puckered nylon dress to wear for church usher. She will pay me when cotton chopping comes or anything I have for her to do.

A request like this could be refused only by a heart of stone, so she gets the money.

The rural mail carrier arrives with 100 baby chicks C.O.D. for a family on the other side of Big Cypress Bayou. I pay for them and take the crate of baby chicks to the store and send word to the owner that they are here.

So the day goes on, with repair orders to be written for broken fan belts and gaskets and radiators and truck springs, and sick children to be sent to the doctor, and requests for hay and corn and lespedeza seed to be taken care of, bills to be checked and paid, and I am trying to get some flowers and shrubs planted.

I am fairly busy now, but if you want to know what running a cotton plantation is really like, come trail me for a day in chopping or picking time! Sincerely yours,

Mrs. Mills' article on Lily was never published; however, it came to the attention of the editor, John McKinney, and later when in Arkansas, he spent a day with Lily. He wrote her on his return and said, "All women farmers I had known in the past were 'battle-axes.' I was astonished to find you so exquisitely feminine."

By hard work and long days and frugal living, Lily and Jesse paid off the indebtedness for Ratio by 1954. Jesse's only indulgence was following the local ball teams. He loved to get up a car load of the high school students and take them to games. Often the cheerleaders depended on him before the days when schools paid for their transportation. He loved to be around them, but he never took advantage of them. Every candidate for football queen for miles around (whose victory always depended on fund raising at so much per vote) sought his support. It was generally conceded that if Jesse Peter backed a candidate, that one would win. He was exceedingly generous to such projects.

He was instrumental in organizing a tri-county baseball league, and he bore all of the expense of uniforms, equipment, and transportation for the local team. He even built a two-hundred-seat stadium on his land. John Kirkley, who worked for the Peters from 1948 to 1982, played on that team and said that there had not been a community activity that everyone enjoyed so much since Jesse died. Kirkley's wife, Alvern, kept the Creigh store open a half-day for Lily until the eighties.[3]

Lily did not consider herself a partner to Jesse. She deliberately kept him in the foreground of all their dealings with others. She gave credit to him for all she knew about farming, having been involved with him ever since she loaned him money for seed corn when he was nine years old. But he always listened to every idea she had with patience and kindness. She loved and admired his creative way of farming which was highly productive, just as she had admired her father's efforts. She was never able to alter his record-keeping methods; she thinks she eventually would have, had she not perceived the symptoms of his fatal illness and hated to worry him. Although he never complained, he tired easily. Earlier in the forties, he felt so bad that Lily persuaded him to go to a specialist in Memphis whose thyroid treatment improved his health for a while. The local doctor had treated him for malaria.

It was not known that his illness was leukemia until the last two months of his life, but by 1954, Lily knew that something was dreadfully wrong and begged him endlessly to seek medical care. She enlisted the aid of Dr. Patrick McCarty in Helena, who was Lily's former student; and because he was fond of Jesse, he deviated from the usual ethics and begged Jesse to come in for examination. Jesse consistently refused, and all Lily could do was re-double her efforts to help him all she could.

Because of his health, she did not wish to pressure him for figures. She submitted their income tax returns, knowing they were inadequate, deciding that she would take the consequences of paying interest on back taxes rather than bother him when he was obviously ill and exhausted.

Aware as she was of Jesse's condition, Lily, at his insistence, attended the Moravian Music Festival at Winston-Salem, North Carolina, in the summer of 1955. Thor Johnson and other church leaders had pushed for a foundation for Moravian music, arranging for the appointment of Dr. Donald McCorkle as the first director of the foundation in Winston-Salem — a most appropriate appointment considering that the subject of his doctoral dissertation was *Moravian Music in Salem: a German-American Heritage.* Lily met him that summer and renewed her acquaintance with friends and cousins who sang in the festival.

One evening several of them were being entertained at the estate of a cattle man and his wife. He loved wildlife and kept a spacious game preserve around his home; she loved music. After dinner, they were all sitting on the long porch with its Greek pillars and were looking out over the valley. McCorkle proposed to Lily that she found a library in connection with the foundation. They discussed the prestige, stability, and caliber of attention it would bring to the foundation. Lily said, "I am just not in the financial position to build a structure for housing it. The best I could do to give it a little beginning is donate $2,000 now and commit myself to giving $2,000 annually until I see I can do more." McCorkle was pleased to have that start and asked Salem College for space on its library shelves. This was a mutually beneficial arrangement — and the Peter Library was begun. Lily thought this most appropriate, since several of her forebears were instrumental in founding Salem College back in the eighteenth century.

When she came home and told Jesse about this promise, he was pleased and completely approved. Their work through the fall went well, and for the Christmas holidays, he went to Vicksburg to spend some time with his brother, Ted, his wife, Mary Lu, their son, Ted, born in 1939, Uncle Brutus, and Aunt Ada. Jesse was taken so ill while there that he had to be hospitalized. He could not return home on schedule; the doctors were making extensive tests. But he was so miserable that when one of his foremen came to see him he walked out of the hospital with him. Mary Lu, who was out on an errand, saw them driving down the street toward the Mississippi River bridge. She was appalled and waved frantically to no avail. Ted conferred with the doctors who told him that, although they had not completed their tests, Jesse was seriously ill.[5] Ted and Lily begged Jesse to return and he did so. By the first of February, he was so much worse that he was transferred to the Baptist Hospital in Memphis. Except for one weekend, Lily remained there with him at his bedside until his death on March 31, 1956. Jesse weighed only seventy-two pounds when he died, but he was courageous, always courteous, and alert to the last. The event was heart-breaking for Lily.[5]

Lily could say at this point that she was glad that she had quit teaching and devoted her full time to working with Jesse those last years.

James King, the farm manager, stood at Jesse's funeral in a state of grief. He had worked for Jesse for twenty-six years and had much affection for him. But he had the additional grief of thinking that he would have to look for another job. He could not imagine that he could work for a woman who had the last word in all matters. However, Ted, Lily's brother, walked over to him and said, "James, you know it's the middle of the planting season. Will you please stay on at least until it is over?" He readily agreed, and by the time planting was over, he was convinced that he did not wish to make a move. Lily never once reproved him publicly or privately, even in cases when she had found he had used bad judgment. She would say, "James, I know you did the best you could and will not make that mistake again." In later years, he told many of his fellow farm managers who liked to question him about working for Lily that "he had it better" than any he knew of in the country.

James King stayed with Lily as farm manager for twenty-two years until 1978, when he had to retire for reasons of health. He was a part of all of her experiments in farming. He takes pride in the fact that he learned to tell when "Miss Lily was tore up," although it was difficult. The deaths of her two brothers and the possibility of the channelization of Big Creek were the times she was in the worst state of anxiety, but she never allowed her anxiety to affect her demeanor with the people around her.

James and his wife, Ellen, tell of many good times they had with Lily. Once Lily determined that she would learn to drive the riding lawn mower and insisted that James teach her. Reluctantly, he showed her the sequence of starter, gears, and fuel feeding. Right away it achieved a high speed. Round and round the yard she went, shouting half from glee, half from fright. All observers shouted instructions. James held his breath as she headed for the corner of the truck shed, but she missed it by inches and finally aimed toward a bush which she felt would stop the mower without hurting her too badly. She and everyone present often laughed recalling this episode.[6]

Another boon to Lily, and a tribute to her, was that Brooks Griffin agreed to take over the management of Ratio. He had farmed for Jesse and had already shown his ability by becoming the owner of the largest farming operation in Arkansas. He rented Ratio on a crop percentage basis which Lily considered the fairest to all concerned. But Brooks could not take over Ratio until he disposed of the huge Ben Laney plantation which he had purchased a few years previously. It was too far south of Ratio for him to move his farm equipment back and forth. Also, Brooks had almost completely changed over from tenant farming to big machinery farming, so Lily had to give those families deprived of work time to make other arrangements for income. She had the management of Ratio for another three years. The presence of farm managers never did, as far as Lily was concerned, allow her to turn her back on farming. She had her own gin. She had no use for absentee ownership and paid attention to what was taking place on every single acre. It was a credit to King and Griffin that they recognized her intelligence and were capable of adjusting to her disposition and temperament.

The first three years after Jesse's death were by far the most difficult and strenuous Lily ever experienced. They were the ones which plunged the ore of her being into the crucible for testing her mind, body, and emotions. Jesse had willed half his estate to Lily, and the other half was divided in thirds between his sisters, Oma and Ethel, and his brother, Ted. The IRS came. Lily was involved with the agent for two years, struggling to gather accurate information for him and defending accusations. She told that he was crude and ill-mannered, and constantly insinuated deliberate fraud.

The estate was finally settled in 1958, and Lily was confronted with a tax bill of one and one-half million dollars. This included estate taxes, back taxes, and interest fees. To meet this obligation took strenuous effort and management. In order to settle the estate, her siblings wanted to sell land to Lily. She arranged for money to buy out the other heirs. Her mortgage commitment was staggering. She was advised by her attorneys, accountants, and bankers not to think of attempting to take on that kind of indebtedness. Many, many "so-called friends" were on hand to "relieve her of her burdens by taking her land off her hands." The testing of her metal would not be complete for years.

Mr. J. J. White, Chairman of the Board and President of the Helena National Bank and Trust Company, said that her handling of these affairs and eventual payment of that indebtedness was nothing short of genius, that he had never seen it done nor heard of it done anywhere. He said, "Lily Peter is by far the most brilliant, far-sighted farmer I have ever dealt with in all my years of banking." He added that she was impeccably courteous and completely honest.[7]

Carrie Johnson, whose husband had farmed the Creigh place for the Peters during the thirties until his death, and who cooked for Lily and Jesse through the fifties, observed Lily's suffering. She said, "She was a very brave woman, smart, not lazy. I caught her crying lots of times, but she always kept herself straight. I could tell when she was upset. She would not eat hearty, never have much to say, go into a deep study and would not answer

Carrie Johnson in the back yard among the zinnias

when spoken to except as an after-thought. Yet, she was lots of fun to work for, a working woman who planted many flowers, vegetables, entertained company often. At those times, she would have me in to help and give me extra pay. She was always ready to help people who worked for her—would always come to the rescue. I was a widow, and she said I would never have to move. When I came to Marvell to live with my daughter, I just slipped off because I knew it would worry me and worry her to say goodbye."[8]

By 1958, Lily was listed as one of the music composers of Arkansas recommended for study by the Arkansas Federation of Music Clubs. The president of the Dardanelle Musical Coterie (this biographer) invited her to come and present a program. She and her accompanist, Margaret Van Meter (now Triplett), came. Three of her songs were performed, and she recited the entire poem, "Forty Singing Seamen," and then played a violin number she had composed in the spirit of the poem. She and Margaret stayed at the Carl Jaggers home, and she entertained Carl, a pharmacist, until 3:00 a.m., with the pharmaceutical practices of the Elizabethan era, excerpted extemporaneously from her Vanderbilt thesis.

Her compositions placed second in the state federation's composition contest in 1958 and first in 1959.[9] She continued to go to the Moravian Music Festivals held every other year and sang in the chorus. Her friendship with Thor Johnson deepened; he asked her to marry him. He arranged for the recording of one of her songs. Malcolm Johns utilized them at Wayne State University. Malcolm told her one time, when she explained her way of composing (hearing all the sounds in harmony at one time), that, if he hadn't known her so well, he would have accused her of lying because it just wasn't done that way. Getting her compositions down on staff paper was so difficult for her that, when she completed one composition, she would take it to Helena and put it in her lock box at the bank for fear something would happen to it at home.

Lily was remodeling her house in early spring of 1959. One day she was in her living room sorting and discarding papers in preparation for moving into her new rooms. She ended up with two stacks of papers, one to put away and one to take to the incinerator. A young girl was there helping her with house cleaning, and Lily told her to carry out the trash and burn it. About this time Lily was called to the store for something, and when she returned, she found to her horror that the girl had burned the wrong stack. In it were all of her original songs which she had brought home a few days in order to revise. Had Thor Johnson not encouraged her to have three of them published, they would have all been gone forever. There were some twenty of them destroyed. She could have rewritten them, but her schedule was getting to the point that she could not take the long stretches of time they required.

Now that Lily had the sole responsibility for the farming operation, she was doubly determined to discover every method that would allow the farm to achieve its maximum productivity without compromising quality. One situation which had bothered her even while Jesse was alive was that the Ratio cotton was always considered by buyers superior to cotton grown around Marvell, including her own. She knew that this was not true of all Marvell cotton, certainly not hers, because she had employed the same methods and seeding practices as Jesse and had fertilized her land equal to his at Ratio.

During the fall of 1956, when she had to sell the cotton from both places, she had a bumper crop of good cotton and made up her mind she was going for the top price, which was ranging from thirty-three cents to thirty-five cents with thirty-five and one-half for premium. She contacted friends in her area for opinions about who were the most reputable cotton buyers. Following the advice of her friend, Jim Matthews, a Holly Grove banker, she finally chose Brooks and Coffin on Front Street in Memphis. She called and told them that she had about five hundred bales and wanted the top price. They asked to see the samples, and she sent them. They liked the samples and offered thirty-five cents, but she refused to sell. She figured they would wait awhile and that she might have to accept the same offer; however, she noticed a development that would surely affect the market. A Caribbean storm, Hazel, was gathering and if it turned up the Mississippi Valley, it would drench all the cotton in its path. This encouraged Lily to hold out, but, of course, had Hazel, the storm, gone to sea, she would have had to be satisfied with the thirty-five cents. Brooks and Coffin also noticed Hazel and knew that if it came, it would mean the last of the pretty cotton; so they capitulated. Lily was pleased with this victory. The half-cent meant only two and one-half dollars a bale, but she wanted as many of those extra dollars for her tenants as she could get, and she wanted them to know that she could do good managing for them.

She knew, however, that she couldn't depend on "Hazels" to give her bargaining power, so she made arrangements the next year to attend cotton grading school in Memphis. A local friend of hers, Decatur Jackson, went too. They stayed in Memphis unless something called them home between sessions. One drive home was made because there was an anaplasmosis epidemic among their cattle. They were hurrying home. Lily was entertaining Decatur on the drive with a detailed account of the apparent death of Sir Walter Scott's mother on her wedding day, her semi-burial, and her accidental resuscitation by grave robbers. A state patrolman stopped Decatur for speeding, but Lily intervened and explained that her tale had caused him to be distracted and begged that he be excused that time and promised not to divert him again. The patrolman was so amused that he let Decatur off with a warning.

She and Decatur attended to the vaccination of their cattle, returned to the cotton school, and studied hard. It accomplished Lily's purpose. She learned the many variables involved in cotton grading, learned the way to spot that 1/32th of an inch in the length of the staple which can alter quality and price. She learned the principle and the use of a new invention, the Micronaire. Every cotton fiber, although it is finer than a human hair, is as hollow as a stovepipe. The "mike" forces a current of air into it which makes the fiber swell, and the instrument gauges the resistance of it. It is a simple instrument which looks like a thermometer. One takes a tiny pinch of cotton, places it in a slot, and an electrical impulse forces a strong blast of air through the fiber, and a needle records the reading. A low reading indicates that the fiber is too weak to spin into a strong fabric; a high reading indicates that the fiber is too coarse-walled to spin to a smooth fabric. The invention of this instrument eventually became an important innovation in cotton grading. The U. S. Department of Agriculture used it and stamped the farmers' samples with the grade, staple, and "mike" reading. This eliminated the inaccuracy (and often the skullduggery) of the small cotton buyers, who became obsolete. The cotton could be sold directly to the mills.

Lily enjoyed the advantages of her training until the direct method (selling to the mills without having to go through a middle man) became prevalent. When she still used local buyers, they hated to see her coming. They had to be polite, and they were often not polite when haggling with men farmers. Aggravating them further, she stated her offer and stayed with it, refusing to play the game of giving a little this time, getting a little the next. She wanted exactly what she had coming, no more, no less, and did her home work well enough to know.

Another factor altering cotton buying methods was that it was taking a far larger capital outlay to be a cotton buyer. Rich cotton brokers could make such investments, and many mills bought through them.

That fall (after attending cotton school), Lily had a call from a cotton buyer in Helena who was representing one of the largest cotton mills in the East. He wanted a hundred bales of her Ratio cotton; she had it for him, and shortly afterward he called for another hundred. This time she explained that she only had Marvell cotton, but that it was as good as the other. He rejected it, and she didn't press the matter. The same sort of exchange took place a couple of more times. She reasoned that she must have an advantage and that, even though she did have almost another hundred bales from Ratio by this time, she would insist on his taking the Marvell cotton. When he called again, Lily said, "I still have this cotton from Marvell, and I will let you have that at the same price." He fumed and said he would never pay the same price, that he would have to look at the samples to see what he would offer. Lily's response was that she would like him to know that her word was good when she said the Marvell cotton was as good as the Ratio cotton, that since so many times buyers "pawed into" cotton samples and made a mess of them, he would just have to take the cotton without looking at the samples if he really wanted it. He was so angry that he hung up on her.

Lily knew that she was talking high and beyond legal bounds, because buyers have a right to see samples. She concluded that she would probably have to sell it somewhere else. But about an hour or so later, the gentleman called and said, "Miss Lily, I need that cotton, so I will just have to accept it on your terms. Just tell me how to proceed." Lily's behavior had been risky; however, it did establish her reliability which, along with her quality goals for her cotton, established many a good market place for her. She learned later that the broker was representing Cannon Mills.

Lily could look back at the fifties and see that it was a crucial, strenuous decade.[10] She had gained much self-confidence. She could see potential wealth. No one was dependent on her. She could look forward and dream of future accomplishments, as she entered the sixties.[11]

During the first two years of the sixties, Lily devoted most of her time away from farming to performing her duties as Regent of the Arkansas Society of the Daughters of the American Revolution (DAR). Its membership reflects rigid principles of decorum reminiscent of Victorian social views, and the organization appealed to Lily since she loved history, social events, and the accessibility of a platform for expression. While she was state regent, she set in motion an effort to make the DAR marker of the Louisiana Purchase accessible and appreciated by the public. The marker was a large bronze plaque embedded in a monolith of marble, set in place at the point of the original survey on October 27, 1926. The marker was surrounded by swampland, and its inaccessibility was offensive to Lily. She wanted the marker to be in the center of a hundred-acre park, an arboretum, which would include at least two specimens of each tree native to Arkansas, and she wanted each tree to be clearly identified. She procured the promise of three of the four twenty-five-acre plots around the point, but the fourth owner adamantly refused to donate his land. Lily offered to buy it, but the price he asked was exorbitant and she withdrew her offer, not only because she felt the fourth owner was holding her up, but also out of fairness to the other owners. After some time, two of the three donors withdrew their offers, but Lily did not give up the project entirely. It would be years later until something was done about the marker.

Lily did give more time to her writing and attended poetry society meetings in neighboring states, often as speaker.[12] She sang at the Moravian Music Festival at Winston-Salem in June of 1961 and continued her annual grant to the Moravian Foundation. She also contributed to the Moravian Colleges in Winston-Salem and Bethlehem[13] and became more active in the Vanderbilt Alumni Association. Philanthropy became a major part of Lily's life.

During the 1960's Lily continued her rapid pace of farming which would not diminish until the late seventies when she retired from farming directly. Few around her would have dreamed that she was in her early seventies, and she told no one. One could see that she valued worthy memorials, and, just as "the word is the estate the world has left us," she wished to leave the world at least one book of poetry, binding her poems together for posterity, rather than leaving them scattered in various magazines. Her wish came true. Two volumes of her poetry would be published in the next few years.[14]

NOTES

[1]Even though Lily's time at farming had increased, the relief from teaching gave her more time for social and creative activities. In addition to the DAR chapter, she joined the Pacaha Club in Helena, a serious study group which was organized in 1888 (the oldest study club in the state). She wrote more poetry for the Arkansas Writer's Conference outlets. She increased her already lively pace of letter writing. She submitted poems for publication with some success. For example, Ferdinand Earle, Editor of a poetry magazine in Hollywood, California, wrote on March 27, 1950:

> Dear Madam: I am investing a drop of ink and one red penny [it was a postcard] to inform you — with your permission! — that we consider your sonnet (though not strictly iambic pentameter) — delightful — full of feeling and power.
> In order to get you to send another contribution, I gladly extend the date-line on deadline to April 20th for you. Thanks for the contribution. It is one of the very best in the Earlean form!

[2]William Alexander Percy. *Lanterns on the Levee.* (Baton Rouge: Louisiana Univ. Press Paperbacks, 1973) pp. 22-24.

[3]Personal interview with John and Alvern Kirkley, 24 Feb. 1981.

[4]Personal interview with Mary Lu Peter, 22 May 1981.

[5]Details of Jessie Peter's last days and death may be found in letters Lily wrote O. B. Emerson on March 22 and March 30, 1956.

[6]Personal interview with James and Ellen King, 8 Aug. 1980.

Dedy King, brother to James, who has farmed on Peter land since 1944, told the biographer about his long relationship with Lily. Dedy King was a self-taught singer and guitar player, who emulated the late Jimmie Rodgers. He also wrote songs, and one year after he had bought a cassette recorder and taped some of his songs, he took it to Lily and said, "Miss Lily, I know you do not like this kind of music, but I want you to listen a few minutes." He said Lily graciously listened, and when he had finished, she said, "Dedy, you wait here just a minute." She came back in the room right away and handed him $120 and said, "You're right, Dedy; I don't care for that kind of music, but for what it is, it is very good. Now, you take this money and go and buy yourself a good guitar." He was so pleased, he readily added another $30 and bought himself a $150 guitar (Personal interview with Dedy King, 8 Aug. 1980).

162

[7]Personal interview with J. J. White, 6 Aug. 1980.

[8]Interview, Carrie Johnson, 30 Sept. 1980.

[9]Even though Lily's work schedule was longer and more intense, she took some time, often out of the middle of the night, for her composition of songs. Passages from a letter from Don Brooks, August 23, 1958, give details on how they worked together.

[10]The last days of the 1950's were pleasant but touched with more sadness. On December 15, she played second violin in the orchestra which accompanied *The Messiah* presented at Arkansas State University at Jonesboro, commuting 250 miles round trip for each rehearsal. She chose to spend the Christmas holidays in Vicksburg with her Uncle Brutus. His wife, Aunt Ada, had died in 1959, and he was still grieving. The fact that they had no children intensified his loneliness. Of course, she got to visit the Ted Peter family.

[11]During the period of time since the death of her brother Jesse, Lily had proven to herself that she was capable of handling the large farming operation. Her records contain evidence of attention to the most minute details about expenses and yields of her various crops, e. g. the fiber tests of the cotton on every acre. She had procured the services of Hennigin, Croft & Cotham, Certified Public Accountants, Little Rock. She was confident that she was going to meet her financial obligation to the federal and state government in the matter of taxes; however, it was clear to her that she would rather give her money to causes which she valued than to pay taxes.

She did not alter her manner of living simply in the country, wanting all her relatives and neighbors to feel comfortable about dropping in to see her as they had always done. Her extravagances were confined to those occasions in which she saw herself as "representing the state of Arkansas." She wanted to do so in the most favorable light possible. Such an instance was an Arkansas luncheon which she gave at the Mayflower Hotel in Washington during the 1961 DAR Congress. She entertained the Arkansas delegation to the DAR Congress, the national officers, the regents of the states adjoining Arkansas, and the wives of the Arkansas Congressional delegation of the government. She saw that the food and decorations carried out the Arkansas motif. This cost her hundreds of dollars. She enhanced her wardrobe with an autumn haze mink stole from Macy's.

Don Brooks came down to Washington to visit her. Because of her love for good photography and desire to identify with excellence, she sat for a portrait at the famous Hessler Studio in Washington. She said of that occasion, "The studio vestibule was filled with pictures of the great and the near-great all over the world. There on the wall was a very handsome picture of Queen Elizabeth and one of Prince Philip. Mr. Hessler asked if he might use my picture in his exhibit at Palm Beach the following spring if it came out as he hoped. It did, and it was exhibited in Florida. I can say now that, although I have never been presented at court, at least, I have been a wall-flower with the Queen."

A more detailed account of Lily's work with the DAR can be seem in the organization's publications. One issue contains a full account of her Arkansas regency, 1960-62, the national magazine of the DAR, January, 1962.

[12]She attended poetry society meetings in Oklahoma and Texas and Tennessee. Letters from Martha Sherwood Johnson, Tahlequah, Oklahoma, April 30, 1961; Lucille Glasscock, Corpus Christi, Texas, June 20, 1961; and Anna Nash Yarbrough, Benton, Arkansas, March 10, 1961, all give insights to Lily's work with the Arkansas Writer's Conference.

[13]In 1961, Lily attended the Moravian Music Festival at Winston-Salem, North Carolina in June. She sang and visited, but more significantly, committed herself financially. Moramus, the foundation, issued the following news release on July 23, 1961:

> The Moravian Music Foundation has begun a long-range development program aimed at making the institution's library resources of maximum significance in American music research. The program has been initiated by a library grant of $20,000 pledged by Miss Lily Peter, of Marvell, Arkansas, an honorary Trustee of the Foundation and a prime mover in the rediscovery of American Moravian music, especially the compositions by her ancestors, John Frederik Peter and Simon Peter. . . .

[14]Personal interviews with Lily Peter, tapes 7, 16, 17, 18, 22, 28, 39, 40, 42, 50, 51, 55, 56, 60, & 61. Torreyson Library Archives, University of Central Arkansas.

Chapter VI

PAINFUL CRITICISM AND
PROUD PUBLICATION, 1962-1967

I wrap my thought in the green linen of summer
Against the terror of the dragon wind,

And pray that the linen may not too soon be threadbare,
Its texture thinned.

For by and by I know will come November
With its wintry blast;
And what is there to keep body and soul from freezing,
If the linen do not last?
                              Lily Peter
                              The Green Linen of Summer
                              Title poem

Lily devoted five years, from 1962 to 1967, in part to the preparation, publication, and responses to her first book of poetry, *The Green Linen of Summer* (1964), and her second, *The Great Riding* (1966). The green linen is Lily's metaphor for the creative impulse. Like linen, creative impulses turned into poetry are meant to last, and she feels that unless the poem ends up on the printed page, the poem has not achieved its reason for being.

Lily was approaching twenty years of work in state and regional poetry organizations. She set out to have her poems published in book form, as if she were ready to seek an image of herself beyond that of the stereotypical literary club woman. She had already established herself as atypical on a number of counts. She had become a truly independent woman, having proven her capability as a farmer, ginner, and finally business investor, as she was about to enter into a partnership with Brooks Griffin and others to form the Elaine Implement Company. But to some the most atypical feature of her life was the fact that she had, for whatever powerful reasons, eschewed a commitment to one man, yet she nurtured and treasured many diverse and satisfying Platonic friendships with men of varied ages. She had borne no children, yet she had been devoted to many as a teacher, aunt, neighbor, friend, and benefactor.

After a fairly busy spring, including going to Washington for the DAR Congress, to Fayetteville to be honored as an Arkansas composer by Sigma Alpha Iota, a music sorority, to Little Rock to speak to the Arkansas Writers' Conference on our human heritage of poetry, she submitted manuscripts of her poetry to the Vanderbilt Press. Dr. David Howell Jones was director, having come from the University of Texas Press in 1959. In a letter to Lily on August 1, 1963, Jones wrote:

> Dear Miss Peter: Thank you for your charming letter of July 18 and 24. I have found a reader for the poems whose judgment of new poetry I have hitherto respected, and I have sent all the short poems and all of "The Great Riding" to him. I didn't tell him anything about you: I simply told that this was poetry that we felt was worthy of serious consideration and would like his comments.

Jones also told Lily something of himself as a musician and gave some of his background and experiences in Texas and closed:

> This autobiographical excursion represents a sort of self-indulgence, and I really shouldn't do it, but I have been so cap-

tivated by your letters that I feel like writing more of a personal letter than a business letter anyway. I'll certainly let you know what our critics have had to say about your poems when the opinions are in.

Lily experienced the writer's usual anxious period of waiting to hear about work submitted. She worked on getting the gin cleaned and repaired for the fall season, and when it was ready, she took some time to visit her Uncle Brutus Mobrey and the Ted Peter family in Vicksburg. She always stayed in Uncle Brutus' home since his wife, her Aunt Ada died, and this was one visit she was glad she made, because he died that November, even though he was sharp and energetic until the end.[1]

Another diversion for Lily while she was waiting for a decision about her manuscript was to help the Moravian Music Foundation become permanently housed. The year before, Lily's cousin, a wealthy, generous Moravian, had bought and given to Moramus for its permanent home an old mansion in Winston-Salem.[2] The previous owners, also Moravians, had extended a reasonable offer so that the settlement was amicable. Lily contributed $5,000 of the $55,000 which was needed for the remodeling to accommodate the foundation. The second floor was given over to the Peter Memorial Library. The dedication was set for November. Lily eventually purchased two southern landscape oil paintings from DeWitt Jordan, a Helena painter, to be placed in the library. Jordan was a Negro who had studied art in Paris and whose work had received acclaim.

Finally, in early October, Lily heard from Jones at Vanderbilt Press. He wrote on the second:

> ... For about a month I have had the comments of the reader to whom we sent your poems in the summer. I have been debating whether to go ahead and get another opinion first or send them on to you, with the result that I haven't done any-

thing. I enclose herewith a Xerox copy of the reader's comments, believing that you meant it when you said you wanted complete frankness from us. The reader incorporated the comments in a letter, and I have removed those parts that would tell you who he is and where he is, because as a matter of policy, we always present readers' reports to authors anonymously. This man is widely recognized as a critic, though, and I have read reviews by him of new poetry and thought him a most perceptive critic. I tend to agree with his comments here on the whole, though I should like to do what he suggests and submit the poems to a practicing poet. I am right now casting about for a suitable poet to send them to. . . .

Jones included in this letter other paragraphs, telling her that he accepted an appointment as organist-choirmaster of a new Episcopal Church in Nashville, commenting on Lily's friendship with his friends, Worth and Virginia Conkle at UT in Austin, and apologizing for his delay in writing. Those paragraphs somewhat alleviated Lily's reluctance to turn the page and confront the critic who said:

I feel rather less than adequate to evaluate these poems, and perhaps you should have a practicing poet do it for you. My recommendation would be not to publish them. The author undoubtedly has talent, considerable of a way with words. But there is a sameness to this verse, which after a short time becomes monotonous. It's rather old-fashioned poetry, the sort of thing that was being written in the 1910s and 20s by an avant garde not taught by Eliot and the Fugitives to discipline their craft. It very much reminds me of the poetry of . . . who had a real feeling for words but who never learned to discipline her work, cut out the soft spots, eschew lush description when it did not get her anywhere. So with Miss Peter — good lines, good figures, but a general impression of vagueness, softness, lack of focus. At times it's little more than spangled prose, and seems poetry only by courtesy of being arranged so on the page. I felt this especially about the DeSoto poem, the long narrative of Spanish conquest—what's the point of telling it this way? . . .

The long nature poem at the beginning has some fetching images, some very nice evocations. But it keeps going on and on, making about the same point, and you keep waiting for something to add up, to amount to more than just some more description, and it never does. . . .

The one group of poems that I felt did come off well, and which I thought quite successful, was that entitled "Runes." Here she knew what she meant, and she didn't just describe without comment or point.

I wonder about the author. Is she young? If so she ought to be encouraged strongly, but told to go to school to modern poetry, to read the best modern poets to learn what she needs to know—what, indeed, Donne and Dickinson knew very well—which is that it isn't enough to describe, but that she must amputate all vagueness, laxness, soft material from her work, and make everything just right, tense, muscular, able to stand of itself. . . . To play the natural scene against the meaning, to make the former embody the latter, fit it exactly—that's what makes poetry exciting.

But after all, who am I to say all this? I'm no poet. What would a practicing, dedicated poet say about this? Maybe you should try these on such a person.

Lily was offended. Certainly for her poetry—the offspring of her very soul. And was she not educated? A degree in modern literature? Continuing self-education? How ludicrous to her that anyone not senile is too old to learn!

Although Lily was a voluminous letter writer, she never kept copies of them; however, if she made a typographical error beyond facile correction, she started over and retyped the letter and often left the unfinished copy with her correspondence. There remained with the Jones letters the first two pages of her reply to Jones. On October 8, she wrote:

> Dear Mr. Jones: Thank you for your very gracious letter which came last week, and thank you, too, for sending me the comments of the Critic who read my poems. He sounds Olympian enough to be deferred to, and I am writing to tell you that you may return the mss. to me, since his recommendation is not to publish them. And now let's have a little fun out of the situation, now that it's settled for good and all, by doing a small bridge post mortem on it — dealer, would be poet, vulnerable, bids one club, down four — the Critic liked just three poems only!
>
> I wish I could tell you that the comments of the Critic would be helpful to me, but unfortunately, his diagnosis is too superficial: he does not probe deeply enough to recognize my very real difficulty. For this, he would have to go to Plato, to those passages in which he is discussing the two great basic elements of becoming, the Masculine and the Feminine, the Masculine representing Form, and the Feminine, Matter. And Plato is so right! In all fields of human endeavor in which form is prerequisite, only men can excel. For this reason, no woman has ever built or designed a great bridge, composed a great symphony or has written a great narrative poem — the requirements of Form in these areas and others that might be mentioned are totally alien to the feminine make-up. To restrict this comment to literary matters, there are many fields in which women can write extraordinarily well, as well as men — the novel, for instance, which can be quite formless and yet distinguished writing.
>
> As for poetry, anybody who can put two words together — I, Why? — can write mediocre verse, which is relatively formless, but the upper ranges of really fine poetry, in which form is a *sine qua non*, are almost unattainable to a woman — consider how few great woman poets there are — you can count them on less than the fingers of one hand! — unless by some

mysterious chance of heredity she has within her enough of the masculine component to give her the intuitive sense of Form that is necessary to great poetry. And the more feminine she is, the greater the difficulty and the more baffling the barrier! So it does no good whatever for your Critic to refer me to Donne and Dickinson — Donne was a man and a very masculine one and Form was as intuitive to him as the breath he drew, and Emily Dickinson had in her a sufficient masculine component to give her a diamond-hard sense of Form.

In my own case, this intuitive sense of Form seems to be completely lacking, and I have never found the way to acquire it. Discipline, so-called, is not the answer; at least, not for a woman, though at this point I make my best curtsey, both to the well-meaning Critic and to Vanderbilt Press, for their kindliness in trying to set me on the right path, but they might just as well tell me to go out into the yard and look at the sky for three hours every day and my eyes would turn blue instead of being the color they are. Discipline is good advice for a man. If he wants to be a poet, all he has to do is to develop his sense of Form, because he was born with it, but for a woman, alack and alas! she is not born with it!

Since I was a mere child, I have loved to write verse and have written quantities of it, most of which was written for the simple pleasure of creation and then thrown into the waste basket. On reaching the age of reason, or a reasonable facsimile thereof, I realized the fatal flaw, the lack of intuitive Form, with which, being feminine, I must come to terms somehow, and I have truly tried in every way I know to compensate for it in my verse, through freshness of subject matter, originality of treatment, vividness of imagery, through morpheme and semanteme to leave my small testament of beauty of the world, moods, impressions that seemed worth recording.

But this, evidently, is not enough, and the most chilling thing about it is that the Critic was bored by my work — "sameness to this verse," "becomes monotonous," "no variety to speak of," etc., etc. All this is pretty crushing, since I would rather commit any one or all the Seven Deadly Sins than bore anyone, especially with poetry! It is plain that I must do a great deal better or else abjure poetry altogether!

But all in all, we're getting the wrong slant on this! It is your Critic who needs cheering up, and here I am mourning over what is to be will be! What a dreadful fate to be a Critic and have to read collection after collection of dismal poetry like mine — no wonder he feels weevily! After ten thousand poems they would all become monotonous, with no variety to speak of! We simply must not let our Critic suffer the sad fate of the Book Reviewer who had reviewed one too many books and finally cracked up. The psychiatrist who was called in tried to jar him into reality by putting the city telephone directory before him and asking him what he thought of it. The Book Reviewer glanced at it briefly, then rose to the occasion: "Very short on plot, but what a cast of characters!"

So let us cheer up the Critic — after all, he paid me a gorgeous compliment, and for that, he deserves some cheering, even though it must be done anonymously! Listen to this. "I wonder about the author. Is she young?" With such flattery as this bestowed upon me, I will presently be thinking I am Cleopatra — "Age cannot wither her — " you, of course, can easily place me in my niche of time, if you know my Nashville classmates in Vanderbilt, as I am sure you do. Bob Purdy and I did our Master's degree the same year, and so did Frances, Bob's wife, and Sally Hamilton Sell (Dr. Sarah Sell, of the Vanderbilt Medical Faculty) and I were roommates, and Ed and Ivar Lou Duncan were in our classes, though they were ahead of us, as already working on their Ph.D. But we must make the Critic happy, so that he will not feel that his golden words are wasted, so please assure him that I am young enough to learn something new every day, that I am being encouraged strongly, and that doubtless in a few years I shall be doing such semantic ballets, tense, muscular, with no lush description anywhere around to bother us,

Lily's letter stops off there (it's the bottom of the page), but one can surmise that she did not add much more, other than that, if it were possible, she would like Robert Graves to look at her work. Jones wrote to Lily on October 18:

> Dear Miss Peter: As I began your letter of 12 October, I was sorry to see you give up readily and ask for the return of the manuscript. I don't know that I think any one critic is Olympian enough to be deferred to, though I did think that this was a perceptive set of comments. I knew that you knew the modern poets — in all likelihood as well as our critic does — and I knew that your master's essay was on Donne.
>
> ... I do not know that I can go along with you and Plato about the masculine element of Form and the feminine element of Matter except as I see specific instances where it seems true. Besides, wouldn't the successful operation of a plantation normally be considered a masculine undertaking, and Bob Bahnsen thinks you are probably the best in the business at this job. [Bob Bahnsen was in charge of institutional development at V.U.]
>
> When I got to the last page of your letter, I was delighted to have your suggestion that we try Robert Graves. I shall forthwith try to compose a letter to him that will make him want to read your poems and offer you some helpful advice. In a way, it seems to me unfair that the critic who has already read the poems knows who you are and you do not know who he is — though this is a situation I cannot do anything about. I can conceal from Mr. Graves, though, the fact that you made the suggestion that we seek his advice. I will just tell him that you are a poet whose works seem to us already to justify book publication, and that we should like to be able to offer you some concrete suggestions. ...

No matter that Lily's stated assets are approaching the two million mark and no matter that the artist loves his or her creation, the ordeal of waiting for creditable reinforcement continued for Lily some time longer.

Lily received a letter in the fall of '63 from her congressman, E. C. "Took" Gathings, First District. Senator Weltner of Georgia had investigated the amount of cotton subsidies paid to all farmers whose acreage exceeded one thousand acres and charged that Brooks Griffin, Ratio manager, along with many others, had received payment on all bales produced as if they had all moved into the export program. Gathings asked for data to negate the charge and help him deal with the Cooley Cotton Bill. Lily had to sift the 1961 records to support her refutation of the charges and report it to Gathings. He wrote her on December 2:

> Dear Miss Lily: Portions of your letter and of several others from our area were read into the Congressional record to refute the information that was incorporated in the Record earlier by Mr. Weltner of Georgia. I have only included a portion of your letter which so well told the story that I was so anxious to get.
>
> With kindest best wishes, I am Yours sincerely,

In October Lily received the message that her Uncle Brutus Mobrey had suffered a heart attack. She immediately dismissed her plans to go to the dedication of the Moravian Foundation Library and left for Vicksburg. He died shortly, and Lily stayed for his funeral. She stood at his graveside during the Masonic ceremony, remembering their last evening together and contemplating the small diamond engagement ring on her left hand. It was Aunt Ada's ring which he had given Lily when Aunt Ada died. She was full of grief, as were the other members of the family.

Lily returned home and concluded her year's work. Her holidays were routine except for subnormal temperatures. Some business concern sent her a New Year's greeting accompanied with a spiral notebook called "The Ready Reference Weekly Memo Calendar." She nearly always recorded her trips on wall calendars, but this one appealed to her more. She made her daily entries on this calendar, starting with the first day of 1964. It had a space of five lines for each day, and she packed them full.

On January 9, Vice Chancellor Bob Bahnsen and two of his Vanderbilt colleagues came to see Lily, and Bahnsen returned on the 17th. Undoubtedly the matter of publishing Lily's poetry had been discussed on the first visit, because, this time, Bahnsen presented to Lily the idea of having her work published by Robert Moore Allen. He was a young man on the staff of Vanderbilt who, with his wife, was publishing books of poetry. Bahnsen and Allen came to see her on February 1. She liked him, and they entered into an agreement to move forward with publication of *The Green Linen of Summer* on a royalty basis. Lily said that Allen bore all the costs, that it was not a vanity publishing arrangement: however, the writer found evidence that Lily helped Allen bear the costs.

The night before, Lily had written to Jones at Vanderbilt, asking him whether or not he had sent her poetry to Robert Graves. He replied on February 4:

> Your letter of 31 January makes me very much ashamed that I had not written you sooner. I took rather a long time in getting a letter off to Robert Graves, because in a particularly busy period I did not find the time to reflect on how to approach him, and when I did have a moment to think about it, it seemed rather unlikely to me that he would take on the assignment. A recent article of his in the *Saturday Review* suggests that his duties at Oxford are about all he is willing to leave his own projects and the Island of Mallorca for. I finally did write him, though, and as yet have had no reply.
>
> By now I trust you will have received a visit from Messrs Robert Bahnsen and Robert Allen and that they will have brought the poems back to you. . . .

Jones continues in an apologetic vein, assuring Lily that she had not troubled them at the Press and that her poems were certainly worthy of "serious consideration." He commended Allen to her.

Lily was not at all sure that Graves would read her poetry, so the anxiety of hearing from him wasn't too great. There was no lessening of her club work or farming. She corresponded often with Allen.

April had always been a favorite month for Lily, but this one was especially rewarding. She was busily working to get ready to make a trip east. Dr. Don McCorkle (Moramus Director) had summoned her to Winston-Salem to see the new Foundation home and then go on to Bethlehem where she would receive the Moramus Award for devotion to recovery and preservation of early American Music. This would compensate somewhat for her not being able to attend the dedication of the Peter Library.

In the midst of this preparation, she received a letter from Robert Graves, truly a surprise. She recorded in her diary, "Letter from Mr. Robert Graves!! Delightful! Cleaned house all day & Gracie helped me this P.M. Mr. Graves letter was dated March 28 and came by air mail." Lily promised the writer that she would search for the letter and gave the writer access to her correspondence to search for it and other letters from Graves, but they were never found.

In April, after the spring planting was mostly complete, Lily felt she could take time to go to see the Moravian Music Foundation's new quarters and attend the DAR Convention in Washington.[3]

According to her daily log, Lily wrote a reply to Robert Graves' letter on April 26. On May 5 she received another letter from Graves. She noted, "Letter from Robert Graves — astonishingly quick reply. Very interesting."

While Lily was in Little Rock in June, presenting a program

she prepared on Spanish and Gypsy poetry, Bob Bahnsen, who had Vanderbilt business in Little Rock, delivered to Lily the proofs of *The Green Linen of Summer,* as a convenience for her publisher, Robert Moore Allen. She was excited and pleased to do the proofreading. She re-read each page dozens of times. Lily did not dawdle about getting them back to Allen. He wrote her on June 19:

> . . . You did a fine job on the proof. I am glad for your decision on the use of capital letters to begin the lines of the poems. I changed the poems you indicated and have gotten the type done again. Also I corrected all the mistakes you marked and worked the changes in the copy. Everything is ready now for the plates to be made. . . .
>
> I am more pleased than ever with the book and how it is working out. . . .
>
> Bob told me that you are corresponding with Robert Graves. This pleases me very much. We must send him a copy of your book. I think he will like it and if he does what a joke this will be on David Jones and his critics. I would love to be able to meet Robert Graves. . . .
>
> By the way. I myself have a talk to give. I am supposed to make a talk at the Converse College Writers' Workshop this summer. I am supposed to tell them about my publishing and the poetry I am publishing. It will be a chance to show off your book and I am very pleased at being asked. There is so much I want to do to help writers and poets in this area which is almost wasted because we are so for away from the great centers of publishing. I have eight or nine manuscripts in my file now. . . .

On June 16, Lily departed for Bethlehem, Pennsylvania, to attend the Moravian Music Festival.[4] Upon her return, she had a letter from Robert Allen, written June 17, 1964, excerpts of which follow:

Everything is finally worked out. The book has just gone to the bindery and will be ready by the time I return from North Carolina on July 1....

Of course I want to bring some of the books over to you at the first opportunity. I also want you to sign the special edition. Would it be all right with you if JoLynn and I come down to see you on the 4th of July? This is a very patriotic coincidence.... My only hope is that you will be pleased with what I bring you.

One other item. You mentioned in your letter about perhaps making a visit up here sometime in July. If you do I wonder if you would be willing to help me promote your book up here among the people in Nashville who I know would like to have a copy and meet you. I have talked to the manager of the bookstore here, about your book and he suggested that if you were coming we might arrange an autograph party one afternoon in the bookstore....

Robert and JoLynn Allen came over for the Fourth, and Lily went to Nashville on the nineteenth for the autographing party at the Vanderbilt bookstore and many dinners and luncheons. She wrote about each in her diary, even noted what she wore. Three radio stations featured her on programs, and Ivar Lou Duncan invited her to read from her book at Belmont College.

Bob Bahnsen came to her home on July 31, bringing a Miss Lee from the *Nashville Tennessean* to interview Lily and have her autograph more copies of her book. The first printing was 1,400 regular copies, two hundred of a special boxed and autographed edition.[5] Allen wrote and told her how proud he was of the book and said, "Sales so far are good and I would say that as a result of your very excellent appearance in Nashville you are selling more than Robert Frost and T. S. Eliot combined, at least in Nashville." He emphasized his desire to begin working on the publication of her epic poem on DeSoto's exploration.

By mid-August Lily was swamped with correspondence about her book. On the nineteenth she wrote, "Finished writing letters to my Nashville hostesses, with Emily Post shaking her finger at me from somewhere in the Elysian Fields for my delay." She started noting the number of letters received in the margin of her diary, and it ran from four to twenty-nine every day the rest of the month. Her friend and fellow Arkansas poet, Edsel Ford, wrote on August 20:

> My dear Lily, I don't know when I have ever been so happy, so delighted, so downright *grateful* about a new book of poems as I have been since your GREEN LINEN OF SUMMER arrived. It is pure pleasure to the eye, to the heart, and to the mind. Lord, it even *smells* good! It is my deep, fond hope that it will meet with uncommon success; you can be sure that I will speak of it and from it wherever I can, to help assure that success.
>
> I am terribly proud of it, and of you.

Lily also heard from a number of other friends.[6]

It was on that trip to Nashville that Lily worked out the details of awarding scholarships in English with Ed Duncan, then chairman of the department at Vanderbilt. She provided two a year ($3,000 each) until conditions altered the need in 1971.[7]

Lily received an especially pleasurable letter from Don Brooks, who wrote her on August 23 after having received a special-edition copy of her book. He said:

> Dear Lily, . . . Even after the preparation afforded by your letter, the arrival this past week of your exquisitely realized book was one of the most joyful surprises of my life. . . . I am already well along in a re-reading of the volume which will be more lingering — . . . One of my favorites, by the way, has always been "Delta Rain," the fourth line being expecially

spellbinding. ["in the cool dimness of the cloudy May afternoon"] An apparently simple line, I don't know whether its magic is intrinsic or the effect of some forgotten association. But the book is full of magic and music of your own special kind. . . .

Lily had every reason to expect approval from Don Brooks, but what had she expected from Robert Graves? Her log states that she received a letter from him on August 28, that she replied on August 31 and sent him a copy of *The Green Linen . . .*, and that he replied on September 10. It is a genuine loss that the Graves letters have not been found, but it is possible that Lily intended just that.

John Ciardi had been sent a book. She recorded that he replied on September 14, but that letter was also missing.

Book reviews of *Green Linen* were beginning to appear in papers, and more letters came, but Lily attended to her farming. She recorded, "Took Loydell to Marianna this A.M. to get gin truck . . . To Helena in P.M. with 92 cotton samples for Allen Keesee. . . . Cut all the cockle burrs & careless weeds in N.E. corner South bean field . . . to gin, all's well . . . had a good rain this A.M. It was needed . . . to gin in P.M. to make up pay roll & copy cotton. Cut some weeds in soybean field. New 2-row cotton picker delivered."

In October, Lily drove to Nashville to give the banquet program for the Tennessee Press Woman's Association, reading from *Green Linen*. She went to Little Rock for Poetry Day and gave another reading and stood in the receiving line at the tea at the Governor's Mansion.

Neither Lily or Robert Allen, her publisher, had time to attend to a wide-range promotion of *Green Linen*; however, it received favorable attention from several quarters in the region. Some sample reviews follow:

. . . Here is a person who can not only run two huge cotton plantations and participate on the cultural horizon of her state, but who has found as well the meaning and flavor of life around her, and who had been endowed with the great gift of being able to capture it in her songs. . . .

. . . We have here not only poetry of very high quality but the testament, as well, of someone who has lived among us, that life can be good, rich, and meaningful. In this collection there is only praise of beauty, and delight in the flavors of life, including the bittersweet. Kenneth Beaudoin — *The Commercial Appeal*, Memphis, Tennessee.

. . . In this world of bitter words and troubled minds, it is refreshing to find so delightful a book of poems as *The Green Linen of Summer* by Lily Peter. . . . Sidney Owen — *The Nashville Tennessean.*

. . . Lily Peter. . . is most persuasive when she writes of the cotton and bayou country where she is virtually an institution. She . . . has technique equal to a brilliant mind, and her interest in music, history, mathematics, and mythology results in a varied, but always rich poetry. . . . Edsel Ford — *The Ozarks Mountaineer.*

There were also a number of favorable reviews in Arkansas newspapers.

On October 27, 1964, Lily recorded, "Still catching up at home. Yesterday was Joe's birthday, which I always remember so vividly. [Joe was her brother who died at age nine.] This is the anniversary of the day I made my first money, a 2c piece Mother gave me for shelling a dishpan full of peas. I was five." And she told about all the appearances she made during the rest of the year.[8]

Lily closed out the very special year of 1964 by noting just before Christmas in her log:

> 3303 bales today. There is something you can say about farm-
> ing. It comes up every morning, like the sun, in a cloud of
> witnesses, items expecting to be attended to that very day, and
> if they are not, the next morning they are right back on your
> doorstep, adding their clamor to that of the troop of newcom-
> ers that are lined up to wish you a good day. . . .

It was her ultimate love. Farming was poetry to her.

Lily kept no log in 1965; however, newspapers and maga-
zines, where there is other source of information, show Lily's pace
to be one which few could match. In January, she was active in
organizing a local branch of the Cotton Producers' Institute
(*Brinkley Argus*, the 28th). The sales of cotton to fabric mills were
dropping; the large mail order catalogs listed few 100% cotton
garments. A promotion campaign was adopted by the national
organization, and the rapid trend to synthetics was altered. In Feb-
ruary, *The Christian Science Monitor* carried a feature article
about Lily written by Edsel Ford.[9]

All this time Lily was working diligently on finishing *The
Great Riding,* her epic poem about DeSoto's explorations. On
February 28, Robert Allen had written from Madrid, Spain, tell-
ing her that he and JoLynn had taken an excursion to Segovia.
He said:

> . . . you probably know from your reading that [it] is a very his-
> toric city, most notable for its famous castle The Alcazar, where
> Ferdinand and Isabella lived at times during their reign. . . .
> visited by Columbus twice. We went all through the castle,
> seeing many interesting things including some armor used by
> the Conquistadors in America. I was continually reminded of
> *The Great Riding.* . . .

This inspired her all the more. Lily was studying books she had procured from the Vanderbilt and University of Texas libraries.

Lily's June activity was interspersed with planning the grand opening of the Elaine Implement Company set for July 4. It was during this occasion that an incident occurred that gave rise to the legend that Lily drove tractors in evening dresses. Lily planned down to minute details to make the event a memorable social occasion: printed invitations, personnel for hosting, decorations, even the clothing. The men on the board of directors took care of the food, a noon fish-fry.

Lily had chosen a white sheer cotton shirtwaist dress with a skirt of tiny knife-sized pleats. This made the skirt so full that when Lily sat down, the sides would drape to the floor. The International Harvester photographer asked Lily to climb up into the seat of one of their largest machines. She did so, and because of the side angle of the photograph, it looked as if she were wearing a long dress. When Harry Pearson, a reporter from *The Pine Bluff Commercial*, wrote a story on Lily's financing the Philadelphia Orchestra's trip to Arkansas in 1969, that picture among several others was chosen to illustrate his story.

Lily was quite happy with the success of the opening of the implement company. They received over seven hundred visitors during the long day. She had even gotten up at 4:00 a.m. to gather tubs of day lilies from her yard to display along with the many congratulatory floral gifts. Local newspapers, grateful for extensive advertising, gave the opening more than adequate coverage. This business event also added to the volume of her mail.

The year 1966 began with Lily's continuing to work on the final draft of *The Great Riding*. She had mailed a portion of it to Robert Allen in Spain, but it was missent by surface instead of air mail, causing a delay in delivery of three months. That delay frightened both Lily and Allen, but he came back to the states in January and they were in constant touch as they worked on accuracy.

The famous photograph of the grand opening
of the Elaine Implement Company

She was much in demand as a speaker, but she had to reject
several invitations because of the demands of the U. S. Depart-
ment of Agriculture on cotton farmers. Each farmer had to file a
statement of the production of cotton for the previous three years,
providing bale number, weight, compress numbers, names of con-
tract growers, and date of ginning. That was a monumental task
for Lily because Ratio had produced from 1,600 to 1,800 bales a
year, and her own place had produced from 1,500 to 1,700 bales.
She did take time from gathering those records to accept a request
from Jessamine Gist of Marianna to speak to students in the En-
glish Department at University of Arkansas at Little Rock.

On June 5, 1966, Lily went to Little Rock for the Arkansas
Writer's Conference and was speaker at the Celebrities' Banquet.

Robert Allen wrote on June 24:

... The book [*The Great Riding*] is printed as JoLynn told you over the phone. We are in the process of assembling it now. We are doing it by hand so as to insure the quality. . . . It should go to the bindery in a week or so and then it will be only a short time before I bring the first copy to Marvell to celebrate the publication. I will also bring the news release I am preparing to send to all the newspapers I can think of. . . . I am determined that this book get the attention it so richly deserves. . . .

The Great Riding was released in September, 1966. Lily went up to Vanderbilt. Julie Kerling wrote the following in the October issue of the Vanderbilt *Hustler*:

Lily Peter composes songs, writes poetry and is the only lady cotton ginner in the United States.

Her second volume of poetry, *The Great Riding*, which tells the story of Hernando de Soto's explorations of the Mississippi River, has recently been published.

At an appearance at Vanderbilt on October 14, Miss Peter read from her book and told of her reasons for choosing the subject.

Born and raised in the Delta region of Arkansas, Miss Peter read of the early explorers as a child. Although not impressed by Columbus, she explained, she was fascinated by the figure of DeSoto because of a steel engraving in her book that showed him in full armor, topped with plumes.

When she learned that he had explored her beloved home county, he became a living presence, and she often expected to see him riding up to the front gate.

This childhood impression, combined with her deep love for the county in which he had traveled, prompted her to write the book as a contribution to cross-roads history.

Miss Peter's visit was sponsored by the English Department, and she talked with visitors at a tea in the book store. . . .

Her love for the land on which she has spent most of her life is clearly revealed in her words and poetry. The prologue to *The*

Great Riding is a lyrical tribute to the beauty of the country seen by DeSoto, which is exactly the same today with the exception of "the carrier pigeons his men saw, which are now extinct."

"Have you ever heard a panther scream?" Miss Peter asked her audience. "I have."

Near her home is Big Cypress Bayou. . . . Miss Peter can understand the misery of DeSoto's men, who spent hours crossing the Bayou when the tide was in.

Interrupting her reading, she asked her audience, "Fancy those men in water up to their waists, plagued by mosquitoes and gnats, and," she added spiritedly, "carrying their pigs in their arms." . . .

Marshall Falwell, one of the first recipients of a Lily Peter Scholarship, was present at that reading. He said, "She was a fascinating woman. When she was reading from her epic poem about DeSoto, a long reading, I had the feeling that I was listening to an original in the peculiar medieval sense. She was like an anachronism in the very best sense of the word, an old patron. There was an other-world, other-time-and-place aura about her as she read."[10]

Despite a car collision in March which hospitalized Lily for six weeks, 1966 was a year of accomplishment, but her summer activities were comparatively few.[11] It was eighteen months before she felt that she was fully recovered from the accident, and her right shoulder never ceased to give her pain when she lifted her violin. While recuperating in the summer, Lily made a study of architecture. She wanted new housing for her cotton gin, so she set in motion plans which would bring her unique "beautiful turquoise gin" into reality in 1967.

By the beginning months of 1967, Lily was back at her normal speed: accepting speaking engagements, performing civic duties, and contributing to various causes. She remodeled her gin;

she renewed her efforts toward a fitting site for the Louisiana Purchase marker. But two events occurred that would engender the birth of two of her "giant children." We shall digress for an explanation of the metaphor.

During the mid-seventies when attending a Moravian Music Festival, Lily had a conversation with Dr. Malcolm Johns, brother-in-law to the festival director, Thor Johnson. Dr. Johns was relating something about his two children whom he adored, and Lily remarked that it would always be a source of sorrow to her that she had never married and borne any children. Dr. Johns immediately remonstrated, "Lily, how can you say you have borne no children? You are like the ancient earth mother, the goddess Cybele, who bore giant children. Without your genius and vitality, there would have been no Moravian Music Foundation. Think of the power and influence you have exercised through your forty-year teaching career. Your personal subsidy of scholarship students, both financial and psychological, is a giant production. And your books are children."

Dr. Johns went on to name other things Lily had done, and she protested somewhat; however, the more she thought of it, the more comfort it was to think of her creative efforts in that way. She knew she tended to be matriarchal, in her family and with her tenants and laborers, yet she had striven for nurture rather than dependence. So Lily began to think about her projects as her children. She re-read the myth of Cybele who had to bear the god's offspring in a dark cave and was intrigued with that myth as a metaphor of her experience.

The two seminal events of 1967 for Lily were these: Governor Winthrop Rockefeller appointed her to the Sesquicentennial Commission to plan the celebration of the 150th anniversary of Arkansas' achieving territorial status. A Big Creek Drainage District, which had as its goal the channelization of Big Creek and its tributaries, was organized. The former was an honor and a joy to contemplate; the latter was a horror which filled her with the utmost dread for the next seven years.

Robert Allen, Lily's publisher, was disappointed that *The Great Riding* did not achieve international or national acclaim. He sent a notice to *The London Times* and got no response. Neither the *Atlantic* nor the *Saturday Review* gave it a review as he had wished. But Lily had long since learned to expect little realization of her dreams and to rejoice in what she received, knowing acclaim in this world is whimsical. She was gratified, as was Allen, at the regional attention the book was given. *The Great Riding* was reviewed by about the same number of papers as had reviewed *Green Linen.*[12]

All the year up to ginning season, the transformation of her gin was taking place. In February, Lily heard from the Varco Steel Company at Pine Bluff by letter that the materials alone for the outside walls would be nearly $15,000. *The Commercial Appeal* on November 10 carried an article by Barbara Warnken which said:

> East Arkansas' only lady cotton ginner has put her faith in the future of cotton and built the prettiest and perhaps the newest cotton gin in the state in a year when many gins failed to open because of reduced cotton acreage and short crops.
>
> Miss Lily Peter, the lady ginner, runs her cotton operation. . . . She acted as her own architect for the new gin which is a $36,000 turquoise and white building with all white interior walls.
>
> It was built over the equipment which had been the heart of her old gin.
>
> "We wrapped the equipment in plastic to protect it from the weather during the rebuilding, then found out that the plastic held moisture and it had rusted some of the equipment," she said.
>
> "I have been ginning for 20 years, so when I planned the

new gin I used everything I had learned, plus the good advice of my ginner friends. I planned it right down to the size of the doors and skylights. Being a woman I had to dress it up. The enameled steel building is as fireproof as possible," she said. . . .

The baked-on turquoise enameled steel was much more expensive than the customary galvanized sheet iron, but it unquestionably added to the beauty of the countryside. And the ginning crew took pride in it. Warnken's article was illustrated by a picture of Lily with her gin foreman, J. R. Smith, observing the operation of the deseeding equipment. The extra light provided by the white inner walls made it easier to achieve safety. The gin customers owned dozens of cotton trailers all painted in a variety of colors. Neatly parked in the open shed on the gin yard near the road, they added to the zest of the vista seen from State Highway 1 across the small cotton field between the highway and the gin. Lily could now say to her many nonlocal visitors, "Travel about eight miles south from Marvell on Highway 1 until you see a turquoise gin on your left across a field, etc." Many others in the neighborhood would use the same directions. Lily's gin had become a landmark.

Lily again made an effort to establish a creditable, accessible site for the Louisiana Purchase marker. Congressman "Took" Gathings in Washington wrote to Stewart Udall, Secretary of the Interior, recommending at least the endorsement of establishing the site as a state park, referring to Lily and her efforts, as well as those of others. However, the involvement of John Fleming, Outdoors Editor of the *Arkansas Gazette,* seemed to generate more response than had been achieved in the past. In his column of April 30, 1967, he said, under the headline, "Lonely Monument Needs Some Help":

If you look at the official highway map of Arkansas, at the point where Lee, Phillips and Monroe Counties intersect, you will find a little triangle which is identified as the Louisiana Purchase Historical Monument. Although not pin-pointed so definitely, you will also find this marking on every piece of map literature distributed by the Publicity and Parks Commission.

However, if your curiosity is titillated by this imposing reminder of a great event in the history of our nation and you make an effort to see this well advertised monument, you are going to be sorely disappointed.

Fleming went on to tell of his own efforts to find the marker and his contacting Lou Oberste of the Publicity and Parks Commission. Oberste had referred him to Lily Peter. Fleming then gave an account of his interview and correspondence with Lily on that subject and why she had given up the project of the arboretum. He effectively emphasized the historical value of clearly marking the spot, applauded the efforts of the DAR to do so, and headed up a paragraph, "Why Not an Arboretum?" He told of Lily's trying to procure the land, and concluded:

> . . . It is regrettable, but understandable, that Mrs. Peters [sic] has given up her quest.
>
> There are two obvious choices and the latter one would be tragic. Either find some method of establishing the Louisiana Purchase Historical Monument State Park or erase any mention of the name from all state literature and let the monument fall into decay in the middle of its little swamp.

This was one time when the appeal to reason and pride in one's history was effective. Letters came in to the paper. Local papers again carried long articles, including not only the history proper, but the history of the project itself. Abe Davidson of Marvell renewed his interest and contacted Fleming. (Davidson was one of the original owners willing to donate acreage.) On June 18 the *Gazette* printed a story on the accuracy of the survey that established the point, featuring a picture of Eldridge P. Douglass,

an engineer then living in Fayetteville, Arkansas. After an intro-
duction, it related the following:

> In 1813 the government of the United States became acutely
> aware of the necessity to survey the Louisiana Purchase, the
> area that President Thomas Jefferson had bought from France
> in 1803 for $15,000,000. A team of engineers from Washing-
> ton sailed down the Ohio River to the Mississippi and then
> down the Mississippi to Arkansas. At the mouth of the St.
> Francis River the group split into two parties. One party be-
> gan to survey westward while the other dropped on down to
> the mouth of the Arkansas River and began to survey north-
> ward. The point where the lines cross was the base point for
> all surveys of the Louisiana Purchase, an area that included
> most of the land west of the Mississippi River.
>
> To this day every property description in the states which
> have since been cut out of this huge land mass stem back to this
> point in Arkansas. However, the point lay unmarked and un-
> attended for 107 years—from 1813 until 1921.
>
> In 1921 there was a dispute over the exact boundary be-
> tween Lee County and Phillips County and a younger engi-
> neer at Helena was hired to find the line and draw proper
> maps. The engineer's name was Eldridge P. Douglass. The 33-
> year-old engineer enlisted the help of an old-time surveyor,
> Thomas Jacks, a Yale graduate who became a surveyor be-
> cause his father, a Helena doctor, had acquired large property
> holdings in Eastern Arkansas and it was necessary for some-
> one to establish the property lines. Thomas Jacks actually
> bridged the gap between the methods used by engineers in
> 1814 and the more modern methods used in 1921.
>
> Today Eldridge P. Douglass is a spry 79 and he lives at
> Fayetteville. Recently he recalled the hot day in 1921 that he
> and Thomas Jacks found the long lost point of beginning for
> the Louisiana Purchase survey. The two men had the original
> notes written by the 1814 party. But this did not insure quick

results because back years ago surveyors actually used chains (now a steel tape is employed) and as the chain was stretched the links would spread. After days of use the chain would be slightly longer than the exact distance. Over a long span of time the margin of error could become considerable.

The two men started the survey from a point 10 miles east of the point they were seeking. When they reached the approximate area of the Purchase survey point they discovered two tupelo gum trees, gnarled with age and hollow. The 1814 survey notes had used two tupelo gum trees to establish the exact point. . . . After 107 years the slash marks on the gum trees were still visible.

The article gave Jacks' exact words at the moment, "Under the law of probability there could be no two other trees on the bearing distance." It told of the work of the Marianna women who commissioned a monument marker, saw that it was placed, and planned a dedication with Senator Thaddeus Carraway the principal speaker. The account also mentioned Lily's one-woman, fourteen-year campaign to get a park established and held out some hope of the accomplishment.

Concern was aroused. The *Gazette*'s John Fleming, accompanied by Clarendon attorney John Moore and his son Burton, Abe Davidson, and Max Love of the Arkansas Publicity and Parks Commission made the trip to the site and made photographs of the marker, surrounded by the men, all in hip boots wading around it. Fleming wrote about the trip to the site at length, and it was published in the Sunday paper, July 23. The state legislature had approved the creation of a park in 1963, and it looked as if the land were going to be acquired. Fleming had secured an opinion from the attorney-general that the Highway Department was mandated to build a road to the site. Fleming concluded saying:

Strangely enough, the swampy nature of the land should enhance rather than detract from the possible purpose of this "maybe" new park. A boardwalk could be built out to the monument in the same manner as the Audubon Society has made available the wonders of Corkscrew Swamp in Florida.

But the establishment of the park was to take a few more years.

On November 15, 1967 the *Arkansas Gazette* reported the organizational meeting of the Sesquicentennial Committee, appointed by Governor Winthrop Rockefeller to plan the celebration of the anniversary of Arkansas' becoming a territory.[13] Lily was made chairman of music for the celebration, and, given the hindsight of knowing that her appointment eventually led to her single-handed importation of the Philadelphia Orchestra for the occasion, one can imagine that Lily's fantasies instantly took flight.

At the same time, the stress and strain and misery of the potential channelization of Big Creek began. To Lily channelization meant an insult in the medical sense, a harmful shock, just as harmful to the water supply, the soil, the plants, trees, and wild life of any area as the penetration of a knife into flesh. As early as June, meetings were held "to discuss the organization of the proposed Big Creek Drainage District" (*Helena World*, June 12). Opposition to the proposals of the District was already rising, but not nearly so much as was approval of the drainage project. The Brinkley papers were touting the project regularly. A strong battle was developing, and it would not be concluded for seven years, not until 1974.

Nevertheless, Lily took some time to write for sheer fun.[14]

A Nude Singularity

NOTES

[1]Lily conjectured that she may have married, had she met any man who measured up to her Uncle Brutus. She admired him immensely. Brutus Mobrey grew up at Greenville, Mississippi, and suffered the same deprivations as a child as had his sister, Florence, Lily's mother. At age twelve, he earned money by carrying water to the towboats and barges which docked at Greenville. This contact with the transportation on the river caused young Brutus to become fascinated with river transportation. He gave up formal schooling and became a fireman, the lowest of jobs. He steadily moved up the hierarchy of river work: from fireman to deckhand to engineer. The latter called for passing an examination on the maintenance of compression engines, and he had learned all about them from a long and hard apprenticeship. Many river men were rough, hard, eccentric, and abusive because of the long periods of isolation while navigating the length of the river system. Many drank whiskey to alleviate their feelings, but Brutus always sought to rise above the common level. He went through the ranks of engineer: second, first, chief, then boiler inspector. He married and settled at Vicksburg. In spite of his lack of formal schooling, he spent much of his spare time reading, educating himself so well in this way that he became informed on many subjects. He had an excellent memory.

On Lily's last visit with him in the early fall of 1963, they spent a long evening together. He told her about his experiences as a Mason (he had reached the thirty-third degree) and recited one entire ritual from memory. Then they discussed the world of business and investments. He told Lily had would have liked to have been a stock broker. He could quote the assets and liabilities of all the blue chip corporations. It was as if the conversation foreshadowed his leaving Lily stocks and bonds in considerable amounts.

The final topic of the evening was about his plans to redecorate his home, work he did not like to do. But Lily was amazed at his knowledge and taste in architecture and furnishings, even though she had always known that he had taste in his personal appearance. He was quite dapper, "dressed to the nines" in whatever clothing was suitable for the river, and immaculate. Lily said, "He was one of the few men whom I've known whom I could praise from every angle."

[2]Lily's cousin was Clarence Leinbach, past-president and chairman of the board of trustees of the Wachovia Bank and Trust Company, Win-

ston-Salem, North Carolina, the largest financial institution in Western North Carolina.

[3]Lily traveled to Winston-Salem by train on April 13-14. Her cousin Clarence Leinbach met her at the train; she visited with Cousin Margaret Kolb. The cousins entertained her with a dinner which included Dr. and Mrs. Gramley (President of Salem College), Dr. and Mrs. McCorkle, and other friends. The next day McCorkle took her to see the foundation's new home, and she was delighted. After more celebration and an interview for the local paper, she went on to Bethlehem where the awarding took place on April 17. Lee and Tom Butterfield had a party for Lily. The event was reported in the papers in North Carolina, Pennsylvania, and Arkansas, and in the January 1965 issue of *Pipes of Pan*, national magazine of Sigma Alpha Iota. The latter gave a full account of the significance of the foundation and information on Lily's musical accomplishments and concluded:

> A surprise feature of the April 1964 evening occasion at Bethlehem was the singing of two of Miss Peter's compositions by Soprano Juanne Lotz and the reading of one of her poems, "The Death of the Wild Crane," by Dr. Donald McCorkle, at that time director of the Moravian Music Foundation. The Moramus Award presentation to Miss Peter was made by Mr. McCorkle. (39)

Lily was fortunate that this tour coincided with the DAR Congress at which she had regional music chairman duties. Her cousin, Tom Butterfield, drove her to Philadelphia to get a train to Washington, D. C. One of his treasured memories of Lily was her entertaining him during this sixty-mile drive with the recitation, from memory, of 1,100 lines from her epic poem about DeSoto which she was preparing for publication. (Letter from Lee Butterfield to author. 12 Mar. 1981)

Besides full attendance at the various DAR events, Lily took time for hair styling and complexion and make-up analysis at the Elizabeth Arden Salon. She was pleased enough with her Hessler portraits to have some more made.

Lily barely got home in time to attend a national meeting on watershed construction held in Little Rock. She did her homework, as usual, and made her contribution to the discussions in the presence of Governor Faubus, Congressman Wilbur D. Mills, and Orville Freeman, Secretary of Agriculture.

⁴At Bethlehem at the festival, besides the usual singing and social activities, Lily got to meet the new director of Moramus, Dr. Ewald V. Nolte and his wife. She was among the eleven who were photographed because they had attended every festival so far. She loved every minute of her time spent with Thor Johnson. One performance was given in Lititz, formerly a mission near Bethlehem, now a thriving town.

⁵First and second printing, 1964, third printing, 1966, by Robert Moore Allen, Nashville. Fourth printing, Little Rock: Pioneer Press, 2,000 copies, 1974. Lily bought many copies and gave them away.

⁶Typical is a letter from her friend, Virginia Conkle, at UT, Austin, she heard along with a lengthy report on Virginia's trip to Europe, these comments written September 17, 1964:

> Dearest Lily — One of the nicest things we came back to after two months in Europe & Mexico was your charming book! Especially the bird poems — They are wonderful. I plan to read some of them to our local Audubon Society. . . .
>
> . . . That ornery Lyndon Johnson badgered Frank into going to the White House a few months ago — & Frank came home exhausted — had to go to the hospital. I'll never forgive Lyndon. He & Lady Bird <u>both</u> got on the phone. He felt he <u>had</u> to go. Still I can't vote for Barry Goldwater. What a choice! . . .
>
> Thanks again for the dear, <u>dear</u> book — I love it —

⁷Vanderbilt asked her to contribute her money without designation. In that way, it could procure grants as high as three dollars to one.

⁸In mid-November, Lily drove to Hattiesburg to William Carey College for appearances there. Soon she heard from Dr. Benjamin Dunford and his wife, Nancy, both on the music faculty. They sent her a copy of the local publicity in the *Hattiesburg American* on November 18 showing a picture of Lily standing between the two of them. A subscript said:

> FIND MUCH IN COMMON — At a coffee in her honor. . . Miss Lily Peter (center) finds many interests in common with . . . [the Dunfords] Miss Peter, who presented a reading of her own poems Tuesday evening in Tatum Court as the third feature of the Carey Fine Arts Series, is the founder of a library. . . . Both Dr. and Mrs. Dunford are graduates of Winston-Salem College and are particularly interested in study and performance of Moravian music. (2)

On November 28, Lily left for Spartanburg, North Carolina, where she gave a program of poetry at Converse College. She was shown the usual courtesies and entertainments. She particularly enjoyed being received at the Faculty Club "in the Block House, built in 1743."

These sorts of appearances continued, and the time intervals lessened. Lily rejected no invitation unless some farm business demanded it.

[9]Edsel Ford, Fort Smith, Arkansas, wrote an article which carried his by-line and was designated "Special to the *Christian Science Monitor*" and headlined "Miss Lily Harvests Culture." It appeared on page 4C on February 19, 1965.

Gladys Cope Powell, a fellow-poet from the Arkansas Roundtable, placed an account of Lily's publication and activities in *The Pen Woman* in February of '65 (p. 8). Lily attended the Arkansas-Missouri Cotton Ginners' Association meeting and was among those who received the annual safety award. This was reported on page 19 in *The Cotton Gin and Oil Mill Press*, Dallas, 13 March 1965.

From New York City, Don Brooks wrote Lily on July 3, 1966, and told her how pleased he was that she had received national, or even international, publicity from having appeared on the pages of *The Christian Science Monitor*. He said:

> . . . Your epistolary silence is sufficient indication that you continue to be totally occupied in your two worlds of farming and poetry, plus sundry civic or social activities as usual. I of course can offer no such excuse — in fact, I seem to have almost nothing to relate as to activities. Come to think of it, <u>that</u> is an excuse! . . .

He had been doing some things, though. He told of his vacation trip to Florida, and his visiting with their mutual friend, Jack Carter at Winter Park.

[10]Telephone conversation with Marshall L. Falwell, August 28, 1980.

[11]In late March, '66, Lily was working all of her spare time on finishing her manuscript. She typed late in the evening night after night. On the sixteenth, she typed until 2:00 a.m. so she could get it into the mails the next day, a day on which she felt morally obligated to attend two funerals. The one in the morning was that of her old beau (long since married to another), Jimmy Jackson, who, along with his brother, had been

killed in an automobile collision at the crossroads of highways 49 and 79 in Monroe County. The afternoon funeral was that of Minnie Asbury Mixon, the mother of Louise Mixon Griffin, the grandmother of her Ratio manager, Brooks Griffin. She sat at the service of the latter in Citizens Funeral Home, West Helena, and struggled to keep awake. In this state of exhaustion, she pulled out of her parking place on 4th street directly in front of a gravel truck. The driver could not avoid hitting her car broadside. Louise Griffin told that she and others at the graveside ceremony wondered why Lily was not there, since she had said she was coming. As soon as Louise and Frank got back to Helena, they made numerous phone calls about Lily only to find that she was in the Helena Hospital in critical condition. She remained there six weeks.

Lily's hospitalization caused her to miss many engagements; however, the one that grieved her most was an invitation extended to her by O. B. Emerson. He was chairman of the committee of the host institution for the Southern Literary Festival. The April 21 issue of *Crimson-White*, the University of Alabama newspaper, carried six front-page articles on the impending festival, for example: "Atlantic Grant Winner Ford Here Thursday" (Jesse Hill Ford, author, *Mountains of Gilead*); "Sewanee Editor Andrew Lytle to Lead Welty, Gordon Panel"; "Peter to Conduct Poetry Workshop."

Ivar Lou Duncan wrote her on May 7:

> Since hearing from you personally we have evidence on which to build our hope for your recovery <u>soon</u>. You wrote as if the pace of your getting well were the principal deterrent. But we could see your determination shining through!
>
> You missed a handsome room in an old governor's mansion in Tuscaloosa. Months ago, as you know, O. B. had arranged this for you and me, an amenity that no one else had. That was the only bedroom in this 1820 mansion, the bath large enough for at least four at one time! In your place I invited Carolyn Moore, whom you met (in charge of student enlistment, a kind of Belmont hostess). We were at lunch there with 54 others and at a reception for all 300 guests. . . .
>
> All praise goes to O. B. for an unusually good program. He gave the luncheon himself. . . . He moved around behind the curtain in a modest manner, but the university committee did not forget the prime mover. We all missed you. . . .

Shirley Ann Grau and Robert Fitzgerald were also on that panel, and Lily regretted that she missed the opportunity to meet those Southern authors. As she said, as she often did on those occasions when she felt she was keeping company with people who had achieved status, "I would have been walking in tall cotton."

[12]In October 1966 Lily traveled to Fort Smith where the Arkansas Writers' Conference met and where she received the *South and West* annual award for literary achievement based on her authorship of *The Great Riding*. Daisey Middleton said to her, "Lily, I love you, but I'm not going to read anybody's poetry which sends me to the dictionary every other line — two dictionaries at that." (Interview, cited)

Through the Tennessee Poetry Society, Kenneth Beaudoin honored her with his famous Gemstone Award for the best book of poetry of the year. (*Helena-West Helena World*, 25 April 1967, p. 4) The Arkansas-Oklahoma joint sponsorship of the Tulsa Poetry Festival in the fall featured Lily reading from *The Great Riding*, at which time she was awarded a handsome trophy for writing the book.

[13]The Territorial Sesquicentennial Committee was to function as an adjunct to the standing Arkansas Commemorative Commission of which E. P. Pyeatt, Searcy, was chairman. He exhorted them to plan such a celebration as would merit national commission. Besides Lily, the committee included Governor Rockefeller as honorary chairman; Dr. Boyce Drummond, Arkadelphia, active chairman; Bernard Campbell, Hot Springs; Cleon Collier, Gillette; John L. Solomon, El Dorado; David R. Perdue, Pine Bluff; John Morrow, Batesville; Senator John L. McClellan, (D-Ark) Washington, D. C.; Mrs. Rockefeller, Edwin Cromwell, Dr. John L. Ferguson, Louis Oberste, and Ellis Doyle Herrin, all from Little Rock. Lily was the only woman on the committee, but she worked closely with Mrs. Charles F. (Agnes) Loewer, secretary of the standing commission. The group met often from the time of its appointment until the year's celebration was over.

[14]A letter Lily wrote to Ivar Lou and Ed Duncan in January of 1967 shows that it is no wonder that Lily's house is filled with replicas of owls. It also illustrates her imaginative personifications. She said:

> Dear Ivar Lou and Ed: This time I'm writing you both together, because first of all I want to thank you for the charming, the fetching, the intriguing little Mexican owl you sent me at Christmas time! This owl is a treasure indeed, and none of the adjectives I have used to describe him do justice to him at all, such

is the depth of his nature. He is inscrutability itself, with a personality that is quite fathomless, and his aloofness must be quite baffling to the group of owls in which he finds himself on top of my bookcase. The patriarch of the group, the handsome owl that Mr. Cecil Sims conjured out of a cedar fence post for me, beams down upon him in a friendly and magnanimous way, the little white French owl regards him with a genially cocked head, La Lechuza, the tiny barn owl with her brood of four owlets, *hijuelos de buho*, is not too distant in her manner, but El Buho, completely unmoved by these neighborly overtures, ignores them altogether, himself the very incarnation of Spanish metaphor, the Unsociable One, *El Buho* indeed! And he goes on staring into the direction of Outer Space, with his mind evidently on extra-terrestrial and super-mundane matters too deep for our comprehension.

The Spanish language, by the way, has some delightful circumlocutions about owls. The very word <u>owl</u>, as I have just intimated, means also an unsociable person. <u>Owl</u>, as a verb in Spanaish, *verbo neutro*, means to smuggle, *matutear*. The red owl, *el mochuelo*, for some unknown reason, operates in a somewhat sinister context — *cargar con el mochuelo* is "to get the worst part of an undertaking." And <u>owllight</u>, which most of us think of as a poeticism invented by Dylan Thomas — "Altarwise by owllight in the halfway house" — is a familiar and accepted word in Spanish — *crepusculo*, the twilight — in onomatopoeia, that tenuous echoic principle underlying all language, "the time of day that gives one the creeps."

But enough of this nonsense! . . .

It is this very "nonsense" in her correspondence and her conversation that has endeared her to many of her admirers.

Chapter VII

MORTGAGING A FARM FOR MUSIC BY THE PHILADELPHIA ORCHESTRA, 1968-1969

How can I say with bitterness,
"My friend has changed, Love had failed me!"
when I myself
am the most deviable of all phenomena.

. . .

Since you struck the first note of that sonata,
having heard what the music would say to me,
I have passed through all the phases of the Moon
from its faint silver circle above the sunset
to the completion of its jasmine mask,
in all I reach for but may not become.
And my journey is not yet done; for my spirit, driven
by itself, compelled by the music, like a point of light
rotating through the revolving planes of the Four
Dimensions,
swerves through Space in unpredictable parabolas,
rising above all I have ever been,
and I am not now what I was five minutes ago.

I shall return to you from where I have been —
the music was, after all, a hair's breadth digression,
compared with other mutations of being and becoming
through which the spirit must pass. . . .

> But unless you have been where I have been,
> when I return you will not have all of me.
> How then can I make a reproach:
> "My friend is changed. My Love grows cold to me."
> > Lily Peter
> > from "Concert"
> > *The Green Linen of Summer*

When Lily Peter said, "I love music," she did not say it casually. She said it with emotion and solemnity, and music was, to her, a fulfillment of love. The time and energy she gave to bringing about those fleeting moments of perfection are immeasurable. Her appetite for great music was insatiable, and nothing exemplifies it more specifically than her underwriting the costs of bringing to Little Rock, Arkansas, the Philadelphia Orchestra for two performances in June, 1969. It is the event that more readily identifies her than any other.

Preparation for the arrival of the orchestra occupied the major portion of Lily's time and thought for the years 1968 and 1969. Her meticulous planning broadened the range of her farming, her creativity, her public appearances, and her philanthropy. By the end of 1968, Lily had received fourteen letters from Eugene Ormandy, about that number from Norman Dello Joio, and a number from their associates such as Boris Sokoloff, manager of the Philadelphia Orchestra Association, and Felix Greissle, Managing Editor of Marks Music Company. At the same time, such heady correspondence didn't turn Lily away from sixth graders at Helena Elementary School who asked her to read from her epic poem, *The Great Riding*, which she also read to an international audience at HemisFair in San Antonio, Texas, about this time.

She continued to write. In January, she received a check for seventy dollars from *The Delta Review*: forty dollars for an article on DeSoto's journey through Arkansas to appear in its February issue and thirty dollars for a long poem, "Not Even a Rose for Emily." (The latter was never used.) This magazine began its life in 1964 in Greenville, Mississippi, and was bought in 1966 by William King Self of Marks, Mississippi, was moved to Memphis. He had chosen Henry Clay Mitchell to be editor with Sara Kearney and Elliott Jones as assistants. It had an attractive format and increased its subscriptions until a rival magazine appeared on the scene in 1969 supported by the Memphis Chamber of Commerce. The rival so effectively dispersed the sources of revenue from advertising that *The Delta Review* had to suspend publication. The magazine had sought to appeal mainly to readers in four states — Arkansas, Tennessee, Mississippi, and Louisiana — while the Chamber wanted a magazine with a focus on Memphis. The demise of *The Delta Review* was a loss to southern literature because it published the most gifted writers in the four-state area, not the least of whom was Eudora Welty. One edition was devoted entirely to William Faulkner, and another edition included "Faulkner and the Mule," an article by Lily's friend, O. B. Emerson.

Lily was happy to be among *The Delta Review*'s contributors. After Lily's story of DeSoto's journey appeared in the regular feature, "Accent on Arkansas" in February, 1968, the *Review*'s editor, Henry Mitchell, invited Lily to tell what it was like to run a large plantation, and she responded with "An Arkansas Plantation . . . A Poet Runs It," and it appeared in the May 1968 issue. For the November 1968 issue she wrote the copy for "Accent on Arkansas," giving an account of S. D. Warfield, who in 1967 bequeathed to Helena's people, regardless of race or creed, the rare and unprecedented gift of one or more free concerts of classical music a year, in perpetuity. For March 1969 she furnished the magazine with the story of the program entitled "Salute to Arkansas Post" which the Territorial Sesquicentennial Committee had planned for the purpose of launching its activities.

When Dello Joio, Ormandy, and others expressed their natural curiosity about their new patron, Lily not only furnished them with copies of her books of poetry but also sent them copies of *The Delta Review* which contained her articles.

This association with people of stature in the world of music contributed to Lily's life-long dream of making her mark in that world. Further, it contributed to bringing about some of the things she wanted for Arkansas. She wanted Arkansas to have a creditable symphony orchestra and the essential strings programs in the public schools; she wanted to dispel the caricature of Arkansas which had been generated by the late, but unlamented, radio programs, such as Lum and Abner and Bob Burns, and the Arkansas Traveler writings.

Since there was no question in her mind that the ultimate in a musical experience was hearing a polished and refined performance of classical works of music by an outstanding orchestra, she was sure that such an event would provide the impetus that would make her goals become real. In her capacity as chairman of music for the Sesquicentennial, she had the opportunity to move toward these goals, especially if she were able and willing to underwrite the costs.

By this time, Lily was beginning to see the end of the huge indebtedness incurred by the estate taxes and her subsequent purchase of the property inherited by the other heirs to her brother's estate. Therefore, she told the committee that she would pay the bill to bring a full orchestra to Arkansas for the celebration of the Sesquicentennial. Lily imagined a musical event so thrilling that it would touch the hearts of all the men of means and influence in Arkansas, especially those in Little Rock, where the largest concentration of wealth existed.

What would inspire a well-established, prestigious orchestra to come to Little Rock, Arkansas? Lily knew that money was not enough, but she had read that the great orchestras were constantly looking for new compositions of quality to include on a program with traditional classics. To discover such a work, to master it, and to give its premiere performance was considered a worthy feat. All orchestras eagerly embraced opportunities to do so.

That was the answer, thought Lily. She would find a composer, commission a work to honor Arkansas on its territorial anniversary and then invite the orchestra. Unquestionably, the Philadelphia Orchestra was her first choice. It also excited Lily to think that Arkansas would be the first state to have a suite of music composed in its honor. But how could she procure a composer when she had only known one in her lifetime and him only slightly?

This composer was Dr. William Schumann, who was at the Juilliard School of Music when Lily had studied there in 1935. She wrote to him and told him that, because of her pleasant memories of him, she would like to commission him to compose this work, thinking her slight acquaintance with him might be enough to gain his attention. He replied that he would be happy to do it, but that he unfortunately had so many other commissions for the next few years that it would be impossible for him to accept one from her.

Lily was disappointed but not deterred. She certainly knew famous names in composition circles. She was interested in Aaron Copland, but discarded the idea of commissioning him because the works she had heard of his contained some jazz elements, and this she disliked. She did, however, like some contemporary music. Dissonance and atonality, handled as a part of an effectively synthesized whole, did not offend her. She regarded it as fresh and exciting despite its lack of the harmonic richness of the works of the 18th and 19th century composers.

Continuing her search for a composer, she came across a little brochure that contained a list of the Pulitzer Prize winners in music composition since the inception of the awarding of the prize. Aaron Copland was the only one on the list whose music she knew, and since she had already rejected the idea of asking him, she studied the others. She read the titles of the compositions over and over and was attracted to *Meditations on Ecclesiastes* by Norman Dello Joio. This gave her a clue. Anyone who could take the book of Ecclesiastes from the Old Testament and compose from it a Pulitzer Prize winning composition must be a true creative artist. Such a composer would be aware of the terrific ironies in that great philosophical free verse poem and would undoubtedly be capable of conveying a sense of those ironies in sound. Such a one would have to be good.

Lily found out where she could get a recording of this work performed by a Yale University group; she ordered it and played it repeatedly. She felt that Dello Joio had indeed realized in sound something of the spirit of Ecclesiastes. It was pessimistic, but realistic, *verissimo*.

Lily wrote to Dello Joio, telling him what she wished him to do, the reason for it, and the deadline; it would have to be completed in time for performance in 1969. He replied on March 2:

> Thank you for thinking of me as someone who might contribute in some meaningful way to your state's sesquicentennial. I am indeed flattered at your complimentary remarks on my music which makes it hard to resist an immediate acceptance of your offer. However, before I do I ask a question or two. . . .

Dello Joio questioned Lily as to what she would like in such a work. Lily was delighted. She sat down and wrote him a long letter of eight or ten pages, single spaced, setting forth the musical ideas which she wanted embodied in the composition. In this undertaking Lily was again reminded of how she had yearned for an adequate musical education. Had she had the kind she wanted, she, herself, might have been able to compose the suite for the occasion. Lacking that ability, she utilized all her vocabulary to tell Dello Joio what she envisioned in the work.

Dello Joio responded:

> I was delighted at your response to my questions, and I shall be glad to accept your invitation to compose for the Arkansas Sesquicentennial.
>
> To get to my fee, I tend to get paralyzed and have asked my close friend and my publishing editor to propose the size of the commission. He has relieved me of this for several years as a personal favor. I trust you will not mind carrying on negotiations with him.
>
> I might state that my publishers are delighted with the possibilities. . . .

The date of the above letter was March 9. On March 13, Felix Greissle, Editor-in-Chief, Edward B. Marks Music Corporation, wrote to Lily:

> Norman Dello Joio was good enough to let me read your letter, showing such extraordinary understanding of musical matters. As you know, Norman would very much like to write a work of major proportions. You are, therefore, absolutely right in saying that you would have to invite an orchestra like the Philadelphia Orchestra. Knowing Eugene Ormandy for many years, I cannot agree with you that he would turn down your offer because he would not care for going west of the Mississippi. . . . The difficulty lies rather in the fact that the Philadelphia Orchestra is fully booked for several years ahead. However, you should try anyway, especially since Ormandy likes Norman. . . .

Greissle offered the names of other orchestras for consideration in case Ormandy had to reject the engagement. He then discussed the fee. He told Lily that she would have exclusive rights to the premiere of the work, the privilege of giving any number of repeat performances without charge, and that complete performing material, score, and parts, would be at her disposal. Finally he suggested that she offer Dello Joio "the usual fee for a work of this kind by a leading composer, namely, the sum of $8,000."

Lily agreed to the fee, but with some objections. Greissle wrote on March 21:

> Thank you very much for your wonderful letter. First of all let me tell you that I envy you your soybeans and cotton fields. I think I would prefer them to having to see so many conductors, composers and other nervous, jittery people. At any rate, your letters are a most welcome, refreshing and interesting change in my daily routine and I give myself the pleasure of reading them several times. . . .

Greissle provided the addresses of orchestras which Lily had requested and offered to help her in negotiations. In reply to whatever protest Lily had made about the fee, he said:

> . . . I must object to your statement that you will return to your cotton fields, "to be lost in anonymous oblivion." This will not be easily possible because your name will appear on the printed score, etc, etc. As regards the performing rights, this means only that the particular orchestra which plays the work first would have the privilege of repeat performances without charge. All other institutions, orchestra societies and so on will of course have to pay if they wish to perform the work. Consequently neither publisher nor composer would gain from retaining these rights. I wish I could be helpful as regards the commission fee, but this is more a matter of acknowledging the status of a composer so that any reduction would create too difficult a problem. . . .

Boris Sokoloff, Manager of the Philadelphia Orchestra Society, wrote Lily on April 3, "Mr. Ormandy has turned over to me your very interesting letter of March 26, 1968, in which you inquire as to whether or not The Philadelphia Orchestra with Maestro Ormandy would be able. . . ." Lily had directed her letter to Ormandy because she thought it the proper avenue of approach. Sokoloff explained at length the problems involved: the special rehearsal required to present a new work, the time involved in shipping the instruments which would cause some cancellations of performances, that a Little Rock appearance would not coincide with the usual tour. He suggested that two concerts would cost little more than one and made her a price based on two, $45,000.

There continued the exchange of letters through April. At one point Lily canceled her offer, but on June 12, Sokoloff wrote, "I herewith acknowledge with deep appreciation your remittance of $9,000 as a down payment for the appearances. . . . I must tell you that we look forward with a great deal of pleasure to the fact that you have selected The Philadelphia Orchestra to help celebrate the Sesquicentennial of your distinguished state." Throughout the summer Lily had more letters from Sokoloff, and ones from Joseph H. Santarlaschi, Assistant Manager, and Mary Krouse, Mr. Ormandy's secretary. There were many details to attend to. It was September before she heard from Ormandy himself, but she was enjoying her close association with Greissle and Dello Joio. The latter wrote on March 25:

> Thank you for all the material you sent me about yourself. I must confess that corresponding with a woman like yourself is a new experience for me. Aside from your cotton gins and the complexity of keeping cotton and beans behaving, I am amazed at your varied cultural interests. I note that you went to Juilliard — I did too, for a spell. . . .

He wrote on April 3:

> Thank you so much for sending me your poetry which I have dipped into and am enjoying. I am taken with the lyric quality in your work. May I have your permission to set "Note Left on a Doorstep" to music? I think this poem most apt as a song. . . .
>
> Forgive me if I am a tardy correspondent at this time as I am deeply involved with the rehearsals of a new ballet I have completed for Martha Graham to be premiered here in New York in May. The subject is Heloise and Abelard. . . .

Greissle wrote on April 25:

> Now in turn you have made *me* the happiest man. I am sure everything will come off fine and what you have done for Arkansas will be one of the biggest events in the history of the state. . . .
>
> I enjoyed the magazines very much. . . .

He wrote on July 25:

> Thank you for your letter of July 20, 1968, and above all for the records which arrived yesterday. I had no idea that you were related to this best American composer of the 18th Century. I only knew some of his anthems and the records were very welcome. I spent the whole evening listening to them and was most amazed by the powerful invention and perfect "professionalism" of your great-great uncle. I am now really curious to see your songs and hope they will arrive soon. As soon as I have seen them, I will write again immediately. . . .

On August 8:

> Please forgive my delayed reply, but this is the time of the year that I have to visit music festivals and I am in and out of the

office. (By the way, I may see Mr. Ormandy tomorrow).

As to your songs, I really liked them. Could you let me have the ones to which you wrote the accompaniment yourself? The reason is, we do not like to publish works that have two authors and I am seriously considering a couple if it could bear only your name. . . .

On August 20:

Thank you very much for your delightful, long letter and the newspaper clipping.

In regard to your songs, please take your time. There is no rush and as soon as the accompaniments are in, we will send you an agreement. I would suggest that you pick about four songs of your own choice and send the first two when the accompaniments are finished. It is quite possible that these might be the ones we select for publication. However, I hope you won't take it too badly if I would like to see the third and fourth ones too before making a final decision.

I am going on vacation today and will be back by the middle of September. . . .

Lily still suffered much discomfort as a result of her 1966 accident; further, she had to wear wigs because her head had been shaved, and the hair had not yet grown out. There was much scar tissue on her scalp. She disliked the wigs. Nevertheless, Lily carried out an all-day-and-half-the-night schedule. There was an increase in the number of invitations to appear on programs. She considered it an honor that she was invited to a Conference on the Arts called by Texas Governor Tom Connally to be held at Dallas in early April, 1968. It was for the purpose of shaping the program of the Texas Pavilion at Hemisfair in June. Lily went to Dallas and contributed to the planning by offering awards of $200 and $50 "for the best poems on the confluence of civilization in the Americas," the theme of the exposition. And she attended

Hemisfair, appearing on the program as a reader of her own and other works on four different days.

She and Brooks Griffin had formed a corporation for land investment and had bought a large ranch near Hugo, Oklahoma, which held out productive possibilities; Lily found herself hopping over to Oklahoma with Brooks in his airplane. She loved it in good weather, hated it in turbulence. Brooks would often drive back and forth during the night, and Lily was concerned that exhaustion or speed or both would cause him death or injury. They eventually disposed of the ranch for that reason, but it was an interesting new adventure for her.

That year, Lily and Jeff Carr (then assistant to the chancellor of Vanderbilt, now Vice Chancellor and Legal Counsel) developed a congenial relationship based on their mutual interest in photography. He came to the area to interview her and make pictures for an article in the Vanderbilt publication, *Alumnus*. She speeded up her pace of making pictures, and the letters and photographs went back and forth through the mail.

Most of Lily's friends have observed that she was attracted to handsome, intelligent young men like Jeff Carr, as well as beautiful young women. Of course, this is not to say that Lily surrounded herself with beautiful people; her ego seemed to be entirely dispensable when she encountered someone interesting. She became intensely absorbed by their world and was often an attentive listener.

Besides being the festival poet, Lily was asked to give a one-person show of her photography at the Grand Prairie Festival of the Arts at Stuttgart that fall, and similar invitations followed so that she had some twenty odd one-man shows from the Arts Center in Little Rock to the Art Gallery at Vanderbilt University and the Fine Arts Center in Winston-Salem, North Carolina.

It was one of Mother Nature's more whimsical years. The cut worms invaded the area, and the cotton crop had to be replanted. It was such a wet fall that Lily sold the cotton in the field, a thing that assured lower prices, yet she was glad that she had done so when it continued to rain through October. Once a tornado had skipped and hopped across her home place close enough to frighten her and cause thousands of dollars worth of damage.

On June 2, "Red" Wilkerson, her bookkeeper, left her a birthday card and affixed the following typewritten message:

> Wishing you many happy returns of the day. May you continue to maintain your excellent health. Sincerely hoping that you will accomplish all of the many goals, which you have outlined. With vitality which you possess, no mountain can stand in your way.[1]

As if Lily did not have enough to do, she decided this year that she would fill in as a bookkeeper at the Elaine Implement Company. The main bookkeeper had resigned early in the year. By July 11, she was able to write in her log:

> To Elaine to help with the books — spent the time posting our June bills, balancing out the journal, taking out-dated pages from our price book for parts and inserting pages for present prices — Revision 46.
>
> To date I've been driven down to Elaine 51 days this spring and summer to help with the bookkeeping, and I have enjoyed it very much and have learned a tremendous lot, most of which I should have learned years ago, but glad I'm learning now.

Lily continued doing this task until November. Sometimes the payroll would have to be brought to her to sign. It was her first involvement with double-entry bookkeeping, and the struggles with balancing were sometimes amusing and sometimes maddening. She often noted in her log what she wore to the office; one notation, for example, is "wore the pale pink whipped-cream crepe."

She watched the proceedings of the Big Creek Drainage District out of the corner of her eye. One gratifying note of the year was that at one hearing, Judge Elmore Taylor ruled out the channelization of the tributaries of Big Creek: Big and Little Cypress Bayous and Coffey Creek. All three were near Lily's home.

The Sesquicentennial Committee was meeting regularly. Dr. John Ferguson (executive secretary of the state history commission), observed that it was Lily, Agnes Lower, David Perdue, Dr. Boyce Drummond (chairman), and himself who met every time and that Lily was the most hard working of them all. He also said that it was she who maintained the highest level of vision and enthusiasm and, therefore, inspired them all.[2] The committee was eager to share its plans with the people of the state, so, in August, the chairman called a press conference. Because of this publicity, Lily's mail doubled. An example is the following letter written to her by Aleta Jessup on August 8, 1968:

> Dear Lily, How could one ever imagine a more queenly bestowal on a beloved commonwealth than that revealed in the enclosure? Truly "man does not live by bread alone," but by "whatsoever things that are lovely" — I'm sure I am only one of thousands who feel deeply grateful to you for your royal gift to your state — a priceless incomparable gift. I shall be among those. . . .

There were many like the above, but there were other kinds too. Some wanted to appear with Mr. Ormandy in one way or another. Compositions were sent to her for examination. Letters came from people wanting to play instruments all the way from small parts to concertos, from the saxophone to the pipe organ. There were all types of offers to help, some genuine, some exploitative, but all needing some response.

But no letters made Lily happier than those from Dello Joio
and Ormandy.

The former wrote on September 13:

> . . . It does not seem possible that the summer is over. . . . I
> am taking up our project now. Some time ago, I wrote a little
> work for winds on a lovely tune of Haydn's. I want to now use
> that tune again for a totally new examination of what its real
> potential offers, and what I now know can be a major creation
> as different from the unfulfilled feeling I am left with about
> my initial attempt. The "Meditations on Ecclesiastes" which
> you know was also the result of a past attempt on a Gregorian
> melody that initially in my opinion failed. I feel as satisfied
> with it now (as one can be) as with anything I have done, and
> the fact that it won a Pulitzer for Music would seem to affirm
> my feelings about it. It takes some effort for a composer to be
> objective about his work but I find that as I mature this be-
> comes a demand.
>
> I shall be sending you shortly a little song set to one of your
> poems which I was so taken with. It will be published but
> shall need your permission. Publishers are that way. . . .

Lily was excited and eager to see the song, and she couldn't
have been more pleased that he was going to take a theme from
Haydn as a basis for the commissioned work. She readily con-
nected Haydn to the early settlement of this country and remem-
bered that her great, great Uncle John Frederick had hand-copied
and brought to America scores of Haydn's works. Dello Joio
wrote later in the month (September 29):

> Thank you for all the clippings and programs you sent. I am
> amazed at the scope of your interests and activities. You make
> me feel positively lazy.
>
> You may have received the original manuscript by this time
> of my setting of your "Note Left on a Doorstep." I do hope you

will not take amiss a couple of word changes I felt musically necessary from a rhythmic standpoint. If you find what I have done objectionable, do not hesitate to suggest alternatives, since it is going to the printer soon.

Our project I think is going well.

Lily had just received her first letter from Eugene Ormandy, parts of which follow:

When your letter arrived some months ago I automatically turned it over to our Manager, Mr. Boris Sokoloff, who handles such matters. At the time he informed me of his very pleasant correspondence with you, and also of your desire to have a work by Dello Joio given its world premiere. I gladly accepted it.

Since that time I have been away from Philadelphia and I just returned to open our new season, so before we get into the hustle and bustle too deeply, I want to first thank you for your warm letter and, secondly, to tell you that it will be a great pleasure for our orchestra and me to be a part of the Arkansas Sesquicentennial on June 3rd and 4th and we look forward to it with happy anticipation. . . . (September 26)

Ormandy continued his letter with a proposed program which included, besides the Dello Joio work, Wagner, Beethoven's 7th Symphony, and Mahler's 1st. He closed, telling her that he was looking forward to meeting her personally. On the same date, Sokoloff wrote Lily and said:

I want to take the opportunity to thank you very much for your detailed and heartwarming letter of September 22. . . .

I noted with great interest your photography show and I would just love to see it myself. In fact, what I was wondering is whether or not when we are out there in Arkansas in June whether it might be possible to have some of these pictures

216

exhibited in Little Rock as I know several members of the Orchestra are amateur photographers and I am sure they would be most interested in seeing these pictures of yours. . . .

Without a doubt, in giving these people information about herself which they asked for, Lily proffered her songs, poetry, photography, and news of her activities, and hoped for approbation; but these responses were thrilling beyond measure. All it took to accommodate Sokoloff's suggestion of a Little Rock exhibit for the photography was her telling Townsend Wolfe, Director of the Arkansas Art Center. He immediately scheduled it to be displayed for a period which included the dates of the orchestra's concerts. What about the song? Lily ever so delicately mentioned its inclusion on at least one of the programs, but neither Dello Joio or Ormandy agreed to it. Dello Joio wrote on October 22:

> Thank you for the lovely photos of the places and people that keep you so busy. There is something so impressive about the scope of what your plantation covers, and despite this, I do gather that your interests go so far beyond the land itself. To a native N. Y. boy it is indeed far removed from my own life.
>
> I am glad that you like the song. When you wrote of hearing it done, did you mean at one of the orchestra's concerts or simply a solo recital? If the former I do not feel that a soloist with piano would be wise at this kind of concert. If the latter, I would be happy to suggest names that would fill the bill. If you wished someone to do a full recital of varied repertoire, I might suggest our song at which time I would be glad to accompany the singer in any thing of mine.
>
> I have listened to the album and enjoyed it. I so envy the comfort that men of bygone day must have had in their work. We of today, engulfed in complexity might do well to try and recapture the simplicity of the spirit manifest in the work of men like your ancestor. . . .

Finally, the work for you is finished. It is entitled "Homage to Haydn."

Ormandy had not had time to hear from Lily by the time he wrote his next letter (October 11). In it, he told of having had a personal visit from Greissle, who brought the album of the Peter Quintets. He said:

> . . . Until then I had no idea that you were related to him, or that you, yourself, are also composing. . . .
>
> Would you please let me know if you would be interested in having us play your ancestor's quintet, enlarged for a full string orchestra? I am willing to obtain the score of the one I consider the most effective for a large string body such as ours and then I would probably arrange it for string orchestra myself (although Mr. Greissle offered to do it). If you are interested in it it would make a good opener for the second program and we would take out the "Meistersinger" Overture. . . .
>
> Could you send me a diagram of your concert hall and your stage set, and let me know the seating capacity of your hall? The size of the stage and the acoustical shell are of great importance to us. . . .

Soon after Ormandy had heard from Lily, he replied on October 21:

> . . . First of all, I will be delighted to play the Dello Joio Suite at both concerts. Secondly, I also will be very happy to perform one of John Frederick Peter's quintets at one of the concerts. Mr. Greissle tells me that it is very difficult to obtain these scores, so I will have to await the receipt of one of them from him. . . .
>
> If we play the John Frederick Peter quintet, I wonder if we should also have a singer at one of these concerts. This breaks up the architecture of the program, and since Mr. Dello Joio is the composer it may take something away from the success

of his Suite. Don't you agree? Naturally, we will have to completely revise the programs and as soon as I know the exact length of the Dello Joio piece, and receive whatever quintet score is available, I will be in a better position to balance the programs, so this will have to wait for a little while. Please forget any fee for me for arranging the quintet for string orchestra.

My wife is a great lover of poetry and, being Viennese, she has famous poems in three different languages in our library. She will be happy to receive your two books, but being in the process of moving to a larger apartment and buying new furniture she will have to wait until our vacation period in February to read them. . . .

Will you forgive my wife if she doesn't answer your most kind letter personally? As I said, she is extremely busy these days but she thanks you very much for your kindness.

Lily did agree or certainly did acquiesce gracefully because nothing more is noted about the song's appearance on the concerts' programs. Dello Joio said in a November letter that he would be happy to suggest that "our song be done at the University of Arkansas though I think this will be contingent on whether a solo song recital is part of the planning for my stay." He was scheduled for an appearance at the university the following April. Lily had asked Dello Joio if he wished his fee immediately or after the first of the year (her preference), so she was not surprised when he concluded the letter with a request for a check before the year was out. He said, ". . . I seem to be perpetually hounded by bills — what with 3 children in private schools who also like steak for breakfast." Lily sent the check, and he acknowledged it and told of a friend of his who wanted to do a human interest story on Lily and the Arkansas celebration, but the story never came about.

Lily had no more long letters from Ormandy until after the

concerts; the remaining details were attended to by either Sokoloff or Krouse, Ormandy's secretary. The year 1968, a difficult and strenuous one in many respects, came to a close. Her sisters came home. She spent Christmas Eve with the Frank Griffins and Christmas Day with niece Marjorie and family, a practice that had become a tradition for her. But her most tantalizing fantasy for the new year was the vision of her association with the world's finest musicians. She meditated on this happening and speculated on the possibility that her great uncle John Frederick and Franz Joseph Haydn, himself, somewhere out in the far reaches of the universe, might be having a conversation such as the following:

JFP: Have you heard the latest? A great, great niece of mine has commissioned a suite of music to be performed at the Arkansas Territorial Sesquicentennial Celebration, and it is to be named "Homage to Haydn."

FJH: Well, I'll declare. That's almost as surprising as my symphony. How do you suppose it happened? I never heard of Arkansas.

JFP: It seems that she was music chairman for the occasion and wanted to have the best music possible, and this composer chap had won a notable prize. When he accepted her commission, he told her he had done a small work on one of your themes which did not satisfy him and suggested that he would like to re-work it for the symphony. That pleased her because she loved your music, and mine, and thought using one of your themes would tie our tradition to the modern day.

FJH: You a composer too? Oh yes, you're the Moravian minister who migrated to the new world — even carried some of my scores. I suppose Arkansas is somewhere over there.

JFP: I'm sure it is, although I certainly did not know there was such a place in my lifetime. It seems this niece of mine is a farmer who loves music enough to pay for the com-

position and the Philadelphia Orchestra. Philadelphia I
certainly know about. It was a thriving city, home of the
founders of the United States. And the conductor is or-
chestrating one of my quintets for the occasion. I feel
pretty good about appearing on the same program with
a tribute to you. I'm proud of that niece of mine.

FJH: Well, young man, I certainly won't mind the association.
After all, all that hand-copying of my compositions
when you were in London, supposedly on a holiday. I'd
feel it would be safe to say that that niece of yours is a
lady we'd enjoy knowing. Funny the turns of immortal-
ity!

It occurred to Lily that if such far-reaching speculation
seemed egotistically grandiose, one had only to remember the gal-
axies beyond galaxies and the millions and billions of atoms in
the universe, to say nothing of the speed of light and Einstein's
$E=mc^2$. That recollection would always serve to place one's own
little bundle of energy in the proper perspective.[3]

The Sesquicentennial Committee had decided that three
months would be enough time to give adequate publicity to the
Philadelphia Orchestra concerts, so they called a press conference
in March to give the public more details. Lily had considered hir-
ing someone for the publicity, but decided against it, feeling she
could handle it and save the money. She set about writing the
many releases she thought would be necessary to attract every
shred of attention possible to make the event a success. Many said,
even members of the committee, that she would never get more
than two hundred people in the auditorium. Many thought she had
lost her mind.

Lily planned to give the lion's share of the publicity to the
two state papers in Little Rock, the *Arkansas Gazette* and the *Ar-
kansas Democrat*. Between them, nearly everyone in the state
would be reached. The editors of the *Democrat* agreed to carry

any articles Lily sent them every week in its Sunday recreational section. The editors of the *Gazette* chose to print one full report after the press conference and print no more until the week prior to the concerts, at which time they would publish something every day.

The Philadelphia Orchestra management had sent Lily a huge press book with many pictures, both of the whole orchestra and individual members of it, but Lily thought the material should be rewritten and localized as nearly as possible. She found it very useful; in fact, she couldn't have done without it; however, the rewriting took hours and hours of her time, not counting the preparation of mailing lists and the actual mailing.

Lily kept the weekly articles going to the *Democrat*. In addition, she decided that she wanted the county papers to have material. She got an old press book from the *Helena World* which contained the names of all the papers in the state and their editors. Then there were sixty-five daily papers and one hundred thirty-odd weeklies. The same article which she wrote for the *Democrat* each week, she amended or revised and sent to those papers. She chose every variety of approach imaginable, long and short, general and specific, to make her articles as interesting as possible and appeal to as many readers as possible. She had them mimeographed, but she worked late many a night. She admits that she was handling this publicity on the basis of near ignorance other than the use of common sense. She did not know that she could have sent one article to a central bureau to be sent to all the state papers.

She had some amusing responses from some of the papers, for example, "I would have been glad to use your article but my readers would not know anything about a symphony orchestra," and "Received your article. Would have been glad to use it last week but do not have room this week," and ". . . just what is a symphony orchestra? Is it not just another kind of band?" One editor said he couldn't run the article because he had to run the pictures of the members of the graduating class of the local high school. She could not believe that the parents and students would not have been just as happy if the pictures were published the next week.

However, rural newspaper editors know they can't survive without photos of their readers, and Lily's news of the Philadelphia Orchestra always had to compete with photos of someone who had brought in the most beavers for bounty or a farmer standing by his first cotton bloom or similar subjects.

However, the news did get distributed over the state, and Lily felt good about the money she saved in this way which would have had to be taken out of the money from ticket sales. She had another idea for this income. She planned to give it to the music departments of the state universities for scholarships.

Out of Lily's efforts as publicity director came one single incident that did more to fill the auditorium than any other factor, and it never could have been dreamed up by the most clever of publicity agents. Lily was sure that the powers of the universe were on her side in the outcome. The first week in May prior to the concerts in June, Lily received a phone call from a young newspaper reporter on the staff of the *Pine Bluff Commercial*. Neither of them had any knowledge of the other before this. Harry Pearson called and asked her if it were true that she was underwriting the cost of bringing the Philadelphia Orchestra to Arkansas. Her first rejoinder was that she had been sending articles to his paper for some time, and she asked if they had been received. He disclaimed seeing them and continued his questioning. He seemed to have an unusual knowledge of music, declaring that her providing the orchestra was a beautiful thing to do, that he was excited to know that he was going to have the chance to hear the orchestra. They chatted a good while because there was nothing Lily liked better than to talk about music to someone knowledgeable on the topic.

She was unaware that he was getting an interview. She regarded it as his being pleasant and sociable in the process of finding out where to go for a news story.

Then all at once, like a bolt out of the blue, this young man whom Lily had never seen or heard of before asked her how old she was. As quick as a flash, she thought that any young man who would ask the age of a lady he didn't know deserved any answer he might get, and she came back with the statement, "Oh, I'm nearly one hundred years old." He said, "You can't be that old." She responded, "Oh, yes, I am, and all my friends here think I'm a lot older than that, I've been here so long." At this point Harry Pearson hung up the phone. (Harry Pearson writes that this is "absolutely not true," in a letter to the writer dated September 1, 1981. This is how he explained the circumstances: "We talked on until I was facing deadline. I knew the story I had and was determined to get it in that day's paper. Scooping the *Gazette*, whose Bill Lewis had completely missed the real thrust of the story [her mortgaging her farm to give the state a birthday present of the Philadelphia Orchestra], was the reason I hurried off the phone. . . .")

Lily was more concerned that he was so angry that he would not give the concerts any publicity than that he was rude to her. She reprimanded herself for committing the *faux pas* of giving him a "smart alecky" answer. She felt that he deserved what he got, but was glad when he called her the next day and asked if he might come to her home on Sunday for an interview which, according to Pearson, was already scheduled to run in the Sunday Pine Bluff paper and which was later also run in the *Washington Post*. Of course, Lily gave him permission and directions to her house. Despite them, Lily says he got lost and was late, while Pearson, who claims he would be "shocked" at anything less than "professional courtesy," wrote to the biographer that he never got lost and furthermore says, "I was early."

But Lily says he finally found the turquoise gin and arrived.

She found him to be a personable young man, and they had the following exchange:

"Have you planted any cotton yet?"

"Oh, yes, my cotton is all up and it's up to a beautiful stand in this field across the road."

"Let's go down to the field and look at it."

"Oh, Mr. Pearson, it's raining and we will certainly get wet."

"That won't make any difference to me if it won't to you. Let's go and look at the cotton."

Lily thought to herself that any fisherman who minded getting wet when he's catching a fish was indeed no fisherman, so she replied, "Okay, we'll go right on."

So they walked out in the rain (Pearson says it was "misting), bareheaded across the road to the field of cotton. He asked her to walk a little bit ahead of him, and Lily says she did so not realizing that he was taking pictures of her. She says she did not find out until a whole week later when a picture of her in that cotton field appeared on the music page of the *Washington Post*. (Pearson maintains that the photograph used by the *Post* speaks for itself. He says, ". . . you'll see her there, big as life, staring directly at the camera." Lily might retort that she wouldn't want to be known as foolish enough to turn her back on free publicity.)

After walking in the cotton field, Lily and Pearson came back to the house and continued visiting, disregarding damp clothing, until supper time. Lily offered him supper. She could always put together a meal of sorts on short notice. It might be peanut butter and crackers or "beany-weenies," but it would suffice. Pearson accepted and stayed until 10:00 p.m. It was six hours of conversation. Although Pearson denies it, Lily says he asked if she had any pictures of herself at farming operations. She did not have many because she was usually the one making pictures of people farming for her, a thing she loved to do. But she ransacked her house and found the picture of herself made by a Memphis photographer at the 1965 opening of the Elaine Implement Company — the one on the big tractor with her in a seemingly long dress and a corsage at her shoulder as big as a tea-plate. Pearson asked to take it, and she assented.

After that pleasant time with Harry Pearson, Lily, in her "busy-ness," thought nothing more about him. She had not even asked him what paper up East he was writing for.

The following week she had to make several trips to Little Rock to see about the radio and television coverage. Many of the stations in Little Rock give publicity free; but Lily says that some stations charged for it and that she paid them. (Harry Pearson, however, maintains that "Nobody does this: she was big news then.") Lily says she always offered to pay the stations in any event.

The next week she had to make trips to Little Rock on both Monday and Tuesday. She returned home so late the first day that she didn't see anyone, but the first thing the next morning, Helen Copeland, the store clerk, greeted her with the news that she had received calls from people from all over the United States. Since those calling had not left messages and she had to get back to the city, she did nothing about the calls. Wednesday morning, Helen told Lily that the phone had rung all day Tuesday.

While at the store that Wednesday morning, she had another call. It was from the publicity and public relations director for the Philadelphia Orchestra, Wayne Shilkret, with whom Lily talked several times but never got to see because he was sent to Atlanta on orchestra business when the group came to Little Rock. Shilkret told Lily that she could now consider herself famous all up and down the East coast, that she had managed to do something that the orchestra had never been able to do: get the news of its appearances on the front page of the *Philadelphia Bulletin*. Lily thought he was teasing because he had shown a sense of humor in previous conversations, so she teased in return. But he finally convinced her that he was serious, that there had been an Associated Press release which had been picked up by many Eastern papers, and that all connected with the orchestra were excited about the large amount of publicity. He promised to send her copies of all the papers he could find. He read some copy to her; one began, "An elderly spinster who says she is nearly one hundred years old has mortgaged one of her farms. . . ." She recognized that this was the writing of Harry Pearson.

Pearson's article "Miss Lily: Mortgaging the Farm for Music," appeared on page L7 of *The Washington Post* on Sunday, May 18, 1969. Excerpts from it follow:

> MARVELL, ARK. — She lives alone in an inelegant white frame house beside a dusty Delta dirt road, about eight miles from nowhere.
>
> To find it, the woman who is bringing the Philadelphia Orchestra to Arkansas will probably tell you: "Look for the turn-off just west of my cotton gin. You cannot miss my cotton gin. It is the only turquoise cotton gin in the state of Arkansas."
> Her name is Lily Peter and she will never again see 70. And if you could not find that turquoise cotton gin at first (and chances are you wouldn't), then she would say, "Enjoy yourself until you do."
>
> Watch the slow gathering beauty of a dark summer storm rolling across the forever flatlands, the still bayous. Or listen to the song of the summer tanager; or get out of your car and pick the burr marigolds which swathe the roadsides.
>
> When you do find that humble white house in a grove of oak trees, next to her desolate-looking plantation store, you will find Miss Lily uncertain and a-quiver and already talking, the words pouring over each other and out like raindrops rolling off a tin roof.
>
> In the first few minutes, she has offered you cool cider, fudge cake, ice cream and "Co-cola," and she has imparted to you

that a goldfinch is nesting in the panel of her go-to-town truck and that she has a woodpecker who, after living near her front door for six years, now talks to her each time he spies her out tending the day lilies.

Miss Lily has just put a mortgage on her plantation near Ratio, Ark., to bring the Philadelphia Orchestra to Little Rock for two concerts, June 3 and 4.

Bringing the Philadelphia to Arkansas for these concerts commemorating the state's Sesquicentennial is costing her $45,000, not one penny of which she will recover.

There is an admission charge for the concert — $5 top — but the money will go to set up scholarships for the music departments at the University of Arkansas in Fayetteville and Arkansas State University at Jonesboro.

"I don't have that much cash just lying around," Miss Lily says, "nor the sort of financial assets which can be easily converted to cash; and so I went to the people at Equitable Life Insurance and put a mortgage on my farm."

Furthermore, she wrote to Norman Dello Joio last year — in her official role as music chairman for the Sesquicentennial — and commissioned him to do a piece in honor of the occasion.

That cost her $8,000. And that isn't all. She is paying the publicity costs, including the cost of newspaper advertising all over Arkansas.

How is she going to repay the loan?

"I guess," she says, "I'll just have to hoe more soybeans and chop more cotton. You'd be surprised at what a good cotton chopper I am."

Of her parents' five children, only Miss Lily and her brother Jesse cared about the land. Since Jesse died 13 years ago, Miss Lily has been solely responsible for 8000 acres of the richest soybean and cotton land in the Delta plains.

And she made it make a profit — as she, like the other farmers in the Delta country, phased out the share-croppers and the old way of life and phased in automation. . . .

Pearson told that she wrote poetry and quoted "The Green Linen of Summer" in full. He continued with the account of her contacting Dello Joio and the Philadelphia and her telling him how much she longed to be a violinist. He closed his article with the paragraph quoting Lily.

> "That's why I am bringing the Philadelphia — because I want the people of Arkansas to be exposed to good music, to have a chance I didn't have."

Perhaps due to Pearson's youth and perhaps because Lily felt it was such an accomplishment, she believed that Pearson had gone back to Pine Bluff and written an article for the *Commercial* and put it on the desk of his editor, Paul Greenberg, who liked the article and suggested that he put it on the AP wire. Lily thought it was Greenberg's reputation as a Pulitzer prize-winning editor, as well as Pearson's capable writing, which made the AP pay attention to the article. (Pearson writes: "This is a serious misconception. I was sufficiently powerful in Pine Bluff to get the story on the front page and on the AP wire. If anyone got behind the story other than me at that point, it was Gene Foreman [originally from Helena] who is now managing editor of the *Philadelphia Inquirer.* . . .)[4] Lily eventually learned that the article had appeared in thirty-seven states.

Pearson wrote this biographer on September 1, 1981:

> . . . It is essential that you understand what happened. The Associated Press picked up my story and ran it big across the state. That put the other newshounds on the trail. It was The Associated Press that asked for — and got — the picture of her [Lily] on a tractor. I used no photographs of Miss Lily until I used my own (I'm an expert photographer and wouldn't think of using anybody else's work). That AP story went out across the nation, thus alerting TV and the national media that some-

thing was afoot in Arkansas. Yes, I did start it and it was heaven-sent. . . .

Pearson is capable in his field and knowledgeable in many other fields (and personally charming), yet it is interesting to note that his longer, sensitive story which appeared in the *Pine Bluff Commercial* on Sunday, May 11, 1969, (page 25) was illustrated only with the photograph of Lily on the big tractor taken at the opening of the Elaine Implement Company, an early sixties photo of Lily standing by a bale of cotton, and "one of Miss Lily's photographs of the cypress bayous of East Arkansas" (the cutline).

Television stations all over the nation called Lily asking for interviews, but she accepted none except those in Little Rock because of time. The editor of the *National Observer* called her for a half-hour phone interview, asked her many questions, but not once mentioned her driving tractors. When his article appeared, it stated, ". . . and she frequently drives a tractor wearing a long white gown." Most included the question of her age. Lily heard of many arguments about the matter, but she would never tell her age and had lots of fun on that topic. Most important to her was that ticket sales to Robinson Auditorium shot up dramatically.

Lily envisioned more benefits from the Philadelphia Orchestra concerts and cast about for ways to achieve them. She wanted as many people as possible to become truly interested in a symphony orchestra for Arkansas; she wanted Dello Joio, Ormandy, the orchestra members, the press corps, and anyone else coming for the celebration to take home with them a fine impression of Arkansas and its people. She must see that they had a good time. She wrote Sokoloff and told him to tell the players in the orchestra that provisions would be made for them to enjoy their recreational interests and that they should bring with them whatever personal gear they required, such as fishing tackle, golf clubs, or tennis rackets. Still she wanted some one occasion which all would enjoy and settled on a dinner in the best facility available with the best food available. At the time, this meant the Little Rock Country Club. How could she accomplish this when she thought she must have a man to host the dinner? She had no husband, and she knew few men in Little Rock.

She went to the Mayor of Little Rock, Mr. Haco Boyd. She told him what she would like and that since he was the highest official in the city, he would be the appropriate host for the dinner. He declined because of poor health. He suggested that the Little Rock Chamber of Commerce would help. This suited Lily because it would involve so many men who held positions of leadership and influence, so she said, "Oh, Mr. Boyd, that would be wonderful. But I have to tell you, I do not know a single member of the Chamber personally. How would I possibly approach the matter?" Boyd reached Bill Walters, president of the Chamber of Commerce, and introduced Lily to him by telephone. She left Boyd with the assurance that she wanted him to be an honored guest at the dinner if he were able to attend.

When Lily met with Walters, he caught her contagious enthusiasm, and it was not hard to persuade the chamber members to adopt the project. They organized committees for all phases of the dinner and the varied sports, such as golfing, fishing, tennis. The Monday night closing policy of the Little Rock Country Club was perfect for the dinner since the concerts were on Tuesday and Wednesday nights. Lily thought that magnolia blossoms would be an appropriate decoration for the dining room and even wrote to Sokoloff to ask if any members of the orchestra were allergic to them. None were, so the dining room was made into a bower of magnolia blossoms by Lily's friends in Little Rock.

On Sunday before the concerts, Lily's color photography show opened at the Art Center. A tea was given at which Benny Selman (piano teacher, UALR) played selections including *Pic-*

tures at an Exhibition by Moussorgsky. Benny and Lynnah Selman were Lily's hosts during her stay in Little Rock.

To add to the festivity and significance of those days and to show that the state of Arkansas could respond to such an undertaking, Governor Winthrop Rockefeller declared Tuesday, June 3, Lily Peter Day. Because of a Republican Governor's Conference in New Orleans, the governor could not attend the concerts or the dinner; however, Lieutenant Governor "Footsie" Britt delivered the proclamation to Lily at the intermission of the concert on Tuesday night. Jeanette Rockefeller and some out-of-town guests were there; when Lily learned Mrs. Rockefeller had guests, she provided them with tickets.

Eugene Ormandy and the orchestra arrived by plane Monday afternoon. Mayor Haco Boyd was there to meet them along with Chamber of Commerce officials. Carrick Patterson wrote for the *Arkansas Gazette*: "Ormandy accepted an honorary citizenship certificate and the key to the city from Mayor Boyd but seemed most excited at meeting Miss Peter for the first time. 'I thought you would be taller,' he commented. Miss Peter is about 5 feet, 4 inches tall, and Ormandy is slightly shorter." Patterson quoted Ormandy (who also spoke to the press in his room at the Albert Pike later in the afternoon) as having said that being in Little Rock was a wonderful experience, that he was impressed with Dello Joio's composition, that he was delighted with the J. F. Peter quintet. He said, "Miss Peter is a new lady in my life, but very close to my heart already."[5]

Lily said that in one conversation with Ormandy, she told him about the many countries of Europe represented on her family tree, including Kristoff Paus, the "one Hungarian," and he immediately replied, "Then we're kin. Everybody in and from Hungary is kin to everybody else in and from Hungary." He said this with enough enthusiasm that she felt he was enjoying possible kinship with her.

At the Monday night dinner, there was no formal program *per se*. Walters, the chamber president, was master of ceremonies. He introduced some guests. He called on Ormandy for a few words, and Judge Mackey conferred upon him the order of Count Pulaski. Lily was also called upon and given the same honor by being made Countess Pulaski. She said, "All my life I've dreamed of how wonderful it would be to be a countess, but I never had a chance at all to marry a count, and here I have become Countess Pulaski anyway!" Walters introduced the men in charge of each recreational activity so the orchestra men would know them. Afterward they met together and made plans for their day of recreation Wednesday.

Lily felt that the dinner was a complete success. Although it was an *ex officio* affair with a select list of guests, there were nearly two hundred people there, filling the large room to capacity. It cost her around $2,000, but she thought it worth every penny. The men who served as hosts felt important because they had such enthusiastic guests; the guests felt important because it was obvious that their pleasure was being considered.

On Tuesday morning, the orchestra rehearsed for three hours. Lily was present and reveled in it. On Tuesday afternoon, a garden party was given for the orchestra at the D. D. Terry mansion in the Quapaw Quarter hosted by the orchestra guild of the Arkansas Symphony. On Tuesday night, there was a dinner at Trapnall Hall for the Arkansas Commemorative Commission, the Sesquicentennial Commission, and Territorial Restoration Commission, and guests. It was indeed a full day, but Wednesday was left free except for the final concert and the individual recreation.

The committee's provision for fishing recreation for orchestra members produced an amusing incident. Dick Elwood from the First National Bank was the contact man. Determined to make sure that the one musician who wanted to go fishing could go back

Lily and Eugene Ormandy tête-à-tête at the Tuesday rehearsal

to Philadelphia with fish stories to tell, Elwood tried to locate a professional fishing guide, but had no luck. He found someone who had a large pleasure boat for rent which would accommodate twenty-five or thirty people. The boat was equipped for fishing, and other water sports. He rented it for the whole day. That evening Elwood called the member who wanted to go fishing, described the boat, telling him he could invite others. On Wednesday morning, Elwood discovered that his "fishing party" had grown to twenty-six men. They spent the day on the Arkansas River, swimming, lounging, and fishing. All of them came in with glowing sunburns. But so did the golf and tennis players and the group who went canoeing.

There was one thing which Lily did not think of in advance. Soon after the orchestra arrived, the men in the woodwind section wanted to know where they could find the Arkansas whetstones which they used to sharpen their knives for trimming the reeds for their instruments. When they found that they came from Hot Springs and that it was only a comparatively short distance, they wanted to go there and visit the quarries. Craig Hines, UPI reporter, volunteered to provide three cars for the trip. He notified the quarry people, and when the party got there, they were received with much courtesy and given all sorts and sizes of whetstones free of charge, enough to last the next hundred years.

The two state newspapers in Little Rock gave the occasion the sort of complete coverage that it deserved: careful and appreciative. Each had adequate advance notice as well as full and interesting feature articles. Early on, the *Gazette* saw fit to editorialize about it when it looked as if there might be an embarrassing attendance. "We should mind our manners" was the heading of the last paragraph on the editorial column which said:

> In view of the fact that we quite regularly turn out 40,000 persons to see a football game and 3,000 for a wrestling match, it will be something of an indictment of Arkansas if we fail to fill up Robinson Auditorium June 3 and 4 to hear what is one of the world's greatest orchestras. . . . This appearance is a real treat for most of us, because this orchestra does not regularly go on tour. And if it did we would have to pay $8 to $10 a seat to hear it. But in Little Rock, seats are available for $5, $4, and $3. This is because Miss Lily Peter, an eastern Arkansas woman of means and good taste, is paying the major cost of bringing the orchestra here as a gift to the people of Arkansas on the state's 150th birthday. Surely we wouldn't want it said of us that we had such bad manners as to turn down a gift.

On May 29, the front page of the Food Section (page 1C) carried a feature on the dinner being given at Trapnall Hall for the various commissions by the Territorial Restoration Commission. This account written by Harriett Aldridge, Food Editor, said:

On the rare occasions when the Territorial Restoration enter-tains, it strives for a setting and theme in keeping with its abid-ing interest in bygone days. . . . In 1963 it honored the new members of the House of Bishops of the Episcopal Church with an old fashioned supper. . . . The late Mildred Woods, former food editor of the *Arkansas Gazette* and a sixth gen-eration Arkansan, was the food consultant. . . .

Itemized bills among Trapnall family papers provided a fas-cinating source of information for Mrs. Albert Vernam Forbes and Mrs. George Rose Smith, members of the . . . Commis-sion in charge of arranging the dinner. These papers included a grocery order delivered from New Orleans to Trapnall Hall in 1858 — the order is reproduced in part on the above illus-tration and a facsimile of it will form the cover of the souve-nir menu card at the dinner Tuesday — a $20 receipt for playing the violin at a party in 1851, and a local order for over a hun-dred pounds of ice. . . . Place cards will bear the Territorial seal and flowers decorating the damask laid tables will be seasonal ones, including some lilies in honor of Miss Peter. . . .

The article included several pictures. One of them was of York Willborn at the door of Trapnall Hall dressed in his white coat; he was to serve as butler for the evening and announce guests. The "1969 Menu From 1858 Grocery Order" listed the fol-lowing: sparkling catawba, ardent spirits, summer fruits in com-pote, quail on rice with almonds, scalloped oysters, hot biscuits, fig preserves, yard beans, asparagus vinaigrette, little fellow tarts, and coffee. Recipes for these foods were included.

Lily with her intense love for Southern refinement was, of course, thrilled beyond measure to be so celebrated. Another ad-vance story in the *Gazette* by Bill Lewis, art critic, gave a full account of the week's plans. It appeared on the front page under the headline, "Miss Peter Supplies Music and U. S. Lends an Ear." He told the whole story from the beginning of Lily's idea to the present and said this about the social arrangements: "Although

Ormandy is besieged with social invitations on tours, most of which he declines in the interest of conserving his energies for music, rarely are members of the entire orchestra invited any-where. Little Rock will be the exception, thanks to the generos-ity of Miss Peter. . ." (Sunday, 1 June 1969). This was surely the reason Ormandy entered into the festivities and attended all the social functions.

Both Little Rock papers covered the city's anticipation of the Philadelphia's arrival and sent reporters to meet its plane Mon-day. Each paper gave front page coverage including photos of the festive reception at the airport.

The day after the first concert, Wednesday, June 4, the *Democrat* went all out with its coverage. A large picture of Lily in a white evening gown holding a sheaf of roses and blowing kisses filled the center of its front page, accompanying Bob Lancaster's feature headlined, "Seats are as Scarce as Bad Notes as Ormandy Leads Musicians." In addition to its front-page story, the *Democrat* ran Lancaster's story on the concert and a critique by Mary Lowe Kennedy headlined, "Philadelphia Musicians Play Precise, yet Inspired Music." The *Gazette* gave somewhat more copy space with fewer photos than the *Democrat*, including two detailed articles by Bill Lewis. One was "Backstage Ormandy Warms up; on Stage He Comes on Strong" (page 8A); the other was "Ormandy, Orchestra Provide Highlight of Sesquicentennial" (page 20A), the latter critical in nature and full of praise. (Harry Pearson, not known to miss an opportunity himself, points out that the reason the *Gazette* gave this publicity to the concert was that his paper, the *Pine Bluff Commercial*, "had scooped them.")

Both papers carried critiques by Lewis and Kennedy the day after the second performance, June 5. Kennedy of the *Democrat* quoted Ormandy as saying that the orchestra did not wish to leave "this wonder state," and that he thanked Lily Peter, "this wonderful little lady," and the people of Arkansas and asked to be invited

A Nude Singularity

back. She said the applause was tremendous (page 9A).

Richard Allin, writing in his popular, satirical column, "Our Town," in the *Arkansas Gazette* and who played the tuba in the Arkansas Symphony for a number of years, devoted all his space to the event for four straight days. Richard Allin would have been excited and involved in the concerts in any case; he was reared in Helena and had known Lily since he was old enough to remember, because his older brother, John, was a pupil of Lily's when she taught in Helena. Lily gave Richard a special invitation to come to the Albert Pike and meet Ormandy. There follow some selections from his columns. On Monday, June 2, he wrote:

> HAVE TUBA... The Philadelphia Orchestra arrived in town by airplane yesterday but the call I expected from Dr. Ormandy has failed to come through. I had tried to send him word that I would be available to fill in for the tuba player if he wanted to save a little money and not bring him.
>
> After all, when Ringling Brothers comes to town, or the Ice Capades, or a stage show, they pick up local musicians to augment a central roster of musicians. It looks like the Philadelphia could do the same.
>
> I have a tailcoat and white tie lined up just in case the call comes, and I know where I can borrow a four valve double B-flat tuba.
>
> . . .
>
> PROGRAM NOTE While the Philadelphia Orchestra is playing upstairs at the Robinson Auditorium on Tuesday night, the wrestling matches downstairs will feature a bear.

Allin attended the Tuesday rehearsal and discussed that in his Wednesday column, as well as his visit with Ormandy. He said:

> "Ah, so you want to play tuba with us," Ormandy responded with a good natured chuckle. "Have you practiced?"

"Well, no," I said, "but I'm a pretty good sightreader and could follow along."

"Very good," he said, "You must get in touch with our tuba player, Abe Torchinsky, and tell him you want to take his place."

"Tell me," Mr. Ormandy said, "Do you want to play both concerts — Tuesday and Wednesday?"

I didn't want to be greedy about it. Mr. Torchinsky could play the Tuesday night concert, and I'd sit in on Wednesday. I told him I could use the extra day for practice.

"Yes," he said, "Play the scales very, very slowly. Play each tone twenty seconds."

Then Mr. Ormandy held out his hand. "That lesson will be five dollars, please."

That whimsical exchange will give some idea of Mr. Ormandy's jolly nature and sense of humor. He is exactly unlike what one has come to think of the classic symphony conductor. He sets his visitors at ease, banters easily with them, is eager to hear what they have to say. . . .

After watching Mr. Torchinsky and listening to his part in the ensemble, I decided he didn't need any help. . . .

On Friday, June 6, Allin said, "NOW THAT IT'S OVER... One of the greatest tributes that could be paid to Miss Lily Peter and to the Philadelphia Orchestra was paid by those who didn't have tickets to the concerts, but slipped in anyway." He described several instances and admitted that he had done so himself because he liked to watch the conductor from the wings. He concluded with a few paragraphs on the response of the orchestra members to their visit, saying, "They . . . seemed genuinely impressed with Our Town and the way they were treated. They participated heartily in all the arrangements that had been made for them. . . ." Allin told an amusing story about three of the musicians who wanted to walk (and did so) from the Little Rock Country Club to the Marion Hotel, a goodly distance. (All of Allin"s columns appear on Page 1B.)

It is interesting to note that *The Daily Leader*, Stuttgart, Arkansas, gave almost as much space to the event as the state papers, although it is generally considered a county, or sectional at most, paper. It had a reporter, James O. Foxx, covering the occasion and carried an AP article by Robert Shaw. Lily had enjoyed a good relationship with the citizens of the town for years, and they seemed to like to identify themselves with her as a neighbor. The mayor made her an honorary citizen in 1971.

Many other papers out in the state also carried items. The following Sunday, the *Gazette*, which features each Sunday a number of excerpts from editorials about the state, contained several which commended the event and Lily's generosity.

One, clearly laden with respect and admiration, was written by Katherine Payne Leftwich, society editor for the *Forrest City Daily Times-Herald* (9 June 1969, page 3).[6] She combined description bordering on the extravagant, and high praise for Lily and the orchestra, and, courageously, a reprimand for her own paper. She said:

> It was Arkansas' shining hour, that wonderful week in early June when the eyes of the nation were turned to Little Rock where the Philadelphia Orchestra, under the direction of Eugene Ormandy, played for two nights to point up the Arkansas Sesquicentennial, and the state suddenly gained cultural stature it had not previously claimed from afar.
>
> The "musical evenings" were an out and out gift from a little lady from East Arkansas. . . . Through her largesse, the image of Arkansas with barefoot Ozark mountaineers, poverty-ridden sharecroppers, cold corn pone, and bazooka music was changed. . . .
>
> The event went unheralded—because of the pressures on time and space of more urgent local events—in the Forrest City press. . . . However headlines in state, national and international

press releases keep bringing to the mind of this writer the magnitude of the Sesquicentennial gift of a fellow Arkansan, and it seems improper that Miss Peter go unacclaimed in the Forrest City Daily Times-Herald. Hence this piece. . . . "This world is not all violence, dissent, protest, tragedy and despair. It is beauty and soul and mind and heart — and selflessness!" This is what that 70ish Arkansas spinster planter seemed to be saying when she gave . . . [the] gift of fine music. She exhibited an artistic bent, a gentle heart, and an exciting spark of enthusiasm, and she proved that her life has a touch of magic, a fierce chauvinistic loyalty, and a glorious satisfaction. . . .

National attention was given to the event. A Philadelphia paper, *The Evening Bulletin,* on its front page carried pictures and an article written by Walter F. Naedele, who had come to Little Rock, and made a trip to Marvell and Lily's farm neighborhood where he interviewed local residents. *The Dallas Times-Herald* published an article about the concert with pictures. Many others carried AP or UPI stories. There was a paragraph on the "People" page of *Time* magazine (13 June 1969, page 52). *Look* magazine sent reporters, but its feature didn't appear until November.[7] Peter Jennings from the news staff of American Broadcasting Corporation came to Lily's home, taped an interview and requested that she play her violin standing near the edge of Big Cypress Bayou. While she was playing, a water moccasin slithered along the surface of the stream, raised its head, and commanded a moment's attention from the camera.[8]

The one critical review with any negative comment came from Harry Pearson with the *Pine Bluff Commercial.* He raised the question of whether the event was worth the money, writing, "It was an evening three-quarters music and one quarter schmaltz last night as Miss Lily Peter 'presented' the Philadelphia Orchestra. . . ." He named the instances of "schmaltz," then downgraded Ormandy's program selections and his interpretation of Debussy.

He called Dello Joio's work "a whipped cream confection long on homage and short on Haydn." He continued:

> Several orchestra members, chatting informally afterward, opined that Miss Lily didn't get her money's worth.
>
> She paid Dello Joio more than Dvorak was paid for his last three symphonies and any resemblance between "Homage to Haydn" and the occasion for which it was written was purely coincidental.
>
> "Homage to Haydn" was a sort of show-off concatenation — all right, a distillation — of just about every light classic written in the past 30 years, with exactly one theme traceable to Haydn — and more than one hint of George Gershwin and Ferde Grofe.
>
> THE ORCHESTRA played it magnificently and there is every reason to believe that once it is recorded, it will make a fine stereo spectacular. It is a nifty little piece — but that's all it is. There is nothing wrong with nifty light classics but it seems a shame to pay $8,000 for one and then — as Miss Lily has hinted she would do — pay the $10,000 or so it would cost to get the piece recorded. . . .

Pearson's review appeared Wednesday, June 4, on page 2. It created a considerable stir. He wrote to Lily on July 2 and said:

> Dear Miss Peter, What a delightful and gracious letter you wrote.
>
> . . . [two paragraphs on Photography]
>
> As you probably know, the review certainly set off a tidal wave of criticism (toward me). I will send you the original and the letters we published. (We did not publish the ones without signatures). Unfortunately, no one defended my right to call the performance the way I saw it, and no one ever noted that my review specifically credited you for what I consider to be the finest single flourish for Arkansas that it has been my pleasure to see. The critics did not, sadly, note that I found no

fault with the orchestra's playing per se (that's why the Phila-
delphia is the Philadelphia, because it can even sight-read a
score like it has been playing it for years). I assume that an
artist such as yourself understands the function of criticism.
. . . I shouldn't be surprised that the public doesn't. However,
the outrage is really quite complimentary to you. The ratio-
nale behind the comments about my review seemed to be that
it was "ungracious" to say anything unpleasant after Miss
Lily's marvelous gift.

At any rate, we can discuss everything on a rainy (hope-
fully) Sunday afternoon soon and believe me I look forward
to it.

In 1981 Pearson told this writer that the reason he was caus-
tically critical of the Dello Joio number was that the indignation
of several of the orchestra members and even Ormandy had crept
into his writing. He talked to them backstage, and they were out-
raged that Dello Joio had passed off a work which he had barely
altered as a new one. But they had had such a wonderful time and
had been treated so spectacularly and were so fond of Lily that
they didn't have the heart to tell her. Pearson seriously consid-
ered writing a separate story on the matter but could not find spe-
cific proof, so decided to say that much and no more. Although
Lily and Ormandy made plans to record "Homage to Haydn," the
recording never came to pass.[9]

Pearson said further, in retrospect, that it turned into a big,
splendid event, that it was one of those things that really helped
turn the state around from its dark, we-are-good-for-nothing at-
titude. It was 48th or 49th on the list of everything. It was just
about this time that the state began to develop a sense of self. The
Buffalo River and other scenic beauties of the state were vital in
waking the state up. It was remarkable to many in the nation that
someone in Arkansas did something like Lily had done.

(Harry Pearson expressed much fondness for Lily. He got to

see her on two or three occasions after the concerts. He invited her to a party given him at Jay Dickey, Jr.'s place in Pine Bluff because he had won the National Business Journalism Award for a series of stories examining the state's inequitable tax system. She sent word that she couldn't come unless the baby prothonotary warblers had left their nest in the back of her pickup truck. But the night of the party, she arrived in her pickup truck dressed in the tradition of a southern belle, looking like Melanie in *Gone With the Wind*. She fluttered in saying, "I just couldn't know whether the birds were going to get out in time for me to make it." He said she was the hit of the party. He said, "The orchestra was a big gesture, but the small gesture [for the warblers] showed me that she was consistent from one end of the spectrum to the other. Both were life-affirming.")[10]

Bob Lancaster, a reporter for the *Arkansas Democrat* at the time, generally concurs with Pearson about the atmosphere surrounding the event, yet injects a note of caution. Reflecting on the times, he says:

> . . . This was the period when Winthrop Rockefeller was governor, and he and his wife, through the Arkansas Arts Center and other such uplift projects, had heightened public awareness of the arts to an extent. The public attitude was vaguely approving toward this more sophisticated pose, and that approval derived from the state's image-consciousness, which the Faubus years had made so acute as to be almost pathological. In that context, Miss Lily's dramatic gesture meant something special to many Arkansans, although I'd have a hard time articulating it. It was something we could point to with pride — and there weren't many such somethings — even if we knew nothing about classical music and had no interest in attending the concert. . . .
>
> . . . But it didn't cause near the stir that, say, an Arkansas-Texas game at Little Rock always does, or even an Arkansas-

Rice game. The fine arts just aren't a part of the ordinary life of most Arkansas people, and a certain sense of the obligatory characterizes the general interest in an event like this. The publicity surrounding the event, viewed in retrospect, is usually therefore misleading. You have to carefully guard against that any time you're doing work that involves historical review. . . .[11]

How did Lily feel about the event? She felt that she had indeed achieved some of her goals. The orchestra had a very good time, and Lily gives the hosts in Little Rock full credit. She and the Little Rock committee received aggregate and individual letters full of lavish praise and gratitude for the reception they had been given and asserted that it was a unique experience in the history of the orchestra. The newsmen wrote, Herbert E. Marks wrote, Dello Joio wrote. Eugene Ormandy wrote a personal letter. And Lily received between four and five hundred letters from over the state and region. It was an embarrassment to her that she could not answer them. One result which she felt was certainly partly due to the effort was that the budget for the Arkansas Symphony Orchestra increased from $18,000 a year in 1969 to $286,000 in 1974, five years later.[12]

Lily eventually found out that Dello Joio had not given her a new work and that the Philadelphia Orchestra had charged much more than their usual concert fee. Was she angry? No. As Lily wrote in her poem, "Concert," ". . . the music was, after all, a hair's breadth digression, compared with other mutations of being and becoming through which the spirit must pass. . . ." She agreed to the prices quoted her and furthermore feels there was no way to estimate the ultimate value of the concerts.

One result of the Philadelphia's performance in Little Rock was that Helena people were more determined than ever to have a home for their Warfield Concerts. Work began immediately on another of Lily's "giant off-spring," the Lily Peter Auditorium.

That competitiveness is not confined to love, war, or big sports is illustrated by Memphis' invitation sent to the Philadelphia Orchestra to come to Memphis a few years later. Lily wrote to Sokoloff about having the orchestra at Helena while it was in the area. He told her that Memphis had written into the contract that the orchestra could not sign a contract with any other community within range of one hundred and fifty miles within six months. Lily was terribly disappointed. She almost wished that she hadn't promised the Memphis Society $5,000 to help with the fees. Lily and Cleon Collier went to the Memphis concert, however, and she got to chat with Sokoloff and Ormandy and meet Mrs. Ormandy.

Another pleasure for Lily at the time of bringing the Philadelphia to Little Rock was that she was able to entertain her dearest friends and relatives. She feels that the occasion could not have been more nearly perfect. Love and pride and attention and pleasure had come together in music.[13]

An afterthought? Yes. How did Lily choose to record the experience for herself and posterity? Photography, of course. Lily engaged the John F. Bruton Studio in Little Rock to stay by her side for three days. The result was three handsome white albums stamped with gold designations filled with eight by ten color photographs. Bruton's fee was seventy-five dollars a day above the cost of the photographs. John F. Bruton wrote Lily on July 2, 1969:

> Dear Lily Peter: How does one write to Lily Peter — especially after receiving a complimentary letter, aglow with nineteen sparkling adjectives touching my most sincere interest and empathy?
>
> Perhaps by confession — understood only by those who are young at heart — so in answer to your lovely letter of appreciation for my photographic coverage of your extraordinary conquest of Arkansas on June 3, 4, and 5, 1969, I confess, the degree by which I capture the moment is in ratio to the degree

I fall in love with my model.

Lily Peter, in those three days you dazzled me.

Now, may I thank you for something else — for giving to our wonderful Arkansas people a common heartbeat for great music. Sincerely, . . .[14]

Notes

[1]Lily certainly felt as if she had confronted an immovable mountain when she accepted a request to be on a committee to bring into being a suitable concert hall for Helena and the surrounding area. The marvelous S. D. Warfield bequest precluded the continuing use of the high school auditorium for community concerts because it was a facility full of limitations. Warfield had stipulated that the core of administration should always be three persons: the mayor of Helena, the rector of St. John's Episcopal Church, and the rabbi of Temple Beth El. Each of those three members would then appoint one member of the concert committee to serve a term of three years. The mayor appointed Sam Anderson, director of radio station KFFA; the rector appointed Mrs. Aubrey Solomon, the former choir director at Temple Beth El; the rabbi appointed Mrs. Winston Mosby, choir director at St. John's Episcopal Church. It was this group that Lily met with in the fall, and their first decision was to travel and look at existing facilities which were similar to what they envisioned for Helena. Lily could not go with them because of the pressure of harvesting, ginning and the work of the sesquicentennial committee, but she kept in touch with them. The conclusion was that they could not count on the cost's being one penny less than a million dollars. They were determined not to abandon the idea; Lily encouraged them and contributed the first gift of $5,000, but said her time given would have to wait until the Philadelphia Orchestra concerts were over. But the project of a concert hall for Helena was always in the back of her mind.

[2]Personal interview with Dr. John L. Ferguson, head of the Arkansas Historical Commission, 14 Apr. 1981.

[3]An exchange of letters between Lily and O. B. Emerson shows that

she did a few other things in early 1969 besides get ready for the Philadelphia Orchestra concerts. Emerson wrote Lily on February 12:

> Dear Lily: This letter is more in the nature of a business communication because I need to have all issues of the *Delta Review* for a project which I am engaged in and must complete before March 1. The project is a bibliography for the study of southern literature. . . .
> I miss very much the good letters that I used to receive from you on a variety of subjects. Someday I plan to collect the letter from Lily to O. B.. I have some excellent ones in my collection. Please add to them when and if your time permits. I still have not heard from the article I sent the *Delta Review* on Faulkner and the Mule.

Lily responded to O. B.'s letter on February 16:

> Dear O. B.: Thank you for your good letter which came today — you are certainly a true and loyal friend to forgive me so graciously for the way I've neglected you this winter! This past year I said Yes, Yes, to my friends a few times too often, . . .
> . . . how sweet you are to be collecting my letters — you make me feel very famous and important indeed! Where did you learn to make such beautiful compliments! It's really too late to write any more this evening! . . .

Emerson did save everything Lily directed to him. He wrote to the biographer:

> I have saved (collected) letters from Lily Peter over the years (They were so good I could not possibly have thrown them away). Your recent communication has forced me to confront the issue that has been lurking in my mind for some time now — that is what I should do with these letters (photographs, programs, newspaper clippings, etc.). I had thought of . . . giving them to some college or university in Arkansas, interested in collecting material on Lily Peter. . . . If you gain her approval I'll send you all the material I have in my possession. . . (Letter from O. B. Emerson, Ph. D., Department of English, Univ. of Alabama, 13

Apr. 1981).

Lily's approval was obtained. Dr. Emerson has lately given his William Faulkner and Robert Penn Warren collections to Vanderbilt University in memory of his students. Emerson died of cancer in January, 1991.

[4]A letter from Bob Lancaster (cited below) says that since Greenberg was editorial editor of the *Pine Bluff Commercial*, he had no control over what went into the other parts of the paper. He further says that the Associated Press office in Little Rock reads the state papers and picks up what it chooses, ignoring "influences." Lancaster doubts that Foreman had anything to do with it, since he had become by this time managing editor of the *Arkansas Democrat*. It was Foreman who assigned Lancaster to review the concert.

[5]*Arkansas Gazette*, 3 June, p. 1A.

[6]Katherine P. Leftwich. "An Affair Remembered—East Arkansas Planter Gives State a Birthday Gift." *Forrest City Daily Times Herald*, 9 June 1969, p. 3.

[7]John O'Conner. "A Gift from Miss Lily." Photography by Bob Lerner. *Look*, 18 Nov. 1969, 4 pages lettered M following p. 94.

[8]Lily did not see Peter Jennings' report because she didn't own a television set, but many spoke to her of it, and Peter Jennings mailed her a film clip of it, and she stored it in its postal wrappings which show it was mailed from New York on September 23, 1969.

[9]When Lily was told that a young woman who had attended the University of Wisconsin the previous summer had played the near-identical number by Dello Joio as a band composition, she was offended, but that didn't bother her nearly as much as the fact that she, herself, didn't care for the piece because it contained the despised (by her) jazz elements and did not (to her) express the spirit of Arkansas. She did not fully decide to withdraw her offer to subsidize the recording, however, until she learned in the fall that her brother, Ted, had leukemia. Explaining that development, she wrote a courteous letter to Ormandy, and told him that the future was too uncertain for her to commit herself financially to the cost of recording.

[10]Telephone interview with Harry Pearson, Editor and Publisher of *Absolute Sound*, Sea Cliff, New York, 7 Mar. 1981. Letters received from Harry Pearson, 2 Feb. and 1 Sept. 1981.

[11]Letter received from Bob Lancaster, 22 Jan. 1982.

[12]The writer asked Townsend Wolfe, Director of the Arkansas Art

Center, to what degree Lily's bringing of the Philadelphia Orchestra to Little Rock was a factor in the Arkansas Symphony's growth. He responded that it was certainly a large factor and the biggest thing that any one individual had done in the sense of taking the initiative and following through. He remarked that he would say, at the risk of erring in an off-the-cuff remark, that the beginnings of the orchestra owed most to the persevering strength of Polly Kellar, Gene Showalter, and Francis McBeth, the conductor who preceded Kurt Klippstatter. (Personal interview with Townsend Wolfe, 12 Sept. 1980)

[13]Lily bought and reserved sixty seats each night and invited her cousins and her college friends. Lee Butterfield from Bethlehem, Pennsylvania; Peggy King from Prince Frederick, Maryland; Drs. Ivar Lou and Edgar Duncan, Drs. Sally and Gordon Sell and children; Nancy (Mrs. C. Darby) Fulton and her son from Nashville, are just a few of them. Lily gave a luncheon for all her invited guests on Wednesday at the Albert Pike, and Mr. Ormandy and the Dello Joio family attended. Sally Sell said her sons groused about going to Little Rock for the event, but that now it is one of their favorite memories (interview cited). Lily's sister Ethel was on hand for all events, but her sister Oma was present for one concert only. Lily regrets that there were some of her nieces and nephews who did not come because they were not interested.

[14]Personal interviews with Lily Peter, tapes 4, 6, 8, 9, 10, 11, 18, 23, 31, 44, 63, 64. Torreyson Library Archives, University of Central Arkansas

Chapter VIII

STANDING UP FOR ARKANSAS
WITH NAIL KEGS AND
COCKLEBUR CUSHIONS, 1969-1972

> Where and when did I begin to become what I am?
> There will always be problems,
> with this intractable Jackdaw
> and the Nine Sextillion Ancestors to cope with,
> in keeping this ramshackle House in some sort of order.
> I was not asked beforehand to accept this legacy:
> I was given no voice in the ordering of its terms.
> Before coming into possession, I had no knowledge
> as to what it would entail:
> but, being in possession,
> I have found compensations beyond measure. . . .
> > Lily Peter
> > "The Mansion"
> > *News from Camelot*, unpublished

Lily's reference in the poem, "The Mansion," above is to her body which houses her psyche; however, if she were ever required to say whether or not she had built a mansion for herself on this earth, she would undoubtedly refer to the Lily Peter Auditorium at Helena, or the *Miss Lily Peter*, a towboat on the Arkansas River, or the Lily Peter Fire School at the National River Academy at Helena, or Peter Hall which houses the music department of Moravian College, Bethlehem, Pennsylvania. Only a week after the Philadelphia Orchestra performances, Lily was talked into heading up a committee to raise money for a community center in Phillips County.[1] Her other cultural activities did not stop.[2] A personal injury and problems with fund raising added to the tension of Lily's year of 1969.[3]

The bids for the center were opened in January of 1971 on the day that Dale Bumpers was inaugurated governor. Since Lily appeared on the governor's program, she could not be present for the opening of the bids. Upon her return from Little Rock, she called Dr. Easley, who had appalling news. Since the estimate of the cost of the Center had been made in 1968, the rate of inflation had increased to the extent that the cheapest bid for the building was $1,350,000, over one-fourth more than the funds available. This bid was made by the M&M Construction Company, Jonesboro, Arkansas. Dr. Easley's appeals for a lower price were unsuccessful. Acceptance was called for in sixty days. Lily said, "My Dears, we are just going to have to cut some of our specifications. It is no more possible to get $350,000 from the community in two months' time than it is for us to build a bridge to Neptune."

So the committee met and met, again and again, going over the features that could be omitted. The first cut was that of a hydraulic stage for theatre in the round. The local Little Theatre group had raised a thousand dollars for the center and had requested it. Lily thought theatre in the round might be an essential dimension of the evolution of theatre, but that it could be omitted. She and the others assured the Little Theatre group that the stage could be added later. They then considered the wiring that was so elaborate as to seem "gold-plated" and managed to cut $20,000 off the estimate and still meet the requirements of the underwriters' code. The original plans called for kitchen facilities and equipment for large public dinners costing around $65,000. Lily amused the committee members (according to

Helen Mosby) by saying, "Let's get the auditorium and the room and worry about the equipment later. If worse comes to worst, we can always have a community skillet shower."

That sort of shaving of costs continued, and the matter of the fairly luxurious seating was confronted. Another quip by Lily, "Boys and Girls, let's get this auditorium, and if we don't have a single seat, we can just tell people to come to the first few concerts bringing their own nail kegs with cocklebur cushions."

After making every cut thought possible, the committee members were still faced with a $150,000 deficit. Lily made another canvass of possible donors with few results. Dr. Easley "found" another $100,000-reservoir of grant money and was able to qualify for it; however, when they came down to the wire of letting the contract, they were $46,000 short. Lily volunteered to go to the bank and borrow it, but Dr. Easley suggested that they ask the state legislature for it. Legislators dipped into some fund for $50,000. To the discouraged committee members that act seemed some sort of a miracle. The genuine feeling of victory came when the building contract was signed. In the *Commercial Appeal* on December 5, 1971, there appeared a picture of the community center under construction, merely skeletal at that point.

The consummation of this project was the happy coincidence of three important factors. Helena was the only city in the United States that was willed an estate of an adequate size to assure one or more concerts of high quality a year. Following S. G. Warfield's death in 1968, his lands were sold and the amount realized from the sale was placed in the Trust Department of Union National Bank in Little Rock. Of the interest earned, only three per cent was to be used for concerts, the remaining earnings to be placed with the principal after administration costs were deducted. In that way the amount of the principal increased. The very first year gave the Warfield Concert Association $14,000 to spend, enough for three concerts. In 1980, eight concerts were presented. This was certainly a rare bequest. The second factor was that the needs of Phillips County Community College and the need for a community center coincided in time. A community center supported only by civic funds would have faced the tremendous expense of maintenance. Many communities had built centers only to have them fail because of the cost of custodial care. The college could and did assume this responsibility. It is the only college campus in the United States with a community center on its campus. The third factor was that the atmosphere for both federal and state assistance was favorable. Even though aesthetes will readily admit that cultural events are not essential to survival, all of them believe that they are essential to total health of mind, body, and spirit, but only at certain moments in history are aesthetic leaders able to convince governments of this fact.

It would be reasonable to conjecture that Lily Peter was a fourth indispensable factor. She was devoted to good music and eventually gave $35,000 to the center, besides countless hours of her time and innumerable units of her energy. When the Lily Peter Auditorium was dedicated on December 3, 1972, it was unquestionably a triumphal day for her. Dr. John Easley, president of the college, concurs.[4]

In the fall of 1970 Lily participated in the Grand Prairie Festival of Arts in Stuttgart, and along with her photography and other collections, displayed King Solomon the Owl. Lily tells his story.

"Well, King Solomon came into our lives in this way: He was a great horned owl; they are very rare now and very beautiful and enormously intelligent and charming birds. Poor King Solomon was living in our pasture woods down below our old home. He had a family evidently, whom he was trying to feed and having a very hard time of it because the land above our house had been cleared until little wild life was left, and owls cannot live except on wild life. So this great horned owl was coming up to raid the Copeland's chicken house — they were living down there in the home house then and Virgil was my store manager, but Helen kept the store more than Virgil did. Virgil worked at the gin in the fall, and he was also my farm carpenter.

"Well, Helen and Virgil were very unhappy because the owl was carrying off their chickens. Virgil told me about the owl, and he said, 'He's an enormous owl and I'm going to kill him, because I just can't have my chickens carried off that way.' So I said, 'Oh, Virgil, I will be glad to pay for the chickens that are carried off, for that owl is a great horned owl and very, very rare. Please don't shoot him under any circumstances, but keep up with the chickens that are carried off, and I'll pay you well for them. I'll pay for his board and keep.' So Virgil did as I asked. The owl kept coming to their chicken house, and they tried every way they could to scare him off. He would even come into the yard in the day time, he was so hungry and so wanted to get food for his family — they can't see too well in the day — and he would sit on the fence post in their back yard hoping to get a chicken. Helen is a good shot, and she shot at the post. She didn't want to hit him, but all he did was jump off the post and come back and sit on it. He was too desperate for food to be frightened.

"One evening at dusk Helen heard a great going-on in the chicken house and ran out to see what was happening, and this great horned owl had caught a big three-pound broiler and was fixing to eat it. Helen ran out of the chicken house to see if there was any way to find someone to help her catch him. Since there was no one, she picked up a tow sack lying on a bench near the chicken house and threw it over him and held his legs real tight so he couldn't claw her. She called Virgil, and he came and helped her get the owl into an empty chicken coop they had for taking chickens to market. But the coop was built for chickens and was only tall enough for them. The great horned owl was seven inches taller than the coop.

"That was on a Friday evening. I was over at Stuttgart that day setting up the 1970 exhibit, and I didn't get home that evening until dark. When I went by the store to get my mail, there was a note from Helen telling me that she had caught the great horned owl and named him King Solomon and asking me to come down to see him. I was tired and had many more things to gather for the exhibit and was going back to Stuttgart the next day, so it was Sunday before I got to see him. I did, however, on Saturday call the zoo-keeper at Little Rock and told him we had the owl and asked him what he should be fed. He said, 'First of all, you must remember to give him a varied fare. It must be fresh meat, and he must have some fur and some kind of feathers every week for his digestion.' That meant he had to have some birds of some kind and some mice or rabbits or something of that sort every week.

"When I finally got to see him, I never saw a more pitiful creature. He was just all huddled over, unhappy, dejected and furious that he had been made a prisoner. He was a king, and here he was a prisoner, angry with the whole world. I was so sorry for him I said, 'Your Majesty, we'll have you more comfortable in a day or two.' I asked Virgil to build him a cage that was eight feet long, four feet wide, and six feet high and told him I'd pay him to do it. I then sent some of my men to Helena to get the materials — chicken wire, wallboard, and framing — on Monday, so it was two or three days before his home was ready. We put some tree limbs in it for him to sit on if he wanted to, and in one end we placed a big old mail box we had used years ago when we lived down at our old home. That was where he spent the night. I had a great big oval dish pan. We filled that nearly full of water and put that in his cage so he could have a bath — owls are very clean. He used it and we refilled it every day. We did everything we could think of to make him comfortable.

256

"And we remembered what we should feed him. I went to town and bought him steak and ribs and bones. We found out by trial and error that he liked bones, especially chicken and turkey necks. And we gave him all the wild creatures we could come by. One day Helen's old mother cat brought in a great big bull frog. She traded the mother cat a saucer of milk for that frog, and King Solomon ate that frog with all the gusto and aplomb of a royal gourmet enjoying frog's legs in a Parisian restaurant. Another time the cat brought in a garter snake. Again we traded and gave the snake to King Solomon. Word of the great owl got around the neighborhood, and it wasn't long before the boys were bringing rabbits to him.

"It was incredible how his appearance improved. When he first came to us, he was so bedraggled and so skinny and bony. We examined his body to see what condition he was in, and we found that someone had shot the poor creature. In the flesh of his leg was a bullet. Now I couldn't have done this because of my phobia about blood, but Helen could and did. She took a good pocket knife and sharpened the blade on a whetstone as sharp as she could make it, heated the blade red hot to destroy any germs on it, let it cool, and to make sure it was sterilized, dipped it in alcohol. Then she took this great bird in her arms as if it were a baby, slit open the place where the bullet was and took it out. That bird was so intelligent it knew she was helping it and didn't offer any resistance. He always liked Helen. She was the one who caught him and made him a prisoner, but he knew what she had done for him; she had rid him of that misery, so he always liked her better than all the rest of us put together. And he never liked me at all. I did everything I could to propitiate that beautiful bird and to make friends with him; nevertheless, he thought he was my prisoner because he was at my house. I was out there every day to see about him, but he didn't want to have anything to do with me. I had given him a palace to live in, but for him it was a prison.

"I did hold him on occasion. We took him to Stuttgart to show him to the school children. And they came in droves to see him. We couldn't take the cage because it was too unwieldy. It would have to rest on a big truck, and then the children couldn't see him very well. So we had to improvise a kind of carrier. We had over at the store an old cookie container that long years ago we used for selling loose cookies. We now sell only packaged cookies, but we still had this big wire container, and we could put King Solomon in it comfortably and put it on a pickup truck. We showed him in two places. He didn't seem to mind it, and he did not protest. So the children could see him better, Helen took him out of the cage. I always let her do the handling because he didn't mind her approaching him. But I wanted to show him too and explain how to handle him. I told the children, 'Don't try to play with him, because he has a powerful beak, and he can bite off the end of your finger. And don't touch his feet except above them. Don't touch the sole of his feet at all because an owl has a terrific grip — that's the way it catches its prey.' And in spite of all that warning, a gentleman came up out of that crowd, and he touched that owl's foot. That owl cracked down on his finger right to the bone. So we had to call a couple of men to extricate those claws from that man's finger. Of course, it hurt him. He had to go to the doctor, but he had only himself to blame. I know he had heard what we had told about the owl's grip. I can assure you nobody else came up there and touched the sole of the owl's foot.

"So anyway, King Solomon created a sensation at the festival. He was the center of attraction and was greatly enjoyed by the children and the grown-ups too. We made lots of pictures of him over there, and they were in several of the papers.

"He had four ways of expressing himself vocally. If he were mildly displeased, he would hiss like a goose. And he was displeased one way or another most of the time because he didn't like being a prisoner. If he were more than mildly displeased, he would

Lily and King Solomon

blow HH, HH. And if he were extremely angry with the whole world and hated everybody in sight, he would go scriptural, and he would do what I call a gnashing of teeth. Now an owl doesn't have any teeth, but he has a big strong beak, and he would crack that beak in a way he thought most terrifying. And if, on the other hand, he was pleased, which was very seldom, he would make a sound like blowing over the top of a bottle. We never heard him do this except at night when he was talking with another owl that would come down here on the bayou to talk to him along toward morning. They were very discreet in their conversations. Some

259

nights I would wake up about three o'clock in the morning and King Solomon would be carrying on a conversation with another owl back in the woods and the sounds were similar. His voice had the sound of pleasure as if he were talking to his sweetheart, or it may have been his wife who had found out where he was.

"I had only intended to keep him until after Christmas so that my sister Ethel could see him. She was greatly intrigued by what I had told her about King Solomon; however, he got away from us the second week in December. One of the boys from the farm had brought him a fine rabbit which would do him for three or four days in the winter when it would stay fresh. That night the dogs in the neighborhood smelled that rabbit and tore a hole in the cage to get it. Of course, they couldn't get to King Solomon; he was up in the top of the cage, but when he saw that great gaping hole, I know he must have said to himself, 'Well I don't like these folks anyway, so I'm going to take this chance for a French leave.' So off he went, and we never saw him again up here. But he did come back down home to Helen's place the next year looking for food for his family. Helen told me about it, so we fed him. Every day we put some food by a certain tree down in the pasture. Helen would hide and watch him and his mate come and get it. We never tried to catch him again because he was so miserable in prison.

"He didn't come back again after that summer, so we don't know what happened to him. He may have died of natural causes, or someone may have shot him. Oh, people are so unkind to our wild birds — shooting them for no reason. We knew he was elderly because his legs were scaly. King Solomon was obviously a patriarch, a beautiful creature, every inch a king, and we were richer for having known him."

Lily has told that story to audiences many times to illustrate the need for conservation.

She and King Solomon were the focal points of interest in most newspapers' accounts of the Festival; however, Richard

Allin in "Our Town" in the *Arkansas Gazette* devoted most of his column to the unusual quality of Lily's photography and expressed amazement that she used "only a box camera."[5]

Lily's love and respect for the land is such a strong and tenacious aspect of her character that it is unthinkable to her to sell any part of it. Her only exceptions have been in cases wherein loyal employees or neighbors have wanted a homesite. That fall Lily deeded to Helen and Virgil Copeland (at a give-away price of $150 per acre) ten acres of land near the old home place where they had lived a number of years. Helen and Virgil worked together and built a home out of the lumber from two tenant houses.[6]

Lily often remarked that she was like a cat which has nine lives, except that she lived them simultaneously: farmer, ginner, educator, philanthropist, environmentalist, civic worker, poet, musician, and photographer. This multifaceted existence became more and more obvious during the decade of the seventies.[7]

After a bout with pneumonia in January of 1971, Lily resumed her activities in February. During the previous year a National River Academy was established at Helena. Lily considered it a remarkable feat for freshman legislator Bill Alexander to get the academy located there. He had stepped in the breach caused by a competition for the institution between St. Louis and Greenville, Mississippi, and he had offered the solution of placing it in Helena. It was to be an institution supported by tow-boat companies in the Mississippi River Valley; however, federal approval and financial help were essential to getting it started.

This support from the private sector did not come forward in the amount expected, and the academy was suffering from lack of funds. Captain Pierre Becker, the director, having heard of Lily's love for and interest in the river, asked his secretary, Elizabeth Ashcraft, to go with him to visit Lily. When she heard his story, she immediately contributed $5,000. No doubt Lily's concern for the training of young men and women for work on the vessels which plied the inland waterways was based on the fearful conditions of the apprenticeship system she had heard about from her Uncle Brutus. She continued her support and acted as early as June of the same year when the academy was threatened by the attempt to found a rival institution at Lake Dardanelle on the Russellville side. Sponsored by the Ozark Regional Commission, the group promoting the rival wanted to draw on the funds of the Manpower Development and Training Act. Lily was pleased that Governor Bumpers and Congressman Alexander rejected the rival proposal.

On March 24, 1971, amidst all the pomp and ceremony of such occasions, Lily was honored by getting to turn the first shovel full of dirt for the Lily Peter Auditorium. Dr. John Easley and the mayors of both Helena and West Helena were present, and Lily's efforts were praiscd in the speeches.

The state papers announced on March 28 that Lily had been elected the *Arkansas Democrat*'s 1970 Woman of the Year. Letters of congratulations poured into her mailbox, including one from Mrs. D. D. Terry, the matriarch of one of Little Rock's oldest families.[8]

The more publicity Lily received for her activities the more invitations for appearances she received. She accepted all she possibly could, and one of them in April was to the Beethoven Club in Searcy. Her thank-you letter to her hostess, Mrs. Ernest (Helen) Forbes, gives us a rare glimpse of Lily's emotion. Usually her self-discipline is impeccable. She wrote:

> Dear Mrs. Forbes: It was a joy indeed to meet you on my visit to Searcy for the program for the Beethoven Club, and I want to thank you for the pleasure of being in your lovely home and for the hospitality of the pleasant night at the Motel. . . . I want to apologize, too, to you and Mr. Forbes for the sudden return of what Elizabeth Barrett Browning would call "my child-

hood grief," which upset me in the last moments of my visit. I am not a person who is given to tears and this never happened to me before, but because of our parents' great love for us as children, my childhood memories are very vivid, and the loss of my father, happening so suddenly as the result of an accident, when I was fifteen, was a severe trauma to me.

It has never before happened to me that in one evening there was built up such a sudden and overwhelming flashback of those childhood memories — and please remember how much I did enjoy the evening with you and your husband in your beautiful home with its exquisitely planned flowering plantings and orchard and gardens. Walking with you in the spring twilight among the fragrant blooming shrubs and trees and flowers reminded me so vividly of our walking in the evenings with our mother, who loved all growing things. In meeting your husband I have never known anyone who reminded me more startlingly of my father, not so much in appearance, though Mr. Forbes has the same clear rosy complexion as my father had, but in manner and personality. We sat, chatting pleasantly, by the fireplace, which evoked more nostalgia, though ours was only an old-fashioned brick fireplace and not a handsome marble one like yours; and the fireplace brought on more memories, so that when I was saying good night to you my eyes were brimming with tears, in thinking of the long ago death of my father. I never want my friends to be saddened by my own personal feelings, and when I turned to say good night to your husband, since I was already blinded by the tears and did not want you all to be grieved by my sad memories, I turned my head to try to cover my emotion. Mr. Forbes' kindly gesture and your own gracious understanding helped me in quenching the sadness as quickly as possible, but even so, I could not recover my poise readily enough to make my adieux as cheerful as I would have wished. And I do want to ask both you and Mr. Forbes to forgive me for this sudden welling-up of what another poet has called "memories too deep for tears." . . . (April 16, 1971)

Obviously Lily took her mother's admonishment against a display of emotion quite seriously and was embarrassed whenever she showed her feelings. We can conjecture that in the case of the visit to the Forbes other emotions were also present. In this family setting, Lily was surely reminded of the high price she had paid for her independence and singularity. She was fully aware of life's intrinsic tragedy: the collision of genuinely good values.

Lily went to Washington in September 1971 to attend the opening of the John F. Kennedy Center for the Performing Arts, where one of the events was a concert of Moravian Music sponsored by the Moravian Music Foundation. Having heard of it in advance, the foundation had requested to be a part of the two-week musical celebration. All its personnel were thrilled to have been given a time on Sunday afternoon to present the third concert of the festival. They were confident that they could marshal their talent to present an excellent program; however, they had considerable misgivings about filling the 2,800-seat auditorium. They sent their message abroad; Lily responded by buying twenty-four tickets in the Horse Shoe Circle at $100 each. Even so, she was not sure she could give them away since the expense of the trip to Washington would keep a number of her friends in Arkansas from attending. Nevertheless, she telephoned all of her friends and cousins who she thought might like to go. She was disappointed that only two people from Arkansas could accept, Mr. and Mrs. Max Worthley from Fayetteville.[9] Lily also invited to the concert the members of the Arkansas Congressional Delegation and had acceptances from the McClellans, the Hammerschmidts, the Alexanders, and the Fulbrights. Betty Fulbright invited Lily to stay at their home, but Lily could not accept because she was helping the Moravian Music Foundation sponsor a Sunday luncheon at the Watergate and had twenty-four personal reservations. Included in her guest list were relatives in Bethlehem, Pennsylvania, and Jane and Orville Freeman, her cousins, who were living in New York. She had not heard from them, but she held their tickets, knowing that they traveled a lot and thinking they might return home any time.

During the blessing at the luncheon, in walked Jane and Orville Freeman, who had been on a trip to Europe and returned home barely in time to come to Washington. Lily was pleased that their chairs and tickets were waiting for them. The luncheon went well; they all went to the concert, and all were proud of the performance. The hall was filled, and Lily regarded it as a peak experience. The reviewers were complimentary, except for one, who, Lily said, missed the point that it was a reproduction of the earlier historical performances and expected something on the scale of Beethoven or Brahms.

Lily had procured a schedule of the concerts at the festival far in advance, and when she noted that Leonard Bernstein's opera, *Mass*, was to be the first presentation, she immediately ordered a copy of the score and libretto at an exorbitant price, only to find that she did not like it at all. She regarded it as "blasphemous, sacrilegious — vulgar even — because it was a travesty on the Catholic mass in many respects." She did not attend the opera and was able to attend only one other, a program by the great violinist, Isaac Stern.

All connected with Moramus and its biennial music festivals deemed the appearance a culmination of their twenty years of hard work to keep their musical tradition alive. Lily's only regret was that Thor Johnson had an engagement elsewhere which he could not break. She had grown quite close to Thor, especially since he had become director of the Nashville Symphony.[10]

Lily did not waste this opportunity to promote Arkansas. Chairman of the Moramus Board, R. Arthur Spaugh, wrote her on September 9, apologizing for a delay in getting the tickets to her and said:

Thank you for enclosing with your letter a copy of the publicity you have sent out. This is excellent. We are delighted that you are capitalizing on the fact that Mr. Edward Durrell Stone, the architect of the Kennedy Center, is from Fayetteville, Arkansas. Can't you make him a Moravian also?

While in Washington, Lily renewed her friendship with Henry Clay Mitchell and his wife Virginia, the former editor of the *Delta Review,* now on the staff of *The Washington Post.* He wrote a feature article for his paper headlined "Arkansas Traveler" published on September 13, on page B1. It said:

Lily Peter, of Marvell, Ark., who knows she is a good farmer and hopes she is a poet, stood up for rural America at the Kennedy Center yesterday, merely by being present. For she is an enthusiastic Friend of the Center, and a link with the music of both yesterday and tomorrow.

A sponsor of the concert of Moravian music — the first chamber music concert in the new Center — she also is a descendant of Johann Friedrich Peter, who in the 18th century was one of those learned Moravians who produced the first body of chamber music in America. His second quintetto, composed the year the American Constitution was adopted, was featured yesterday.

The music, like the descendant, was neat, polished; and if the composers were farmers, you are pretty sure they had fine barns and careful records.

Miss Peter, who sat in a box at the curve of the horseshoe, said she thought the Center was charming and its music glorious. She wore a high-necked, long-sleeved brown silk dress, with a cross of white and blue enamel that belonged to the last Russian czarina.

But most of the year, she's out in the fields. She is one of the few women in the world who operates a complicated cotton and soybean plantation. She lives in a plain house, got up at 5 a.m. for years to open the farm store, can run a cotton gin herself, and the Lord only knows the last time she ever lounged on the gallery with a julep.

She is the first woman ever to build two sky-blue cotton gins. [Lily planned to build another one at Ratio but never did.] The usual old-gray-wood-and-tin gins look dilapidated and she decided a gin might as well look nice. (She is also quite proud of the plantation's safety record).

Her home plantation, out from Marvell, is one on which International Harvester tested its prototype cotton-picking machines back in the '30s — an invention that as much as anything changed the Delta Country. On her farm (she did not own it then) in those days there were 95 tenant families. Now there are 11.

In the old days, nobody on a cotton farm would have upped and come to Washington the second week of September.   In the Delta Country it doesn't rain in September and October, but it pours in November. The trick is to get the cotton picked before the late rains. But with cotton machinery, you don't start picking until a great deal of the crop is ready — fewer and later pickings, but vastly cheaper than hand labor. So now you don't have to be home in early September.

Though she has seen a few changes in her day, Miss Peter is not altogether old-fashioned. She spends much of her year racing her farm truck over Big Cypress Bayou to the Elaine Equipment Co., 40 miles away, for machine parts. And from time to time she's spotted in small Delta towns looking snappy in her polished black vinyl knee-height boots.

An authority on Hernando de Soto's route through her country in 1541 (though as she points out she was not actually present at the time) she once sent a picture of a locally famous cypress tree to a magazine, as an example of a tree de Soto passed by and must have seen.

A photographer among other things, Miss Peter shot the top of the tree at a distance, then moved in and shot the great base of the tree. The center of the ancient giant she could not shoot at all, since a forest of lesser trees obscured it. When the editor complained the tree didn't have a middle, she said why not just run the top of the tree at the top of the page and the bottom of the trunk at the bottom and just sort of fill in with type. Which was done, and the effect was fine.

A very serious farmer, she knows cockleburs are botanically Xanthium and she's a walking encyclopedia on the uses of alpha, alpha, alphatrifluoro-a, 6-dinitro-N, N-dipropyl-p-toluidine, one of the well-known weedkillers.

She has also published books of poetry, is an enthusiastic amateur historian and, perhaps above all, a music lover.

Two years ago she sat down and wrote Eugene Ormandy on her plain farm note paper and asked if he'd consider bringing the Philadelphia Orchestra to Arkansas for some concerts. Ormandy later told reporters he was afraid, at first, that Miss Peter didn't understand the Philadelphia Orchestra didn't just pick up and plop down in Arkansas for the hell of it, but the upshot was the orchestra went to Arkansas, presented some sell-out concerts, and Mr. Ormandy kissed Miss Peter right in front of half of Little Rock on the auditorium stage — a thing Miss Peter remembers with pleasure.

She mortgaged her land for the concerts and dictated that no ticket could cost more than $5 — otherwise how could anybody but the rich afford to attend?

. . .

Yesterday's program, hugely supported by North Carolinians and Pennsylvanians, nevertheless, found in the farmer of Marvell a sponsor. Roger Stevens, Kennedy Center chairman, was saying at a luncheon before the concert (attended by box ticket holders at the Watergate Terrace) that the Center really belongs to the nation, not just Washington, "in spite of what some Washingtonians think."

But the problem, as one guest said in a whisper, is whether Lily Peter may not get the whole thing shipped down to Arkansas.

The article included a photograph of Lily at "the wheel of the tractor." Actually it was taken at the airport in Dallas when Lily attended Governor Connally's conference on the arts. Someone had asked her to pose on one of the small vehicles which transport luggage from the plane to the lobby. But since the photo was trimmed from Lily's waist down, one could easily take it for a tractor — and it was a reinforcement for the legend that Lily drove tractors. Lily appreciated the feature story by Mitchell and considered it an honor when Senator William Fulbright, with an appropriate introduction, placed it in the Congressional Record.[11]

Governor David Pryor sent Lily a tearsheet of the article by Mitchell and accompanied it with a hand-written note on his official stationery saying, "This is a beautiful story about a beautiful woman" (September 14, 1971). Lily had supported David Pryor in his campaign for governor and had cordial relations with him while he served. On one occasion she had gone with Rex Hancock of Stuttgart to present a set of wildlife prints to the governor and make some sort of appeal in the interest of conservation. They had arrived early and had been able to observe the conduct of the governor's office nearly all morning. The governor received the rice princess and her court and treated them like royalty. He performed other duties while she was there, but what impressed Lily was the way he handled a press conference. Some particularly incensing event had occurred in Southern Arkansas, and the press came armed with controversial questions bordering on personal attack. Lily said that David kept his "cool," never losing his temper, never offending anyone so that the confrontation took on the delicacy of a fencing duel which ended in a draw.

When Lily was attending an institute on politics and government in Little Rock, she heard David tell a story which captured her sympathy and admiration for his wit. He said that on one cold, dark wintry afternoon he had stayed at his desk pondering the answer to some dilemma, until he was the last person to

Lily, with Rex Hancock, presenting wildlife prints
to Governor David Pryor

leave the building besides the custodians. His phone rang and an irate lady gave an account of her fury and stated, "I won't speak to anyone lower than the governor." His reply was, "Madam, there is no one lower than the governor of Arkansas."

The other exciting event of the year brought much publicity and momentum to Lily's beloved, but stress-filled, project, a suitable setting for the Louisiana Purchase Monument. *The Twin City Tribune*, West Helena, reported on October 13, 1971, under the headline "French Visitor Retraces Trail of Hernando DeSoto" (page 1) that Pierre LeLong, a delegate from an agricultural district to the French National Assembly, was being hosted on a tour of the area by Congressman Bill Alexander and members of his staff, Harry Truman Moore and Ginger Holmes. Alexander was considered LeLong's American counterpart. Also on hand were Nan Robertson, a writer for the *New York Times* and John Fleming, outdoor editor of the *Arkansas Gazette*. It was Fleming who gave the visit a humorous treatment, reporting these items among other things:

> Morlaiz will never be the same again. The Department of Finistere will never be the same again. There is a possibility that all of France may never be the same again. Certainly, Pierre LeLong will never be the same again.
>
> Pierre LeLong is a delegate in the National Assembly of France. He represents the area around Morlaiz in the Department of Finistere. In France the National Assembly corresponds to our House of Representatives. Pierre is one of the 627 delegates and he represents about 80,000 persons. Last week and part of this week, he got the fastest tour of Eastern Arkansas since the Quapaw Indians ran one of DeSoto's conquistadors from the salt deposits above what is now Guion to the Spanish camp just below Helena.
>
> What a delegate from the French National Assembly was doing in Arkansas takes some explaining. There is an interna-

tional program wherein members of the United States Congress and their counterparts from other countries exchange visits so that a legislator from one country can see how the system works in another country. Thirteen French delegates were nominated to make the trip and 13 United States representatives were invited to play host to the visitors. Two considerations were involved in deciding who should entertain who and where. Officially it will be explained that the selections were made geographically. My version of what really happened is this: whomever [sic] arranged this trip got the physical records of the members of the House of Representatives and selected the hardiest 13. . . .

Among the more healthy members of the House is Arkansas's First District Representative Bill Alexander. He got the call. The French selectors must have had the same idea. Bill Alexander is 37 and Pierre LeLong is 40. That's the last time I'll ever give away 25 years in an out and out endurance contest.

Delegate LeLong started out with a disadvantage. The other 12 Frenchmen came to Washington a week ago Monday for a briefing but he was delayed. So it was that he flew directly from Paris to Memphis.

NO LANGUAGE BARRIER. Pierre LeLong, who was making his first visit to the United States, speaks highly passable English. He was, however, subjected to some confusion in the language department on his first full day in Eastern Arkansas. Within a period of six hours he had heard Miss Lily Peter, the recently named state poet-laureate, recite two of her poems, and also heard Lewis J. (Red) Johnson, president of the Arkansas Farmers Union, preside as master of ceremonies at a session held at the end of the newly constructed state road into the Louisiana Marker in Monroe County. Suffice to say, there is a wide range between Miss Peter's flawless rhetoric and Red's colorful Arkansasese. This gap confused some of the more erudite natives, so what chance had a stranger on our shores? . . .

The journey covered approximately 800 miles from the banks of the Mississippi at Helena, to West Memphis to the Ozarks around Batesville, Mountain View and Greers Ferry Lake, back to the Mississippi at Blytheville, to Oceola, to Jonesboro and to the point of the beginning at the Memphis Airport.

Vehicles used for transportation included a private plane, a 10-seat bus, sedans, a john-boat, a cabin cruiser, a station wagon and the rear end of a pickup truck. The number of formal speeches was at least 10 and Pierre kept getting better and better as time went on. Entertainment ran the gamut from attendance at a black church to the nightclub at Fairfield Bay where a sexy, blonde vocalist from the Good Times Singers sat on Pierre's lap and did a throaty version of "Help Me Through the Night."

Delegate LeLong was the first Frenchman to ever visit the point at the confluence of Lee, Phillips, and Monroe Counties which marks the point from which surveys of the Louisiana Purchase began 12 years after France sold this 125,000 square miles to the United States for about $27 million. Bill Alexander became the second member of the United States Congress to visit the point. The first was Senator Thad Carraway who made the monument dedication speech in 1926. This old man came within a few seconds of being the first American ever to die of exhaustion at this historic site. . . . (October 17, 1971, page 4B)

Lily's account of the event also has its moments of hilarity. Hers was the last of a six-car entourage to the marker site of the Louisiana Purchase, and when the lead car came to a dead end, Lily's became the lead car. Sure enough, she too came to a dead end, and the process was again reversed, so that the parade to the marker looked like an old cops-and-robbers silent comedy. Even after they finally arrived, confusion ran riot because they couldn't find a dry enough site for the flat-bed truck that was to be the stage

273

for the program. Publicity pictures show Alexander, the congressman, and LeLong, the French legislator, along with a half dozen others, clad in hip-boots, standing in water up to their knees. Lily caught a look of pure bewilderment on the Frenchman's face, and she was sure that at times he wondered whether or not he'd ever see home again, surrounded as he was by a strange landscape, peopled by even stranger young men with football numbers on their chests, "volunteer" students from a local high school to help the day run smoothly. All in all Lily enjoyed the surrealism of her first mandate as poet laureate of Arkansas, an appointment recently conferred by the state legislature.

And 1971 was the year in which the Ozark Society had used several of Lily's best photographs of the wetlands and a poem or two. It had been a good year. The crops were good. She had been able to give away lots of hundred-dollar gifts, one of which went to the Alban Berg Society, Limited, which Igor Stravinski had founded prior to his recent death. It was solicited by her Philadelphia Orchestra-days friend, Felix Greissle, who acknowledged it personally. It was her last letter from him. He said of the gift that she gave it without knowing much about Berg. "She just assumed it must be for a good purpose if I asked for it. I found this rather moving and disarming."[12]

The year 1972 began with another ground-breaking ceremony, that of the National River Academy. It was a bitter cold day, but a platform had been devised, and flags of several nations were flying, representing the international use of the Mississippi River for shipping. The Memphis paper described Lily as ". . . outfitted in a red suit and cape, red boots and scarf. . . [reading] one of her poems, 'Song of the Mississippi.'"[13] Lily's brightness may have matched the international flags blowing in the cold Mississippi winds, but she recalls that it was not so bright underfoot. There had been some heavy rains, and that low land right at the Mississippi River levee was solid gumbo. About a hundred tons of hay had been brought in and scattered to provide some ground cover, but still when one stepped anywhere, the hay would sink into the mud, along with everyone's feet and ankles. All the participants ended up with "hay-feathered" feet, and Lily was learning again how true is the delta farmer's description of his gumbo fields: "the longer yuh walks in it, the taller yuh gets."

With the National River Academy, Lily felt that another of her "giant children" had been born, and its operation was one of her foremost interests until it closed. She was invited to speak to the students of the Academy often, and the director, Tom Tooker, considered her presentations on history, tradition, and the telling of tall tales of the river of inestimable value to the students.[14] A visitor to the academy could see included on its grounds a small building with a sign on it which said, "The Lily Peter Fire School."

There was no let-up in her invitations to speak, often at women's clubs which have been and are the butt of satire, labeled as superficial in purpose or "show cases" for indolent, rich women. Lily would own a grain of truth to such claims, yet she would assert that the clubs fulfill a genuine need for a place to exercise courtesy, in the courtly sense of the word, and the discipline to suppress petty competitiveness. She concedes that although the social relations between some club members were often shallow, the groundwork was laid for some genuine and straightforward friendships.

Recognition of Lily's name was extending farther and farther. During 1972, feature articles about Lily appeared in six publications: *Pan Pipes, The Paper, The Pen Woman, The Nashville Tennessean*, the *Winston-Salem Journal*, and *The Progressive Woman*. On February 8, Lily wrote Jeff Carr, her Vanderbilt friend:

. . . Since last spring my life has been like a tidal wave — all kinds of events, innumerable duties. . . .

The tidal wave hasn't slackened any, either. Since the first of the year I've been building — having built would be a better verb — a new wing to my house — 800 square feet in all, and it is going to transform the looks of the place. My farm carpenters are doing the work for me, but I am being my own architect, contractor and errand boy, so you can imagine the complications! . . . I will claim that I can do this chore about as well as anybody, having this good, stout little step-side pick-up truck to fetch and carry in. But when it comes to the intricacies of architecture and the logistics of being a contractor, I have to function on a cavewoman level, and the results of all of this architectural ado may turn out to be without rhyme or reason. . . .

This "architectural ado" was caused partly by Lily's insistence that a very narrow sun-porch attach the new, large room to her kitchen. To have attached the two rooms directly would have crowded an elm tree that had a long history of protection. Back in the mule age, there had been a mule lot at the back of the house, beyond the elm sapling, and Lily observed that every time this young tree got any growth to speak of, some mule would reach over the fence and bite the top out of it. She finally persuaded brother Jesse to set the fence back so the mules could not reach it. She then trimmed and nurtured the elm until now it is a huge, mature tree with the most unusual, spreading shape of any elm tree in Arkansas. Her bird feeders were under it.

During the summer, she worked on a book about the Mississippi River, a project she'd been asked to do as a member of the Joliet Commission which was planning a celebration of the anniversary of the Marquette-Joliet exploration of the Mississippi River. A young French teacher, Reid Lewis, from Illinois, taking the part of Louis Joliet, would reenact the expedition with his students as part of the celebration, and Helena would be Lewis' last stop. The committee members thought this called for an outstanding reception. They invited thirty-eight Cherokee Indians from the Carolinas and among other things planned to build a facade of a rustic church for holding the Catholic services as the original expedition had done. The committee realized they would have spent the $5,000 federal grant money before they had hardly started. They later enlisted a commitment of $10,000 from the state legislature, but at that time the chairman of the committee, John King, asked Lily to write a history of the expedition which would not only be educational, but financial, as its sale would raise money to defray the costs of the reception of the expedition. Lily sent to Vanderbilt for material, but the research for "the little book which could not be more than one hundred pages" turned out to be a monumental task. Lily, determined to stay with original sources, had to rely on memoirs of early explorers and translations of the journals of the Jesuit priests, the Sulpitian friars, and the Franciscan friars, and much to her consternation, she found conflicting accounts, reflecting considerable controversy. It became clear to her that she could not treat the subject without careful sorting to see what she could tell authentically. It took her well into the next year to complete it, entirely too near the time for the week-long reception.[15]

June of 1972 saw the conclusion of the Louisiana Purchase Marker affair. Not the hundred acres Lily wanted, but forty acres to be left natural was the amount of land eventually acquired. The asphalt road was completed, as well as the board walk to the monument, raised above the swamp water level on piers with natural wood railings and planks, treated but unfinished, to preserve the rustic atmosphere. Governor Bumpers set a date for a re-dedication of the park and monument.[16]

During that busy summer, Lily excitedly watched the completion of the Lily Peter Auditorium.

Wanting the most excellent event imaginable for its dedica-
tion in December, Lily and Helen Mosby, chairman of the Warfield
Concert Association, met frequently. Lily wanted to display Ar-
kansas artists, and what would be better than the Arkansas Sym-
phony Orchestra? But to disclaim regionalism, they engaged an
internationally known violinist, Guy Lumia, from New York City,
to be guest soloist. They invited every dignitary who would have
the remotest interest in the event and wrote to every out-of-state
contributor to the center.

Lily and Helen Mosby divided the task of the publicity, and
Lily day-dreamed about an extensive write-up in *The New York
Times*. All fall she would ask anyone she was conversing with
whether or not they knew any of the reporters on the *Times*. She
was having no luck whatsoever until she was in Stuttgart talking
to Calvin Manning, editor of the local paper, telling him about
the unique features of the auditorium. He commented that he
knew the southern representative of the *Times*, Roy Reed, and that
he would love that sort of a story. Lily responded, innocently, as
if she were having a spontaneous idea, "Oh Mr. Manning, would
you call him and tell him about it and that he will be receiving a
personal invitation from me very soon?" Of course, Mr. Manning
would.

As the date for the dedication of the auditorium came closer
and closer, Lily realized that she hadn't heard from Roy Reed.
Finally late Saturday afternoon while she was paying off the farm
hands, she received a phone call from Roy Reed and was elated.
However, their conversation was cut off immediately, and Lily
waited at least an hour in the store before he called again, explain-
ing that he was in a storm which had suspended phone service
in North Carolina, but that he would be in Helena for the dedica-
tion concert Sunday.

The dedicatory program began at 8:00 p.m. Lily was the em-
cee for the preconcert music remarks. Some say they lasted an

Lily, Senator John McClellan, and his wife Norma
at the opening concert in the Lily Peter Auditorium

hour; some say an hour and a half. Helen Mosby said that some complained to her afterward that Lily had, as usual, talked too long, but she told them that it was Lily's night and she deserved every minute she wanted to take. Lily was adamant that all donors should be recognized and planned her program around that idea. She categorized the donors according to whether they represented the federal, state, or local governments and invited donors to speak about the government they represented. So Senator John H. McClellan spoke for the federal government; the secretary of state of Arkansas spoke for Governor Bumpers who could

279

not attend. Mr. Clay Bumpers, Vice Chairman of PCCC board, spoke for the college; Helen Mosby spoke for former-resident donors; and Alma Faust spoke for local donors. The Reverend Cartwright from the original steering committee (he had since moved to Memphis) gave something of the history of the project.

After the concert, the show piece of which was Guy Lumia playing Mendelssohn's Violin Concerto, many attended a reception in spite of the late hour. Lily certainly did. She enjoyed the fun with the champagne set aside for the celebration, imbibing to the extent of her one dutiful sip. She never wavered from her lifelong resolution not to drink; her mother's stories of her grandfather's alcoholism loomed large in her memory. Besides, she claimed she could feel exultation naturally, without chemical stimulation, and could control excitement without sedation.

Local papers covered the event extensively, but the report that gave Helenians and many other Arkansans the most pleasure was Roy Reed's in *The New York Times*. It appeared on December 6, 1972, and included three-column pictures of both the interior and exterior of the auditorium and one of Lily in her gray silk brocade evening gown with a large orchid on her shoulder. But the sheer delight was a little map of Arkansas and the borders of Tennessee and Mississippi pinpointing the more populous cities and naming them in small print, but designating Helena in larger white print on a black block. Reed's opening paragraph read:

> A hundred years from now, when history records how this Mississippi River town of 21,422 persons became a famous musical center during the last quarter of the 20th century, there is a risk that the story will be dismissed as a Jack and the beanstalk legend.

He told of the Warfield inheritance, described the center and the history of its fruition and summarized the high points of Lily's activities. He announced that Van Cliburn would play there in

February. He concluded:

> A member of the orchestra said after Sunday night's dedica-
> tion, at which Miss Peter was the master of ceremonies, that
> some of his fellow musicians had grown restless waiting to
> play. But he said that he had told them, "Well, it's her audi-
> torium." (page M41)

That national publicity compensated for the slight which
Lily and Helen felt keenly over the fact that the Memphis *Com-
mercial Appeal* had used hardly any of the material which Helen
had carefully prepared, confining its account to a small notice on
one of the inner pages.

Lily would often compare this gala event to the appearances
of the Philadelphia Orchestra in Little Rock, but she felt it would
take some sort of electromagnetic instrument for measuring ec-
static impulses to determine which occasion gave her the most
pleasure. To be associated with Eugene Ormandy and the mem-
bers of his staff and orchestra, even for a short while, was a mar-
velous experience. Could anything be more pleasurable? Or could
anything be more pleasurable than providing, with the help of
others, a showcase for her fellow-Arkansans? Who could say?
She couldn't. And she could hardly wait for February and Van
Cliburn.

The harassment of the year was her fight with the White
River Drainage District over the rechanneling of Yellow Bank
Bayou (the "small river" DeSoto may have crossed) on Ratio. She
had offered two counter-proposals, but the matter was concluded
with a compromise to the satisfaction of no one. She learned les-
sons she would later use in opposing the channelization of Big
Creek, a matter still pending.

An unheralded, but truly triumphant event of 1972 was that
Lily paid off the one-and-a-half-million-dollar indebtedness in-
curred by the estate and back taxes, sixteen years after Jesse's death.[17]

Governor Dale Bumpers proclaims Lily Peter
Poet Laureate of the State of Arkansas

Notes

[1]Helen Mosby, Carlos Smith, and W. B. Cartwright came to Lily's home in June, 1969, and reported to her that they had begged a number of people to head up a committee to raise the money for the center with no success. They begged her for nearly two hours to accept the leadership role. Finally Helen said, "Lily, if you don't do it, it will never be done; we'll just have to give up the whole idea. Many people have suggested that you are the logical one to do it. We will help you right down to the wire." That was the statement that persuaded Lily, although she could take little pride in the position since they had already "scraped the barrel."

Early in July, the *Helena World* carried a full-page letter form Lily, as chairman, appealing for funds. This was a paid advertisement; however, she wrote many articles explaining the projected plan for the center. In July, she personally wrote and mailed the "native son" letter to former residents. By August there was such an impressive response that the committee thought the community should know and bought another page-spread and reproduced a dozen or so of the letters in it. During those months there was not a week in which something about the proposed center did not apprear in the local papers.

[2]Lily was displaying her photography often. She appeared at four different colleges for lectures and readings, besides at innumerable civic clubs. At the Poetry Society of Texas, she was awarded its Citation of Merit given every five years to the person it considers to have contributed the most to the arts. She was made "Guardian of Scouting" for a $5,000-contribution to boy scout work. The Sigma Alpha Iota Yearbook for '69-'70 was dedicated to her. Lily was honored at the Grand Prairie Festival of Arts in two ways: her song for which Dello Joio had written an accompaniment was premiered, and the recipient of one of her music scholarships at the University of Arkansas, Dean Kauffman, played an organ recital.

Other feathers were being ruffled, as were Harry Pearson's when he invited Lily to his award party. The *Commercial Appeal* in its "Arkansas-at-Large" column on September 14 gave the following bit of publicity. After telling of Lily's various projects, it said:

> Miss Lily, who is past 70, attends to her farm business in a pick-up truck. She has been having sort of a transportation problem the past five months.

It seems that for the fourth year in a row a family of gold-finches has taken up summer residence in a stake pocket of her truck. "I wouldn't disturb them for anything," she quipped. So the truck has been parked since last April while the goldfinches hatched out three separate families.

The birds had had it timed just right — because Miss Lily's car broke down last week about the same time that the birds finally vacated the truck.

Miss Peter reportedly remained unruffled last week when she was to attend a formal dinner in Little Rock — she drove up in her truck.

It was some years later that a true Audubon-type bird watcher came to visit and discovered that the little golden birds were not goldfinches. They were prothonotary warblers. And they were back to the vehicle shed in the blistering summer of 1980; however, Red and Lily had diverted them from the stake pocket to a tomato can sitting on the two-by-four ledge of the shed just a few feet away. As Harry Pearson said to this biographer, "You will never capture Lily directly. She vanishes like a fog. She is an American Original, and there are not many of them." (Telephone interview with Harry Pearson, 7 Mar. 1981.)

[3]On May 27 Lily was in Little Rock on business and was getting ready for speaking to the Arkansas Writers' Conference. She had left her car at Rebsamen Motors for some minor service, had returned for it, and after having paid the bill, was walking toward it rapidly, hoping to leave Little Rock before the heavy afternoon traffic. All at once, she turned her ankle and "measured her length" on the concrete sidewalk. Some gentlemen in the motor company saw her fall and rushed out to help her; she hadn't moved because she was stunned from the fall. They gathered her up most solicitously, carried her into the lobby, and laid her on a couch which was there for customers. She assured them that she would be all right in a few minutes, but she was in extreme pain and unable to stand. She attempted to alleviate their concern by making light conversation between her attempts to stand, but she was finally sure that she wasn't going to be able to. She could move one foot and thought about asking the men to carry her to the car, but she realized that that would be putting herself and others in danger.

Lily finally called her friend, Lynnah Selman, a doctor, and told her what had happened. Lynnah, of course, said she would come for her immediately, and upon arrival told Lily that she had already called Dr. McKenzie, an orthopedist, who would meet them at St. Vincent Infirmary.

Lily had a broken pelvis bone. Even though she was hospitalized for six weeks at an age when many have given up, she fully recovered and resumed her busy schedule. She just vowed never to hurry again and that her name from that day on would be "Miss Sorghum Molasses in Winter."

[4]Personal interview with John Easley, Ph.D., President, Phillips County Community College, Helena, Arkansas, 4 Aug. 1980.

[5]"[O]nly a box camera" is quoted from Richard Allin's column, "Our Town," *Arkansas Gazette*, 22 Sept. 1970, p. 1B.

[6]Helen and Virgil Copeland related many pleasant experiences in their years of working for Lily and her brother Jesse. Virgil said that every leap year he would say quite often, "Miss Lily, you had better get on the ball and find you a man." She took teasing well and always answered, "Oh, Virgil, you're so cute." (Personal interview with Helen and Virgil Copeland, 14 Feb. 1981.)

[7]During January, 1971, there was a lull in the drive for the Lily Peter Auditorium. Resulting from what could very well have been stress and exhaustion, Lily's bout with pneumonia caused her to spend several days in bed. She was determined, nevertheless, to participate in Governor Dale Bumpers' inaugural ceremony. It was not surprising that she was invited to do so. In December she had received a personal letter from Bumpers thanking her for her contribution and support in his campaign in which he defeated Governor Winthrop Rockefeller. She was invited to bring a show of her photography to be placed in the capitol rotunda, where the ceremony was held, and to read a poem of her own composition. The day before the ceremony, the 11th, she declared herself well and, with the help of her great-nephew, Harold Crisp, she went to Little Rock and set up the exhibit. They stayed the night, because the reading of her poem, "This is Our Arkansas," was the first item on the afternoon program and the ceremonies started at 10:00 a.m. There was a musical concert given by the Arkansas Symphony Chamber Orchestra and the Bach Society of Greater Little Rock under the direction of B. Cecil Gibson and the Schola Cantorum of the University of Arkansas directed by Richard Brothers. She was in the receiving line at the Governor's reception.

[8]There follows the text of the Terry letter:

Dear Lily Peter, Congratulations! Actually the people to be congratulated are the members of the *Democrat's* committee who chose you — It is a salute to cultural affairs through you.

My Admiration and good wishes, Adolphine Terry (28 Mar. 1971)

[9]Dr. and Mrs. Maxwell Worthley (Edith) from the staff of the University of Arkansas at Fayetteville accepted Lily's invitation. By a happy coincidence, Dr. Worthley's brother from Australia, whom he had not seen in several years, was in Washington on business, so they combined a family reunion and attendance at the concert. Dr. Worthley wrote a letter to the biographer January 27, 1981, which contained a touching tribute to Lily, extravagant yet poignant.

[10]Ivar Lou Duncan told the biographer that when Vanderbilt invited Lily to show her photography there (in the spring before the Philadelphia Orchestra concerts), she attended the showing in the company of Thor Johnson. She said that he stood before each photograph for long periods of time, seeming totally engrossed with each of them and that afterward on many occasions he praised the beauty and composition of many of them by name. This was somewhat more than the usual intensity of his praise of Lily's talent and accomplishments. (Personal interviews with Ivar Lou Duncan, Ph.D., Head of Department of English, Belmont College, retired, Nashville, Tennessee, 27 August 1980.)

[11]*Congressional Record*, 14 September 1971, p. S14282.

[12]Letter to Lily from Felix Greissle, Flushing, New York, 8 Feb. 1981.

[13]*The Commercial Appeal*, 4 Jan. 1971, p. 15.

[14]Personal interview with Tom Tooker, 31 July 1980.

[15]Another spring event and the occasion for the article in *The Tennessean* was Lily's visit to Vanderbilt in April. Its introduction stated:

Lily Peter, having probed successfully into the area of letters, music, teaching and large-scale farming, tried her hand Monday at gaining some knowledge of microbacteriology at Vanderbilt University.

The little lady from Arkansas is in Nashville to attend the two-day conference at the children's Regional Medical Center on H-flu meningitis which she underwrote, after learning of the need from her friend, Dr. Sarah Sell, associate professor of pediatrics at Vanderbilt.

Scientists from across the country are here sharing knowledge on research toward a vaccine to prevent the disease that afflicts 20,000 children annually.

"This is my first time to sponsor a medical conference." Lily said, "I had read of the disease in the Little Rock papers and was very interested, so here, I hope I can do some good in helping save the lives of little children. I've always been interested in medicine and read medical books as a child.". . . (25 April 1972, p. 10)

Lily's sponsorship of the conference had come about while she was visiting friends in Nashville the previous summer. Dr. Sell, Lily's Vanderbilt room-mate, had often invited Lily to visit her at her laboratory to save time and to please Lily, who found it fascinating. Sally had been doing research in the field of H-flu meningitis for years; in fact, she discovered the means of diagnosing it and had received acclaim in the medical world. She was called to Washington for consultation when President John Kennedy and his wife, Jacqueline, had a son born with the disease. The best consultants, however, were not able to prevent his early death. Sally told Lily about the research that was being done at several medical centers and about her efforts to raise funds to hold a conference for giving researchers a chance to compare their findings. This might implement a break-through in finding treatment. So far all that had been volunteered was $2,500 from the Eli Lilly Company. Lily immediately said, "Why Sally, I'd be more than happy to give you the money since it would help save the lives of little children. How much would it take?" Sally responded that she thought they could put it on for $10,000 more, provided they were careful about expenses. Volunteers had already offered to house the delegates. Lily wrote a check for the amount.

The Vanderbilt University Press published a hard-back compendium of the papers given at the conference and a summarization, and on the fly-leaf is a dedication to Lily. An epigraph contains a quotation from one of her unpublished poems, "Meditation on an Electron Microscopy." (Sarah S. W. Sell, Ed. *Hemophilus Influenza* [Nashville: Vanderbilt Univ. Press, 1973].)

Dr. Sell said that Lily referred to her (Dr. Sell's) laboratory as a wonderland and that Lily would remark that she would just have to take a day off and learn chemistry. This was laughable on the surface, also somewhat symbolic, but, Sally said, it was amazing how rapidly and with what comprehension Lily could read technical material. (Personal interview with Dr. Sarah Sell, 29 Aug. 1980.)

[16]*The Marvell Messenger*, 23 June 1972, p. 1.

[17]Tapes 8, 9, 11, 15, 18, 38, 339, 40, 43, 52, 53, 56, 65. Torreyson Library Archives, University of Central Arkansas.

Lily and Brooks Griffin with the next governor,
Bill Clinton and wife Hilary

Chapter IX

RIDING INTO THE SILVER DAWN
1972-1975

Let us now praise all brave men who have faced the morning
    With the sun in their eyes, knowing their burden is danger;
Scorn and hardship and toil their reward, the warning;
    Their home, the land of the stranger.

The track of the Dream is blood on mountain and river.
    Call it obsession, delusion, the Dream is the Maker
Of all man has that is worthy — it is the Giver,
    The Preserver, the Earth Shaker.

We never can pay our debt to those who discover:
    They give us continents, moons, for six feet of clay.
Like mythic shapes of the past, their presences hover
    In the vague hodden-gray

Of our mind's back corridors, now that we are the arrogant
    Heirs of all of their goods, being the living;
The sole custodians of the treasures of which we are celebrant,
    That live only in the regiving,

The sifting of dross, the rechallenging, reaffirmation
    Of the gifts our Discoverer-Dreamers have left for our need.
Let these words of praise be as a rededication
    Of mind, of heart and of creed!
                Lily Peter
                "In Praise of Dreamers,
                Who Are the Only Discoverers"
                The Sea Dream of the Mississippi

Van Cliburn performed at the Lily Peter Auditorium in February of 1972, and the clamor for tickets started the moment the concert was announced. It was only a short time until all of the 1,200 seats were taken, and the Helena Fire Department was called to see what would be allowed for temporary seating. By using portions of the stage, they could seat another three hundred. Van Cliburn was called in New York for his permission, and he said, "Put all the seats you need on the stage. Just do not put anybody on top of the piano." Surprisingly, no one was turned away.[1]

The great night came, and Lily, clad in a long Scotch plaid woolen skirt and a bright blue turtleneck sweater, received in the aisles of the auditorium. She was given the assignment of reserving two rows of seats near the front. Ernest Cunningham, the representative from Phillips County, had asked the governor and a number of state officials, and they had accepted. By the time Lily explained to a group in one aisle that the seats were reserved for the Governor and his party, some other groups had seated themselves on the opposite aisle. She felt as if she were "running circles" and wished that the building committee had not had to delete the velvet rope markers for reserved seats from the original building contract. She was glad that she had taken time to ask people to keep sending money until there was enough to make up the deficiencies caused by cost cutting.

In the midst of this task, she did not have time to know about the furor that was taking place back stage. Van Cliburn had not arrived. Everyone was either concerned about his well-being or irritated at his tardiness or both. Dr. Easley, President, Phillips County Community College, suggested calling the highway patrol; others wanted to call the Memphis airport. The late Sam Anderson, member of the Warfield Concerts Committee, suggested, "Well, if Van Cliburn does not get here, we'll ask Governor to make a speech." Thinking that Cliburn would arrive any moment caused a delay in doing anything, and finally at 8:20 p.m.,

Lily, Senator Dale Bumpers, and wife Betty
talk with Van Cliburn on stage after the concert

he strode across the stage (his height making the strides seem like those of a giant), sat down at the piano, and started playing immediately with such fire and brilliance and aplomb that the audience soon forgot their waiting. Lily noticed right away that he could hardly get his knees under the piano, but he played his program and gave many encores.

Immediately after Cliburn concluded his playing, Lily went straight up to him to compliment his performance, but before she could say a word, he asked her what had happened to the casters on the piano legs. He actually shook his finger at her, thinking she must be in authority, and gave her a good-natured scolding. It was a sight that *The Commercial Appeal* photographer did not fail to record on film.

There was no member of the committee who dared stage the usual reception for that crowd at home, so arrangements were made for the Helena Country Club. A huge crowd gathered there, drank punch, ate hors d'oeuvres and cakes, and waited and waited and waited.

Why the long wait? The summer before when Lily was showing her photography at Winston-Salem, she conversed with a young man who had been Van Cliburn's host when he gave a concert at Nashville. The man had contacted Cliburn in advance and learned that his favorite food was turnip greens and cornbread. Lily told Helen about this, and they decided that party food just would not be adequate for a healthy young man who had come from expending the amount of energy required to give a concert and arranged that Cliburn be served a full dinner which he ate alone in the dining room of the club. Helen and Lily guarded the door. Then as a publicity stunt a small table was set in the pro shop, where Cliburn and Lily were served his favorite southern fare, turnip greens and cornbread. Lily treasures her picture *tête-à-tête* with Van Cliburn in candlelight and her visit with him. They discussed history, music, and Lily's ancestry, and he did explain why he was late. He had visited an old friend in Memphis, Gary Witt, and both of them completely misjudged the amount of time it would take to drive to Helena.

Needless to say, many were angry about the waiting. Some did not wait. It is safe to say that, in any typical gathering of a number of the civic leaders in Helena-West Helena, one could easily elicit an argument between those who thought Lily should not be allowed to monopolize the attention of visiting artists and those who knew how much such brief encounters meant to her and considered that her contributions to making the concerts possible merited the patience required to indulge her desires.

This time the publicity more than exceeded expectations. The men from *The Commercial Appeal* placed their report in a feature article, "Miss Lily of Marvell," in *Mid South*, the Sunday magazine of the paper (page 4). It was a four-page feature with several pictures. The entire front page (no margin at all) was filled with a color photograph of Lily and Cliburn on stage, with him wagging his finger in her face. She was enchanted (one of Lily's favorite words to express great pleasure).[2]

A pleasant relationship between Van Cliburn and Lily developed and endured. He sent her flowers many times. In 1976 he had his Memphis friend, Gary Witt, call Lily and ask her to send him an account of what musical events were occurring for the Moravians on July 17, 1776. He had been invited to give a television program in New York on July 19, 1976. He was in Japan on concert tour, and the TV talk would take place immediately after he returned to the states. Lily had told Cliburn about the Moravian celebration, but because she wanted a precise account of the day, she called her cousin, Lee Butterfield, for help. Lee told the Moravian archivist, who wrote a complete account taken from the journals of the Central Church in Bethlehem, the one at Nazareth, and from John Frederick Peter's diary. (All Moravian ministers were required to keep diaries of their tenures.) There were formal *singstunden* at the churches, and on that day a group departed from Bethlehem for the Muskingham River in Ohio. Lily added an explanation of the *singstunde* and more general information and forwarded the data to Cliburn's friend to send to the agent in New York City in time for his use.[3]

But much of her time was devoted to her history of the Marquette-Joliet Expedition which was taking more than she had estimated. She pushed herself to fatigue because she knew it should be out well in advance of the reenactment if it were to fulfill its purpose. She finally got her manuscript to an eastern Arkansas printing firm which had been engaged to publish it. It took the workmen much longer than it should have, and Lily was aghast at the galley sheets. The copy was riddled with errors, and it was obvious the firm was not equal to the task. She took it to the Democrat Printing and Lithographing Company in Little Rock, only to find that Lawrence Harper, its manager, had promised to take a holiday with his family, another cause for delay. When the galley sheets were ready from this firm, someone incorrectly mailed the package to Marianna where it lay in the post office for five days before being traced.

One night in March the area had a bad storm with eleven inches of rain that interrupted telephone service. A neighbor who had no outage brought Lily word that Ethel, her sister in Falfurias, Texas, was trying to reach her. Lily was working on the very last of the correction sheets to her manuscript, stopping every so often to walk over to the store and try to reach Ethel. She completely forgot her pledge to move like "Lady Molasses in winter" and slipped on her wet sidewalk and hurt herself so badly that she had to crawl to the house. Examination revealed two hairline fractures to her right leg. This injury necessitated immobility for six weeks, but she managed to finish her little book which she named *The Sea Dream of the Mississippi.*

In June, *The New York Times* printed an article on the celebration of the Marquette-Joliet expedition entitled, "6 Intrepid Voyageurs Paddling Into History," a month before the expedition was to arrive in Helena.[4] Eastern Arkansas folks involved in Serendipity Week (an annual event with which the arrival of the expedition serendipitously coincided) were stimulated by the *Times* article, and the momentum of preparation increased. Lily wrote every friend and relative she had and invited them to the "landing," including Van Cliburn, to whom she sent the *Mid-South*'s magazine story.

It was July 1 before *The Sea Dream* . . . was ready, a real disappointment since the celebration was only two weeks away. Lily made several appearances autographing the book, and the sales and publicity went comparatively well. To Lily the highlight of the week's festivities was the landing of the voyagers. The river was indeed the focal point that day. Thousands of cars were parked on the levee. The U. S. Navy furnished boat rides all day long prior to arrival of Lewis and his group. Governor Dale Bumpers arrived the night before aboard the *Brown & Surf*, a seventy-foot Chris Craft yacht belonging to Charley Meyers who was taking it on its maiden voyage from the factory at Holland, Michigan, to its home in Little Rock. A young man who was trying to set a long-distance record by water skiing from Minneapolis to New Orleans was also on hand. Lily saw the canoeists pull up on the levee; she heard the Hendrix College Choir sing; she observed the celebration of the mass by His Excellency Andrew J. McDonald of Little Rock assisted by Father Charles McEnery (portrayer of Marquette on the journey).[5]

The party of jubilant young men dramatizing the historic event arrived, each one of them tanned, handsome, and healthy. They were entertained with a large dinner at the community center in the evening, and they entertained with storytelling and singing French *voyageur* songs of the 18th century in a series of appearances. Lily visited with all of them and, as was her custom, invited them to come and see her. Reid Lewis was so intrigued with her that he did so at Christmastime when he returned to speak to the historical society. He told her how he had underestimated his costs and was in financial trouble even though he had had excellent support from a federal grant and even some subsidy from Canada and France. Lily surprised him by saying that she would give him $10,000 if that would help. He was astonished, but certainly accepted it. Even though Lily deemed it a good cause, she regretted her generosity in that Reid returned a number of times with financial troubles.

Lily was quite happy with the event. As a background for the Cherokee Indians who were featured, there was an excellent display of Indian artifacts and a mockup of an Indian Village. Her book continued to sell, and the proceeds were given to the Phillips County Bicentennial Committee after all the expenses of Serendipity Week were paid.

Writing the book and participating in the tricentennial festival whetted Lily's appetite for the nation's bicentennial. She was soon deeply involved in local, state, and national bicentennial planning, giving it all the energy she could muster outside her farming and ginning. Although she designated no specific amounts to any one thing, she told a number of her friends that she intended to contribute $200,000 to the bicentennial celebration.

The Arkansas Federation of Music Clubs held its annual convention in April 1974 in Little Rock. Lily was there because the federation had named her its U. S. Bicentenial Coordinator. There she made public her intention to spend $200,000 on the commemoration, and Tommy Yates, a UPI reporter, interviewed Lily about her gift and other activities and sent out the story. All the rest of the year Lily heard from friends who sent her twenty-odd copies of releases from out-of-state newspapers. One was from a former Marvell student who had seen it in *Stars and Stripes*. It amused Lily to see what portions of the story were selected and the variety of headlines which were used.

It had been a wet, tedious spring requiring several replantings of the crops. She had influenza, was not feeling good, and embarked on the highly strenuous task of estate planning, employing Gaston Williams and Lawrence Burrow of the Worthen Bank & Trust Company, Little Rock. They worked out a last will and testament with which Lily was never quite satisfied, and codicils were regularly added and removed.

Another frustration in 1974 was that two of her favorite politicians, both of whom she really considered statesmen, were running against one another for the U. S. Senate. On June 14, she had this letter from William Fulbright:

> Dear Lily, I cannot tell you how pleased I was to receive your cordial letter, written after the election. Indeed, you and Phillips

County performed magnificently, but, unfortunately, there is only one Lily Peter in Arkansas — and most of the other voters seemed determined to have a change.

One of the great pleasures of public life has been the opportunity to meet individuals such as you, and to see what one person can do with spirit and imagination. I believe you have made a greater impact on the cultural life of Phillips County and Arkansas than any other person in our history — in addition to being a good farmer.

I do hope that our paths may cross in the future so that I may have the opportunity to thank you personally for all your help. In the meantime, Betty joins in sending our affection and good wishes. Sincerely,

Dale Bumpers wrote to Lily on June 20, 1974:

Please accept my sincere apologies for the delay in answering your very thoughtful and considerate letter of May 23. Much of the mail that came in during the campaign was held and accumulated by my staff for my perusal following the campaign. However, I had to make quick plans to attend the National Governors' Conference in Seattle, and then come home and start preparing for a special Session of the Legislature. . . .

Running for the Senate was a very trying experience because I know that many people had mixed emotions and strong allegiances to both of us. I certainly understand fully the happy relationship you have enjoyed with Senator Fulbright, and would fully expect you to support him. Your support of him will in no way diminish the great respect and admiration Betty and I have for you and we will look forward to seeing you on many more happy occasions.

Betty sends her love.

That Dale Bumpers won a senate seat would have made her quite happy at any other time, but that he had unseated Bill

Fulbright grieved her.

Despite her being in her ninth decade of living, Lily studied and learned a new art, that of fashion modeling, in the year 1974. The Phillips County Cotton Wives Association asked Lily to become a special member of their group of married women. Its purpose was to promote the use of cotton fabric by giving style shows of all-cotton outfits. The group hired a young woman from the Powers Modeling School to come to Helena, and she gave a course to all the members. So Lily had another schooling to add to her varied curriculum. She loved perusing the many catalogs which came in her mail box looking for all cotton outfits. Once in the fall of 1980, the group was staging a show at the Mid-South Fair in Memphis. During one of Lily's walks, something about the lighting made her dizzy, and she "measured her length" on the stage, but it did not daunt her. The style shows were a regular activity for Lily until the group disbanded in the early eighties.[6]

Nineteen seventy-four was the year Ethel retired from teaching, coming home and living with Lily until such time as she could move into the old home-house which Lily had begun remodeling for her. Sister Oma had retired, but her health was such that she chose to live in Park Manor Retirement Home in Memphis. In July, Lily was named to the "CIRCLE OF FIFTEEN" of Sigma Alpha Iota, a national music sorority.[7]

By September the very real possibility of the channelization of Big Creek was looming large on the horizon. Big Creek rises from its tributaries, a number of smaller creeks including Big Piney Creek out from Brinkley, near the Woodruff-St. Francis County line near Interstate Highway I-40 about sixty miles west of Memphis. It flows through these counties and Lee, Monroe, and Phillips Counties in a general southerly direction until it reaches the 49.1 mile marker on the White River. Lily had made a thorough investigation of every aspect of the Big Creek Drainage District project of straightening and deepening Big Creek's channel and acquiring acres and acres of floodlands, excellent wildlife habitat. She was, as a lover of nature, opposed to it; as a practical caretaker of the land and the water table, opposed to it; as a tax payer, opposed to it. But to add to all that, her very home and birthplace were in the mitigation lands. She was terrified that it might come to pass. As James King (her farm manager) said, "It upset her more than anything besides the deaths of her brothers."[8] She went to the Memphis office of the Corps of Engineers and paid them a visit. The entire Big Creek episode is to be accounted for in the next chapter.

In connection with Lily's bicentennial gifts of music to the community, one was a total failure. She thought an international gesture of good will would be most appropriate and arranged with Columbia Artists for a program called "The Carnival of Mexico" to be presented on December 8, 1974, at the auditorium. It cost her $3,250, and she imagined that it would be a glorious opportunity to bring to the community beautiful Spanish music and dance, fostering better understanding of a neighbor-nation. She admitted that the costumes were gorgeous and the dancing superb, but to her horror the music was electronically amplified and "jazzed up" to the degree that after fifteen or twenty minutes, she left the auditorium and went out into the foyer. Helen Mosby came to see about her, thinking she was ill. When Helen found out what was the matter with Lily, she turned off the amplifiers. In minutes, they were back on, and the manager informed Helen that the use of them was required in the contract. Some others came out to commiserate with Lily, but most of the audience loved it, and Lily received many thanks for it. But nothing ever altered Lily's determination not to accept jazz elements in music.

The Big Creek Protective Association was meeting in every community in the area, so that Lily would often be occupied with it several nights in a row. She was so busy that all correspondence was neglected, and she didn't realize when she received a lavish bouquet of flowers from Thor Johnson on Christmas Eve, that he had arranged for its delivery from the hospital. (Thor was director of the Nashville Symphony, a Moravian friend from the days of his initiation of the Moravian Music Festival.)

It was a painful shock to her when she learned that he had died on January 16, 1975. She had been in touch with him as late as the past November. They had made a plan for another recording of Moravian music to help celebrate the bicentennial. Thor was going to conduct the Nashville Symphony Orchestra and the Peabody Madrigalians (a chorus) in a performance of a work of music, "Psalm of Joy," which John Frederick Peter had composed for "A Solemn Day of Thanksgiving for the Restoration of Peace" at Salem, North Carolina, at the end of the Revolutionary War after the treaty of peace was signed in Paris in 1783, the first and only celebration of that first "Fourth of July." Other states were asked to celebrate the day, but Carolina was the only one that did. This would be on one side of the disc, and for the other side, Director of Moramus Karl Kroeger had composed a work in keeping with the other. For this project Lily had contributed $25,000.

Lily was not able to attend Thor's funeral in Nashville or burial in Winston-Salem, but close friends to both Thor and Lily told her about his illness and death. In late November on a trip to be a guest conductor for a young people's orchestra in North Carolina, he had noticed that his right thumb would become periodically numb. It continued to become numb more often, but he was so busy, he ignored it as long as possible. When he did consult a doctor, he was hospitalized for tests, and it was discovered that he had a rapidly growing, inoperable brain tumor. Lily said, "And so he passed away in just a few weeks. But, my dear, when he was dying, to think he would remember to have someone send me those flowers; you know how it touched me and how sad it made me feel. I didn't even know that he was ill. And I was ill myself and he didn't know it." But it was one of her most treasured memories that Thor had loved her and had asked her to marry him.[9]

Thus began two years in which Lily was to feel so weak and listless that she could hardly rise in the morning. There was no pain, but there was no zest. She refused to believe that she was ill; she was sure that, if she could just slow down and rest a few days, she would be all right. But in spite of this, her fervor for the bicentennial and her fear of the channelization of Big Creek were powerful emotions that pushed her on and on. It was two years before she consulted a doctor.[10]

On January 29, Lily gave the second in a series of fifteen organ recitals which she was financing to celebrate the Bicentennial and display the seventy-five-thousand-dollar organ she had given the community college the previous year, housed, of course, in the Lily Peter Auditorium. Early in 1974 Lily had started the necessary correspondence to get one of the finest organists in the world for the dedication of the organ. She had known that the Episcopal Church of the Virgin in New York City had a reputation for upholding the finest standards of excellence for organ and choir work and had written to the rector for recommendations. It happened that the rector was the agent for McNeil Robinson, organist at the church, and he had just arranged a tour of England for Robinson to play at Chichester and Durham Cathedrals and a number of smaller churches. In addition to having to make this trip, Robinson became ill in the fall from hepatitis, causing great difficulty in establishing a date at Helena. Lily had wanted him for the first organ recital, and he came.

At the program of dedication, Lily presented "The Instrument and the Artist," and Dr. John Easley gave a speech, the "Acceptance of the Instrument." The last item on the recital program, which followed a traditional group of selections, was "Improvisation on a Submitted Theme." All involved knew McNeil Robinson had invited Lily to submit the theme. It was the melody of one of her songs, "Ballad for a Tapestry." In their correspondence, Lily had revealed that she had composed some songs, and Robinson had suggested such an item be included on the program. Lily was overwhelmed with what he did with the theme and thought it one of the loveliest numbers on the program. She had a visit with him, and, as he drank his milk (a requirement for those recovering from hepatitis), he told her of his experiences in England. He also allayed her fears that the Allen electronic organ might be a lesser instrument; he praised its capability and sound. If anyone has doubts about Lily's love for music, her capacity to experience ecstacy in the presence of its beauty, the letter which she wrote on January 31, 1975, should allay such doubts:

> Dear McNeil Robinson: This evening I must write about the concert! It was all superb, all glowing with the strength and beauty of your musical concepts, for you brought to the works of Bach, Dupre and the others the element of magic that the notes cannot convey unless they are recreated, given a life of their own through the medium of the mind, personality, technique of the supreme artist, which you are indeed!
>
> It is when we come to the improvisation that I am almost speechless in my wish to communicate to you what this music meant to me, but I will try.
>
> In one of her later, heart-breaking poems, Sylvia Plath has this line:
>
> "Once one has seen God, what is the answer?"
>
> I can say more than that. I have not only seen Apollo, I have held converse with him, and he did me the honor of performing a miracle for me, in accepting from his altar a small offering of a few bars of music that I had composed years ago, in honor of Apollo, not dreaming that I should ever have the privilege of seeing the god face to face, much less of having

my offering noticed by him; and in creating from the theme of these few bars an improvisation of such incredible imaginative power and beauty that it transcends all description. I can only write about it indirectly, by making of it a symbolic narrative in the present tense. This was the most glorious moment of my life, and I am living this moment over again.

"All in green went my Love riding
on a great horse of gold
into the silver dawn."

It is you, McNeil Robinson, in the guise of Apollo, who in this music is riding the great horse of gold into the silver dawn, and I am riding with you, for it is my theme that is the motif for this empyreal flight. It is fitting that I should know something of horsemanship, for you will recall that my sign of the Zodiac is Gemini, and the Gemini were originally the gods of horsemen, along with their other powers and attributes.

"Horn at hip went my Love riding,
riding the echo down
into the silver dawn."

The sound of the huntsman's horn! The zest! The eagerness! And the echoes! — ah, the echoes! They remember what we had almost forgotten! The four lean hounds and the tall, taut deer! What are we searching for? Shall we ever find it?

"Bow at belt went my Love riding,
riding the mountain down
into the silver dawn."

The deadly bow and the mountain's hidden claws! What dangers lurk in these dense catamount shadows that the dawn has not dispersed!

"the famished arrow sang before."

It is too much! I cannot write of it all! There come to mind four lines of my own, from THE GREAT RIDING.

"the Star-Seekers, the Sun-Treaders, riding,
riding forever, forever riding — oh, never
walking! — they on their seraphim-tended horses of
gaunt flame, through the flowering lanes of eternity."

Are not you and I of the race of the Star Seekers, the Sun-Treaders? And here we are riding into the silver dawn together! What could we not accomplish together! Will the famished arrow cheat us of this destiny?

All this, and much, much more, your music said to me in those enchanted moments, and I am still lost in this enchantment. When the Law of Gravitation drags me back to earth again I will write of other things. In the meantime, I can only say Thank You, Thank You for the power and the glory!

Yours in the daffodil weather, . . .

Of course, the Law of Gravity brought Lily down off that cloud of delight, but she was sustained from a complete let-down because another thrilling event was in the offing. On February 5, the *Twin City Tribune* printed on its front page an account of an interview with Jim Walden, president of Helena Marine Services, excerpts of which follow:

"Miss Lily Peter" will begin working for the Helena Marine Services sometime this summer.

Lest somebody get the idea that Miss Lily Peter . . . is forsaking her farming interests, quitting writing, forsaking her multitude of civic projects and going to work for Jim Walden . . . that's not the case at all.

Rather, by mid-summer, there will be two "Miss Lilys" in these parts.

The first Miss Lily will, of course, be at her farm. . . . The second will be on the Mississippi River — a towboat which will bear Miss Lily's name.

Walden, a long-time friend and admirer of Miss Lily, made the announcement today, saying that Calumet Ship-building Company at Morgan City, Louisiana, has been awarded a contract to build four towboats for Helena Marine Services. "The first is due to be commissioned in early summer," said Walden. "It will be commissioned as 'The Lily Peter' in recognition of Miss Lily's contributions to the State of Arkansas, Phillips County, the National River Academy, and the river industry."

Walden said he had felt for some time that an appropriate method should be found to honor Miss Lily. . . .

Why was a towboat named after Lily Peter? It happened this way. Lily was going into the First National Bank at Helena to see Francis Thompson, long-time chairman of the board, to enlist his help in the Big Creek matter. She saw Thompson, James Bush (another member of the board), and Walden sitting at a table in the back of the bank discussing something so serious that all three looked as if they were at a funeral. She chatted with the receptionist and was about to decide it was an unpropitious moment, when Thompson saw her and invited her to come back and talk with them. He told her they were concerned because it looked as if they were going to lose the river academy after all. Lily knew that the academy had experienced all sorts of difficulties as a pioneer institution — inexperienced teachers, lack of textbooks, students who knew not what to expect — and she knew that St. Louis and Greenville had never withdrawn their "eager eyes" from its potential for failure. Neither was she sure that these cities had nothing to do with the academy's problems with the Environmental Protection Agency inspection which was threatening to close the school unless an adequate sewage plant was installed immediately.

The men relayed these facts to her. They also told her that they had canvassed the town for sources of money and that there was none in sight. Lily asked how much money it would take, and when told, she said without blinking, "I'll give you all the $62,000 it will take to build the sewage system." She explained that she didn't have her checkbook with those "little wiggly numbers" that are required, but that she would get a check for $25,000 to Jim Walden the next day for him to take to the board meeting in New Orleans. She suggested that he get a "signed and sealed" commitment in exchange for that earnest money that there would be no more talk ever of moving the academy. This was just what was needed, and Walden accomplished the task. Lily paid the remainder of the sum when it was needed.[11]

March 19, 1975, was the date of the Corps of Engineers hearing at Helena, the focal point of the final efforts of both sides of the question of channeling Big Creek. Lily says she was kept on even keel the day of the hearing because she enjoyed the Arkansas Symphony in Helena the night before.[12]

Because the ruling at the hearing was favorable to the opponents who had Lily on their side as a prime mover, that following October the Arkansas Wildlife Federation presented Lily with its "Conservationist of the Year" award. Her picture and a commentary on her deeds appeared in the elegant program. It said:

> As Chairman of the Big Creek Protective Association, Miss Peter was instrumental in setting up a public hearing this spring in Helena, Arkansas, on the Big Creek Project. The overwhelming majority of the testimony presented at the hearing was in opposition . . . and none of the pleas for common sense in dealing with the water resources of Arkansas were more eloquent than Miss Peter's. . . .

The program also had her poem "I Hear A Hawk Calling" printed in a frame on the inner side of the back page; on the other side of the page was reproduced one of her photographs, "Autumn on Big Creek." This event received regional publicity. One picture showed Lily receiving a kiss from gubernatorial aide, Richard Howell.[13]

What had she done about Big Creek? The next chapter tells.[14]

Notes

[1]Lily's role in bringing the auditorium into being placed her in the center of the musical events which were to come to Helena. She had told the Warfield Association not to let any opportunity for a great concert slip by because of lack of funds, that she would be glad to supplement the cost. Such was the case in the Cliburn concert; she paid half of his fee of $8,500.

Her friendship with Max and Edith Worthley (UAF music staff) made her want him to see and enjoy the new facility, so Lily underwrote performances at the Lily Peter Auditorium of his university opera production of *The Bartered Bride* on March 9 and 10.

There were other 1972 subsidies of the arts. In September, she donated $20,000 to Phillips County Community College "to enhance its music studies." This would partially pay for a teacher and the expenses of a department. For the Grand Prairie Festival at Stuttgart, she provided a fifty-dollar prize for paintings and paid for a performance by the chamber music group from the Arkansas Symphony Orchestra. She closed out the year by giving $5,000 to the Hendrix College Choir Fund. She had watched the work of the late Robert McGill and was glad to subsidize his and the choir's efforts. The Hendrix Choir had come to Helena for the Tricentennial and Serendipity Week and had actually gone out to Lily's home and sung for her there.

[2]*The Commercial Appeal* featured the event in its Sunday magazine Mid-South on p. 4, "Miss Lily of Marvell." Senator William Fulbright had the article placed in *The Congressional Record* (p. S12255, 27 June 1973).

[3]When Lily appeared on the campus of Arkansas Tech University in the fall of 1980, Richard E. Chalmers, an executive at Valmac Indus-

tries, Russellville, approached her telling her that he was happy to bring her greetings from Van Cliburn. In a telephone interview Chalmers told the writer that he had become well enough acquainted to be recognized by Cliburn during a period of time when both of them were in Houston, Texas. They had recently met by accident in the lobby of the Waldorf-Astoria Hotel in New York City and while visiting, Cliburn told Chalmers that if he ever saw Lily, to tell her that he had asked about her and sent her good wishes. When Chalmers saw in the local paper at Russellville that Lily was to be on campus, he made a special trip to see her and tell her about Cliburn's greetings. Lily said that Cliburn never wrote her; he loved the notes of music more than the written word, and Lily accepted him gladly the way he was. (12 Oct. 1981)

[4]Seth S. King, *The New York Times*, 18 June 1973, p. L18.

[5]Other assistants were Jesuits, Father Thomas H. Clancy, Jr., Head of the New Orleans District, and Father Francis J. Coco, both natives of Helena.

[6]The Phillips County Cotton Wives gained such a reputation that invitations came so often that they were forced to be selective in making appearances. Many of the members made their clothing, developing expert tailoring techniques. Margaret Van Meter Triplett furnished appropriate piano accompaniment for the members while they modelled. It made an entertaining show.

[7]On July 18, 1974 Jeanne Grealish, Chairman, Sigma Alpha Iota Foundation, and Constance Eberhart, Chairman of its "CIRCLE OF 15" Committee, wrote to Lily and told her that she was among the fifteen honored as follows:

Marion Anderson	Lily Krause
Mrs. August Belmont	Ruth Martin
Sarah Caldwell	Dika Newlin
Dorothy Chandler	Lily Peter
Nancy Hanks	Mrs. Jouette Shouse
Margaret Hillis	Louise Talma
Marguerite Hood	Alice Tully
Olga Koussevitsky	

Despite Lily's not feeling "up to par," she attended the Foundation Banquet at the Hotel Muehlebach in Kansas City, August 11, a part of the National Convention.. She was proud to be honored with her fellow-Arkansan, Sarah Caldwell, and Mrs. August Belmont and Mrs. Jouette Shouse who had developed Wolf Trapp. This event was, as usual, given much publicity, and Lily had another set of clippings and photographs for her collection and to send to friends. What would Lily say to that cynic who must utter, derisively, "All honors do not mean a thing. They are purely political"? Probably, "Oh, my dear. That's so true. . . but I just can't help but accept them."

[8]Personal interview with James King, 8 August 1980.

[9]Nashville and all Moravians grieved for Thor Johnson. There was an account of the tribute paid to him by the Nashville Orchestra Association written by Louis Nicholas in the January 26, 1975, issue of *The Tennessean* (p. 9F). In the same paper on the 31st, Natilee Duning wrote a full account of the recording which proceeded under the direction of Thor's brother-in-law, Dr. Malcolm Johns, complete with the research data provided by Marilyn Gombosi, musicologist, another good friend of Lily's (p. 39). Lily did not go to Nashville for this recording event because the date coincided with the presentation of her second organ recital.

[10]Phillips County officials had appointed Lily and Carolyn Cunninham, Head Librarian, Phillips County Library, West Helena, as co-chairmen for the bicentennial celebration. They, in turn, appointed a Heritage '76 Committee to emphasize the past; a Festival '76 Committee to plan and sponsors activities to represent every endeavor of human need: agriculture, manufacture, distribution, athletics, all arts and crafts, churches; a Horizons '76 Committee, for planning for future challenges and rededication to valuable enterprises. Specific programs had to be submitted to the state commission early in 1975. This took untold hours of imagination and strategy, and Lily did more than her part.

[11]Telephone interview with Jim Walden, 31 July 1980.

Walden also told of another experience he later arranged for Lily to make her happy. He made reservations on the *Cooperative Spirit*, a towboat owned by AgritransCon, for Lily and Dorothy Sanders, an executive secretary at the river academy, to travel from St. Louis to New Orleans. Walden furnished his plane to take them to and from those points. Dorothy said she never enjoyed anyone's company more. Lily was intensely interested in the operation of the boat and wanted to stay in the pilot house most of the time. They shopped in New Orleans, and Dorothy told the author that Lily bought a beautiful rug with blue birds on it at a price of $4,000, but changed her mind and canceled the order, saying, "My dear, it was just too luxurious for my house" (Personal interview with Dorothy

309

Sanders, 31 July 1980). Lily told of the trip with relish. She said the pilot welcomed her to the pilot house, listened to her and showed her things until it came time to pilot the string of barges between bridge supports. "That called for absolute precision in handling and certain knowledge of the river and its currents." Lily gave an entire history of shipping on the river in personal interview tape number forty-five, and one item was that she and Dorothy enjoyed in their suite solid gold bathroom fixtures which had been salvaged by the Rose shipping line from the passenger steamboat era.

[12]This Arkansas Symphony concert on 18 March 1975 was another concert credited to the Warfield Concert Association paid for by Lily at the Lily Peter Auditorium. On March 23, Lily presented her third Bicentennial organ recital given by Herman Hess, Jr., and his wife, Patricia, soprano, from Arkansas College, Batesville.

She went to Southern Baptist College at Walnut Ridge for a reading in early April and prepared for the fourth organ concert (the final one for the season) on April 18. This time she had procured the talent of Roger Fisher, Organist and Master of the Choristers in Chichester Cathedral, England, on tour in this country. Bach and Mozart, Harris and Vierne, all were a joy to Lily. She had chosen 3:00 p.m. on Sunday afternoons for most of these concerts, and she was broken-hearted at the size of the crowds. Brooks Griffin, Lily's farm manager at Ratio, said that he knew they would be small, and for that reason he attended all of them. It was his least favorite music because it was so serious and was associated with funerals in his mind. He and Winston Mosby often took long intermissions together (Telephone interview with Brooks Griffin, 17 Aug. 1980).

[13]*Stuttgart Daily Leader*, 13 Oct. 1975, p. 1.

[14]Tapes 1, 11, 12, 13, 14, 16, 18, 22, 25, 27, 29, 31, 53, and 57. Torreyson Library Archives, University of Central Arkansas.

Chapter X

MISS LILY VERSUS
THE U. S. CORPS OF ENGINEERS

None remember this beauty:
the March diaphony
of leaf and bloom: the April madrigals:
the nesting of the white cranes in the cool branches:
the towering cypress trees:
the blue herons,
marigold-eyed, moving like tall-stemmed flowers
through the shadowy marshes — O lovely bird,
loved by Athene in the Homeric years,
no more is your spear-like speaking heard in the green
glade!
Gone forever are the iridescent pigeons, their passage
set to the sun's circle, impaneling the sky.

Here come the deer to drink,
stepping proudly through the vine-tangled cane,
the blackbird thickets:
the bear with her frolicking cubs,
greedy for June dewberries: the tawny panther,
wary in the web of muscadine vines:
the otter,
glossy and sinuous in the lynx-striped shadows.

The colonnades of cypresses, tupelos, cottonwood:
on the ridges between the bayous, white oak, sweet gum,
hickory, maple: all a green dominion
governed by the colures of solstice and equinox,
from the yellow budding of the February willows
under the high black clouds of the spring storms,
the midsummer calms of the moon-shade branches,
    plangent
with the appoggiatura of coomb and coppice
castanet antiphon of cicada and jar-fly, bird song:
to the persimmon-colored autumn, leaf and berry
translucent in wild-orange, carmine, russet,
through the trailing folded grey November fog,
the cypresses cinnamon-brown, the kildees crying:
the patternless hoarfrost shrouding the January trance
of the wilderness moving to the March epiphany
that only the bird and the veined leaf may know. . . .
           Lily Peter
           The Great Riding

The images in the poem above were the vistas of Lily's childhood, born, as she was, on the banks of Big Cypress Bayou, which runs into Big Creek, only a short walk away, with the Mississippi River within twenty miles of both waterways.

Some enthusiastic environmentalists say that Miss Lily Peter stopped the channelization of Big Creek singlehandedly. That, of course, is an exaggeration; however, there was no question that her organization of the Big Creek Protective Association was a factor; also a factor was the constant stream of her letters to those conservation organizations which were in sympathy with her efforts, as well as her letters to those politicians whose support for implementation would be needed in either outcome. Nothing she had ever undertaken was more tedious, strenuous, or took more courage, because her work angered those who perceived the completion of the project as being in their financial interests.

The final hearing of the public meeting, held to decide the channelization proposal, has been recorded by the Corps of Engineers in a transcript which is several hundred pages long, the longest ever published, Lily was told.[1] The hearing was held in the Fine Arts Center of the Phillips County Community College, and the place was packed with people. It took eighteen pages to list those present with approximately twenty-five names and addresses to a page. Besides a record of the spoken remarks, there were sixty-three exhibits of written testimony.

The Big Creek Drainage District was formed in 1967. Hearings were held at Brinkley, Marianna, Marvell, and Helena, but public notices in the newspapers were small and attendance poor except for the one at Helena. The *Helena World* (November 20, 1967, page 1) stated that the Phillips County Circuit Court room was jammed as the hearing took place before Judge Elmore Taylor, but the room was not large. Many present were opposed to the project from the beginning.

As a farmer who had studied soils and crops all of her adult life, she regarded the benefits of drainage as difficult to achieve as was the Aristotelian Golden Mean. She had found that if her lands were contoured properly, the natural rains could be counted on for the right amount of moisture, either by adequate absorption or evaporation and proper cultivation. Plant roots must have both oxygen from the air and water from the soil which they can pull up from amazing depths—the reason that the water table levels are so important. And she had observed from her experience in ditching and planting near natural streams that, if drainage is too rapid, erosion and lack of absorption take place; if it is too slow, the soil packs and the plants rot. The proper amount of drainage makes it possible for plants to absorb the needed water; the proper amount furthers the decay of organic matter and enriches the soil. Therefore, it is easy for a farmer to conclude that clearing and draining right up to a natural stream is beneficial, because for the first few years, he will get a rich yield because of the fertility of the soil. But Lily was convinced that tampering with the natural curves of a free-flowing stream was eventually self-defeating. Then there were the other considerations of what happened to the flora and fauna of natural wetlands.

Lily watched the developments of the project out of the corner of her eye as best she could in those busy years, and the time lapses between hearings caused her to think it might be abandoned. She admits it was wishful thinking. Then she accidentally heard that there was to be a hearing at Brinkley on January 24, 1974. The newspaper notice (January 3, *Brinkley Citizen*, page 1) had recommended that those wishing to testify bring written statements; however, Lily, not having seen the notice, had no time for that, but went anyway. She had to insist that she be allowed to speak. She and those who went with her were not greeted with smiles; in fact, the atmosphere was heavy and hostile. Lily delivered an eloquent, but obviously spontaneous, speech, charged with emotion, excerpted from the transcript as follows:

> I am Lily Peter. My home is in the south end of Monroe County where I have lived all my life, and I have lands in both Monroe County and Phillips County. I have lands along Big Creek which is being affected very adversely by this project and, in addition to that, so are my homelands where I farm. So I am not in favor of it.
>
> I want to say that I am altogether in agreement with everyone who is opposed to it, from whatever viewpoint, because it has so many points which is [sic] damaging to our countryside, that I won't stand here and mention, especially since we have been asked not to be repetitive. . . . Having myself suffered agonizingly from the results of the White River Drainage District in Phillips County, I can appreciate some of the disadvantages that can be brought to a plantation or to lands by this kind of undertaking.

Furthermore, I should like to say to the good people of Brinkley — I have some very good friends up here and I am not saying this in any unkind spirit whatever — but I am just calling attention to the fact that in the course of the comments made by some proponents of this undertaking to the effect that the people up here are people and the creatures living at the other end of the county must be less than people. We, we think we are people anyway, and for that reason, we wonder if it would not be more to the advantage of the people who live up here, who are our friends and whom we regard very highly, if they haven't considered, since they are drowning in their own sewage, according to a report of the — or one report we had from this platform, why not get a big city cesspool out here somewhere, as many other cities do, and obviate that difficulty, and if they need drainage for their homes, why not make a handsome habitat — [have the] Corps of Engineers get a handsome big lake for you out here on Piney Creek and then you have recreation, you have drainage, you just have everything you need, and you wouldn't have to be abandoning us in the sewage at the other end of the county. . . .

I am not going to repeat all the advantages that leaving Big Creek alone will bring to the people of this county. We have got on beautifully this afternoon by those who are opposed to the project, and I am so unalterably opposed to it that if it comes to drainage and destroying our property in the way that this accomplishment has consistently started, I can promise you in turn that I would leave my part of the country and go somewhere else to live. Thank you.[2]

This hearing was being conducted by Colonel A. C. Lehman from the Memphis District Office of Engineers. T. Bay Fitzhugh, dentist and environmentalist from Stuttgart, was there, and he said that it was hard to imagine the astonishment, the mixed emotions of sympathy and amusement which intermittently appeared on the faces of Lehman and the others present when Lily spoke.

Fitzhugh thought Lily was powerful and effective.[3] Robert Apple, Regional Director of the National Wildlife Federation, Dardanelle, Arkansas, was also present at the Brinkley hearing. He said, "As gentle as she was, she could be adamant and formidable on the destructiveness of channelization. She wrote a letter to the Corps of Engineers in Memphis which was a masterpiece. She compared their work to ruthless surgeons and applied her metaphor to every aspect of their dealings with our waterways. Yet it was clear that it was distressing for her to pit herself against people who were her friends and associates. (She and all of us in environmental work were aware that the majority would be for immediate gains, and we learned to insulate ourselves against this and 'take our lickings.' Lily took a lot of abuse more gracefully than most of us.")[4]

Tom Foti, then Director of the Arkansas Ecology Commission, thinks that meeting, electrified as it was by Lily's speech, was the critical action in turning back the channelization proposal, although many did not feel confident about it at the time. He said, "Proponents were arrogant to opponents, particularly Lily. Though not in the record, asides could be heard, such as, 'This is one time that Lily Peter won't get her way. We'll take her land as quick as anybody's.' They even tried to inject racial prejudice by bringing old, black people to testify that they often had to sleep with water under their beds. I could tell that Colonel Lehman was affected by this treatment of Lily and this willingness to appeal to emotions. Lily was polite, but hard, powerful, and firm."[5]

It was at that hearing that Lily and the opponents learned that the project had been authorized under a Flood Control Act in October of 1965, a kind of blanket bill, one that left it to local interests to conceive and recommend measures for flood control. The drainage district had been formed under that directive, which made it amazingly easy for a few citizens to form an organization and go before a judge and get approval for such engineering projects, apathy and inertia of the disinterested being the ingredients that made their approval possible.

The results of that hearing were inconclusive; however, both the proponents and Corps of Engineers proceeded with plans. And Lily was concerned enough about antagonizing her friends at Brinkley to look further into why the people at Brinkley were so strongly in favor of the project. She asked lots of questions. She knew that Brinkley was in the midst of a highly irregular terrain brought about by the upheavals and shiftings of lands during the New Madrid earthquakes. She found that the land west of Brinkley had a fall of about six to eight feet a mile, but that the level land east of the town had a fall of only a half inch a mile; thus, in the latter case, drainage was practically nil, almost totally dependent upon evaporation. But there had been some dry years during the thirties, and some of the flat lands had been bought cheaply and opened up to farming, which was some help to drainage.

The city leaders came by monies from a variety of sources and added three other projects utilizing those lowlands east of town, undoubtedly influenced by the property owners of the area. One was the building of a municipal airport on land given by Frank Federer; one was a municipal fishing pond built with government funds and placed in the midst of the only natural drainage point of the town, Greenlee Creek; one was a group of houses which had been built and given to his tenants by landowner Frank Andrews. When the rainfall returned to normal, all three of these developments were in trouble. The airport, confined to serving small private planes, would remain flooded for days, precluding landings; the fishing pool had been made by levees surrounded by ditches of only six feet, inadequate to carry water around the pool. Water would get into many of the homes in the housing project or surround them, cutting off access. Lily was fully aware that the town had serious problems which needed solution; however, she firmly believed that the proposed channelization of Big Creek would merely shift the problem to those people living at the other end of the creek. Therefore, she remained stubbornly opposed to it.

Her continually active opposition came to a head in the fall of 1974. J. C. Crisp came to her house with a newspaper from Brinkley which not only said that the project was to be started right away, but also displayed a map of the project which showed, as Lily strongly suspected all along, that her home on Big Cypress Bayou was included in the mitigation lands to be acquired. She knew that the right of domain would give the Corps the authority to buy the lands. She felt that her back was against the wall. When J. C. asked if there was anything at all they could do at this point, Lily replied, "J. C., there are some things we cannot stop. We cannot stop an earthquake, and we can't stop a tornado. But what people start, people can stop if they go at it the right way and work hard enough."

It was in the harvest season, and Lily and all the other farmers in the area were busy. Nevertheless, she wrote up a petition, got copies made, and J. C. distributed them to people who would carry them. When signatures were obtained, Lily filed them with the Corps of Engineers and the governor's office.

Then they rapidly formed an organization, the Big Creek Protective Association. She asked her farmer friends and other opponents to call a meeting at the Legion Hut in Marvell. They elected officers (all farmers from Phillips County): D. T. Hargraves, Jr., was secretary-treasurer, Ray Fuller, vice chairman. Lily reluctantly accepted the chairmanship. They met often in all of the towns where they could make arrangements, the main thrust being to increase membership. There was disagreement on the amount of cost for membership, suggestions ranging from $500 to $1. Lily was on the side of the latter figure. She said, "Boys, many people will give a solicitor a dollar to get rid of them." An executive committee was formed of people who would give every minute possible to writing, calling, and talking against the project, in addition to getting members into the association. Lily called on every articulate speaker she could think of to appear at the meetings: men from the Arkansas Game and Fish Commission, the Arkansas Ecology Center, and as many state legislators as she could persuade, as well as nationally known authorities. One state legislator was Senator Paul Benham, Jr., from Marianna. When asked if he had not taken a considerable risk in opposing the project, considering that so many of his constituents in the northern part of his district were in favor of it, he answered that he listened carefully to Lily, checked her facts and figures at various sources (such as the UAF Agricultural Experiment Station at Marianna), and he decided she was right.[6]

The unlettered and inarticulate were by no means excluded. They were sought after and given an opportunity to testify. Lily spoke at every meeting. She telephoned; she talked the project to nearly everyone she met. At one point she had laryngitis so bad that she could not speak above a whisper. The organization grew to 7,000 people. Lily observed that that number was fairly insignificant in New York City, but that no Arkansas politician would ever ignore such a figure.

On January 19, 1975, the *Arkansas Democrat* headlined an article on page 6A by Susan Keilhauer, "Complaints Force New Hearing on Big Creek Plan." She gave a careful account of both sides of the issue. In the same issue, another article tells that Colonel Lehman planned to proceed with the project despite Governor Bumpers' opposition.

The date of the new hearing was the one in Helena already mentioned, March 19, 1975. In case Lily's group failed to stop the project, the executive committee of BCPA had already anticipated the next step, a law suit. A discussion ensued on the matter of hiring a lawyer and was resolved by following Lily's advice. She already knew that the most informed lawyer on the subject was Richard Arnold from Texarkana, who had represented the

"Save-the-Cache-River" advocates. (Channelization of the Cache River was another project of drainage proponents.) But he had accepted a position on Senator Dale Bumpers' staff in Washington as his legal council. So her choice was his former partner, William Lavender, Texarkana. He was employed on a retaining-fee basis. Many of the members wanted to see him and have him speak at some of their meetings, but Lily advised against it, thinking it inexpedient to threaten legal action unless absolutely necessary and that his very presence might be regarded as such. He, recognizable by few, was invited to the hearing, not to participate, but to observe.

The days prior to the hearing were hectic and dramatic. So many derogatory criticisms of Lily abounded that many wanted her to make rebuttals in the papers, or to do so for her, or take some sort of retributive action. She insisted that they all be ignored, saying, "No, My Dears, don't you say a word in the papers about me. Everybody who knows me, knows my character, and they who don't know me can get acquainted with me on their own initiative if they wish to. I am not afraid of anything in the world those people say about me. If it is true, I will acknowledge it; if it is not, they will eventually find it out."

The association placed a full-page advertisement in the *Twin City Tribune* on March 12, 1974 (page 1B). It was headed "Will Your Taxes Be Raised?" Lily wrote the ad and discussed every phase of the cost of the project, including the gasoline.

An unusual and completely unexpected thing happened just two days before the hearing. L. B. Hughes, vice-Mayor of Brinkley, wrote to Lily, asking her if she would help Brinkley with its drainage problems. She tried to call him, but was unable to reach him, so she made public her willingness to help by telling of Hughes' letter at the hearing. Lily was the fourth speaker; she read her prepared statement (Exhibit 4), but she added these remarks:

... He was under the impression that we did not want Big Piney drained, I think, from his letter, and he was asking my help which I am more than happy to help everybody in this basin to improve our drainage. Remember, I am a farmer and my farms need drainage just as everybody else's farms need drainage, and I realize that the people of Brinkley do have a problem with the flooding from Big Piney. However, when the main channel of Big Creek is cleaned out, that might afford them sufficient relief, but if . . . not . . . we should be very happy to see Big Piney cleaned out. We don't think it would be necessary to channelize it. . . . However, my offer of maintenance for Big Creek would not be in opposition to what those people who live in that area would prefer, and so, I think they should be allowed to come to their own decision. But remember please what I have just said here: that if the landowners in that area felt that more drainage was needed than the cleaning out of Big Creek would afford and they would prefer their tributaries cleaned out instead of being channelized, we should welcome their comments and cooperation, and certainly, I am more than happy to cooperate with all our good friends in Brinkley in every way possible in helping them alleviate their problem. . . .

I am a person who likes to make everybody around me happy if I can. I won't be here in the world very long, and while I am here I would like to leave the heritage of happiness in my way just as far as it is humanly possible, and I would like to see the outcome of these deliberations be one that would bring happiness to everybody living in these five counties that form the Big Creek Basin. I would like to leave the Big Creek Basin the happiest place in the world if I could.[7]

To many, Lily's flowery language has seemed superficial, but even those who think so have through the years become convinced of its sincerity. It was doubly convincing, as it was at the first hearing, due to the timbre of her voice and her delivery. And many who were at that hearing wondered about the identity of the tall, handsome young man escorting Lily. It was Bill Lavender, the lawyer, who said not a word.

Her advice for the other members of her association who were testifying was also effective. She suggested that each one make only one point, limited to a sentence written out on Big Creek Protective Association's stationery and that they should read it. She further saw to it that those who could not attend had sent written statements.

On the weekend after the hearing, she called Bill Alexander and after personal greetings, asked him if he'd like her report of the hearing. He replied, "Oh, I've already heard. Colonel Lehman called me that evening and told me that you all won a complete triumph."

Lily was never more elated with the results of one of her projects. But there was still the matter of Brinkley's problems. She was determined to help them if she could, despite the many caustic and sarcastic remarks directed toward her by many in Brinkley. An example is the testimony of John V. Holliday, the city manager, samples of which follow:

> I don't know how much land Miss. Lily [sic] Peter owns. I do know that she is the principal objector to the drainage district. I have heard that she owns 1,000 acres, and I have heard that she owns 5,000 acres, and I have heard that she owns 100,000 acres of land. I would venture to say that no matter how much ground she has, that at one time it was completely covered with trees. I would also venture to say that in all probability a lot of this ground, this land that is farmed, has drainage canals cut either across it or from the center of a ridge down to the valley that drains water on other people.
>
> I don't personally know Miss Lilly [sic]; I met her the first time when we were having a hearing on the Big Creek Drainage District, before Judge Elmore Taylor, I think in 1968. The battery on her car was down, and I helped her to get her car started. I thought then that this good Lord of ours was frowning at this lady because she had appeared in opposition. . . .

Miss Lilly [sic] has said in her advertisements in the paper that she loves Big Creek, that she wants to keep it as it is. I am sure she is sincere in what she says, but "as it is," it is a detriment to the health and welfare of thousands of people.

Holliday continued by describing Big Creek as cluttered and inaccessible for recreation, fishing, or even the baptizings it was formerly used for, and he concluded:

... and yet Miss. Lilly [sic] says, "let's save Big Creek." I also say, let's save Big Creek, but let's save it in a manner so that the water going down it will benefit humans instead of the way that it is now. The only thing it benefits now is reptiles, beavers and mosquitos.

He then showed a series of pictures of tangles and flooding. He continued and concluded with these paragraphs:

Miss Lily has said, let's save Big Creek for its beauty, its usefulness, for our enjoyment.

Let me ask you, are the scenes we have just shown you beautiful? Are they useful in any manner? Do you enjoy seeing your fellow Americans with their homes, their property under water? There is nothing enjoyable about it to me!

My suggestion would be that if Miss. Lilly [sic] is really interested in trees, ducks and fish she build a lake for fish and a rest area for ducks, then plant the rest of her holdings in trees to be perpetually maintained as a forest with its lake and rest area ... [spelling, punctuation, and mechanics are as in transcript].[8]

Holliday had had no problem in obtaining pictures of the flooded conditions because, prior to the hearing, there had been a series of rains, and they continued for some time afterward. When Lily finally got in touch with Hughes, the Vice-Mayor of Brinkley who had written her for help, he offered to come down to visit her for consultation; however, she said she would be happy to come to Brinkley, not only because the problems would be visibly acute, but also because she wanted to demonstrate her good will to those who regarded her as an enemy. A time was set right away, and she set about more study. She went up to visit with her friend and attorney, John Burton Moore at Clarendon. She knew he would know much about the area because he was known far and wide as "Coon Dog Johnny," an avid hunter, who had, since childhood, tramped every acre of those bottom lands in the county. She asked him to go with her to the agriculture office to study the aerial maps. She then hired Buron Griffin, a pilot, and Ivey Gladin, a photographer, to take more aerial pictures while the floods were occurring. John Moore rode with them so that he could notarize the pictures. With this new information and what she already knew, Lily went to visit with Hughes prepared to make a number of recommendations.

The room in the City Hall where the meeting was held was full of people, representing all contingents of the citizenry. She was introduced with courtesy, and she made her speech offering three different plans, saying, "If any of these plans are implemented, I will give $25,000 to help with cost." She asked for response and got none. Then she said, "I had hoped that one of these plans, at least, might be feasible and satisfactory, but you all live up here and you have a better idea of your needs than I do. All I'm here for is to try to help you. Now, since the plans which I have suggested do not seem feasible to you, I'm going to ask you if you all have some plans of your own."

There was a seemingly long silence, but it was finally broken by a man who spoke up and said, "Miss Lily, what would you say to our cleaning out Big Piney? Do you think that would be of any help to us?" (Big Piney Creek flowed just north of Brinkley and connected with Big Creek east of Brinkley.)

That was just what Lily wanted to hear. She knew it would

help, but didn't dare suggest it because the creek was so choked with debris, old household goods, and similar trash that cleaning it out would be a difficult task. She said as much, but added, "If you would like to do that, I think that would be the finest thing you could do." Someone asked if her financial offer would hold in cleaning up Big Piney. She said, "Because I know that it takes money to do clean-up and drainage, I am willing to contribute to the city of Brinkley the amount I promised, $25,000."

At that point the atmosphere of the meeting changed from skepticism to hopefulness. Carl Geisler, a chief proponent of the channelization project who owned several sections of land along Big Piney (who had already been appointed one of the commissioners to maintain the drainage project when completed) had one of his employees inform the meeting that if Miss Lily was willing to give $25,000, he would contribute $10,000 to the city and, further, see to the cleaning out of all of Big Piney which went through or by his property. That set the ball rolling. One city official volunteered that the town ought to raise money to match Lily's, but that had to wait for an official meeting of the council. But this gathering concluded with all in good spirits.

Lily waited until early fall to see about the progress that the Brinkley officials were making. One day when she had other business there, she called Vice-Mayor Hughes. He said that he was glad that she had come and had much to show her. They drove over the countryside, and Lily felt that what they had accomplished was near-miraculous. They had followed her advice that they not alter the natural, winding shorelines of the creek, that they leave as many trees as possible, and that they do nothing to break the bed of the creek. Geisler had done such a thorough job of cleaning the creek on his land that it looked as if it had been carefully landscaped. He had used the excess dirt and debris to make a firm roadbed along the contours of the creek and finished a road which was extremely pleasant to drive along. Hughes later sent Lily a collection of pictures he had made showing more improvements and accompanied them with pictures made beforehand so that the contrast was dramatic.

On November 30, 1975, *The Brinkley Argus* printed on its front page a picture of Hughes and Holliday captioned "Gift for City," and further stating, ". . . [they] hold a $25,000 check given to the city by Miss Lily Peter to help solve Brinkley's drainage problems. The check was mailed to Mr. Hughes about ten days after he had taken Miss Peter on a motor tour of the problem areas and that section of Piney Ditch cleaned out by Carl Geisler in cooperation with the city."

It would be foolhardy to claim that all involved in that controversy were happy. Many farmers who had stood to gain more acreage were still angry and blamed Lily. Some heavy equipment contractors continued to call her less than flattering names. But many people were happy with the outcome, and it was an experience that added another dimension to Lily's public image.

On June 6, 1977, *The Brinkley Argus* carried an item about Lily, also on the front page. She had pledged $10,000 toward the cost of their building a community center, a project which has never gotten off the ground. She did later give a sizable amount to Brinkley's hospital fund.

Discussion with both Hughes and Holliday revealed that, in retrospect, they feel that the solution of cleaning out Big Piney Creek went a long way toward solving their drainage problems. Holliday said that more work was needed and felt that levees and ditches seemed the best solution. Holliday said that he, at no time, felt personal antagonism toward Lily: that their running arguments at the various hearings were good natured verbal matches; that each always hoped the other would go first so that the other could make the counterpoint. They were, of course, sincere about their positions. Holliday said that the highest compliment ever paid him was made by Lily when she gave her check to the city directors and told them, "Now, I want you to let John Holliday be in charge of spending this money because if he is, I can be sure that every penny of it will be spent on drainage."

Both Holliday and Hughes said that Lily could take more verbal abuse and keep smiling than anyone they had ever worked with. Holliday told of the day he found her with car trouble. He said to her, "Young woman, can I help you with your car?" She replied, "I am a young *lady*, but you can certainly help me with my car."[9] (Lily was reared in an age when there were two categories for the female of the human species: ladies and women. And to her there was a distinct difference.)

John Burton Moore, a Clarendon attorney who represented Lily on a number of occasions (the notary who rode in the airplane) said about stopping channelization, "I have been an environmentalist for years and for a while went to Washington every year and appeared before hearings. But I was known for my love of hunting and fishing, and one time some representative said to me, 'Mr. Moore, if you have no argument against this project except hunting and fishing, I request that you sit down right now and save your time and our time. If you have anything to say on flood control, we'll hear it.' For this reason, I would always have an argument for flood control or some other aspect of conservation and often consulted Lily on the subject. And as long as Wilbur Mills was up there, we could always divert, delay, restudy or something, and Took Gathings never knew what happened. Bill Alexander is not so easy, but Lily Peter did as well as anyone ever has in stopping a channelization project. Now we've got more folks behind us, so we have the Cache River project in re-study, thank goodness."[10]

Senator Dale Bumpers (known for his pro-environment stance) reflecting on the Big Creek episode, wrote:

I'll never forget my meeting with Miss Lily to talk about the

Big Creek Project. I had gone to Brinkley to speak to a Chamber of Commerce Banquet. When I got there somebody told me Miss Lily wanted to visit with me about the Big Creek Project. I knew very little about the project, but when I finished visiting with her, I knew more than I wanted to know. Not only was she violently opposed, but ready to put her own money into an alternative solution which seemed eminently sensible to me. To shorten the story, she won as I knew she would.

One thing that was most inspirational was the obvious respect she commanded from a number of farmers present, whom I thought would have strongly favored the Corps' proposal.

Would that the world had more Miss Lilys. I've never seen more determination and strong will in my life.[11]

Lily thought that there had not been another channelization project approved in the United States since the failure of the Big Creek proposal. Tom Foti, now a professional environmental consultant heading the Olive Leaf Institute, Little Rock, said Lily was correct with the exception of the Tombigbee River project. He said that connecting the Tombigbee River with the Tennessee River was the most ill-advised channelization proposal ever conceived. Besides ruining the clarity and flow of the Tombigbee, it required a canal to be cut through the Tennessee Ledge at the end of the Western Highland Rim and the Cumberland Plateau. This is not only dangerous to the topography of the entire region, but extremely costly. Foti was sure that the reason Congress gave its final approval was that piecemeal appropriations had already sunk a billion dollars into the project. Legislators, he said, just could not admit that such a huge expenditure already made was a dire mistake.

Foti concluded his assertions with this statement: "Lily reaches back in time to the best of tradition; she reaches forward in time to the best of the future. She spans the twentieth century.

I love her."[12]

Notes

[1]The pages of the transcript of the Corps of Engineers' hearing, 19 March 1975, Helena, Arkansas, are not numbered, but the volume is about two inches thick. Department of the Army, Memphis District, Corps of Engineers, Memphis, Tennessee. *Transcript of Public Meeting, Helena, Arkansas, 19 March 1975*.

[2]Corps of Engineers' hearing 24 Jan. 1974, Brinkley, Arkansas, pp. 37-40, enclosure in letter from William H. Reno, Colonel, Corps of Engineers, District Engineer, Memphis, Tennessee, 27 Feb. 1981.

[3]Letter received from T. Bay Fitzhugh, 3 Feb. 1981.

[4]Telephone interview with Robert Apple, 15 Apr. 1981.

[5]Telephone interview with Tom Foti, 29 Dec. 1981.

[6]Personal interview with Paul Benham, 18 Aug. 1980.

[7]Transcript, Corps of Engineers hearing, 19 Mar. 1975, n.p

[8]Ibid.

[9]Personal interview with both L. B. Hughes, Mayor, and John Holliday, Manager, City of Brinkley, 11 June 1981.

[10]Moore further told of his dealings with Lily during the settling of Jesse Peter's estate and blamed himself that he didn't do more to help her get the hundred acres she wanted for the arboretum at the Louisiana Purchase Marker site. He said that she was the smartest person he had ever seen. "The only thing she can't do is drive an airplane. She is the only person I've ever known in my life who can talk on one subject and be thinking on another level about another subject so that she will be ready to speak carefully when the talk on the first subject is finished. I've seen her do it many times. And I've never heard her speak on any topic without having done her homework" (Personal interview with John Burton Moore, 7 Aug. 1981).

[11]Letter received from Dale Bumpers, 7 Jan. 1982.

[12]Telephone interview with Tom Foti, 29 Dec. 1981.

[13]Personal interviews with Lily Peter. Tapes 12, 13, 31, 56. Torreyson Library Archives, University of Central Arkansas.

Lily picking up her mail on the county road
before she financed the asphalt paving

Chapter XI

PEANUT BUTTER MEDICINE
AND LADYBUG FARMING, 1976-1981

We who have looked at our times and felt the clutch
of the nameless sadness that chills the heart, must own
ourselves the Sorcerer's Apprentice.
In our fragile world,
stumbling upon the secret abracadabra
that Newton dreamed of in his alchemy
in our undisciplined ignorance, we have broken the seal
of magic, unwittingly, and now we find,
like the dismayed lout in the ancient legend,
our magic dazzlingly realized, past all fancies
of the *Arabian Nights* — conversing with the lightening,
walking on the air, riding in a chariot of fire
to the Moon, in motion past the speed of sound —
and we, the Apprentice, are confused by our own success,
unable to curb the powers we have loosed on the world:

. . .

Our children are now our heirs, but how shall they cherish
what we have destroyed on river and land and sea?
What can we say to them? How can we expiate
the wrongs that we have done?

. . .

Our work is to dress the Garden.
"My Father worketh
hitherto, and I work," said One who saw the Mystery

more clearly than some of us — a shining message!
Let this be our hope, that we, the fumbling Apprentice,
may learn to use our magic in reverence
for the beauty and wonder and majesty of life!

Lily Peter
"The Apprentice"
The Ozark Society Bulletin
Summer 1973

The second half of Lily's ninth decade was triumphal. She overcame her anemia by discovering a cure in peanut butter, and she retired from farming only after she had succeeded in growing cotton independent of pesticides and herbicides.

As the year of the nation's bicentennial approached, 1976, most Arkansas organizations were aware that Lily had pledged to spend $200,000 on the celebration and were ready with proposals in case they were recipients. When Lily told the Marvell Garden Club that they would receive $500 toward the creation of two gardens, the club erected a wrought-iron sign in one of the gardens that read, "Marvell, the home of Miss Lily Peter."

The beginning of the bicentennial year got off with a christening. Jim Walden missed his estimate of construction time for the towboat, *Miss Lily Peter,* but the boat was delivered, and the christening took place on February 10, 1976. All the planning for dignity, pomp, and ceremony was done. Governor David Pryor officially declared that it would be "Miss Lily Peter Day." Jim Walden provided a large silver tray duly engraved to present Lily as a memento. Many dignitaries were there, and Ivey and Morene Gladin made lots of pictures. Lily wore her red outfit: suit, cape, beret, and boots, the same one she had worn for the ground-breaking of the river academy, except that this time, for a nod to the bicentennial, she had her florist prepare a multiple-looped bow of red, white, and blue ribbon as large as a dinner plate with streamers flowing to her hemline. She saved her beautiful two-orchid corsage sent by Walden for the afternoon reception. No one was ever more colorful than Lily as she grasped the "also be-ribboned" bottle of champagne and smashed it across the bow of her namesake. It was just one more of those events of celebration which Lily loved because she so highly valued human ritual and drama. There was much regional publicity, but one of the most satisfying sentences came from Dee Bailey's report, "Miss Lily Peter of Marvell, who has helped many individuals establish promising careers, experienced a 'first' last Tuesday as she sent an inanimate object to work in a vital field."[1]

The National Wildlife Federation honored Lily early in 1976 in Louisville, Kentucky, by presenting her with a special Bicentennial Conservation Award for her successful opposition to the Big Creek channelization. The Federation gave her a whooping crane statuette which had a special place on the fireplace mantle of her den instead of being crowded among the other awards and citations on the tables and walls.[2]

Arkansas' participation in the bicentennial events in Washington in May was glorious to Lily, exceeding all her expectations. *The Washington Post*'s headline, "Impressive Arkansas Symphony," summarized the review of its music critic, Paul Hume, who wrote, in part:

> The orchestra's excellence is clearly the result of Klipstatter's conducting, which was obvious in both the playing and the music chosen. How few conductors are yet willing to bring us all-American programs. Klipstatter chose with care, including Dello Joio's Homage to Haydn, Barber's Media Meditation and Vengeance Dance, and the Hovhaness Mysterious Mountain. [Spelling of Klippstatter and punctuation are Hume's.]

Hume also praised the singing of Mignon Dunn and apparently didn't realize that she was the wife of Klippstatter and that she is originally from Tyronza, Arkansas.[3]

Teri Thompson, *Arkansas Democrat* sports writer, was assigned to the bicentennial events in Washington, and the headline of her report about the Arkansas Symphony read, "Symphony at Washington — Goodbye to pickin' and grinnin.'" She wrote:

> Before the Arkansas Symphony Orchestra debuted at the Kennedy Center for the Performing Arts at Washington, D. C., May 2, this state's music was best remembered for something Jimmy Driftwood did on the Today Show a couple of months ago.
>
> In that rendition, Arkansas musicians were pictured as a motley group of barefoot banjo pickers — hill-billies, just playin' it by ear.
>
> So what Kurt Klippstatter and the orchestra accomplished before those doubting ears at the Bicentennial concert was, to use the sports vernacular, a home run with the bases loaded.[4]

Lily wanted to believe that Teri was correct because she certainly dreamed of giving Arkansas a new image.

Another event on May 30 made it necessary for Lily to fly up East again. At Lily's suggestion Moravian College had elected to confer an honorary doctoral degree in humane letters upon Eugene Ormandy at its commencement program. Dr. Herman Collier, president, invited her to give the citation and prepare it herself. She did so and memorized it so she could give it without notes. Lily was excited about seeing Mr. Ormandy again; she had only seen him once at Memphis since the Little Rock concerts. She got to the room designated for donning the academic regalia and had dressed in her own gown, hood, and mortar board when she saw Mr. and Mrs. Ormandy over by a window. Their meeting is told in Lily's words:

> I went over to greet them, and they both were very courteous, but they looked very blank, very unrecognizing. But I thought

Lily walks with Eugene Ormandy at Moravian College
on their way to commencement exercises

nothing of it. I thought maybe they were not expecting to see
me. . . . They did not know I was going to be presenting the
citation. They went on chatting, you know, with banalities and
trite remarks that all people make on such occasions. We did
that for a couple of minutes, and then Mr. Ormandy gave up
the trivialities, and I thought what he said was totally perfect.
He said, "I wonder if by any chance you happen to be from
the South?" I thought he had recognized me, so I thought I
would just give him a good time. And so, very noncommitting,
I said, "Yes, I've been from the South for many years." "Well,"
he said, "I thought so because you have such a soft Southern

accent." Then his curiosity overwhelmed him, and he said, "I wonder, if by any chance you would happen to know a Southern lady named Miss Lily Peter?" I said, "I'm Lily Peter." Oh, this poor gentleman was so overwhelmed he just couldn't get over it — that he hadn't recognized me when I had brought him to Little Rock, "Well," he said, "You don't look like Miss Lily Peter. I knew you resembled her in some ways, but I couldn't possibly believe that you were the Lily Peter whom I knew in Little Rock. You look different now. You are wearing your hair different."

Well, of course, I had on that wretched mortar board, and it makes your hair look peculiar, and I don't care how you fix it. Any lady who puts on a mortar board can expect her hairdo to vanish. Anyway, we had lots of fun that day. And that evening we were seated together at dinner. It was delightful.

And then after Mr. Ormandy returned to Philadelphia he wrote me such a charming letter. It began, "Dear Mysterious Lady, You certainly threw me for a loop in Bethlehem because I was so overwhelmed with the fact that I could not and did not recognize you, and you kept your identity mysterious for such a long time and kept me in misery. . . ."

Lily's associations with men and women of celebrity gave her much pleasure. Her genius was such that she could imagine that, had her childhood not been so isolated, had her education not been scattered over so many years, she could have achieved a high professional status in any number of fields. Many people who knew her reinforced these fantasies. Nevertheless, Lily was proud of her achievement in farming. It had provided her with the means to contribute to projects which gave her these associations.

In the middle of all the bicentennial activities, Lily received another honor for her identification with wildlife. It was reported in the *Arkansas Gazette* that two baby pileated woodpeckers were released to the wilderness, but only after one bird was christened "Lily" and the other "Peter." The grand, striking birds are called

"Oh, My Gods" in Arkansas because of their startling, blood-chilling scream, but Lily probably would deny that she's ever evoked such a reaction.[5]

When Jimmy Carter announced his candidacy for President, Lily liked the idea of a farmer as President of the United States and immediately sent him a contribution of $1,000, when everyone was asking, "Jimmy who?" As a result she was the only woman on his National Agriculture Committee of Twenty. Because of a conflict of engagements, Lily never got to meet with the national committee, but she did get to meet with the state committee organized for the same purpose. The *Arkansas Gazette* reported Lily's testimony at the state committee's meeting:

> The leadoff witness was Miss Lily Peter . . . whose advice to Carter was to stop the Army Engineers from channelizing streams. . . .
>
> She called channelization "as stupid and barbarous as bloodletting used to be as a medical practice." She said it killed streams and lowered the water table around the streams, which made farms more susceptible to drouth. Her suggestion was . . . to relieve floods instead by clearing logjams from the streams and to give the United States Geological Survey funds to find ways to recharge the water tables. . . .[6]

Lily had done her homework and submitted a written report to substantiate her advice, and it has been the source of information for a number of spokesmen who have similar concerns.

The reenactment of La Salle's expedition from the Great Lakes to the Gulf of Mexico was completely off schedule because the weather had been colder than it had been in nearly a hundred years. At the outset, the LaSalle Expedition II was forced to carry canoes over miles of frozen water. One young man had broken his leg and delayed the trek about six weeks. When the leader of the expedition, Reid Lewis, and his men arrived in Helena, Arkansas, on March 8, 1977, they were bedraggled and exhausted. Lewis spent as much time with Lily as he could while in Helena, having become one of her greatest admirers. He says that her poem, "In Praise of Dreamers Who Are the Only Discoverers," represents "the very essence of Miss Lily," particularly the line "[we are] . . . the sole custodians of the treasures of which we are celebrant, that live only in the regiving." He adds:

> . . . Miss Lily thrives on this "regiving," as she enthusiastically shares her vast knowledge of the past with those around her. Yet, she is not just a purveyor of the treasures from the past. Miss Lily also shares her own good fortune and the accomplishments which emanate from her wide diversity of interests in the present.
>   . . . Throughout the 2 years of preparation for the expedition, my visits with Miss Lily were creative "shots in the arm." By being with her, I had the exhilarating feeling of indeed being in the presence of a "Discoverer-Dreamer."[7]

Lily enjoyed this young dreamer and beyond her first gift of $10,000 to him, she bought for $9,000 one of the Algonquin canoes so that it could be placed in a museum in Helena and designated that what profits remained after expenses from her history, *Sea Dream of the Mississippi*, be sent to him.

Bicentennial events succeeded one another rapidly.[8] Lily suffered more and more from interminable fatigue, yet she had another project that she felt was crucial to undertake. She had read Rachel Carson's book, *Silent Spring*; it haunted her, and she observed the diminishing population of birds and small animals. She no longer heard the frogs in the bayou or saw the fireflies in the twilight. She was determined to farm without herbicides and pesticides as an experiment in 1977 and began studying how to do so.

Word of Lily's success at farming without the usual chemicals reached Ginger Shiras of the *Arkansas Gazette*. She called Lily for an interview immediately; then Gene Prescott, photographer, came, and Ginger's long and thorough article with photographs by Prescott began on the paper's front page of November 6, 1977.

Ginger Shiras wrote that Lily had decided that the results of her experimentation with nineteen acres the previous year were successful enough for her to put all her own cotton production on the line. She chose 250 acres and began the cultivation using only a pre-emergent herbicide that she found would not damage the soil. She hired two young men, Whitten Lueken and Robert Sparks, University of Arkansas students who were working as cotton scouts for the county extension agent. They inspected her field once a week and reported the findings to her. They would come in, hot and tired, and Lily would get them soda pops from the store, sometimes with cookies. The first few times they found nothing to report. Early in May they were disturbed about the thrips (often called plant lice), which make the cotton look "sick and unhappy." (Thrips appear during blackberry winter, which usually occurs in April.) James King, Lily's farm manager, told her that the tractor drivers were pestering him to tell Miss Lily she had better poison. But she refused the advice from both sources, and the May heat came along, the thrips fell off, so the plants were not badly damaged. In early July the scouts reported plant bugs and wanted Lily to poison. She did not, and the rest of July went smoothly, but the first week in August the boys reported that the fields were crawling with all sorts of worms, all the way from tiny wire worms to big caterpillars with horns on them. Lueken says that he was seriously concerned about the big worms called "cabbage loopers." They were so bad in several fields near Lily's that one could walk into the area and actually hear them chewing on the cotton plants. Both scouts told Lily that she just must poison or she would have no plants left, let alone a harvest, because all those worms were laying eggs. She (as always) promised the boys she would think about it.[9]

339

And this is what she thought based on her long years of experience and her reading. Shiras quoted her as follows:

> I've been taking care of my beneficial insects all summer long. . . . All summer they had a banquet out there on my field, feasting on those harmful insects, and now I have ladybugs and lacewings and ichneumon wasps and three or four other kinds of helpful insects out there by the thousands, and they're still my friends. For them those worm eggs will just be so much ice cream and lemon pie for dessert.

And Lily knew that the worms that were already hatched would have a comparatively short life span because, since her land was so rich that it produced heavy foliage for them to feed upon, they would just eat themselves to death. And they were welcome to eat the foliage because, if she had the usual backlash of a hurricane that came up from the Caribbean about every three years out of five, she would stand to lose about a third or fourth of her cotton bolls from "boll-rot." Such rains would put so much water into the fields that it wouldn't dry out or absorb rapidly enough because the sun could not penetrate the heavy foliage. This was a real problem in fields that were rich and had good cultivation. In addition, the stalks, heavy with bolls and leaves, would often fall over so that equipment could not get down the rows. The worms could prove to be a blessing.

Lily did have some concern about whether or not she had enough Ichneumon wasps — these insects can only reproduce themselves by laying their eggs in nests of worm's eggs which the larvae of the wasps consume. There are not many of these wasps in summers when there are not many worms (as there had not been earlier). But the boys reported that there were some wasps, so Lily knew that there would soon be enough to inactivate the worms' eggs because another generation is born in two to four days.

"Whit" and Bob kept recommending poison, and Lily kept promising to think about it until they were miffed by her refusal to take their advice. But by the third week they came and reported that they could hardly believe their eyes, that the worms were all dead and the eggs were gone. Lily could have told them that many farmers who have poisoned the worms for so long are positive that the poisons kill them because when they inspect their fields they find dead worms. Actually, the worms have died of over-eating or old age or both.

Lily knew from previous records that she would have spent at least $16,000 for insecticides and herbicides had she used them. Her cotton yield was just short of a bale and a half to the acre, somewhat down, because she had left off some chemicals which she had decided were harming the soil, but it was a yield that gave her a greater margin of profit. And it was the margin that counted.

Neighbors and renters had been invited by Lily to try what she was trying, but none of them wanted to join her at all. In fact, many were frightened that her failure to use the poisons might hurt their crops. And when her crop was a success, some even accused her of poisoning at night or explained it away, saying that their poison had drifted over into her fields. But J. C. Crisp, a close neighbor who farmed with his father, Chesterfield, told Lily at the end of the year that, without saying anything to her or anyone else but his dad, he had watched what she was doing, and when she left off poisons, he did the same. When the worms got so bad, he was scared, but he would hold out a day at a time, as Lily was doing, and he never did poison. He was, as Lily was, happy with the results.[10]

Only one other farmer followed her example, Jeremiah Jenkins, who rented small acreage from Lily and owned a little farm of his own. He liked not having to handle and pay for the poisons, which alone do not assure anyone of a crop.

Lily referred to her farming as "the old-fashioned way." She had no objection to the term "organic farming" except that it had become associated with what she called "window-sill gardening," and she truly wanted to influence the large farmers. On November 11, 1977, the *Gazette* gave at least a third of its editorial column to considering Lily's way, headlining it "Farming the Old Way." Its first paragraph underscored an attitude of Lily's which she had voiced many times, and its second is accurate in describing the general response to Lily's experiment. The editorial said:

> To Miss Lily Peter farming the fertile Mississippi River Delta soil around Marvell is easily as much an art as it is a science. The poetic feel she brings to letters as Arkansas's poet laureate and as patron of the arts is visible in her determination to grow cotton without excessive reliance on chemicals.
>
> For some of her fellow farmers, we imagine, she may be thought of in terms of heresy. Many farmers like to pride themselves on their individualism, but the fact is that in many areas of their endeavors they tend to follow under peer pressure the path of least resistance. That is, far too many of them reach for the chemical solution to the myriad of problems encountered in making yearly crops on the assumption that their goal cannot be reached in any other way.

The editorial writer continued with a good summary of Shiras' description of the project and concluded with a recommendation that it was "an example for other Arkansas farmers to ponder. . . ."

George Fisher, the *Gazette*'s cartoonist, drew a cartoon for the same page (24A) depicting a huge giant in typical farmers' clothing labeled Agri-business saying, "Don't get alarmed, Boys — this NEW way of growing cotton won't catch on." In the lower corner is a little lady in a bonnet labeled Lily Peter. Fisher gave Lily a signed copy of the original drawing of the cartoon and she displayed it with pleasure and pride.

Lily's concern for the environment made her wish she could

George Fisher' cartoon in the *Arkansas Gazette*

sell her ideas to everyone; however, she observed that human be-
ings were creatures of habit, that it would take a long time and
more serious damage to the environment to alter the over-all prac-
tices. She did say this to her renters: "Now, you boys who are
farming my land, I'm going to let you go on farming the way you
want to because you are all grown up, and I'm not going to tell
you all what to do. But I'll tell you for sure. I'm convinced my-
self that you can make a good cotton crop, as much as anybody
else, without using any insecticides or herbicides. So, now, if you
boys want to use that stuff, I'm not going to tell you you can't,
but you're going to have to pay for it because I'm not going to."

This clearly was a strong bit of subtle coercion. On summer evenings Lily was seeing the fireflies for the first time in a long time.

Getting through the fall harvest and ginning season of 1977 was a struggle for Lily, alleviated somewhat by her pleasure in her success at farming without chemicals. She had no energy to do the simplest things, and when she went out socially, she was more than happy to have someone at each side to lean upon. She sat down anytime she could rather than stand for any length of time. All of this coincided with the ill health of James King, her farm manager, who had worked for brother Jesse and her for forty-eight years. He was having circulatory problems and was prone to infections that debilitated him. With much reluctance, Lily made the difficult decision to give up active farming. She arranged to rent all of her land, approximately eight thousand acres, on a crop percentage basis and sold her gin to her great nephew, Warren Crisp.

Reflecting on her career as a farmer and ginner, Lily said that she took great pride from three compliments she received on her management of the gin. During the sixties she was being entertained in North Carolina by Mr. and Mrs. Gordon Hanes of the Hanes Hosiery Mills. Mrs. Hanes was on the board of the Moravian Music Foundation, and the dinner was in that connection. Lily was introduced to Arthur Spaugh who immediately said to her, "Oh, Miss Peter, we at Washington Mills want to thank you for your beautiful cotton. We have never seen cotton so clean or cotton that lies more smoothly on the rolls." The second compliment came from Berry Brooks, a famous buyer and fine sportsman from Memphis who came to Holly Grove to buy equities in cotton above the government loan value. He looked over the cotton bales and said, "This is the best ginned cotton I have ever seen. Whose is it?" When told, he came to see Lily, who adds that Mr. Brooks "offered to pay more than I was getting in loan. I had already sold my samples to the compress for 'snakes' used in mills, but in spite of the twenty-five-cent cost per bale to cut new samples, I set about attending to that and getting the loan papers organized which took a week. But by that time the government had closed the doors, and I didn't get to sell the equities to Mr. Brooks. Nevertheless, I treasure the compliment." The third compliment came from her friend and neighbor-farmer, J. C. Crisp, who said to Lily one fall, "Miss Lily, did you know I'm getting four or five cents a pound more for my cotton than my friends who gin at other gins?"

W. A. Henderson, another ginner in Marvell, Arkansas, tells of his association with Lily through the years: "Lily thinks of herself as the only woman cotton ginner; however, the Moore sisters at Poplar Grove inherited a gin and paid pretty close attention to its management, and Mercy Paschal, a black woman, managed an inherited gin efficiently for her family. I concede that Lily is the only one with full ownership and management, and it is remarkable that she was elected to the board of the Mid-South Cotton Ginners Association. She would always call in the fall and discuss payment and charges with me so we could be in line. And I always enjoyed going with her to the meetings. Our Phillips County group would meet and dine and afterwards have some sort of pretty raw stag entertainment. At some point soon after dinner, someone would rise and say, 'We'll now excuse you, Miss Lily, if you don't mind.' And she would always say, 'That's fine, boys. I'll be glad to be excused. I know you must have your fun.'"[11]

Her number-one priority in 1978 was getting medical care for herself. She went to one of the family doctors, Dr. Herd Stone, at Holly Grove. He found that she was seriously anemic and prescribed various remedies, among them large doses of iron. Lily had a fierce allergic reaction to this treatment and seriously thought she was going to die. With this development, Dr. Stone told her that he could do no more and recommended that she go to a hematologist. They discussed the famous medical centers; however, Lily told him that, if she could get as good a diagnosis in Little Rock, she would much prefer to go there. Stone assured her that Dr. Jacob Amir at the Little Rock Diagnostic Clinic had an international reputation for capability and had pleased everyone he had sent there.

Lily's Ratio farm manager, Brooks Griffin, who had been concerned about her health for some time, offered to take her to the doctor as often as she needed to go; in fact, he was insistent upon it. She began treatment in June of 1978. Lily was given every test and found to be certainly anemic: a blood count of 8.5 (normal is between thirteen and fourteen). Dr. Amir knew that her diet had not furnished the necessary nutritive elements and that she needed more bone marrow. He treated her with various nutritive supplements. Lily did not agree that she had an inadequate diet; however, she conceded that she must be lacking something. Through that summer, the blood count got as high as 10.1, but it dropped again.

Lily and Dr. Amir developed a routine. She would come in and get a card for laboratory tests and then go to the waiting room until the blood sample could be taken. Then she would return to the waiting room until the results could be sent up to Dr. Amir. It was not long, however, until Dr. Amir would invite her into his office, and they would chat while waiting. Dr. Amir found Lily to be a fascinating person, entertaining and enlightening. Lily brought him her poetry to read, even some of her unpublished ones, and he was particularly impressed with *Panels of Antiphon* (published in 1983 as *In the Beginning*), a poetic treatment of five different systems of myth, based on Lily's conceptual theme, "Myth is the antiphon of poet and seer, orchestrated by every man in the culture and age of its origin."[12] She, as would be expected, told him of her lifelong interest in medicine, and her thesis on the medieval physic in Donne's poetry. She was somehow invited to present a lecture on her thesis at the Medical Sciences Center of the University of Arkansas. Amir and his wife attended, and he said, "It was that event that convinced me beyond a shadow of a doubt that she was a genius. In her weakened condition, she stood for an hour and forty-five minutes and delivered in perfect language the essence of her thesis without a note or a hesitation."[13]

Lily, in turn, asked to read his medical books on the subject of anemia, and he acceded to her wishes, although warning her that they weren't for the layman. Lily told him that she had taught Latin for years and had studied enough Greek to know her way around many of the roots and prefixes. It never occurred to Lily that she should not assume the responsibility of understanding her case, not only cooperating fully with the treatment, but also participating in the decision making. Neither was she a typically passive patient when it came to the question of blood transfusions. Dr. Amir was confident that tests could determine whether or not Lily was allergic to the transfusions, but Lily was adamantly opposed to the treatment.

One day in the fall, Dr. Amir said to Lily that he hated to tell her that she had one of the rarest of primary anemias and that there was nothing more he could do for her. He told her that medical science did not know the cause of the anemia and that, therefore, no medicine was known which could cure her. He said she would have to resign herself to being in that condition the rest of her life. Lily perceived that information as being a death sentence — that she would become weaker and weaker until her heart went out "like a candle flame from a little puff of air." But she did not accept the prognosis fully; she said to herself, "Then I shall have to be like the little red hen and do it myself."

Dr. Amir did not perceive the situation in quite the same way. However, he knew Lily well enough by that time to recognize the positive power of her will to live and her common sense attitude that only she was ultimately responsible for her health. Dr. Amir thought these dispositions might very well be as efficacious as any treatment he might administer. So he dealt with her gently and with a great deal of understanding. He, therefore, was somewhat surprised, yet extremely pleased, to see her improvement.

After doing her homework reading two of his medical books, Lily gave the following account of her recovery and report to Dr. Amir:

It turned out that there are hundreds of anemias, just no end of them. But for many of them, the primaries in particular, there was no treatment whatsoever that they know of that would cure them. They are totally beyond medical science.

I knew I was not going to be very long for this world because I was weakening so rapidly. I came home very unhappy, but I did not tell anyone, even Brooks. There was no use telling anybody. Nobody could do anything for me and there was no use making them unhappy. I didn't want folks feeling sorry for me. Lots of worse things happen than that. I thought of going to the other famous clinics but felt that wouldn't do any good. They had the same books which Dr. Amir had.

So I took a kindergarten approach. The first thing I did was look in the dictionary and see what goes into the make-up of a molecule of hemoglobin. I keep the Webster's Unabridged, Second Edition, because I think it is superior to the third in that it gives more complete derivations and more information at each entry. I found that it was composed of $(C_{728}H_{1166}FeN_{203}O_{308}S_2)_4$.

I decided that I was getting all of the elements listed except, perhaps, sulphur. I found that it did three things: it helped with digestion; it helped control the amount of perspiration; it was a resolvent needed to produce the amino acids that keep us alive.

Thinking that it might be the very element that I lacked, I looked up those proteins which contained sulphur. After searching and reading articles on diet and foods, I found that the most complete protein known, even superior to milk, was peanut butter.

Well, I knew that I hadn't eaten more than one peanut butter sandwich in my life, so I went over to the store that very minute and got a jar of peanut butter and began eating it by the spoonful right out of the jar. The effect was dramatic and miraculous. In three or four days I was feeling better than I had for three years. I wasn't any stronger, but I felt better. So I continued eating the peanut butter in large quantities.

When I went back to Dr. Amir's within about two weeks, my blood count was up to over ten. Dr. Amir was pleased, but he warned me that it had done that before, only to drop back down.

So I kept on eating peanut butter faithfully all through November. And when I went back the first of December, my count had gone from 10.3 to 10.9. Dr. Amir was so astonished, he could hardly believe his eyes He thought there must be some mistake in the laboratory, so he asked the laboratory people to re-run the tests and check for errors. They did what he asked and the results were the same. I thought it was time to tell him what I was doing, but I decided that it would be courteous to thank him for all he had done because he was a kind and thorough and honest doctor. I started to thank him, but he interrupted me and said, "Don't thank me; I haven't done anything for you. You are curing yourself somehow and the fact that you are recovering from this anemia is defying all the known laws and should be written up in the medical journals."

So I thought I had better keep my mouth shut until I had more to tell, so I didn't tell him that time. He instructed me to wait two months before coming back, and when I went on the 2nd of February, my count had gone from 10.9 to 11.5. Of course, he was more surprised than ever, so that time I told him about the peanut butter. I tell you that poor Dr. Amir was totally astonished.

Of course, he was very happy that I had gone on in my simple way and searched out the information that led me to eat the peanut butter. He then began to tease me. He said, "Now

349

you have not given us a complete medical experiment and proven beyond doubt that it is the peanut butter that has caused this miraculous cure. To do that, you must stop eating peanut butter and see if your count will go back down into the nine-range. Then you would start eating it again, and if it went back up, the proof would be conclusive." I said, "Oh, Dr. Amir, that would be a conclusive medical experiment and very fine indeed, but I'm not about the be the guinea pig." So that was that.

It was not necessary that I return for three months, and when I did on May 7, I was cured. My blood count was 13.4 which is normal for a woman. My hematocrit count was 43, above normal, and it had been as low as a dangerous 29. I asked him about the two-points-above-normal blood count as to whether it was a cause for concern, and he said, "Oh, no. That just means that you have enough vitality to be in an optimum state of health. You will live to be a hundred." I said, "Well, Dr. Amir, I feel fine, but what about the fact that I am still as weak as a dead cat?" He said, "That's to be expected. Your body has been so undernourished that even though your count is normal, it's going to take a year or a year and a half for your body to recover its usual muscle tone."

And I do feel a little stronger each month.

Lily did continue to improve, and she has told the story of her "brush with death" many times and in many an august company. In August of 1979 when Vanderbilt chose to award her its highest honor, the Centennial Medal of Achievement, one of the many festive features of the occasion was a dinner in her honor, given by Chancellor Heard and his wife in their home. It was a seated dinner and included Lily's old friends, the Duncans. Lily told the story to Dr. Heard before the dinner. To her surprise, during the progress of the dinner, he insisted that she tell it to the group. He tapped on his glass and invited all the guests to listen to it. Lily protested courteously, but did not decline the retelling. Present was Dr. Philip Felts, Dean of Admissions to Vanderbilt Medical School.

He was so impressed with the story that he made an engagement with Lily at the medical school television studio, telling her that he felt that a videotape of her experience might be of value to the medical students. He was quite happy to have met her because he was already familiar with her thesis about medieval medicine, as it had been placed in the medical library as required reading for medical history students.

Jeff Carr (Lily's photographer friend, Vice Chancellor of Vanderbilt) took Lily to the television studio as planned and the result is a color videotape of Lily and Dr. Felts done in the style of a talk-show interview. Dr. Felts proved to be a discerning interrogator. His interview progressed from a discussion of Shakespeare to Lily's experiments with peanut butter as a cure for her anemia. The film is shown to all entering freshmen medical students.[14]

Dr. Felts, when questioned on the exactitude of the cure was, of course, good-naturedly noncommittal, yet by no means questioned the honesty of Lily's perception nor the professionalism of Dr. Amir. He said that Lily's story had much value for students, demonstrating the interrelationship of physician and patient, and that the power of her intelligence and personality could be nothing less than inspiring.[15] Dr. Sarah Sell agreed with him and contributed the opinion that, were there no other value, Lily's cure could easily serve to keep the medical profession humble.[16] Dr. Felts invited Lily to appear before a group of medical students to report on her experiment, and since she wasn't able to accept his invitation at the time, she often expressed regret that she missed her chance to lecture at the Vanderbilt School of Medicine.

It's hard to believe that Lily's anemia daunted her. Even though 1978 was her last year to farm, there was no winding down. All her farm machinery had to be retired, in addition to her regular chores. By the end of the year, it was all steam cleaned and painted. She had intended to have a public auction and had asked

Jerry James, manager of the Elaine Implement Company, to put a fair price on each item. Her great-nephews, Warren and Harold Crisp, and their cousin, J. C., asked her to sell it to them. She insisted that they look it over carefully and not take a piece they didn't want. She said she made them an especially good price, and they bought it on a long-term basis at the minimum interest rate.

She made legal stipulations that every one of her farm employees might remain in the houses they were living in rent free for the rest of their lives, with a monthly stipend for James King and an annual stipend for Reuben Wilson, each of whom had worked for her brother Jesse and herself for nearly fifty years.

In April of 1978 Lily traveled to Bethlehem, Pennsylvania, for the dedication of Peter Hall and in June attended the Moravian Music Festival, also at Bethlehem.[17] In May she was pleasantly and artistically satisfied when she received a large envelope containing a letter from Dr. Gary D. Elliott, Head of the English Department at Harding College, Searcy, Arkansas (May 1). He included a copy of a study he had prepared and read to the Arkansas Philological Association's meeting the previous fall. It was on *The Green Linen of Summer*, an analysis of the poetry by topic. He concluded:

> While Peter's poetry seems filled with a celebration of life, tinted with sunshine and joy, marked by affection for creativity, filled with a familiarity for persons from mythology or history, there seems to be a void of intimate contact with "real" persons. I think these final consideration poems [Elliott has discussed three poems called "Considerations."] testify to the loneliness that the poet experiences but refuses to acknowledge because she remains so caught up in living and doing and going, etc.
>
> *The Green Linen of Summer* is good poetry produced by an unusual personality who truly lives life to the hilt. She refuses

to admit that living shall ever cease as she proclaims in the final poem of the collection. . . .

Elliott ended his paper with Lily's oft-quoted poem "Note Left on a Doorstep," the poem set to music by both Dello Joio and Dunham. Lily's reaction to Elliott's critique was, "Oh, that's so true."

Elliott's insight is interesting to compare with what has been said about the poetry of Joseph Auslander, who was Lily's poetry teacher at Columbia. The following is quoted from *The National Cyclopaedia of American Biography*:[18]

> Mr. Auslander approaches poetry with an ear attuned to classic metres and a temperament given at once to classic and romantic traditions, and the criticism commonly evoked by his early work was that it was rhetorical rather than passionate, exalted rather than informed with earthly experience.

The same criticism has been made about Lily's poetry by Lily's Vanderbilt classmate, Roy Purdy, who told the biographer that he firmly believed that if Lily had been in Vanderbilt with "the fugitives," they would have brought her into the twentieth century. He told Lily as much, and she laughingly replied, "They wouldn't have, either."[19] And a few of her readers have commented that when and if we get to the twenty-first century, Lily will be commended for having rejected twentieth century style.

It was during Lily's last year of farming that she could be said to have experienced one of a poet's wildest fantasies, that of reading a caustic poem directly to the audience for which it was intended. While attending the Arkansas Wildlife Federation's 42nd annual meeting in Pine Bluff, she was asked to come to the head table and recite one of her poems to an audience of well over two hundred hunters. She chose to recite from memory her poem, "The Death of a Wild Crane," which includes the following lines:

> ... There is none to inform them
> of the hunter who sees no beauty, his cold eyes staring
> with the thought and the promise of death, as he tramps
>   the clearing,
> carrying his leveled gun, with the bright, obscene
> flash at its end, the frightening roar. And when
> the cranes have seen this, nothing is left but the horror.[20]

According to a member in attendance, it was something to behold how those hunters' eyes darted as Lily spoke those lines. They knew and loved Lily too well to be offended, but the irony and incongruity of the situation was overwhelming, and they covered their laughter with loud applause, wondering always whether Lily's choice of the poem was deliberate. Of course the audience's indecision about Lily's intent illustrates her vast ability to disarm the most riled antagonist.[21]

In the fall of 1978, Lily visited the cotton research center at Raleigh, North Carolina, read poetry out-of-doors at Village Creek State Park, and continued her support of music.[22]

The local history that Lily had encouraged for several years was finally published in November of 1978. The following letter she wrote to the publisher of *Helena: The Ridge, The River, The Romance* reflects the importance Lily attached to her community:

> First of all, Thank You, for the beautiful book on Helena! Your knowledgeable and loving care in arranging and bringing out the best points in all of the photography, the fine quality of the paper required to achieve these excellent effects, the exquisite polish that you contrived to give to the book in the overall matter of publishing — all of this, combined with the straightforward sincerity of the more than a score of neighborhood writers — amateurs all of us — who collaborated in the undertaking — these elements make HELENA: THE RIDGE, THE

RIVER, THE ROMANCE a great and memorable book, even though it is, in physical dimensions, a small book about a small town and ordinary people, like ourselves, going about our ordinary daily affairs. . . .

The important point I want to make is this, a book of this type is about as valuable a source of local history as one is likely to find, and the example that George deMan has set in taking the trouble to bring together a collation of so many of the aspects and interests of a community, from its earliest beginnings down to the present day, represents an approach to local history that any town or community could find pleasure in developing. The noted Spanish novelist, Vincent Blasco Ibanez once said, "It is better to live a romance than it is to write one." Here at Helena we are having the fun of living our romance and writing it as well! With the added pleasure of reading it and hearing our neighbors talk about it![23]

The Director of the American Wind Symphony of Pittsburgh, Robert Boudreau, conceived the idea of bringing poetry, painting, music, and drama to ports on coastal and inland waterways as a part of the celebration of the nation's bicentennial. His "barge of art" was named the *Point Counterpoint II*. While he was in Helena in 1976 making arrangements for his tour of the Mississippi River ports, he met Lily and later invited her to meet the barge in Pittsburgh for the last week of the tour. This was impossible so Lily was invited to meet it in Louisville and journey with them for about three weeks during the 1977 tour ending at Lake Providence, Louisiana. As that time came, Lily was in the midst of replacing a worn-out set of "cyclones" in her gin. She is probably the only poet in history who has canceled a reading by telephoning a grain company with whom she had done business. She arranged for someone in that grain elevator in Louisville to get word to the barge as it passed by on the river.

Lily was invited again to meet the barge in Memphis on its

1978 tour, but she was suffering so much from her anemia that she thought she would have to cancel again; however, she said to herself that this might be the last chance she would have for a good time in this world and decided to go. In collaboration with the other artists-in-residence, she performed at Memphis, Pine Bluff and Little Rock, and Lily, at age eighty-seven, had the good time she imagined she would have aboard a floating "barge of art." A year later Vanderbilt classmate Bob Purdy sent her a copy of *American Way*, the airlines magazine, which included the article, "Good Music Barges In," and among the illustrations was a photo of Lily and artist Herb Scott holding forth from a platform on the barge. Boudreau invited her for return trips, but she was never able to accept again.[24]

Lily fully recovered from her anemia in 1979. And among all her regular activities of arranging for concerts, attending to scholarships, carrying on her correspondence, making her appearances, taking her violin lessons, overseeing the publication of more books of poetry, maintaining a close watch on every acre of her farming operations, she discovered another form of poetry to play with.

On Lily's last trip to Bethlehem, Larry Lipkis, music and composition teacher at Moravian College, had loaned her his copy of a light-hearted book on double dactyls. It was *Jiggery Pokery* by John Hollander and Anthony Hecht. The strict, short verse form was just for amusement. Lily had decided that she must undertake a thorough job of housecleaning, and to alleviate the drudgery, she thought up double dactyls while working. She invented an expansion of the form which she called doubled-up dactyli. By Christmas she had written forty-five of them and eventually wrote enough for a book, but she did not finish cleaning the house. She used the reading and explanation of them as a topic for several ensuing speeches.

Another new interest was in Tanglewood Institute, an extension of Boston University, and the summer home of the Boston Symphony. Tanglewood, of course, tied in with her life-long love of music, and when Nick Hill, her former violin teacher at Helena, was admitted for study during the summer of 1980 and invited her to come up and visit him for a week, she had no idea that she would be invited to be on Tanglewood's national advisory board with the specific imperative of arranging auditions and recruiting talented musicians in Arkansas. She was received and entertained so pleasurably by Dr. Gary Zeller, the director, and was so impressed with the calibre of the musical program there that she was more than happy to accept the task.

Nick Hill met Lily in Albany and drove her to Lenox, Massachusetts, the home of the summer institute. He and Dr. Zeller had arranged for her to stay at Quincy Lodge, an old Victorian mansion which had been made into a lodge by Maximillian and Alix G. Kowler, a couple whom Lily found to be charming hosts. And she found the setting of the institute in the Berkshires beautiful and satisfying in every way — so civilized, yet so natural, where audiences can sit on the grass and listen to music being performed in an open shed. Rehearsals (as excellent in many ways as the concerts) were held morning, afternoon, and evening. A different internationally famous conductor was on hand every week, and Sir Colin Davis of London, England's Covent Garden symphony orchestra conducted while Lily was there. Dr. Zeller's secretary, Ann Kennedy, took Lily to meet him one day after a performance, and Lily "made like" the many students there and asked him to autograph her tote bag, a natural canvas one with bars of a Bach score printed on it in black. He graciously obliged; there just happened to be a photographer on hand, and the picture was one of Lily's many treasured ones because it, too, is autographed by Sir Colin Davis. Dr. Zellar attended to that.

Since Quincy Lodge only served breakfast, Lily usually took lunch with Nick at the cafeteria; however, one day Dr. Zellar took

357

her to lunch at the Red Lion Inn at Stockbridge. They ate on the porch with a breathtaking view of the mountains. Another dining engagement with Dr. Zellar enabled her to meet Dr. William J. Conner, Director of Public Information and Special Programs, Boston University. She would be working with him in recruiting students. One discussion included his role as one of the editors of the new Grove's Dictionary of Music.

For the first time, she met and visited with Alan Burdick, her scholarship student from Heidelburg College, who was there studying conducting. Lily's scholarship program was one more of her "giant children," a composite of highly individualized parts with a variety of characteristics. It had broadened and intensified during the last ten years, yet it was nothing new in her life. During her teaching career, she gave help to aspiring students as she was financially able. A cardinal rule of her tenant farming days was that no child of one of hers or Jesse's tenant families would be without college education if any expressed the desire and had the ability. In this she did not discriminate on the basis of color; two Negro students started college, and Lily regretted that neither of them finished. She had no count of how many she helped and forgot many of the names, but in those last years, she had, for the most part, entered into a close personal relationship with many of those young men and women and shared emotionally their frustrations as well as their triumphs.

Lily experienced both joy and pain from her sponsorship of students because besides being immensely interesting, gifted and talented youngsters are plagued with intense sensitivity. She had to deal with some who were so in love that they gave up their programs. She paid for the psychiatric treatment of some who felt they were not competing at a level commensurate with their self-images and were contemplating suicide. This treatment often was all that was needed. There was another problem which brought her extreme pain. It happened in a few instances that students would start out with modest needs, but in the process of work and study would develop tastes for such items as sports cars or expensive stereophonic sound equipment because they thought Lily's financial resources were limitless. She would, of course, cut off her assistance. There were some instances of jealousy that had all the earmarks of sibling rivalry. With her scholarship program she suffered many of the frustrations of any nurturing parent.[25]

Besides the many chamber and orchestra groups Lily listened to at Tanglewood, she heard choruses and opera renditions. On Thursday evening, she heard John Shirley-Quirk, bass baritone, and his wife, Maureen Forrester, contralto, give a program: "Three Songs" by Faure, "Don Quichotte a Dulcinee" by Ravel (the very ones she had heard in New York and had requested that Gary Kindall sing), and "From the Moravian Duets, Opus 32" by Dvorak. She was inspired to get out, when she got home, the sonnets she had constructed from Dylan Thomas's metaphors and try them with some melodies from Prokofiev, but she found them unsuitable.[26] Another pleasure for Lily was the opportunity to visit a well-stocked music store and buy the scores of several works she had been wanting.

It was a glorious summer interlude. On the way home, she found an article on John Ciardi's new book, *The English Language From A to M*, and read it on the plane. Shortly after arriving home, she wrote Nick Hill:

> It's 5:30 A.M. in Arkansas, I'm feeling on the top of the world, and to prove it, I'm going to indulge in a little aria of semantics, just for fun, to see if I can outdo the Duchess in ALICE IN WONDERLAND in her comment, "Never imagine yourself to be otherwise than what you would appear to others to be otherwise than what you were or might have been would have appeared to them to be otherwise." In other words, "Be what you would seem to be." So now for a little aria

in Arkansas.

"The epistemological permutations of the categorical super-lative are more synergistic to the anagoge of the *sui generis* transcendence of the implicit than to the catachrestical tintin-nabulations of the explicit," or in other words, as John Ciardi tells us in his delightful exegesis, . . . "Sweet style is always more than reason," the word sweet being used not in the sense of saccharine but as meaning agreeable, fetching, delightful to the senses. . . . (13 August 1980)

Lily loved to play with words, and one can see she was in fine fettle. With one exception (the death of her Vanderbilt class-mate, Dr. Edgar Hill Duncan on October 21) Lily had a happy autumn. She gave $15,000 to Moramus, made campus appear-ances at Ouachita Baptist and Arkansas Tech, and began her in-terest in and support of gifted and talented students.[27]

1980 was also the year the biography was begun.[28]

Notes

[1]*Twin City Tribune,* 18 Feb. 1976, p. 1.

[2]The NWF occasion at Louisville was reported on page 5 of the April '76 issue of *Arkansas Out-of-Doors,* a magazine. The article was accompanied by a picture of Lily and King Solomon, the owl, and in a related report on the same page Ralph Gillham, Dardanelle, Arkansas, said that besides him and his wife, Martha, Arkansas was represented by Dr. Rex Hancock, Director of Region 5, Henry W. Meyer, AWF president, and his wife, Desiree, and Robert E. Apple.

Lily had flown up from Memphis and met the Arkansas delegation at the Galt House. Martha Gillham told that, a short time before the reception before the banquet, she received a phone call from Lily asking her if she (Martha) could possibly come up to her room for a minute. When Martha arrived, she found that Lily could not negotiate the back zipper in her long gown. Lily said, "Oh, My Dear, if you hadn't have come, I just could not have gone to this wonderful dinner." Of course, Martha assisted, and she, Lily, and Ralph went down to the party together. Although Lily never drank alcoholic beverages, she did not miss the "happy hours," thoroughly enjoying the conviviality. At this one, she was introduced to one of the banquet speakers, Sir Peter Scott from Scotland, who had been invited to show slides of the Loch Ness monster. He was deeply involved in the search for the creature, and Martha said that Lily was so taken with him and had so many questions, it was difficult to get them to go on to the banquet. Scott received the "International Conservationist of the Year" award at that dinner (Personal interview with Martha Gillham, 11 May, 1981).

[3]*The Washington Post,* 3 May 1976, p. B12.

[4]*Arkansas Democrat,* 9 May 1976, p. 18.

[5]*Arkansas Gazette,* 8 June 1976, p. 8B.

[6]*Arkansas Gazette,* 22 Aug. 1976, p. 3A.

[7]Letter to the biographer from Reid H. Lewis, Elgin, Illinois, 16 Aug. 1980. "In Praise of Dreamers. . ." is from Lily's book, *The Sea Dream of the Mississippi.* (Little Rock: Lily Peter, 1973) p. vii.

[8]While in Bethlehem during '76, Lily conceived an idea for her eleventh organ concert. She wanted her friends at both Helena and Bethlehem to become acquainted and saw a means of bringing some of them together. She invited Monica Schantz, organist and director of music at Central Moravian Church, Bethlehem, to come to Helena to play.

Her husband, Richard, also a musician, had replaced Thor Johnson as Director of the Moravian Music Festival in 1976. Their daughter, Susanne, junior high age, was accomplished in playing the recorder. By means of a series of letters they worked out an elegant program: Pachelbel, Bach, Couperin, Piet Post; and Susanne joined her mother for Corelli's "Sonata in A Minor." Larry Lipkis, a member of Moravian College faculty, composed two numbers based on Lily's poems, "The Subconscious" and "Dogwood." The date was set for March 27, 1977.

Besides the Schantzes, Dr. and Mrs. Herman Collier, Lee and Tom Butterfield, and two other friends came. Lily housed them at the Holiday Inn, and her Helena friends extended hospitality. Betty Faust gave a breakfast, Helen Mosby, a luncheon, and Katherine Hill had a tea for them at her home, Estevan Hall, a well-preserved 1926 structure. The occasion gave them more understanding of Lily's heritage. Betty particularly enjoyed the fact that her daughter, Kate, was the same age as Susanne and that the young girls spent time together, an expanding experience for both of them (Personal interviews with Katherine Hill, Helen Mosby, Betty Faust, 14 Aug. 1980).

[9]Personal interview with Whitten Lueken, 28 Dec. 1981, who said that he had to leave to return to school at the end of August so did not get to see the full results of the experiment, but that he and Bob Sparks both admired her efforts and observed that she had more beneficial insects than the other farmers.

[10]Personal interview with J. C. and Lila Crisp, 28 Sept. 1980. When the biographer asked Lila what was the most valuable contribution Lily had ever made, she said, "This, of course, is a selfish answer, but every day I drive over our asphalt road, I say thanks to Miss Lily." Residents of the community had tried for years to get the counties (Phillips and Monroe) to pave their road which formed the county line, but since it "dead-ended" in the Big Creek swamp, nothing came of their efforts. During the Bicentennial year authorities saw the opportunity to get funds by calling it a historical road, and the project was approved as valid by both counties. Lily personally investigated the federal regulations and involvement, and, finding them unreasonable, volunteered to supplement the road building. The county judges furnished some state and county funds, but Lily gave $45,000 for completion of the asphalt road about four or five miles long.

[11]Both W. A. and Edwynna, his wife, had abundant praise for Lily (Personal interview with W. A. and Edwynna Henderson, Jr., 9 Aug.

1980).

[12]Lily's letters include one from Amir praising *Panels of Antiphon* (Letter from Jacob Amir, 9 Mar. 1979).

[13]Personal interview, Jacob Amir, 12 Sept. 1980.

[14]This videotape, "Miss Lily Peter," as well as the Peter Jennings, ABC, television newscast, and "Arkansas' Lily of the Bayou," (all in Lily Peter's possession) was put on one videotape and is a part of the biographer's materials. The latter was made by the television class at Arkansas State University, Jonesboro, and aired on Arkansas' Public Broadcasting Network, AETN, in early 1980.

[15]Personal interview with Philip Felts, 28 Aug. 1980.

[16]Personal interview with Sarah Sell, 29 Aug. 1980.

[17]An article appeared in *The Morning Call Local* (reprinted in *The Marvell Messenger* on May 12, 1978) which told of the occasion and its program, a part of which was Lily's reading from *Green Linen of Summer*.

[18]*The National Cyclopaedia of American Biography*, Current Vol. D (New York: James T. White, 1934) p. 45-46.

[19]Personal interview with Rob Roy Purdy, 27 Aug. 1980.

[20]Lily Peter, *The Green Linen of Summer* (Nashville: Robert Moore Allen, 1964), p. 13.

[21]Jane Stern told the biographer of the incident in a telephone interview to Pine Bluff, Arkansas, 1 Feb. 1981. She said there was some question of Lily's getting to the banquet because of car trouble, her illness, and the fact that the prothonotary warblers were in the pick-up truck. Jane said that she arrived with Nick Hill (strings teacher at Helena) a bit late. Lily was fluttering and breathless, telling of trouble with Nick's little foreign car. Her poetry reading was not on the program, but Nesbit Bowers, the AWF president, insisted that she come to the head table and recite at least one poem.

In a personal interview 15 April 1981, Robert Apple, Regional Director, National Wildlife Federation, verified Jane's account of the occasion.

[22]*Cannon News*, the publication for Cannon Mills, Kannapolis, North Carolina, carried this item on page 6 in its August 21, 1978, issue:

COTTON GINNERS AND GROWERS from three states are represented by this group inspecting the old spinning wheel on exhibit at the Cannon Visitor Center. Seated at the wheel is Miss

Lily Peter. [names of four others listed] . . . Approximately 30 cotton ginners and growers from Tennessee, Arkansas, and Mississippi were in the group which saw exhibits at the Visitor Center and took the Plant I tour. Cotton, Incorporated, which is funded by growers and ginners, served as host for a meeting of the group in Raleigh and took them on a tour of textile plants and showed them what the organization is doing in their behalf. . . .

On this trip to the research center at Raleigh, Lon Mann, ginner and planter, Marianna, Arkansas, said that he sat next to Lily on the airplane and that she entertained him with stories of her ancestry and childhood. He considered the trip strenuous himself, but he said that Lily didn't miss any portion of it and asked more questions on the tours than anyone. He thought it amazing that, at her age, eighty-seven, she could be so interested in the future (Personal interview with Lon Mann, 5 Aug. 1980).

Larry Lowman, the park naturalist, at Village Creek State Park at Wynne had instituted a series of Sunday afternoon programs for visitors called Art in the Park. On October 15, he invited Lily to read from her own poetry. This appearance was in conjunction with an art exhibit of the paintings of Dixie Hampson Durham, and the two of them attracted such a large crowd that there was not seating space in the theater.

A number of things resulted from this first reading at Village Creek. For one, Lily and Larry began collaborating. He was a graduate from Hendrix in art, but had enough experience with environmental projects to procure the job with the state. He had used his artistic talents to innovate some effective means of nature education, efforts which merited him an award for the best park program in the state. Further, he was a good photographer, and he and Lily worked out a plan to show pictures of the wetlands of Eastern Arkansas while she read her nature poems. Lily contributed enough money to the Arkansas Wildlife Federation (designated for Larry) for him to enlarge and frame the photographs for such an exhibit. The program premiered at Hendrix in October 1979, and since has been presented at Pine Bluff, Pinnacle Mountain Park, Village Creek, and Arkansas Tech. Kay Speed wrote a thorough article on their presentation for the *Arkansas Gazette* which appeared in its January 22, 1980 issue (p. 1 & 2B).

Mrs. Nesbit Bowers (Lee) attended the first program at Hendrix. She said, "I have heard her read from her works for many audiences, but the one that really impressed me was the lovely talk she gave in Conway.

... There was a wide range of people there — young and old alike. Her stories of farming, of the owl she befriended, "King Solomon," captured us before she had been talking even a few minutes. As I looked around at different people, I saw their reaction was just as mine — we were all under her *Spell*!!" (Letter received from Lee Bowers, 3 Mar. 1981).

Larry Lowman told Lily about a tract of land adjoining Village Creek Park which had come up for sale but at a price beyond the purchasing power of the Arkansas Parks and Heritage Commission. It included the historic site of the town of Wittsburg. A gravel company was dickering for it, but no one connected with the park wanted a gravel pit in or near the park. Lily took an option on it. It took three years for the Commission to secure a grant for a portion of the land and iron out the red tape for concluding the purchase. The final cost to Lily was $42,000, donated to the Commission. The Wittsburg land was dedicated in a ceremony on May 14, 1981, which Lily attended with Mina Marsh and Jean Vandiver. Lily also loaned Larry Lowman the money (interest free) to purchase a home site on thirty adjoining acres on which he would build a log cabin for himself. Upon his death the land will revert to park ownership.

It was through Larry that Lily learned of the needs of the young piano student, Reid Smith. He was a nephew of the minister of the Graham Memorial Presbyterian Church at Forrest City, the Reverend Robert L. Smith. On one of Reid's visits to his uncle, Larry invited him to do a concert in the park. Larry, Katherine Leftwich, and others praised his performance so highly to Lily that she provided for him to attend Juilliard School of Music in New York.

On October 18, 1978, a letter from Betty Zane Johnson, Helena Little Theater, revealed another project of Lily's which still exists:

> Dear Miss Lily, ... request your presence Thursday, October 19th at 8:00 p.m. at the opening performance of "South Pacific." This ... is being dedicated in your honor for your generosity in providing the orchestral strings. ...

Lily had promised Bill Stiles (community college staff) that any time stringed instrument performers were needed for a musical production she would pay their fees. Bill said to this biographer that he could never adequately express his feelings of love and admiration for Lily for doing so much for music, that he had known no one who loved it to the extent that she did (Personal interview with William Stiles, 25 Sept.

1980).

[23]George DeMan, Editor, Compiler, *Helena: The Ridge, The River, The Romance,* Pioneer Press, A Division of Democrat Printing and Lithographing Company, Little Rock, Arkansas, 1978. Lawrence Harper was the publisher to whom Lily wrote. Harper, in a letter to the biographer (24 Jan. 1981) told how pleasurable it was to work with Lily in her valuable support to the writing projects of the Phillips County Historical Society and how it was "an amusing sight to see her arrive in Little Rock in Country Club finery with floppy wide brimmed hat & muddy pick-up truck."

[24]Bern Keating. "Good News Barges In," *American Way,* June 1979, pp. 80-85.

[25]There follows mention of eleven young men and women to whom Lily referred to as her "scholarship students." Timothy Moore, Little Rock, at Interlochen Arts Academy, Michigan, was supported for four years. Cullen Bryant, also from Little Rock, a student of Benjamin Selman, was helped by Lily to go to Interlochen along with Timothy Moore. Joella Todd, soprano, from Cherokee Village, Arkansas was employed by the Salzburg Opera Company in Austria. She eventually married Steven Roland, a tenor who had sung several seasons in Hamburg.

Through Harold Thompson, voice teacher at Hendrix, Lily provided the tuition for two years to Susan Dunn from Bauxite, Arkansas, for her to attend Indiana University and take a master's degree. Susan became a singer with the Metropolitan Opera.

All of Lily's scholarship students have been from Arkansas except Reid Smith from North Carolina and Colleen Kennedy from Ontario, Canada. When Lily heard of Reid through Larry Lowman, he had graduated from the Boston Conservatory of Music, had taught at Kent State, and was making some appearances with Columbia Artists. He had entered in scholarship competitions at Juilliard and had won, but did not have money for living expenses. Lily made up the deficit. Reid finished his master of fine arts degree and won a number of honors. He utilized a Rotary Fellowship for a year's study in Vienna, and Lily rounded out his expenses.

Lily met Colleen Kennedy through Nick Hill at Tanglewood in August, 1980. She had graduated from the University of Western Ontario in the past spring and received a scholarship to Tanglewood. She was a competent oboe player, and she told Lily that it was her dream to go to Juilliard where she had been awarded a partial scholarship, but feared she couldn't pay her extra expenses. Lily's dream of international friendship loomed, and she underwrote Colleen's costs which in New York City were formidable.

She had a good year at Juilliard and was presented in the fall at Carnegie Hall, playing some compositions by a young composer whom she met at Tanglewood.

In the mid-seventies, Lily was introduced to Alan Burdick by mail from Max Worthley and Richard Brothers of the music faculty at UAF. Each told of the promise of the young man who wanted a future in orchestra conducting. Having never helped a conductor, Lily responded to Burdick's need for additional financial help to go with his scholarship to Rice University, Houston, Texas. He finished in two years and secured a position in Heidelburg College, Tiffin, Ohio. Later he decided to make a change and contacted Lily for help with his expenses at Tanglewood and again she helped him, as she had done when he went to Germany on the exchange program.

Lily's relationship with Nicholas (Nick) Hill was more nearly that of a peer and friend even though she eventually did supplement his expenses for continued education. The Arkansas Symphony Orchestra proffered a program whereby any school in the state could have one of its string players to come to give instruction on two days of the week. Arrangements were made for Nick to come to Marianna two days and Helena two days. The businessmen of Marianna picked up the tab for the work at Lee Academy there, but Lily paid for his salary at DeSoto Academy at Helena.

With Nick's encouragement, Lily tried one more time to develop her proficiency on the violin, and she took lessons from him the last two years he was there, and continued some time longer by driving to Little Rock and studying with Eric Fried. She often practiced with her violin "propped up" because she was so weak from anemia and because she was never without pain as she played because of her shoulder injury. She finally gave it up with the greatest reluctance when she learned that the strain was elevating her blood pressure.

Nick made many friends while in Helena, and a number of them were in Lily's neighborhood. He would come out often. Ethel was still living with Lily, and she asked him to help her with the musical programs she organized on Christmas and Easter at the Turner Methodist Church. They became devoted friends.

After Lily's commitment to Tanglewood to search for capable students, she found that a young man from Helena was studying composition and conducting at Southern Methodist University, Dallas. Hays Biggs was good enough at the piano for the Warfield Concerts to schedule his appearance for them. He came to see Lily Christmas, 1980, played for her, and they made plans for his auditions and submission of composi- tions. Lily assured him that she would supplement his expenses. He was one of the eight in the United States accepted at Berkshire Music Center for composition study and went there in 1981.

All of the above students are musicians, and one can easily recog- nize Lily's personal identification with them. She has never, though, con- fined her assistance to those studying music. A young design-engineering student who graduated from Princeton in the spring of 1981 has been a great source of pride and pleasure. He is Frank William Conner from West Helena. Carolyn Cunningham wrote Lily in April of '77 telling her of his outstanding high school record. Carolyn further told of his receiving a scholarship to Princeton, but that because it did not cover his living ex- penses, he could not go. Lily came through. The biographer talked to him, and he said that each visit with Lily was a learning experience for him. He expected her to be learned in the liberal arts but was amazed at her knowledge in many fields, even his own. When he showed her his designs or blue-prints, she always seemed to have a sense of the language and seemed to know his aims. He always felt inferior and inadequate in her presence, yet he always came away with a confidence in himself which he did not have before. He said that her financial support had been essen- tial; however, he could put no price on the value of her moral support. He had come home during the holiday his first year exhausted and discour- aged, but she, ever so gently, led him to decide against playing football. As a result, he had become a distance runner and felt that it would be of much more lasting value to his health. He considered Lily's genius rare in that it was so versatile. Bill planned to work for two years and then go for graduate work at either Harvard or Stanford. Lily was confident that the world would hear of the accomplishments of Bill Conner (Telephone interview with F. William Conner, 6 Sept. 1980).

It was in the summer of 1976 that the situation of two more young people from West Helena came to Lily's attention. With Lily's assistance Diane Deitz, having gone to Vanderbilt for a year and a half, had trans- ferred to Hendrix and graduated in psychology with a creditable academic record. Larry Wellborn had just graduated from Harding College, Phi Beta Kappa. Diane was strongly committed to social service work, and Larry had a burning desire to become a competent authority on biblical lan- guages. But their immediate desire was to marry; they had found one another during the last hectic week of their high school days together and had dated as often as possible during their undergraduate years. After visiting with Lily and receiving her assurance that she would supply what monies they needed beyond their own efforts, they took their vows.

Larry was admitted to Yale on a scholarship; Diane found work and attended some classes. She and friends established a soup kitchen in the basement of Christ's Episcopal Church and received regional publicity. Larry's program lasted three years because he had to include the study of a number of the prerequisite languages not available at Harding, such as Greek and Hebrew. During his second year, Lily conceived the idea that he become her literary agent and see whether he could find publishers for her six books of poetry which she was bringing together. She was confident, too, that he would eventually write and felt that the experience would be beneficial to him as an apprenticeship. Lily saw to it that Larry finished at Yale, supported a year's study at Tubingen, Germany (He had received a Rotary Fellowship), a short course in Greece, and finally doctoral work at the Vanderbilt School of Religion. He finally secured a position on the staff of McCormack Theological Seminary in Chicago.

Lily corresponded with all these students. Their letters, in her archives make fascinating reading.

[26]When Lily was hospitalized from an automobile collision in 1966, she had made a thorough study of Dylan Thomas' poetry. She concluded that he was not to be excelled in creating beautiful metaphors, but that he had given them, in her opinion, poor settings as to content. Without altering a word, she excerpted metaphors of her choice and, giving source of each line, she arranged them to form four sonnets. She submitted the poems to James Laughlin of New Directions, Dylan Thomas's publisher, who was enthusiastic enough about them to write to Catlin Thomas for permission to publish them; however, Catlin refused. Later Lily thought of setting them to song, and in that way permission might be granted. Lily never completed this project.

[27]Lily's friend, Sybil Alexander (Mrs. Hiram), an active Baptist, drove Lily to Ouachita University at Arkadelphia for two days of talks and poetry in September.

At the invitation of the biographer and Dr. Gary Tucker, botanist, Lily and Larry Lowman were invited to Arkansas Tech University. It was her first visit to the Tech campus. She talked to the creative writing classes of Clarence Hall and Francis Gwaltney and the Tech chapter of Sigma Alpha Iota. Larry and she gave a program for the public. The Botany Club planted a ginko tree in her honor, a choice that pleased her. Joan Wainright played for her and Larry an impromptu organ recital. To add to the experience accidentally, the Pope County Democratic Women's organization gave a reception for then-campaigning Governor Bill Clinton right in the middle of Larry's photographic exhibit. Together, they formed a double attraction. Marge Crabaugh taped a forty-minute interview with Lily, talking mainly about her farming experiments, and it was played on KCAB the next morning. At a faculty reception, Lily gave an impromptu recitation of poetry, including the witty "Space-Age Mother Goose," and Tom Palko, Head of the Arkansas Junior Science and Humanities Symposium, was so impressed that he, on the spot, invited her and Larry to return the next spring for the annual meeting of the organization. They did so and performed creditably. By this time Larry had prepared slides and availed himself of the needed equipment to make the projected pictures fade into one another at exactly the right moments to illustrate Lily's poems which she read.

While on campus for this second visit, she lectured to AnnicLaura Jaggers' humanities classes and to one of Ecey (Emma Carolyn Calhoun) Gwaltney's honors English classes, explaining her original categorization of poetry according to the four Euclidian dimensions of matter. A number of students seemed to have no idea what she was explaining; however, one student, a young woman named Short, hung on every word Lily uttered and followed her after class into Ecey's office lingering as long as was courteous.

[28]Tapes 13, 20, 23, 25, 27, 34, 36, 39, 45, 46, 47, 50, 59, 62, 64, 65, and 66. Torreyson Library Archives, University of Central Arkansas.

CHAPTER XII

THE FINAL DECADE
TOWARD THE HUNDREDTH YEAR, 1981-1991

And this is the end of the legend:
only the winds,
blowing the length of the centuries, remember
the shape of the deeds, the sound of the words
    they carry:
the scrawl of their shadow in ink — the deeds,
    the words — altered, shriveled, forgotten:
the great beaches
smooth as a worn bone: the world shrunken:
and the time of man a costly thing and a poor one! . . .
                    Lily Peter
                    The Great Riding

The shaping of the life of Lily Peter into words, to be floated into the air and scrawled in ink and altered and shriveled into a book, could be said to have begun in 1980. It was the year the biographer began her interviewing and research. The hottest summer in a hundred years did not stop the taping despite the lack of air conditioning or electric fans. If Lily was tired, the biographer would interview in the neighborhood. If Lily was invited to any speaking engagement or social occasion, the biographer drove her because Lily had stopped driving except in the neighborhood or up to Marvell. She seemed to enjoy the undivided attention and the company of the biographer, introducing me with self-deprecating wit (Why would anyone want to write about me?) and with florid compliments.[1] Announcements of the writing appeared in the local papers.[2]

With the help of Tom McGuire, the business manager of the Arkansas Symphony, Lily arranged for the Tanglewood Auditions in February of 1981. Dr. William Conner came down from Boston, and Lily accepted his praise for the caliber of students who auditioned. Stephen Sims, a violin student to Dr. Barbara Seagraves Jackson of the UAF staff was the first recipient of a full scholarship to Tanglewood provided by Lily. Plans were made for continuing the auditions.

In April, as guest of Chancellor and Mrs. Alexander Heard, Lily was entertained at Vanderbilt. She was informed of the university's acquisition of the Blair-Peabody Music School, which was contributing to the dream of developing a prestigious school of music there. Lily made a $10,000 a year commitment to it, providing the school never offered a program of studying and performing jazz.[3]

Lily went back to Tanglewood that August of '81. She said to the biographer, "Darling, how I would love to take you with me, but I just can't because Reid Smith has invited me to stop over in New York so he can show me Juilliard. You just don't ask another lady to go with you on a date, you know." Her smile was coy. She reported a wonderful time and that she would be going back in the fall for a visit to Boston and a foliage tour.

Shortly after Lily's ninetieth birthday, after a day's interviewing, the biographer spoke with some hesitation, remembering Lily's distaste for talking about her personal feelings, "Lily, some time ago I found an account of the career of Porter Gale Perrin in the *Cyclopaedia of American Biography.* I've brought a copy of it with me. Would you like me to read it to you?" (Perrin was Lily's fiancee from Johns-Hopkins days.) Lily replied, "Oh my Dear, yes, yes."

I read it to Lily. There were nearly two columns of information, telling of his career as a university professor, his several books on rhetoric, his co-authorships, his contributions to journals, and the like. It included his picture, told of his family, and the universities in which he had taught. One of the last sentences said, "His leisure time interests were genealogy, local history, mountain climbing, and *raising lilies*, and in connection with the last-named he held membership in the North American and Puget Sound lily societies. . . . He died in Seattle, Wash., Sept. 9, 1962" [italics mine].[4]

Lily looked at his picture and responded with emotion, "Oh, My Dear, if I had my life to live over. . . ." She did not finish her sentence. The biographer was reminded of Lily's poem, "New England Hillside: August" from *The Green Linen of Summer*, so she read it to Lily:

> Meagre-tasseled corn,
> wind-bitten apples on a neglected tree,
> goldenrod and feverfew among the outcropping boulders,
> purple ironweed in the shade of a hawthorne,
> pines that have seen three summers,
> a birch that is always remembering the spring time —
> even the crickets drowse in this loneliness,
> and one would think that here was utter peace.
>
> But loneliness has many different flavors.
> I do not see
> New Englandly, as Emily Dickinson would say.
> This loneliness has the sharp taste of yellow thorn-apples
> and makes one remember.
> In the loneliness of a cypress swamp one can forget.

The biographer said, "Lily, it seems you have not forgotten, yet you have packed your life with many interests and activities so that one could hardly think it lonely. Your loneliness must have an indescribable variety of flavors, some of which have been good." Lily replied, "Oh, Darling, that's so true. But some have been the bitterest of bitter. But I just must go on."

Sweet publicity continued. No feature articles written about Lily are of better quality than one in *The Atlanta Journal-Constitution* on September 13, 1981, written by Diane Goldsmith who came to Marvell to interview Lily. It displayed a photograph of Lily with Van Cliburn and touched on all her philanthropy. Helen Mosby had met Goldsmith on her annual trip to the Episcopalian Conference Grounds in Swanee, Tennessee, and told her about Lily.

Two other good articles appeared in October because Lily financed the appearance of poet John Ciardi, former teacher at Harvard and Rutgers (a personal friend of Miller Williams) who was the featured speaker at the Arkansas Poets Roundtable for the celebration of its fiftieth anniversary.[5]

A new and different philanthropy which strongly appealed to Lily was support of the Summer Laureate Program for gifted and talented children at the University of Arkansas at Little Rock. During the summer of 1981, she met with Jean Vandiver of Forrest City, Mina Marsh, and Dr. Emily Stewart (coordinator of AG-ATE), each of Little Rock, and contributed $11,000.

The year 1982 included a steady stream of invitations and appointments, but by far the largest honoring event was the celebration of Lily Peter Day at the Phillips County Community Center at Helena. Preceded by all the fanfare of such occasions (a proclamation by Governor Frank White, a full week of publicity in *The Helena World*, notices in state papers), Lily, seated on a throne-like construction which put her at eye level with those who approached, received friends and relatives for nearly two hours before a festive banquet following which seven members of the Arkansas Symphony Orchestra presented a concert in the Lily Peter Auditorium.[6]

In April of 1982 the biographer delivered the manuscript, *A Nude Singularity: Lily Peter of Arkansas* to the Arkansas Endowment of Humanities in Little Rock. One result was that Jerry D. Gibbens, academic staff member of Southern Baptist College, Walnut Ridge, and AEH board member, invited Lily and the biographer to appear on campus September 30. We accepted and the pleasant event took place as planned. Paul Holmes, reporter for the *Jonesboro* (Ark.) *Sun* came over for interviews and photographs.[7]

"Annie Laura Jaggers has performed what well could turn out to be an invaluable service to the state of Arkansas. . ." is part of the lead sentence in Bill Lewis' "Book Notes," a Sunday column in the *Arkansas Gazette*. He told something of the biographer, the AEH grant, the title and scope of the work, and the fact that I had a contract with an agent to investigate commercial publication.[8]

In October Lily was named the Distinguished Citizen of the Year by Channel 4, the NBC affiliate television station in Little Rock. All masters of ceremonies, on occasions when Lily was honored, had the problem of getting her to adhere to the time schedule; she readily pled guilty, because "You see, My Dears, I have so much I want to tell you and beg you to do. . . ." That she was on television made no difference. It was amusing to see the announcer literally having to cut her off.

Keeping company with royalty was another ambition in which Lily saw no fault, and when Prince Phillip came to Houston, Texas, to speak to a meeting of the World Wildlife Federation and she was invited, she didn't hesitate to go. She reported disappointment, however, because protesters and a bomb threat caused security staff to allow no one at all to be introduced to

Prince Phillip. But she could see him at the speeches, the banquet, and on the next barge on a wildlife observation tour on the canals of the coastal wetlands. "A cat can look at the king, you know." She reported that he was, indeed, a handsome young man, a phenomenon which Lily never failed to notice.[9]

Another October event was the National Poetry Day always observed by the Arkansas Poets Roundtable, a special one for Lily since Senator Dale Bumpers had commissioned a poem from her to be entered into the *Congressional Record.* She wrote a history of Poetry Day to be so inserted. Both appeared in the record on September 13, 1982.[10]

"This year Miss Lily opted to keep her money in Arkansas when she selected Dr. Johnny Wink, associate Professor of English, Ouachita Baptist University, Arkadelphia for this prestigious honor" [of featured speaker at the Arkansas Poets Roundtable]. Thus states publicity in *The Helena World,* alluding to Ciardi's appearance the previous year.[11]

Nineteen eighty-three included a steady schedule of appearances: a return to the Tanglewood Auditions in Little Rock managed by Dr. Fred Fox, executive director of the Arkansas Symphony, who with his wife was also her host; a return to Arkansas Tech for the Arkansas Junior Symposium for the Sciences and Humanities; a birthday celebration (June 2) sponsored by the Grand Prairie Arts Council of Stuttgart replete with afternoon reception and evening ball.[12]

An invitation which flattered Lily was one to an International Symposium on World Hunger including representatives from thirty-one nations sponsored by the Winrock Foundation and held at its headquarters on Mount Petit Jean. Mina Marsh went to Lily's home for her, and the biographer met them in Little Rock and drove Lily the rest of the way to the mountain. Before leaving Little Rock, they stopped at a This Can't Be Yogurt store for a small cup of chocolate. Immediately a man got up from a table, introduced himself to them, turned to the young women serving and said, "I want you to know that you are waiting on the greatest lady in Arkansas." He continued with such flattering speech that Lily seemed genuinely embarrassed.

The biographer had not been invited to the Winrock conference, but as Lily's chauffeur, I was readily welcomed and introduced along with Lily, who was not on the program. The first two of the banquet speakers were a man from Bangladesh and a young woman doctor from India who, with her nurses, served two hundred villages. The final speaker was Andrew Young, ambassador to the United Nations during Jimmy Carter's administration. Lily and the biographer were seated at a table with him, a nun from Maine, and a young woman who was implementer of visas and passports from the State Department in Washington, D. C. Lily was able to chat with Young about Jimmy Carter, telling him about her being one of his earliest contributors in Arkansas and the fact that he had appointed her to head a national committee on agriculture. She confided to the biographer later, however, that she would never, ever be comfortable in social situations with blacks and that she wished politicians would not support and encourage them with appointments. Many of Lily's friends who accepted integration appealed to her reason to alter her position on race relations, but she was adamant in her attitude, insisting that she loved many blacks, but only "in their place." Some of the members of the Arkansas Writer's Workshop wanted to invite Maya Angelou to be a featured speaker, but Lily would never approve it.

Ironically, Lily was equally adamant against any aspect of feminism. She regarded assertive women as pushy and said any woman worth her salt "knew her place" and stayed in it. "Why, Darling, I would have been perfectly happy to submit myself to the man I loved and who loved me in return," she said more than once. "Of course, there are times when a woman must control a man, but she must always be smart enough not to let him know it."

Nineteen eighty-three included much communication with the University of Arkansas Press at Fayetteville. The previous fall Director Miller Williams had committed the press to publish a book of her poetry, the one on mythology entitled *In the Beginning.* She was not too happy with the change from *Panels of Antiphon,* nor did she particularly like the illustrations. She confided to the biographer that she was helping with costs of publication and that she thought $7,000 was too large a fee for the artist, that she would have withdrawn her support had not the illustrator been a good friend of Miller's. But her pique was soothed by the pleasure of seeing more of her work in print and the fact that the UAF Press was issuing another edition of her long poem, *The Great Riding. In the Beginning* came out in the fall and Lily was able to go to fifteen or twenty book-signing events, including one at the Arkansas River Valley Art Center in Russellville. She told all buyers that profits from sales would go to scholarship programs. The biographer was never told the extent of the sales, but observed that Lily had bought many copies. When she was at Tanglewood in August, Miller Williams had mailed her fifteen copies "hot off the press" which she gave to friends there.

It was in March, 1983, that the biographer submitted the manuscript to the UAF Press. In April I received a letter from Miller Williams stating, ". . . at Lily Peter's request we have forwarded *A Nude Singularity* to Ms. Peter who said she would like to read it before we go further with it." After a fruitless conversation with Williams asking for further explanation, the biographer called Lily who replied, "Oh Darling, you misunderstood. I did not ask for the manuscript. Miller asked me to edit it. He said it was just too long and that I was just the one to cut the material. Don't worry, My Dear. I shall do the editing just as soon as I can get time." Thus began years of waiting and wondering.[13]

Lily rarely missed performances of the Arkansas Symphony Orchestra, the Opera Workshop, or the Warfield Concerts, all of which received her generous patronage. She and Dr. Ann Chotard were good friends; Ann consulted Lily on many of her decisions. But 1983, Lily's ninety-third year, was her last to move about and travel comfortably. Her feet hurt her often; she had given up wearing any type of shoe other than flat, fabric and rope-soled espadrilles. Late in the year she had both of her second toes removed. They had looped over her big toes making it nearly impossible to put on any kind of shoe. This was a painful procedure and required bed rest and possibly affected her balance. She later said, "During the holidays I had a back-up of dirty dishes in my sink which I was determined to eliminate to uphold my reputation of being an immaculate housekeeper. Some had been soaking in a pan of water. After I removed the dishes, I decided to throw the water out the back door. The storm door stuck, and when I applied extra pressure, it flew open so quickly that I lost my balance and fell out the door on the concrete steps. The pain was excruciating. When I was finally able to get to the phone and have someone take me to the doctor in Helena, I was X-rayed and told that there were no breaks, but that I should have to lie flat of my back for six weeks. You can't imagine how my imagination was stretched to distract myself from the pain and occupy myself. I gave myself every mental exercise I had ever heard of. One thing which occupied a good portion of my thought was the configuration of patterns on my bedroom ceiling caused by a leak of water into the celutex squares. I tried to see how many things the patterns reminded me of."

So 1984 began with a period of confinement at home, but an invitation to be honored by the music department of the Arkansas State University at Jonesboro in March did rouse her out of the bed. The trip proved so painful, however, even riding in the car, let alone moving about, that she went to a neurologist while there. X-rays revealed hairline fractures in several vertebrae near her waist.

Articles in the *Arkansas Gazette* told of Lily's gift to the Arkansas Symphony of her Nicola Galiano violin made in Naples in 1730 and of her feting by Dr. and Mrs. Fox.[14] Gifts of $100,000 for scholarships in the Creative Writing Program at UAF and $50,000 to the university library were duly publicized.[15] Lily was featured and *In the Beginning* was reviewed in *Moravian Music Journal.*[16]

Another source of pain, pleasure, and disappointment was Lily's eye surgery for cataracts performed by Dr. Hampton Roy, not only an ophthalmologist, but also a public figure of considerable stature. She enjoyed his attention and their conversations and declared her first operation in the summer a perfect success with a restored 20\20 vision. The next operation on the other eye in the fall left cloudiness in the eye from a tiny hemorhage. "Entirely my fault, Darling. Despite all warnings, I moved. I am very difficult to anaesthetize, you know. But one thing I can tell you. Eye surgery is no more painful than having one's toes removed."

Lily joined the Saint John's Episcopal Church in Helena. She said she had finally fully reconciled historical, scientific, and philosophical truths with the symbolic truths of Christianity.[17] Pride and pleasure also came in the undivided attention of William Cole, documentarian, and Dale Carpenter, photographer, a team from Arkansas Educational Television Network. Cole, a former CBS correspondent who had served in Russia and the Middle East, was fascinating to Lily, and he was equally taken with her. The result of this project was a half-hour segment for the series, *Arkansas Portraits*, funded by the Arkansas Endowment of Humanities and aired in 1985. The video was quite good in its category. Michael Wooten and the biographer agreed that it contained the images of two Lily Peters: one vibrant, flirtatious, articulate; the other, hesitant, shrunken, fatigued. We conceded that the first three months of 1985 marked a turning point in Lily's sparkle and vitality, but none in her courage and determination.[18]

During the holidays of 1984-85 Lily became ill with some type of respiratory infection, which she called the flu and which caused her to declare another period of immobility. She did, however, receive the biographer and Dr. Earl Schrock, Dean of the School of Liberal and Fine Arts, Arkansas Tech University, who had established an intensive foreign language summer program for youth by means of a series of summer camps. He brought equipment to show her a short videotape, and she seemed quite taken with the program and promised to support it financially, but she could not then because of a $15,000 committment to the Episcopal Diocese for roof repair at St. John's. She never did. Lily had begun to forget some of her promises.

Work on the "Arkansas Portrait" was delayed. It was in late spring when the lilies, magnolias, and other flowers were in bloom that the final filming took place. As she walked about her yard picking these flowers and reciting "The Green Linen of Summer," one can see her cautious walk, some evidence of loss of equilibrium, and the degree to which her spine had shortened. When the segment was completed, Bill Cole brought the equipment, showed her the film, and she was quite happy with it.[19]

Sunday, April 28, 1985, the *Arkansas Magazine, Arkansas Democrat*, published "Miss Lily Peter: In Her 'third incarnation'" by Wes Zeigler (photos by Rick Barrett). "Poet laureate is one of Arkansas' greatest treasures" by Charles Hillinger © *Los Angeles Times* appeared in the *Arkansas Democrat* on Wednesday, November 13, the same year. Dr. Fred Fox came to Lily's home to pick up a check for $50,000 for an out-of-state appearance of the symphony and declared that Lily's home would make a good setting for *La Boheme*.

It was in March of 1986 that Lily told the biographer about her previous year, one in which she accepted very few invitations. She had received Kay Arnold and Frances Cranford from the Arkansas Nature Conservancy and accepted an appointment to the organization's Honor Roll and promised continuing support.[20] She had not been able to appear on the program of the Junior Science and Humanities Symposium at Arkansas Tech that year.

Nevertheless, Lily told the biographer, "I am much better. I have none of the infirmities of old age yet. It is just that it has taken the past year for me to ever so gradually improve from the worst winter of my life, not because of my back which still gives me severe pain, but because of my suffering the bitterest grief and disappointment of my life. Summer before last one of my scholarship students, William Harwood, invited me to be his guest in St. Louis where he was conducting the opera *Beatrice and Benedict* by Berlioz. It's based on Shakespeare's *Much Ado About Nothing*, you know."

"Was this a date, Lily?"

"Oh yes, Darling, and much more. He, a fine musician and a sensitive person, and I, oh we had a wonderful time together, and while there we made plans for me to meet him in New York City in the fall where he was to conduct for the New York City Opera Company at Lincoln Center. But before I could get there, he was suddenly stricken with some type of rare pneumonia and died. My Dear, I was totally devastated. We were to be married. All arrangements were made. He had rented a lovely apartment for us. I was so hurt I could not discuss it with anyone and can scarcely bear to think of it today, because this chance for marital bliss came so late in my life, I may never have another." She was obviously still grieving. Lily's confinement was causing her to become better and better at denying unwanted realities while still striving for the best and the highest.

On this visit, Lily told of her scholarship students. Cullen Bryant was doing fine at the Manhattan School of Music in New York City; John Cheek was taking a master's degree at Stoneybrook; Stuart Sanders (Lily's latest student and her only one to study music composition) was also taking a master's at

Stoneybrook;[21] Reid Smith was teaching and working on a doctorate at the University of Minnesota.

She considered that she was progressing toward further publication of her poetry. Larry Wellborn was acting as her agent and had tentative committments from Howard Dutton in New York and Faber & Faber in London. Jim Whitehead was negotiating with University of North Carolina Press, a fact which held some promise.[22]

Even in the year 1987, Lily's ninety-sixth, she was able to make a few appearances. She always went to the Arkansas Writer's Conference meetings in June and the Poets Roundtable in the fall. She was lecturer at the Joint Educational Consortium of Henderson State University and Ouachita Baptist University in April. Dr. Johnny Wink, associate professor of English, Ouachita Baptist University, a respondent for the lecture, observed that despite Lily's needing someone at her side to move about, she was an impressive lecturer with astonishing sharpness of mind.[23]

It was this year that the biographer noticed that Lily was centering most of her family attention on her great, great niece, Sherry Crisp Wooten, and her husband, Michael. She spent much time telling about the U. S. Department of Agriculture's requirements for the use of land which she considered the best ever and how they related to Mike's schooling and farming. Lily still knew exactly what was being grown on every acre she owned.

It was Michael Wooten who told the biographer that 1988 could be considered the year of the UAF fantasy. Lily determined to go the University of Arkansas at Fayetteville to complete her doctorate, a fact which required several trips for him or Sherry or both. Lily first insisted on living in a dormitory, but with much effort they persuaded her that it would be too strenuous if for no other reason than the noise. Then a plan was made for her to live in the graduate students' apartment building behind the Communications Building which housed the English Department. The university was even going to install doors in the wall so Lily could walk directly across the driveway to classes. Michael did not know why the plan was finally abandoned. He conjectured that the university may have stipulated some requirement she didn't approve, or that Lily may have created the plan as an enterprise to look forward to, quite likely realizing that she could never follow through.

In 1989 Lily did manage to attend her poetry meetings and receive some company. In the spring she flew to Bethlehem, Pennsylvania, where she was guest of Monica Schantz and her cousins and where the Moravian College celebrated her gifts to the school and gave her more honors. Lily liked to fly; she loved to view the clouds from above; she confessed that she thoroughly enjoyed being wheeled through the large airports in a chair which she didn't hesitate to ask for. But this time she came back exhausted and took to her bed for weeks. The cousins, couples Lee Butterfield and her husband Tom, Peggy King and her husband Boyd, returned her visit in the fall. Lily was able to go with Michael and Sherry to meet them and lunch with them at the Holiday Inn in Helena where they lodged, but her back hurt so badly that she had to return after lunch and was too ill to see them again. Sherry and Michael had to entertain them the remaining time of their visit.

Holidays undoubtedly affected Lily because many of her accidents occurred during them. In late 1989, she fell in her kitchen and, besides reinjuring her back, she cut her face on the floor furnace. Luckily she was found soon. This time Michael and Sherry convinced her that it was time to give up living alone, that she must allow them to make arrangements for someone to move in with her or accept their invitation to come and live with them. She agreed with them and chose the latter. Michael and Sherry had recently acquired the Jerry Crisp home about one mile from Lily's home, and it was to this house that Lily's suite was to be added.

In March of 1990 the biographer, her daughter, and sister called on Lily.[24] The house and yard were a phenomenal sight in that many spring flowers and shrubs were in bloom and the house and trees were draped with wisteria. Even though Lily was on her feet in the kitchen, it was as if we had to awaken her from a deep sleep, but when she did recognize us, she seemed delighted to receive us as always. The wisteria tendrils were creeping in under all the eaves. She said, "I just let it go wherever it wants to." All surfaces were stacked with paper except for narrow paths. Lily owned an oversized rural mail box, and it was nearly always full of mail. Her routine was to go through it and remove all first class mail, then set aside the remainder until she could get back to it (and of course she rarely could). This fact accounted for the stacks and stacks of paper in her house. In the piano room all furniture was draped with her clothing, "I'm taking inventory to see whether I shall have to buy any clothes for summer." She did not dispose of a catalog until she perused it.

Lily invited us to the screened porch, the only place where four people could possibly be seated. She recently acquired a high-quality wrought iron glass-top table and chairs for the patio of the new home and was enjoying them on her porch. There the scent of wisteria and lilac was nearly overwhelming. On the table and along a ten-inch plank laid across boxes about half the length of the porch were several hundred rocks and pebbles carefully laid out in various designs, mostly geometrical. She had gathered them from her yard. Lily launched into a lecture on the shapes of nature and moved through several topics. She was as articulate as ever except that she would often stop short of rounding out a subject and fail to pick up the threads, a feat in which she was formerly so adept. It was difficult to get away from her to go home. She followed the visitors to the car, and it was not until then that she said to the biographer, "Oh Darling, I do wish Miller had not asked me to edit the biography. I know how disappointed you are not to have it published, but you know, My Dear, I have just had too many interruptions and too many onslaughts to my health."

Lily had told this repeatedly.

Having determined that Lily was installed in her new home, the biographer and sister called on September 23, 1990. The house, buff brick with some Spanish motifs, a series of twisted columns with half-circle arches connecting them, faced the unnumbered county road which Lily had paid to have asphalted in the seventies. The front door opened into a spacious foyer with red tile flooring. A dining room was to the left and a parlor to the right; above a classic columned mantel and fireplace, anyone entering sees a large oil painting of Lily in the style of a Southern belle commissioned recently to Betty Dortch, an artist from England, Arkansas.

The back of this room opened on a large kitchen with both breakfast bar and table and chairs, ample counter and storage space, and all needed appliances. A large triple door opening at the back of the kitchen revealed an even larger informal room completely glazed on the right wall which extended into the wall of a receding corridor which ran to the right of Lily's suite. The left wall of the room was decorated with a number of paintings, including another of Lily's portraits. Settees, chairs, glass-topped tables of wicker, and Lily's Baldwin grand piano were the main furnishings. Lily received us there with much enthusiasm and proudly showed her suite. A small sitting room was first. It featured a fireplace with marble mantel piece above which was a portrait of Florence Peter as a young woman. Between it and a couch stood her Italian antique coffee table with mother of pearl inlay. A table and the wall on the right were filled with the most impressive of Lily's citation statues and plaques.

Behind the intimate sitting room was Lily's bedroom, large enough to appropriately display her four-poster bed and chests. Her desk and typewriter were in place. When asked if she was keeping up her correspondence, she said, "No Darling. I just can't. I don't like the electric typewriter at all. And my lens implant by

Dr. Roy has not given me the vision I hoped for. I can see to read but not very long at a time."

Her large bathroom just behind her bedroom included a shower stall as well as the highest quality Jacuzzi bath tub, but she said she hadn't ventured into it yet.

After the tour of rooms, Lily led the biographer out onto the brick patio, possibly twenty by thirty feet. It was enclosed by a low brick wall and included on a raised section a gold fish pond which she called "our water garden." We sat side by side on this warm fall day and watched the goldfish. One pink water lily was in bloom. Lily held onto my arm and gripped my hand tightly. With emotion, she said, "My Dear, you have no idea how hard it was for me to leave my old home after so many years. But Sherry and Michael were determined that I live alone no more, so we employed the best to remodel this house to suit us, the Kesl Brothers, famous builders from Helena, and Bob Beavers, architect, from Forrest City. This smart, lovely couple are the only ones of my nieces and nephews who could possibly handle the responsibility of keeping my estate together when I am gone, and they are so good to me, and the children, Damon, Shawn, and Kathryn are so precious, I feel as if I have a real family for the first time since I've been grown. I just love it. And you have no idea how much fun Sherry and I had poring over the seed and plant catalogs selecting just the right plantings for the beds around the terrace and the water garden."

The biographer asked, "Lily, at one time you had willed portions of your estate to universities and other organizations which you loved. Does that no longer hold?" She replied, "No, indeed. I gave to all of them generously for years and feel no need to give more. Except for a small recognition of other nieces and nephews, Sherry and Michael will inherit all I possess. They are the ones I look to for my needs. My sister, Ethel, you know, is in the nursing home in Helena and has her own income, but they will see that she wants for nothing."

The patio wall on which they were sitting was less than fifty yards from an avenue of trees which began at the road in front of the house and extended some distance into a woods. Lily explained that this was the old stage coach trail and that she had driven her buggy or rode horseback down it many a time on her way to teaching school. She owned the pasture land on the other side of the avenue, a corrective square of 94.5 acres. She loved living in sight of the trees, and she could still see the trees of her beloved Cypress Bayou. She seemed quite happy and serene.

In February, 1991, standing beside her bed, Lily fell to the floor and was hospitalized in Memphis. She had broken a hip and a wrist. She was extremely ill and quite difficult to deal with because she was so adamantly opposed to the hated, but needed, blood transfusions. Either Michael or Sherry or both were with her constantly for the shorter hospital stay than anyone expected, because Lily was eager to go home. Sherry was able to procure good women to attend Lily so she could have care around the clock. A capable young man, a physical therapist, came daily, and if able at all, Lily cooperated with him. However, she was quite difficult because circulation to her brain was inadequate on some days, and she would become irrational, stubborn, angry, and accusatory over trifles. It was behavior her doctor had predicted. Often she would not see company, but when she did, she was still capable of dazzling with one of her tales long since memorized down to the least detail; conversation, however, was nearly impossible because her memory of the immediate was virtually gone. On some good days she would play dominoes with one of the children.

Lily went through a period of grief when she received a letter from her cousin, Lee Butterfield, telling her that her husband Tom had died. Michael said that Lily would read the letter over and over and become so distressed that he'd take it from her and distract her by some means.

Sherry made plans for a small celebration of her one hundredth birthday on June 2; however, Lily had no enthusiasm for it. She hated her appearance. Her hair was half-white now for the first time in her life, but she did not feel like going to the beauty parlor or enduring a color treatment at home. Sherry wanted to have a large party and invite lots of people, but Lily objected. Nevertheless, Sherry ordered a large, appropriately decorated cake with plates and napkins to match and made punch, since she knew Lily would have some callers. Several came early. Jim Whitehead and another man from the university at Fayetteville arrived about 10:00 a. m. and stayed for lunch after which Lily retired. A number of others called in the afternoon, but she did not leave her bedroom. She lacked zest and continued to lose vitality. Michael and Sherry could observe her alternating between struggling to live and attempting to pass on. The latter prevailed. And she died gently and easily on Friday, July 26, 1991, possessing some levels of consciousness to the very end.

Her body lay in state at the Citizens Funeral Home in West Helena, a place where she had attended many a funeral herself. Few people ever saw more extravagant easels and vases of flowers than surrounded her casket, lined the walls of the viewing room, and spilled over into the hall. She was beautifully coiffed and wore a simple teal blue silk dress. Sherry had attached a bunch of silk violets to a little comb and placed it in her hair.

The ritual for the burial of the dead was conducted by the Right Reverend Duane Baba at St. John's Episcopal Church, Helena, and was attended by an impressive crowd. Mike and Sherry and the church provided a lunch for out-of-town guests prior to the service. The music would have pleased Lily mightily. Directed by Roger Scott, the regular church choir was assisted by members from other Helena churches for the anthems. A chamber quartet from the Arkansas Symphony added to the organ instrumentals.

The ritual continued from the church to the Turner Cemetery

for interment, some twenty-odd miles South and West of Helena. The cortege was formidable. Several dozen people from the surrounding countryside were waiting there. After the final Amen of the service, Betty Faust read Lily's last poem from *The Green Linen of Summer*, "Note Left on A Doorstep," which follows:

Tell Death I am not here,
When he comes for me.
He will find me standing yonder
Under a quince tree,

With violets in my hair
Jasmine in my hand,
Looking for the last time
At the lovely land:

Feeling for the last time
The wind in my face
Watching the clouds go over
In their tall grace,

Death may have the body
In the room at the head of the stair,
But I shall be under a quince tree
With violets in my hair.

And the many present who had heard Lily wax eloquent on the billions of whirling atoms under the soles of her shoes and hold forth on the primary laws of the conservation of matter were inclined to believe her. Were not all who attended somewhat in her presence, since they were in sight of soybean and cotton fields, the turquoise cotton gin, her last home, and the trees of Cypress Bayou?

Richard Allin's headline sentence was both precise and profound, "A Gift of Grace is Gone."[27]

Notes

[1]The equipment of the biographer's car included two items which gave Lily much pleasure: one, a fully reclining bucket seat for the passenger, making it possible for her to have a nap while riding; the other, a cassette tape deck for playing works of music from the biographer's library. Trips in '80 and '81 were to Helena, Stuttgart, Pine Bluff, and Little Rock.

[2]"Lilly [sic] Peter story to be written by Tech instructor," *The Courier Democrat*, Russellville, AR, May 7, 1980. p3. "Miss Lily's biographer finding plenty of information about renown [sic] subject," by Jane Dearing. *The Twin City Tribune*, West Helena, AR, Aug. 13, 1980. p4B. "Former resident prepares to write Lily Peter's Biography," *The Courier Index*, Marianna, AR, Aug. 14, 198,. p1.

[3]"Lily Peter aids Blair School of Music," *Vanderbilt Today*, Vol. 20, No. 6, Spring 1981 (no page numbers).

[4]*National Cyclopaedia of American Biography*, Vol. 50 (Ann Arbor: Univ. Microfilms, 1968), pp.235-6.

[5]"Poet must learn to find poem," *Arkansas Democrat*, Oct. 19, 1981. p1B. "John Ciardi Is Still Ticking As the Words Keep Clicking," by William Green. *Arkansas Gazette*, Oct. 20, 1981, p1B.

[6]"Admirers Return Kindness Of Their Beloved Miss Lily," by Lela Garlington. *The Commercial*, March 3, 1982, p3A. Beginning on Sunday, February 28, *The Helena World* carried some type of publicity relating to Lily Peter Day. Tributes were even incorporated into the advertisements.

[7]"Miss Lily's Story Told In New Book," Oct. 3, 1981, p11C.

[8]Oct. 10, 1981, p10C.

[9]While in Houston, Lily was the guest of the newlywed couple, Curtis and Claire Erwin (Curtis was the son of Camile Brown Erwin of Marvell). Lily had helped Curt go to law school. The next year while the young couple was attending a La Maze birthing class, Curtis died with a heart attack, as had his father at a young age. When the baby was born, a girl, she was named "Lily," a tribute Lily appreciated.

[10]*Congressional Record* - Senate, S11327

[11]"Miss Lily Peter to gather with bards of state," Sept. 30, 1981, p1A.

[12]"Science speakers." *Courier Democrat*, Russellville, AR, March 15, 1983, p2. "Diversity marks poet's career," by Robin Miller. *Post-Dis-*

patch, Dardanelle, AR, Mar. 30, 1983, p5. "'Miss Lily' Honored On Birthday," by Karen Knutson. *Arkansas Gazette*, Jun. 6, 1983, p3B.

[13]There follows the contents of the letter from Miller Williams, Director, UAF Press, April 13, 1983:

Dear AnnieLaura:

I wanted to let you know that at Lily Peter's request we have forwarded A NUDE SINGULARITY to Ms. Peter who said she would like to read it before we go further with it. When we get the manuscript back from Lily Peter we will begin the screening process.

Warm wishes,

[14]"VONNIE HEWITT." *Arkansas Gazette*, Apr. 29, 1984, p2D.

[15]"Poet Donates $100,000 to UA For Creative Writing Program." *Arkansas Gazette*, Jun. 9, 1984, p3A. "Major Gift By Lily Peter Aids program," *Support*, Vol. 1, No. 1, Sept. 1984, p1.

[16]"Research and Publications: Lily Peter." *Moravian Music Journal*. Vol. 29, No. 32, Summer, 1984, p43-4.

[17]During a personal interview, Sep. 12, 1980, Richard Allin told the biographer that Lily had indicated to some of her friends in the Episcopal Church in Helena that she would join the church if her former pupil, John Allin, would perform the ritual. Allin was the Presiding Bishop of the Episcopal Church of the United States and, according to church rules, deferred to the local bishop. Lily delayed her affiliation.

[18]Telephone conversation with Michael Wooten, Feb. 9,1992.

[19]Cole borrowed a copy of *The Nude Singularity*, manuscript, from the biographer and used it as a reference. He also used some of the photographs collected.

[20]"Miss Lily Peter, Marvell," *The Arkansas Nature Conservancy*. Vol. IV, No. 4, Winter Newsletter, 198 (pages unnumbered).

[21]Stuart Sanders was the son of Lucile Erwin Sanders who grew up in Marvell.

[22]None of these publications have occurred yet.

[23]Dr. Wink told the biographer in a telephone conversation, Feb. 29, 1991, that he took two French exchange students to visit Lily in the fall of 1987. She was able to ride around with them awhile and show them the countryside. On the way back to Ouachita, one of students said over and over, *formidable*, referring, of course, to Lily.

[24]Christi Jaggers Rollans and Margaret Triplett.

[25]"A gift of grace is gone," by Richard Allin in OUR TOWN, *Arkansas Gazette*, Aug. 18, 1991, p1E.

All data in this final chapter, except otherwise indicated, was obtained in personal or telephone interviews with Lily, or Michael or Sherry Wooten or both of the latter. No tape recordings were made because the conversations were for the most part spontaneous. Often Lily was not able or did not wish to make recordings, and the biographer did not press the matter. One contributing factor was the fact that the biographer was not sure that the work would ever be printed.

AFTERWORD

After twelve years of close association, the reading of all of Lily's writings and papers, and conducting over two hundred personal interviews, I assert without equivocation that my respect and admiration for Lily has increased. At the outset of writing this biography, I had no desire for the role of iconoclast and still have no desire for such a role. Nonetheless, Lily's vulnerabilities are a part of her makeup, and no attempt has been made to disguise them. Although the positive responses that Lily elicits far outnumber the negative, it would be ridiculous to maintain that I ran into no derogatory opinions of Lily in the process of interviewing. These derogations fell into three categories.

The first category included those made by persons who recognize or sense great accomplishment in someone and feel the need to "take him (or her) down a notch or two." Typical of this attitude were such assertions as, "Lily Peter wouldn't have all that money if she had not inherited it," and "Lily Peter wouldn't have been all that good a farmer if she hadn't had James King and Brooks Griffin managing for her."

In the second category of derogatory remarks were those made by people whose values do not coincide with Lily's. The dedicated church-goer would say that Lily had neglected the church. The dedicated wife and mother would remark that Lily knew nothing about *real* giving. The specialist in academia would decry her versatility, observing that she rejected the rigors of professional tedium and competition. There were those who could not comprehend her love of music and the other arts and regarded her support of them extravagant and a ridiculous waste of money. Persons living in luxurious surroundings could not imagine the reason for her simple house and her old cars except as undue penuriousness. A few people completely rejected her love of nature as anything other than a facade because of their belief that nature was for human exploitation.

The third category of angry remarks came from those who were firm in their beliefs that they would have been wealthier had it not been for Lily. By far the most caustic statements came from those persons who were furious because the channelization of Big Creek was curtailed. The stopping of the project did, of course, eliminate contracts and jobs and acres of cleared and drained land. Such criticism is understandable and not surprising. Of lesser intensity were the feelings of those who had sought to influence her actions or had appealed to her for contributions and had been rejected. In such cases, she was judged stubborn and intractable.

Of course I would not state that Lily had no personality flaws, no blind spots, but to probe, analyze, and describe them has not been my goal. I have rather chosen to describe the attitudes and accomplishments of this tiny lady, so that we might admire and perhaps learn how to possess the courage that was hers.

One pays for what one gets from life, and Lily is no exception. What did Lily pay? For one thing a tremendous expenditure of energy, working far in excess of the normal daily eight hours. But that was not her painful price. I see Lily's sacrifice to be that of intimacy — not that she deliberately chose it.

I came across a passage which seems to parallel Lily's encounters with love. Margaret Yourcenar says in her Preface to *Fires,* a book of love poems and essays, ". . . the worshipping of the person loved is very clearly associated with more abstract but no less intense notions, and these notions sometimes prevail over the carnal and sentimental obsession. . . . It is not a question of sublimation . . . but a dark perception that love for a particular person, so poignant, is often only a beautiful fleeting accident, less real in a way than the predispositions and choices that preceded it and will outlive it" (Dori Katz, tr. [New York: Farrar-Straus-Ginoux, 1981] xxi-ii).

It is my opinion that Lily possessed that "dark perception" as well as the capacity for sublimation and that her mode of sublimation of her primal impulses was admirable. The energies released by those impulses were channeled into creativity; her desire to express her deepest thought was fulfilled by communion with nature, nature expanded from the poetry of the wild pea vine at her doorstep to the music of the galaxies beyond galaxies.

Index

Index

Index

Index

Index

Of Related Interest from
THE UCA PRESS

The Honorable Powell Clayton by William H. Burnside
An authoritative and fascinating account of the public and private life of one of the most colorful and successful political figures in Arkansas history. Burnside traces Clayton's multi-faceted career through its various manifestations as a union officer in the Civil War, a reconstruction politician who became a longtime Republican leader in Arkansas politics and eventually governor of the state, a successful businessman and entrepreneur who developed Eureka Springs into the "Spa of the Ozarks," a United States senator, and ultimately a respected diplomat. This book illuminates much about politics, life, and culture in Arkansas and the nation from the Civil War into the early years of the twentieth century.
160 pages ISBN 0-944436-10-2 $16.95 cloth

Authentic Voices: Arkansas Culture 1541-1860 edited by Sarah Fountain
From the authentic accents of many voices spanning three centuries, Sarah Fountain develops a picture of a society and culture evolving from stone-age simplicity through the Industrial Revolution. Although it is specifically and uniquely the story of early Arkansas, it is in microcosm the story of the American nation.
325 pages, maps ISBN 0-915143-1-0 $28.95 cloth

Arkansas Voices edited by Sarah Fountain
This newly revised, companion edition to *Authentic Voices* collects literature from or about Arkansas from early Indian tales to modern literature by well-known Arkansans like Dee Brown, Miller Williams, and Jack Butler as well as some emerging young Arkansas poets.
288 pages, illustrations ISBN 0-9615143-7-X $28.95 cloth

Shortline Railroads of Arkansas by Clifton E. Hull
A conscientiously researched and entertainingly presented snapshot of those optimistic little railroads that were the keys to transportation and communication in an earlier, less frantic period of Arkansas history.
432 pages, photographs and maps ISBN 0-944436-00-5 $41.75 paper

To Order, add $2.75 postage and handling + 5.5% sales tax in Arkansas, to UCA Press, P.O. Box 4933, Conway, AR 72032 or order by phone (501)450-5150 on Visa or Mastercard.